The Quest for Prosperity

The Quest for Prosperity

Reframing Political Economy

Raphael Sassower

ROWMAN &
LITTLEFIELD
INTERNATIONAL

London • New York

Published by Rowman & Littlefield International, Ltd.
Unit A, Whitacre Mews, 26-34 Stannary Street, London SE11 4AB
www.rowmaninternational.com

Rowman & Littlefield International, Ltd. is an affiliate of Rowman & Littlefield
4501 Forbes Boulevard, Suite 200, Lanham, Maryland 20706, USA
With additional offices in Boulder, New York, Toronto (Canada), and London (UK)
www.rowman.com

British Library Cataloguing in Publication Information Available
A catalogue record for this book is available from the British Library

ISBN: HB 978-1-78348-929-9
ISBN: PB 978-1-78348-930-5

Library of Congress Cataloging-in-Publication Data

Name: Sassower, Raphael, author
Title: The quest for prosperity : reframing political economy / Raphael Sassower.
Description: London ; New York : Rowman & Littlefield International [2017] / Includes bibliograph-
    ical references and index.
Identifiers: LCCN 2017015243 (print) / LCCN 2017030877 (ebook) / ISBN 9781783489312 (elec-
    tronic) / ISBN 9781783489299 (cloth : alk. paper) / ISBN 9781783489305 (pbk. : alk. paper)
Subjects: LCSH: Economics--Political aspects.
Classification: LCC HB74.P65 (ebook) / LCC HB74.P65 S27 2017 (print) / DDC 330--dc23. LC
    record available at https://lccn.loc.gov/2017015243.

Printed in the United States of America

Contents

Part IV: Reframing Political Economy

Foreword

Raphael Sassower, part Popperian and part postmodernist but all philosopher, offers a critical look at an array of recent attempts to reconceptualize "prosperity," the normative polestar of modern capitalism, in light of changes both to capitalism's mode of production and its social relations of production. Sassower is broadly sympathetic to these changes, which have become part of the intellectual landscape through repeated appeals to "sharing" and "crowdsourcing" as attributes of our emerging economic future. As usual, Sassower's reading here is both broad and fair. Indeed, given that much of the literature in this field is written by people who already are or aspire to be management gurus, Sassower is especially generous in exploring the opportunities for philosophical reflection about the kind of prosperity that is possible when the meanings of such foundational terms of political economy as *labor*, *capital*, and *property* are becoming fluid, distributed, and even virtual. To be sure, Sassower ends on quite a hopeful note, suggesting that this may be the moment in capitalism's development that allows for some serious thinking about a pursuit of prosperity that goes beyond simply acquiring more money.

As someone who has also been following what is normally called capitalism's "digital revolution," which is the substantive focus of this book, I was most struck that Sassower made *prosperity* the book's organizing principle. Indeed, his most distinctive contribution may be to resurrect the original moral force of this concept in the capitalist imagination. Yet at the same time, this moralization of prosperity makes me think that perhaps the concept is not all that it is cracked up to be. In the rest of this Foreword, I shall explore this possibility in the critical spirit that Sassower himself might appreciate as "Popperian."

Prosperity occupies a curious place in humanity's moral psychology, even before the advent of capitalism. Etymologically speaking, *prosperity* is taken from the Latin, *pro-spero*, which means "in favor of hope," a state of mind in which one lives as if one's good fortune will continue indefinitely. The prosperous think of their wealth not as an accident, let alone something obtained by suspect means, but as something that in some sense they "deserve," either due to their own efforts or divine beneficence. The idea that good fortune makes its bearer good—which is the essence of prosperity— was treated with considerable suspicion in the ancient world. The original targets of the Greek god Nemesis were the "prosperous" in this sense. Herodotus appeared to believe that the Persians defeated King Croesus because he said that his great wealth made him the happiest of men. The same point is made more slyly in the Book of Job, as its protagonist slowly realizes that he failed to understand the God to which he claimed allegiance because he too glibly associated his good fortune with divine approval.

In Matthew 19, Jesus clinches the point with his famous quip, "It is easier for a camel to go through the eye of a needle than for someone who is rich to enter the kingdom of God." The suggestion is that too often the rich person carries too much "baggage" from this life to make it successfully into the next. This "baggage" is the prosperous mindset, which is prone to see the wealth accumulated in this life as indicative of one's long-term fate. It amounts to idolatry or fetishizing of possessions, as if they provided a direct measure of one's goodness. To Max Weber's great credit, a self-critical attitude to prosperity drawn from this interpretation of Jesus is now seen as indicative of the early modern capitalist sensibility, understood as the concretization of the "Protestant Ethic."

One long-term unintended consequence of the Protestant Ethic has been a shift in capitalism's balance of power from the class of producers to a class of investors, so called venture capitalists, who regularly shift their funds from established to emerging wealth creators in anticipation of a substantial reorientation of the market. For better or worse, and somewhat counter to more conventional images of capitalism, venture capitalists do not regard a successful founder as entitled to indefinite growth or market domination. Like Nemesis, these capitalists see the prosperous as ripe for the picking. They are made anxious by steady returns on investment, normally seen by shareholders as the hallmark of a well-managed company. Instead, venture capitalists would live by the Schumpeterian imperative that capitalism works best when it redistributes wealth through the "creative destruction" of markets. Thus, the term *disruptor* has come to acquire a positive glow in popular culture.

The resulting "spirit of capitalism" is very different from the spirit in which "prosperity" flourishes as the moral psychology that was so avidly promoted by Adam Smith, Condorcet, and the other early ideologues of capitalism. Prosperity for them was the material concomitant of a dynamic yet stable "commercial society," in which each person could discover his or her unique talent through the process of mutual recognition exemplified in the fair exchange of goods and services in the marketplace. However, even in the eighteenth century, capitalism's promoters realized that were the matter simply left at that point, then a commercial society could become a victim of its own success, stagnating in routinized forms of exchange, eventuating in the sort of complacent economies of the "Oriental" empires that would otherwise serve as the foil for their arguments.

The US founding fathers proposed a constitutional solution to this problem: the Patent Office, a federal registry for intellectual property. Their idea was to ward off the sloth that is bred by complacency in a prosperous society. Their strategy was to render the realm of practical ideas into something over which inventors might enjoy something like property rights for a limited period that would give them the opportunity to bring their ideas to market. If successful, as Schumpeter stressed, these genuine "innovations" would destabilize the market in some substantial way, forcing competitors to raise their game and stop resting on their laurels. Much can be—and has been— said about the overall wisdom of "intellectual property" as a policy. Nevertheless, so I believe, it enjoys the virtue of instilling a self-critical understanding of the concept of prosperity, which in turn nurtures the venture capitalist's soul.

Here it is worth recalling that much more than Condorcet or Smith, the US founding fathers were touched by the hand of Calvin, which alerted them to the endemic depravity of the human condition, given the hereditary character of Original Sin. Thus, government must at least prevent the worst collective outcomes of a society of natural sinners. But it might accomplish much more if society were organized to enable the various forms of sinfulness to play off each other, resulting in a whole much greater than the sum of its parts. Thus, intellectual property may be seen as playing off two sins— avarice against sloth—for a greater societal good that would probably not be achieved simply by removing the already existing obstacles to people doing better for themselves.

Regardless of how the institution of intellectual property is judged as a vehicle for improving the human condition, it sheds a telling light on capitalism's preoccupation with prosperity. Ultimately prosperity is founded on a "success breeds success" principle, whereby once we hit upon a political economy in which everyone is happy with their lot, the main policy question becomes how to maintain comparable levels of wealth across the population over successive generations, come what may. The welfare state is arguably committed to just this project, which in turn explains its fixation on healthcare provision and pension schemes.

Yet to the jaundiced eye, if this be prosperity, then it is a neurosis built on what cognitive psychologists call the "anchoring effect," as that which sticks first sticks best. Once a particular conception of "the good" has been realized by some segment of the population, who in turn attract the envy and resentment from those not yet party to it, then "the good society" gets defined in terms of everyone becoming entitled to this very conception of "the good"—in perpetuity. There is no room for questioning the original sense of self-satisfaction that grounds the entire project.

Put in concrete historical terms, once the European bourgeoisie started to live what they regarded as a satisfying life, that became the life that everyone else first wanted and then, courtesy of the welfare state, expected to live. The presumed momentum of this sense of universal prosperity has generated fiscal crises in welfare states that became victims of their own success, as their members started to live longer lives and produced fewer offspring than needed to maintain the funding of pension schemes and healthcare. Moreover, a somewhat similar dynamic on a global scale helps to explain the successive political stalemates over how to address climate change, a problem that becomes increasingly difficult to solve as newly prosperous nations feel that their time has come to reap the benefits that previously were restricted to the "developed" world.

From a Popperian standpoint, prosperity induces intellectual laziness, a meta-level version of sloth, which discourages reflection on the relatively limited material conditions that make specific images of prosperity desirable and feasible. Just as we should not judge the ultimate validity of, say, Newtonian mechanics based solely on its paradigmatic achievements, we should not judge the ultimate validity of bourgeois prosperity based simply on the success of European-style welfare states. In this respect, in their ideologically opposed ways, both venture capitalism and revolutionary socialism function as potential "falsifiers" of any default sense of moral equilibrium that prosperity breeds.

As suggested earlier, this intuitive suspicion of prosperity's virtuousness is born of a Christianized mentality that regards humanity as "always already" existing in a fallen state, even when things seem good or better than expected. Mindful of our endemic sinfulness, we should remain vigilant, lest we settle too comfortably into depravity, having flattered ourselves that we are getting better at achieving aims that from the outset were set too low. That is the path of a well-trained animal rather than an aspiring divinity. Of course, there are less theologically forbidding ways of expressing the same point. Modern capitalist rhetoric surrounding the "drive for efficiency" and the "maximization of potential" implies that the status quo is never good enough, even if we like it.

The great German idealist philosopher Fichte specifically targeted prosperity as a subethical virtue because prosperity is too often achieved at the expense of Christian virtue, which he identified with a "transcendental" conception of the good. But in lodging this critique, Fichte was not complaining about prosperous people cutting ethical corners to achieve a state that even Christians would find desirable. Given his loathing of any form of economic dependency, even if that entailed domestic sacrifice, Fichte cannot be counted as someone who found prosperity inherently desirable. On the contrary, he was complaining that the prosperous—and their admirers—were prone to "idolize" (in the biblical sense) worldly success as indicative of how one might achieve the sort of transcendental good promoted by Christianity.

Seen in a more secular frame, Fichte associates prosperity's moral deficiency with a kind of confirmation bias at the cognitive level and path dependency at the economic level. The result is deep value confusion, which he believed that only a strong state could resolve in an ascendant capitalist culture. Although Fichte is not usually seen as a political economist, his point remains valid. In fact, in the prior generation, Condorcet had argued—as a defense of capitalism against mercantilism—that states should introduce markets into protected trades to force both producers and consumers to improve their powers of discrimination of what is good. Prosperity would be an *indirect* consequence of this policy whose primary aim would be collective ethical enhancement in line with Christian principles. Condorcet believed, perhaps naively but not without reason, that our species's spiritual and material progress depends on the increase of options. Had he proposed the policy today, it would be dismissed as "neoliberalism."

I believe that Condorcet and the US founding fathers were on the right track with regard to how to think about prosperity in the context of a more perspicuous sense of the public good, be it defined in sacred and/or secular terms. Prosperity is something best pursued as a by-product of an explicit normative project that acknowledges the fallen/imperfect state of humanity. What I do not believe works is the sort of *eudaimonism* originally promoted by Aristotle and updated by Karl Polanyi as a kind of "ethical socialism," one based on a sense of "practical wisdom" that over time would have people learn to want only so much for themselves and leave the rest to others in greater need. Even assuming the psychological plausibility of such a policy, it remains hostage to the multiple levels of human fallibility. Sheer good will could lead to even worse outcomes, in terms of stagnating the human condition by catering to our animal natures. Here Sassower appears to be more sanguine than me, and we would certainly live in a kinder and gentler world were he to be proven correct.

Steve Fuller
Auguste Comte Chair in Social Epistemology
University of Warwick

Preface

Catastrophes provoke reactions. They spur us to rethink what we have accepted on faith or simply were too complacent to question. This is true in our personal affairs when confronted with death or the loss of our homes (because of natural disasters or mortgage bubble explosion) and also in the affairs of the State (American presidential elections are unpredictable, or the unexpected vote for Brexit in the UK). The presumption that the *quest for prosperity* drives the human condition and therefore responds to catastrophes is challenged here. With the first Gilded Age of the nineteenth century and the Great Depression that followed it in the early twentieth century came critical views of market-capitalism that envisioned alternatives to how we should handle any quest for prosperity. The New Deal in the United States came about partially because of the consequences of extreme wealth inequality, the collapse of the economy, and unprecedented levels of unemployment. These were crises of faith (in the markets, in the ability of capitalist growth to overcome poverty and suffering, and in the liberal ideology in general) as much as material crises that exposed the ugly and perhaps unintended side effects of unfettered capitalism. Early critics of classical capitalism, such as Karl Marx, inveighed against the system as inherently unjust and purposefully set up to hurt the working poor and enrich the bourgeoisie. Echoes of their and their disciple's voices resonate loudly today.

With the *age of excess* experienced at the dawn of the twenty-first century (with the celebrity cult of conspicuous consumption) and the Great Recession that ensued in 2008, plenty of critical treatises have emerged. Their authors are the usual suspects, the Marxists and socialists of yesteryear, and committed leftist-liberals who believe their ideals have been unfairly overlooked. This is true when a moral dimension is highlighted among economic variables. In some cases, a psychosocial perspective is explained amid the economic turmoil, so that wealth excess is coupled with the *age of anxiety* (Ehrenreich 2016). Adding my critical voice to this growing cacophony, I plan to revisit some hidden *presuppositions* that guide economic models. Instead of belaboring the consequences of market-capitalism (from wealth and income inequalities to poverty and lack of health coverage), it seems more fruitful to question the basic *assumptions* that have been taken for granted far too long (outlined in detail in part I).

My strategy is to focus on the moral dimension of political economy in a manner reminiscent of classical capitalism's original inception. After all, *market-capitalism* (as it has been labeled since then) was supposed to cure the ills of feudalism and slavery and usher an *age of prosperity*. More importantly, prosperity was promised to all. As will become evident, if we question the foundations of *political economy* we can more fruitfully offer solutions to what are seen as endemic problems. Unlike Joseph Stiglitz, for example, who rightfully argues that we have made policy choices that brought about the sad state of the economy, and with full agreement with his later admission that the "story of the Eurozone is a morality play" (2016, xix), my book exposes fundamental ideas and principles that still guide such policy choices. It's not enough to declare that we can make different choices and that these choices depend on political, ideological, and moral convictions, but rather we must be more explicit about how policy choices should be explicitly guided by *moral principles* we can stand by; otherwise, who is to say that these, too, will not be misguided?

The standard indictments of the internal contradictions of capitalism, from leftists (Harvey 2014) to liberals (Cassidy 2010, Madrick 2014) and those informed by a single, totalizing critique of the neoliberal dominance of the American political economy (Giroux 2004, Brown 2015), have done a marvelous job of exposing that which needs to be exposed: how ideological zeal brought about the ugly side of market-capitalism. These books are political as much as they are about the economy and are complemented by the work of legal scholars concerned with the capitalist influence on the political system in general and American democracy in particular (Lessig 2011, Kuhner 2014). Unfortunately, in our *age of distraction* their biting critiques are sometimes smoothed over if not completely overshadowed by scores of newfound promises of how to remedy market-capitalism. There are those who recommend policy revisions (Stiglitz 2013), while others smugly celebrate the transformation of market-capitalism into its latest version, labeled "crowd-sourced capitalism" or more reassuringly "sharing economy" (Sundararajan 2016). Perhaps we lack the will power to make drastic changes; perhaps we can be consoled with marginal changes. But as is expected here, radical changes in our thinking are possible. Indeed, they require the will to imagine a *moral* political economy.

Sociologists (Goffman 1974) and behavioral psychologists (Kahneman 2011) remind us that the *framing* of questions predetermines what answers we can expect. Questions guide the conversation, as Socrates already illustrated millennia ago. If we dare focus, as laboriously as we have done in part I, on the historical presuppositions that underlie our views of human exchanges, then we are better prepared to tackle contemporary debates over *human behavior* and claims about *human nature*. If we routinely insist that humans are by nature competitive, then of course we couldn't imagine them behaving cooperatively; but they do, and they can be socialized to do so when they are young and in old age. If we are concerned with the *quest for prosperity*, we should examine it on various levels: What do we mean when using this concept? Is it defined exclusively in monetary terms or as the attainment of tranquility and peace of mind? More specifically, should we even concern ourselves with prosperity when viability and sustainability should come first? In other words, is prosperity *sustainable*? If it is, under what conditions should we endeavor to achieve it?

Critically analyzing troubling questions about the frames of political economy and their theories requires what Joseph Schumpeter mentions in passing as the four-stage process by which economic analysis has proceeded historically. The *first stage* includes "the enquiry into the nature of the phenomena we are to study"; the *second* being "the discovery of the relations which, guided by our knowledge of their nature, we conceive to subsist between them"; the *third* is putting "them together into a system (a theoretical 'model')"; and the *fourth* allows us then to "ask whether there is a unique set of values of the elements that appear in this system as variables (or 'unknowns') that will satisfy all those equations which must all hold simultaneously" (1954, 970). Paraphrasing, this means: *first*, choose your area of research; *second*, collect the relevant data and see how they are connected; *third*, systematize your connections into models; and *fourth*, figure out if the system as a whole works as you imagined it theoretically. Since economic conversations have been predicated on the achievement of (material and thereby psychosocial) prosperity, and since they implicitly assume such prosperity to be sustainable, it's a worthwhile exercise.

Unlike Marx who found the bourgeoisie not only the beneficiaries of capitalist production but also accused them and their theoreticians of falsely setting up models to legitimate their unjust exploitation of the proletariat, and unlike some contemporary critics of neoliberal maleficence, my concern is less with pointing fingers (even when they deservedly need to be pointed at culprits); it's more about finding *reasonable common ground* about human behavior, interpersonal relations, the human condition within the confines of our environmental realities, and a just political economy. As the last chapter of this book will show, thinking critically about how a just political economy can be constituted requires a thorough reassessment of the *frames of refer-*

ences we take for granted. For example, *trust* is a moral and not only an economic condition of human relations. This means that what may work well for a small village of the eighteenth century (in terms of neighborly familiarity and ongoing cross-generational encounters) may not be scalable for the digitally connected globe. Where local "politics" were understood in traditional terms and the internal and external tribal relations that extended generations, in modern society politics are institutionalized or even constitutionally circumscribed.

Traditional relations (understood economically) must account for the difference between setting up economic models based partially on colonial or imperialistic realities (where questions of trade are fundamentally skewed and inherently immoral) as opposed to more democratic relations (however defined) where exchange is voluntary rather than coercive. How is trust to be treated within these different models? Likewise, questions of scale—the size of the village economy versus the size of the European Union today—must be reexamined. Just as economists have appreciated "economies of scale" in terms of large-scale efficiency, so must we appreciate *scales of reference* that break down when institutions become too big to manage, when their sheer size changes them qualitatively and the mindset of those operating within their constraints. Likewise, what worked for the transformation of an agrarian and slave age into an industrial one may have little to do with the transformation into the digital age (Sassower 2013), especially as it affects economic relations and the legal protections they enjoy (from intellectual property to bankruptcy laws).

Power and control, exploitation and oppression are undertaken in bad faith when their proponents pretend to present what "naturally" or divinely occurs (and therefore should be accepted) instead of admitting that their fabrications are self-serving. The process of critical engagement is supposed to unveil such pretensions, while acknowledging its own limitations. An ongoing dialectical process should allow our imagination to transcend existing economic and political models even if they, too, will be eventually transcended. Comparing one set of choices to another, assessing one value in comparison to another, should help in making reasonable policy choices. This realization dates back the notion of the logic of the situation (Popper 1957), situational epistemology (feminism), and the predictable irrationality recorded by behavioral economists (Thaler 1992, and Kahneman 2011). In a different form, evolutionary biologists still hotly debate this issue in terms of the unit of selection: Is it the gene, the individual, or the species? (Wilson 1975, 2012) Finally, when we think of political economy, the sphere that brings together our moral sentiments, the material conditions of our existence, and the mechanisms and organizations with which we can ensure long-term peaceful viability (Sraffa 1960) or sustainability, Marx's critique of classical economics still rings true: political economy is set in place as a justification (rather than a critical explanation) of existing modes of exchange.

The Marxist critique resonates today more than ever because of three reasons: *first*, capitalism in its latest manifestation has brought the fruits of its success to only 1 percent of the population (Piketty 2013/2014 on inequality), and as such, it has failed to fulfill its own promises of "prosperity for all"; *second*, the failure of State socialism in the USSR and its satellite States has proven that both socialism and the State needs to be reconsidered (Griffiths 2014); and *third*, the critical dialectical method that characterizes Hegel's and Marx's works remains analytically fruitful because of its dynamic and open-ended methodology (extricating its overbearing determinism). The ongoing process of approaching problems by questioning all assumptions, their internal rationality or reasonableness (no appeal to supernatural forces), and their open-endedness (ongoing intellectual revolution) can even offer provisional solutions. Instead of reverting back to Marx's own analysis, as some more orthodox Marxists still continue to do today (Wolff 2012, Zaretsky 2012, Harvey 2014), I hope to follow a more postmodern orientation that empowers us to liberally employ whatever is still useful from the past without carrying the intellectual or ideological baggage associated with it. This includes Marxism, Institutionalism, Pluralism, and economic heterodoxy. In other words, the resources of the past can be redeployed for novel purposes without the burden of orthodoxy or the dismissal of utopianism.

After discussing some of the standard frames of reference (part I), we move to tease from them the most salient assumptions and then demarcate between those that are intellectually dangerous (intentionally misleading to promote an agenda) and those that can be useful for reconstructing models for political economy. In doing so, it will become apparent the extent to which some of them are interrelated. Two general theories or approaches are then considered, Communitarianism and Institutionalism, as worthy candidates that integrate some of these issues (part II). The next step of the argument is to critically evaluate newer models (twenty-first century ones) and see if they are nothing more than reconfigured older ones or original presentations (part III). An example would be the way in which economic anthropologists (Graeber 2014) reconfigure historically "debt" and "credit" so as to contribute to the current debate over wealth inequality. The criterion of assessment in this stage is whether or not these models are improvements. This critical stage is followed by several case studies from the Catholic Church, the kibbutz movement in Israel, US communes, to the military. Ignoring some of their less attractive features (hierarchy, authority, and power plays), the focus here is on their relational and communal features (part IV). In surveying these case studies, the main concern is teasing out their communal practices as guides for economic exchanges.

For those who are only interested in the provisional model I propose, they can focus on chapter 15 and the Epilogue alone. For those interested in the historical and philosophical issues that arise when critically examining the presuppositions of political economy, the first three parts will be informative. Overall, the intent here is to open our minds to thinking more radically about the conditions under which we interact with our fellow humans without the distraction that seems to capture our attention, if not our imagination. Daring to imagine a future different from the present, where economic growth is not paramount, might alter what we believe we can achieve still in our lifetime. Neoliberal and populist ideologies steer us away from considering alternative models, the ones that arise from the inspiring Marxist, Popperian, and post-modern movements.

Acknowledgments

This long journey into the mysteries of political economy as a philosophical rather than an economic study has taken four decades, since my years as a student. Therefore, I should begin by thanking four of my professors, the late Paul Rosenstein-Rodan, the late Marx Wartofsky, the late Robert S. Cohen, and Joseph Agassi, who in their different ways encouraged me to undertake a lifelong research program.

More recently, my dear colleagues Michael Sawyer (Colorado College) and Jeff Scholes (UCCS) have graciously given me much to think about with their feedback. Other academics that have guided my initial steps were Catherine Mary Lamberton (University of Pittsburgh), Adi Ophir (Brown University), John Watkins (Westminster College), and my dear brother-in-law Sam Gill (San Francisco State University). Special thanks also go to my dear friend and kindred spirit, Steve Fuller (Warwick University), who remains a constant soundboard and inspiration. My students Seif Jensen, Trinity Parker, and Logan Miller read drafts and pointed out deficiencies; I am grateful for their intellectual dedication.

Finally, I'd like to thank my academic home, the University of Colorado, Colorado Springs, whose administrators have not stood in my intellectual way as I pursued this critical line of inquiry.

Part I

Assumptions Underlying Theories

This part is devoted to an exposure of some of the frames of reference we take for granted when we discuss anything to do with political economy—how people behave, how "natural" their behavior is, and under what conditions their behavior is modified. The assumptions that inform these so-called frames of reference are either taken for granted or swept under the intellectual carpet because they have been historically used and once used, not critically reexamined or because they are popularly accepted in the media or daily discourse. This is reminiscent of John Maynard Keynes's final words of his *The General Theory of Employment, Interest, and Money* of 1936: "Practical men, who believe themselves to be quite exempt from any intellectual influence, are usually the slaves of some defunct economist." Ideas take time to gradually find their ways into our collective consciousness, "but, soon or late, it is ideas, not vested interests, which are dangerous for good or evil" (1936/1964, 383–84). Yes, ideas and the assumptions on which they are based have the final word, as far as Keynes is concerned; and their influence is greater than most are consciously aware of.

Moreover, my own reexamination of standard assumptions is worthwhile, as Keynes says about his own critical evaluation of classical economic doctrine: "Our criticism of the accepted classical theory of economics has consisted not so much in finding logical flaws in its analysis as in pointing out that its tacit assumptions are seldom or ever satisfied, with the result that it cannot solve the economic problems of the actual world" (ibid., 378). If our ultimate goal in this book is to explain the quest for prosperity and appreciate the conditions under which it is impeded or enhanced, it's essential that such "tacit assumptions" found in the history of economic thought should be fore-grounded, exposed, critically evaluated, and then either used or discarded, as is appropriate. Simply accepting all of them is a folly that should be guarded against, even if newly formulated assumptions may not fare much better. At least they will be explicit and open to public scrutiny.

Chapter One

Abundance/Scarcity

From the Garden of Eden to Utopia

Most historical or historically informed texts that deal with theories of political economy, from John Locke and Adam Smith to more contemporary ones by Milton Friedman and behavioral economists, assume that scarcity is our natural condition. If indeed natural resources are scarce, then certain other factors are bound to frame the discussion of production, distribution, and consumption. For example, questions of efficient resource allocation become paramount, whether the good under examination is energy or food. But if scarcity is only an assumption rather than a reality, and if instead abundance is the natural condition under which to make political and economic decisions, then many theories and the policy decisions based on them should be changed. My interest here is to outline the genealogy of this frame of reference and suggest that particular ideological interests have foregrounded scarcity rather than abundance. Though offered as brief vignettes, what follows is supposed to offer a picture of natural abundance that somehow has disappeared for a long time, until revisited more recently under the guise of technological innovations, industrial and digital.

I: DEFINITIONS

Among the definitions of scarcity found in the *Oxford English Dictionary*, one can note those associated with positive attributes concerned with saving and preservation, such as *frugality* and *parsimony*. But amid these definitions one can also find some associated with negative attributes, such as *niggardliness*, *stinginess*, and *meanness*. Regardless of one's inclination to consider the term either positively or negatively, one can appreciate the ubiquity of the term *scarcity* and the ambiguous meaning it has in certain social, political, and economic practices. Should society abhor scarcity and try to overcome it whenever and however possible? Or, should society resign itself to the "facts of life or nature" and accept scarcity as unavoidable? Should scarcity be welcomed and manipulated to some advantage? Or, should it be overcome to "create" abundance?

More useful definitions in the *Oxford English Dictionary* (*OED*) emphasize the "insufficiency of supply; smallness of available quantity, number, or amount, in proportion to the need or demand." In support of this particular definition, John S. Mill's *Political Economy* is quoted: "things which cannot be increased ad libitum in quantity, and which therefore, if the demand goes beyond a certain amount, command a scarcity value" (III, iv, section 6, (1876 edition), 283). A comment about value is added: "an enhanced value due to scarcity." This particular definition may be troubling to most economists, since the adjective *enhanced* makes no sense. Either there is value due to scarcity—scarcity is defined as lending value to things—or there is no value; what does it mean to have "enhanced value"? In addition, the *OED* uses the following terms to identify scarcity: "comparative fewness . . . rare," "scantiness," "inadequate provision of the necessities of life—hardship." Here the emphasis is on the problem inherent in certain "things": they cannot be "increased" at will. Things, such as water and air, were considered unproblematic for a long time, so that the notion of scarcity could not be applied to them. Singling out water and air has become a historical anachronism: water and air alike are scarce in the sense described above. So, does that mean that water and air "command a scarcity value" in the sense of "an enhanced value"? Since the answer is affirmative, one must wonder if there is any "thing" left today that will fall outside of Mill's classification. If the answer is negative, according to most environmentalists, then this classification is of no help; it is too broad: everything is scarce by definition.

Can Mill's definition be rescued if scarcity is distinguished from shortage, for example, in the sense that there can be shortage of everything but only certain things are considered scarce? According to Janos Kornai (1980, Introduction), the notions of scarcity and abundance are more fundamental than the notion of shortage. He is not interested in describing or criticizing a system of economic activities, capitalist or socialist, which fails to accomplish a set of goals, such as bringing to an equilibrium the production and consumption of the system, the supply and demand portions of the economy. The notion of shortage is exclusively concerned with the failure of the system, and is therefore an internal problem, not one through which a critique of the whole theoretical framework of political economy can be handled. One may argue that an internal critique, what critical theorists call an immanent critique, can provide insights fundamental to the very conception of the system/model/theory that is criticized. Just as in the case of shortages (chronic or temporary) in a socialist society, one would be providing a parallel but not identical examination of the problem of unemployment and underutilization of resources in a capitalist society.

So, the notion of scarcity is different from that of shortage at least in the sense that the former is considered more fundamental than the latter. More fundamental in what sense? According to Kornai, in the sense of being able to correct shortages, either of capitalist or socialist economies, while being unable to overcome scarcity. Scarcity, then, is not an artificial human construct or invention, but is understood as a natural given. However, phrasing the question of scarcity in empirical terms has itself been open to critical evaluations over the years. That is, it remains unclear what the empirical status of scarcity was, is, and will be.

II: THE GARDEN OF EDEN

The Bible is similarly confusing on these questions. While the narrative of creation in Genesis bespeaks of abundance, and the picture in the Garden of Eden is considered an ideal materialized by divine will for the sake of Adam and Eve, there is also the story of the expulsion from that very Garden. Once Adam and Eve leave the state of abundance, where they roam freely and need not work for their subsistence, Adam's curse is that he should earn his bread by the sweat of his brow. Does this curse turn the human condition around, and change the state of bliss into a state of torture? Must humanity indeed labor continuously and undergo hardship in order to survive in this world? Is this a condemnation or a justification of what actually exists; namely, limited resources for which humanity competes?

Most accounts of the Garden of Eden focus on the serpent's seduction of Eve and her seduction of Adam in turn to eat from the forbidden fruit of the tree of knowledge and their expulsion, or what the Christian tradition calls the Fall (from grace). The running assumptions about the Garden are first, that there is abundance in the garden where "the Lord God caused to grow every tree that was pleasing to the sight and good for food, with the tree of life in the middle of the garden, and the tree of knowledge of good and bad. A river issued from Eden to water the garden"; and second, Adam was placed "in the garden of Eden, to till it and tend it" (Genesis 2:8, 15). What we may miss from the narrative in our theological haste is the fact that though the garden offers abundance for Adam (and eventually Eve), there is an expectation that he will "till it and tend it." What does this entail? As we learn much later when original sin is committed (the eating from the forbidden fruit of the tree of knowledge), and Adam and Eve are expelled from the garden, Adam's punishment is "by toil shall you eat of it" and "by the sweat of your brow shall you get bread to eat" (ibid., 17, 19). It's unclear if abundance has been replaced with scarcity, yet it's quite clear that the custodial responsibilities have been replaced with a cursed existence of hard labor. Leisure has been forever denied in the name of sweat and death, "to dust you shall return" (ibid.).

The image of abundance accepted as the starting point for all the Abrahamic religions is striking not simply because it begins with the opulence of abundance, but because it sets in place a divinely sanctioned starting point for humanity, one that was squandered away. With this in mind, Christopher Jennings argues that the ancient and mystical "Judeo-Christian proposition that history is bookended by golden ages" was coupled with the modern, rational one "that the human race is advancing ineluctably toward a perfection of our own making" (2016, 4). Just as humanity began in the Garden of Eden, so will its worthy candidates end up in Heaven: both are understood as idyllic places where abundance and immortality are guaranteed. It's in the "middle" space and time where humanity confronts scarcity and hardship, pain and suffering. Theologically, the question isn't limited to the relationship between humanity and the divine (where disobedience and lying fractured the intimacy of the two), but is also informed by the human quest for knowledge (realizing nakedness in the garden and eventually more sophisticated attempts to understand the universe).

Between the beginning of life as we know it and its eventual death (return to the dust of the earth), generation after generation must endure work for the sake of survival. There can be no reliance on an omnipotent power for prosperity. If we pay less attention to the theological message and focus on the idea that divine creation brought about a state of abundance, we may also appreciate the Native American view of humanity as custodians of the great Earth gifted to them by the gods. It was clear to Native Americans that "the Creator of life" gave them their lands and that their chiefs and tribal councils have "the responsibility for protecting the lands of our children and the unborn generations to come" (Hill 1992, 171). Unlike the biblical relationship between the divine and humanity, for Native Americans there is a continuity of abundance for which they are responsible as caretakers and which they therefore cannot privately own or tender to newcomers and outsiders. (In this book I use the term *Native Americans* interchangeably with *First People*, *Indigenous Americans*, *American Indians*, and others.)

III: THE ANCIENTS

For some historians, scarcity in the sense of overpopulations has been an empirical reality as early as the sixth century BC. Barry Cunliffe, for example, quotes from Herodotus the incident that led to the establishment of new colonies, in this case off the coast of Libya, with the advice given by the oracle of Delphi. According to Cunliffe, colonization was a standard response by society "when population level approaches or exceeds the holding capacity of the land" (1988, 12–13). Though the conditions that determine the "holding capacity of the land" may vary from city to city, from one island to another, there seemed to be a common appreciation of the need to migrate, to form new cities and colonies, so that issues of scarcity will not undermine the development and well-being of the population.

The sense of the given environment, an environment in which human beings must learn to live with whatever is available to them, has also been discussed by Plato and Aristotle. For both the question was not what is scarce or found in abundance. Rather, it was a question of social and political economic arrangements and structures through which the questions of scarcity and abundance are answered indirectly. And the important question for both Plato and Aristotle is the legitimation of the construction of a city/*polis* in terms of self-sufficiency.

Plato argues in *The Republic* that "a city comes to be . . . because not one of us is self-sufficient, but needs many things" (369b). The multitude of needs we and others have are reciprocally fulfilled. From this argument, incidentally, the notion of the division of labor, as it eventually makes its way to Adam Smith, arises already here quite naturally. Aristotle echoes Plato's sense of justification for the establishment of an ordered city when he says in *Politics* that "now self-sufficiency [which it is the object of the state to bring about] is the end, and so the best; [and on this it follows that the state brings about the best, and is therefore natural, since nature always aims at bringing about the best]" (*Politics* 1253a).

Among the ancient Greeks whose insights have remained the starting point for most Euro-American thinking, we find Aristotle's *Politics* as offering some clues to their view of what nature is supposed to provide humanity. Aristotle explains that "it is the business of nature to furnish subsistence for each being brought into the world; and this is shown by the fact that the offspring of animals always gets nourishment from the residuum of the matter that gives it its birth" (ibid., 1258a). The language here is of "subsistence" rather than abundance, but it ensures full "nourishment" for all living beings, as if it were nature's responsibility to do so. Instead of a moral duty, this responsibility is understood in a utilitarian or functional way. In his words: "As nature makes nothing purposeless or in vain, all animals must have been made by nature for the sake of men" (ibid., 1256b). This view of natural resources, including all animals, as being made for the "sake of men" comes close to the biblical notion of humans' dominion over the animal kingdom.

Underlying this view of perfectly functioning nature, there is also a sense that human subsistence is not simply promised by the gods, but that more specifically human survival is naturally guaranteed. If we were to worry that mere subsistence is offered and no more, Aristotle continues to claim that natural resources "serve to furnish man not only with food, but also with other comforts, such as the provision of clothing and similar aids to life" (ibid.). Natural provisions are mentioned by Aristotle as part of a broader argument about property and the "art of acquisition," topics we will discuss below. As is the case with the general theme of his discussion of the ideal political arrangements among people, the point for him is the discouragement of excess, the moral probity not to accumulate beyond one's needs or the needs of the "household," which for him is the cornerstone of economic relationships. Abundance and scarcity are not mentioned as such because they are at the two extremes of the spectrum of options of what nature offers humans or what humans find in nature; instead, the concept of subsistence is invoked, perhaps what we would think of today as sustainability, the ways in which humanity can provide for itself in the long run.

So, do Plato and Aristotle avoid the question of scarcity altogether? Though appearing to avoid the question, the fact that they emphasize the prudence of the city-state and the inner working of a social, political, and economic arrangement for the sake of self-sufficiency intimates that the backdrop they assume is that of scarcity of resources. The issue of self-sufficiency, now discussed in social as opposed to individual terms, brings us closer to an understanding of the economic organization of society to over-come scarcity. What society can do for the individual is what every individual can do for every other individual: contribute to the social pool from which everyone can draw and thereby overcome any personal sense of unmet need or scarcity.

Self-sufficiency is treated not only by historians and philosophers but also by anthropologists, and more specifically social or economic anthropologists. In a most engaging book, Marshall Sahlins argues that preagricultural soci-eties of hunters may be considered to have lived the life of affluence (even if not abundance in the traditional sense), and not to have suffered from scar-city. According to Sahlins, one need not adopt the familiar modern concep-tion of economists that "man's wants are great, not to say infinite, whereas his means are limited, although improvable" (1971, 2), an assumption that usually leads to an emphasis on industrial productivity and economic growth as the ways by which to minimize the inherent gap between needs and their means of satisfaction. Instead, Sahlins offers what he terms a Zen strategy, claiming that "human material wants are finite and few, and technical means unchanging but on the whole adequate" (ibid., 144). Empirically speaking, this would mean that human needs are finite (tranquility assumed) and hu-man wants are infinite.

If one were to follow Sahlins's road to affluence, one would not be required to adopt the standard features associated with the neoclassical Eco-nomic Man. From anthropological data one could reconstruct a social setting whereby economic needs are easily satisfied, where the ratio between labor and leisure is much more favorable than enjoyed in postindustrial society, and where questions of scarcity are only marginal to the way people conduct their life. Sahlins's ideas provide a challenge to the liberal reconstruction of the notion of scarcity as it developed historically. In other words, Sahlins's treatise provides direct challenge to the empirical basis assumed for the theoretical discussion of the role scarcity plays in contemporary economic thought.

IV: SCARCITY IN THE LIBERAL MOLD

(a) Thomas Hobbes (1588–1679)

Though we are jumping now to the seventeenth century, what becomes clear right into the twenty-first century is that references to divine intervention, the blessings of God, and the plentiful of His creation are still evident in the Western canon. In his *Leviathan*, Thomas Hobbes refers to the "Plenty of Matter" as "a thing limited by Nature, to those commodities, which from (the two breasts of our common Mother) Land, and Sea, God usually either freely giveth, or for labour selleth to man-kind" (1651/1968, 295). This language of the "common Mother" is reminiscent of Native American imagery, and the focus on the sources of abundance—land and sea—makes perfect sense. Given an agricultural society, the cultivation of the land and the fishing of the seas would provide plentifully for a fairly small population (regardless, for writers like Hobbes, of the feudal inequities of the time). God is seen here more of a mediator rather than a creator, the one who either "freely giveth" or "selleth," depending on what natural resources are under consideration. Natural plentiful consists of "Animals, Vegetals [*sic*], and Minerals" that are "in or neer [*sic*] to the face of the Earth," and as such require only "the labour, and industry of receiving them." In this sense, abundance is characterized in terms of the labor and industry of humanity "(next to Gods favour [*sic*])," as Hobbes says (ibid.).

Humanity's labor and industry are neither divine curses nor a burden that shifts the conception of the plentiful of nature into scarcity. Instead, there is a more nuanced appreciation that the maintenance of abundance can be intermingled with human labor and industry, "Native" or "Forraign [*sic*]." There is an intimation that labor itself is bountiful and that industrious humans can fully enjoy natural fruits. This starting point eventually leads Hobbes to argue about the quarrels that are bound to erupt or that should lead to a more just forms of exchange (including human labor as a "commodity exchangeable for benefit") under the ideal Commonwealth (ibid.). Our interest here is to point out that the biblical and Native American images of creation and the abundance of Nature are common and widely shared across various cultures and linguistic domains. These images also inform the construction of the state of nature, as we shall see shortly, and the juxtaposition of an abundant landscape on the behavior of humans.

(b) John Locke (1632–1704)

Just as Hobbes appreciates the fruits of Mother Nature with the grace of God, so does Locke pay homage to the biblical narrative and God's apparent license to humanity to command His creations. Adam is given Earth's dominion twice: once when it is said: "Let us make man in our image, after our likeness. They shall rule the fish of the sea, the birds of the sky, the cattle, the whole earth, and all the creeping things that creep on earth" (Genesis 1:26), and the second time, two verses later: "God blessed them and God said to them, 'Be fertile and increase, fill the earth and master it'" (Genesis 1:28). It's noteworthy that though at this stage of the narrative only Adam is created in God's image, the injunction to rule and master Earth is given in the plural, invoking a sense of human genealogy, where the entire human race is in position of control and power over nature. This is the background story that informs Locke and his contemporaries in matters of government: Who has the authority and under what auspices to rule over others? If God grants Adam the first rule on Earth, then it makes perfect sense for these thinkers to extend the blessing all the way to their monarchs, as we see in his *First Treatise*. As divine gifts, whatever natural resources are found in nature are plentiful and denote a level of abundance Native Americans have appreciated.

As we shall see later, it's Locke's intention to explain how humanity moves from a state of nature to a civil society in the *Second Treatise*, under conditions of a "compact." But as he develops his argument, Locke also allows that "God, who hath given the world to men in common, hath also given them reason to make use of it to the best advantage of life and convenience" (1690/1947, 134). Reluctant to remain in this "common" gift relationship, a condition he attributes to the "wild Indian, who knows no closure and is still a tenant in common" (ibid.), Locke suggests that human reason knows better than to remain in this state of common dominion over nature. The so-called law of reason is what prompts humans through their labor to remove parts of nature out of their "common state" (ibid., 135). It's quite easy, once you agree with these first moves of the argument, to end up with private property and laws that govern exchanges. At this stage, though, our interest is with the question of abundance that was given by the creator and the lack of any notion of scarcity that creeps into the economic literature much later. If abundance is presupposed, is it really the question of common ownership of property that riles Locke? Why is it that the initial biblical gift, whether in the

Garden of Eden or elsewhere, must be identified with an individual rather than with Adam and Eve and their progeny?

John Commons adds the following commentary: "Hence Locke's presupposition of abundance of land granted to free men in common by a beneficent creator, [is coupled] with the duty to work and multiply," as we have shown above. He continues: "The economic term 'abundance' is equivalent to Locke's theological term 'beneficence.' With this presupposition of abundance there could be no contradiction between material things and ownership of the things." The insight is that "not until property means scarcity and labor means abundance does the contradiction appear" (1934/1990, 37). We shouldn't have lost the sense of abundance just because this piece of land or these natural resources are owned by individuals or communities. It's when such an ownership takes on the shape of private property and then is understood by its boundaries and limits that the concept of wanting more is set against a background of something scarce; by contrast, human labor seems to be less limited if not infinite, so that *it* becomes abundant and not natural resources. The infinite potential of human labor, to continue, is more clearly understood with technological innovations, from primitive tools to digital ones, because efficiencies and increased productivity make it look as if the labor canvas can be stretched forever.

As becomes clear from the little evidence provided here, it's the modern world of moral philosophers, such as Hobbes and Locke, which narrows the direction of the theoretical development of political economy. If the starting point of analysis is the political realities of the day, it stands to reason that *post hoc* arguments will be provided against public property rights in the name of private ones. Nature's abundance is thereby taken out of the equation, because if this fact remained intact any human rivalry would seem frivolous: What is there to fight over if we all have plenty to enjoy? The only striking allusion to this situation comes to light when Locke, admitting "the plenty God had given," also warns that "nothing was made by God for man to spoil or destroy" (ibid., 136). In this manner, Locke not only reiterates the "plenty" of nature but also adds a caveat about spoilage and destruction, reminiscent of Native American attitudes toward natural resources. On a different note he also introduces the notion of humanity's power over nature as a reformulation of the biblical injunction to tend and master.

(c) Jean-Jacques Rousseau (1712–1778)

As we are still inquiring about abundance and scarcity before any consideration of human intervention, toiling the land to have a sense of ownership, Rousseau says relatively little about these concepts. He admits at some point in the *Discourse on the Origin and Foundations of Inequality Among Men* that nature offered "gifts" to humanity (1754/1964, 142), gifts that were not fully appreciated, perhaps even squandered. From this perspective, "the earth, abandoned to its natural fertility and covered by immense forests never mutilated by the axe, offers at every step storehouses and shelters to animals of all species" (ibid., 105). Following other "beasts," humans satisfy their needs with the same ease and industry as others of God's creation. Rousseau "sees" man "satisfying his hunger under the oak, quenching his thirst at the first stream, finding his bed at the foot of the same tree that furnished his meal; and therewith his needs are satisfied" (ibid.).

It's much later, in Rousseau's own analysis of the shift from the "noble savage" to the so-called civilized man, that he denounces the kind of inequality that emerges with the initiation of private property. As Marx argues much later, the difference between needs and wants is often confused, even blurred under the aegis of the fetishism of commodity consumption. If humanity's needs are met at every step, then there is no scarcity as such; instead, it's an artificial artifact of civilized society where flaunting one's possessions brings about competition and strife, even rivalry and fights. As long as we speak about the natural condition of Earth, as Rousseau calls it, or the state of nature without humanity as its focal point, there is a seamless continuity between all animals and humanity, a continuum of self-preservation with a modicum of pity toward others (ibid., 95).

However, the notion of scarcity does eventually make its way into Locke's *Treatise* as well in the discussion of money. Money, for Lock, is "some lasting thing that men might keep without spoiling, and that by mutual consent men would take in exchange for the truly useful but perishable supports of life." Scarcity is an artificial product of humans, introduced into their social and economic interactions as a means to overcome the divine injunction against the destruction and spoilage of natural resources. And it is exactly this means, money or gold or silver as means of exchange and savings, that transforms society from living in the state of nature into civil society. And as C. B. Macpherson reminds us (1962), this situation transforms individuals into "possessive" ones and provides a legitimation device for classical capitalism.

Natural abundance is the starting point for liberal theorists, but it quickly gives way to the consideration of scarcity. The notion of scarcity helps explain human relations within a particular economic framework, the capitalist marketplace, where labor itself is a commodity. Without scarcity, the only reason for working is for the provision of one's own needs; without scarcity, there is no argument for establishing private as opposed to public property rights. And finally, from an emphasis on the value of "things" in terms of their use or the labor that is needed to make them useful, there is a shift to a discussion of the tools of exchange and commerce, and money, gold, and silver become themselves scarce and valuable.

V: CLASSICAL POLITICAL ECONOMY

In contrast to Hobbes and Locke, Smith and Malthus no longer speak of the plenty of nature as a divine or natural given, but evaluate nature in social terms. That is, the notions of scarcity and abundance are understood as relative terms, relative to the population and the national boundaries within which societies produce, exchange, and consume. Moreover, what gains prominence in the classical liberal and economic literature is an appreciation of the boundless desires and wants of society, so boundless that nature cannot accommodate them all. The Hobbesian influence of Smith's predecessor, David Hume, is emphasized by Aryeh Botwinick, who explains that according to Hume, "the economic base of society must be positioned between total abundance and absolute scarcity in order for 'justice' to become operative" (1981, 7–15). So, the relative position of the notions of scarcity and abundance in economic terms plays a crucial role not only in economic theory or for the legitimization of a certain economic perspective but also in relation to a conception of the social contract and justice.

(a) Adam Smith (1723–1790)

In his "Lectures on Jurisprudence," Smith joins his predecessors in making some bold statements about nature: "Nature produces for every animal every thing [*sic*] that is sufficient to support it without having recourse to the improvement of the original production" (1762–1766/1978, 487). This sounds like a level of abundance only divine benevolence could have supplied so that all imaginable human needs could be met. He continues: "Food, Cloaths [*sic*], and lodging are all the wants of any animal whatever, and most of the animal creation are sufficiently provided for by nature." But humans are not satisfied with being provided for their needs and wants: "Such is the delicacy of man alone, that no object is produced to his liking. He finds that in every thing [*sic*] there is need for improvement" (ibid.). It's not only the "improvement" upon nature's generous offerings that distinguishes humanity from the rest of the animal kingdom, or that humanity cannot provide for itself more refined "delicacies," but that eventually "conveniences" overtake the mere fulfillment of needs. In his words: "The whole industry of human life is employed not in procuring the supply of our three humble necessities, food, cloaths [*sic*], and lodging, but in procuring the conveniences of it according to the nicety and delicacy of our taste" (ibid., 488). This shift not only from needs to wants, in the Marxian sense, but also to more delicate tastes will eventually lead to an exchange relationship exercised in markets.

While most references to scarcity and abundance in Smith's most renowned work, *An Inquiry into the Nature and Causes of the Wealth of Nations*, are in relation to markets and the supply and demand of various goods, in this chapter our concern is with natural resources and the ways in which assumptions about them were used for economic theorizing. Smith mentions that "the demand for water exceeds that for any thing [*sic*] else whatever, but as the abundance is more than sufficient to answer all the possible demands water bears no price; whilst other things of no real value whose use we can hardly conceive, yet being but in very small quantities bear an immense price as becoming only the purchase of a few. This is the case with jewels and stones" (1762–1763/1978, 358). The point here is less about natural resources and their divine source and much more about the initial understanding of how natural resources enter the exchange relationships in markets, where supply and demand regulate prices. As he repeats, "Every thing [*sic*] is dearer or cheaper according as the quantity of it makes it the purchase of the rich or of the poor" (ibid., 359). The shift from the natural habitat to the markets right away is accompanied by a sense of the rich and the poor and their ability to purchase goods and services at different levels of consumption and price. It is clear from these statements that Smith viewed natural resources as sufficient to accommodate human needs and wants, and that indeed there was abundance before humans developed their tastes and preferences. This improvement of the human condition or the refinement in whose names delicacies were sought after brought about the need to employ others, even though at some basic level humans could provide for themselves. This peculiar human feature disturbs to an extent the harmony or equilibrium of human relations and brings them into a market where some goods are considered abundant, like water, and some are considered dear, like jewelry and precious metals.

Smith continues in his *Wealth of Nations* to say that "whatever be the soil, climate, or extent of territory of any particular nation, the abundance or scantiness of its annual supply" must depend on two circumstances: first, on "the skill, dexterity, and judgment with which its labour is generally applied," and second, on "the proportion between the number of those who are employed in useful labour, and that of those who are not so employed" (1776/1937, lvii). Hence, one cannot assume either scarcity or abundance, but must understand them as relative to the application of labor. The wealth of nations is defined in terms of annual production and not in terms of the amount of gold, silver, or jewelry that is found in the soil. By avoiding the assumption concerning scarcity or abundance, Smith focuses on the importance of the creation of abundance through the efficient division of labor among members of society. Yet Smith's own bias becomes clear, in contradistinction to Sahlins's anthropological studies, when speaking of the "savage nations of hunters and fishers" (ibid.). Though they can provide for themselves and their old, young, and infirm, Smith perceives them as "miserably poor" to the extent that they occasionally find themselves in need of "destroying" or "abandoning" their infant, old, and those afflicted with "lingering diseases." However, among "civilized and thriving nations," Smith continues, "the produce of the whole labour of the society is so great" that it can supply with abundance the needs of all of its members, even those of "the lowest and poorest order" (ibid.).

In this light, then, neither scarcity nor abundance is found in nature; they are socially imposed labels so as to motivate humanity to work hard and efficiently in the classical sense of economic theory. Given these circumstances, it seems that the economic model is predicated on a set of psychological principles and not on a set of practices enjoyed by preagricultural societies, for example. As will be shown later, the psychological dimension that directs the use of scarcity and abundance gains greater prominence in modernity, and it does so without reference to past practices, traditional modes of social interaction, or the reconsideration of psychological dispositions toward happiness or a peaceful lifestyle.

(b) Thomas Malthus (1766–1834)

Society, or more precisely its leading theorists, may motivate people not only to work harder in Smith's terms, but also to control population growth, as Thomas Malthus advocated. With specific acknowledgment of Hume and Smith, Malthus does not consider natural endowments apart from his consideration of the population that is to make use of them. His two principles are by now commonplace, even if refuted empirically. They are said to be based on common sense, vigorously deployed to argue well beyond economic matters. When Malthus argues that "the power of population is indefinitely greater than the power in the earth to produce subsistence for man," claiming that while the "unchecked" growth of population is geometrical the increase in subsistence is only arithmetical (1798/1970, 69), he is in effect arguing for the need to curb population growth. Such a curb can be achieved by imposing controls on the sexual habits of society, and more specifically targeting the lower, less-educated classes.

Malthus's famous *An Essay on the Principle of Population* shifted the discussion from the growing appetites of humans—appetites that could be curtailed—to an inherent natural problem: nature cannot supply enough food for the growing population. More precisely, birthrate growth would outstrip whatever resources could be cultivated. No matter how abundant nature has been in the past, the present human condition is bound to bring about scarcity of food and endanger the survival of the species. The degree to which this doom-and-gloom view was also motivated by a puritan theological posture in regard to human sexuality and the consequences of unregulated mating is beyond the scope of this brief survey.

The main point to remember at this point, as the culmination of the eighteenth century and the Age of Reason, is that despite images of human perfectibility and the progress of history (Hegelian or otherwise), it was Malthus who warned us against the exhaustion of natural resources. Yes, there might be abundance to begin with, but as we consume more and more, as our population keeps growing exponentially, there is a real danger that we might not be able to feed everyone. Malthus's warnings have been repeated many times since his original contribution, and only the ongoing progress in agricultural technologies was able to thwart their veracity. It's exactly this way of thinking about the ability to ensure nature's abundance through technological innovations that remains the hope of humanity in the twenty-first century. We believe that we can, given the proper mechanisms, maintain nature's abundance or at least overcome its potential shortfall. In this sense, it's the danger of scarcity that motivates our work to ensure the maintenance of abundance. And this work is enhanced not simply by hoping that divine intervention will provide for us, as religious texts seem to imply, but rather that human ingenuity will, from the cultivation of lands that were deemed barren to the development of Genetically Modified Objects, such as seeds, more resilient plants, and multiseasonal cultivation in greenhouses.

In some sense, Malthus explains his postulates and predictions on the basis of what nature itself has done. That is to say, nature is responsible for a distribution of the "seeds of life" in a far greater proportion, "with the most profuse and liberal hand," while at the same time being "comparatively sparing" in the space and the "nourishment necessary to rear them" (ibid., 71). So, is nature as such abundant or scarce? Just as Smith does not answer this question directly, or even finds it appropriate to answer without reference to human activity, so does Malthus avoid answering it directly. According to Malthus, nature provides an abundance of seeds and limited resources to nourish them. And in light of this, Malthus continues, there is a natural law of necessity that stipulates a natural equilibrium between abundance and scarcity.

As postulates, scarcity and abundance play a central role in Malthus's theory; but these are postulates that are considered self-evident, not requiring empirical testing; yet at the same time, Malthus assures his readers that his theory and its predictions can and will withstand empirical testing. The evidence that Malthus hoped would vindicate and support his arguments hasn't materialized yet, and even if it were to materialize, it would have been too late since the impact of Malthus's so-called predictions was immediate and served to enlist the support of liberal thinkers against the promiscuous sexual tendencies of British society. In this sense, Malthus's use of scarcity is ideological: it serves to advance a moral agenda with psychologically powerful scare tactics. And therefore it has remained effective in our collective imagination when we think of any sort of scarcity or about population growth.

Saying that scarcity is used ideologically may mean at least one of two things. On the one hand, it could mean that the concept of scarcity is used in a particular fashion regardless of relevant empirical evidence; on the other hand, it could mean that a particular use is due to the absence of relevant empirical evidence. Ideological beliefs constructed from the concept of scarcity, if considered true, then would cease to have ideological status (since they report relevant empirical data); perhaps this is the critical sense in which the concept of scarcity has surfaced in Marx's studies of political economy. One may even argue that the failure to examine the concept of scarcity in ideological terms is itself explicable in ideological terms (because we are already entrenched in our views and refuse to test our working presuppositions).

(c) Karl Marx (1818–1883)

Unlike his predecessors, the German idealists, Marx's view of nature is never separated from his view of human interaction with it. From his early *Economic and Philosophic Manuscripts of 1844* all the way to his mature *Capital*, his main point is that "*nature* too, taken abstractly, for itself—nature fixed in isolation from man—is *nothing* for man" (1972, 102, italics in the original). Any theological or abstract notions about nature, its abundance or the scarcity to which it is subjected by overpopulation, is meaningless for Marx. Instead, he shifts the theological and idealist notions of nature to the ways by which humanity interacts with it, the ways by which nature is imbued with human meaning. "Labour is, in the first place, a process in which both man and Nature participate, and in which man of his own accord starts. Regulates, and controls the material re-actions between himself and Nature." As such, humanity keeps on to "appropriate Nature's productions in a form adapted to his own wants" (*Capital*, Part III, chapter 7). But what about nature in its original form, neither as an abstraction nor without cultivation by humans?

Marx admits that nature does exit independently of humans and that as such it does supply humanity its needs, as it were, with minimal labor. This alludes to a form of initial abundance: "The soil (and this, economically speaking, includes water) in the virgin state in which it supplies man with the necessaries or the means of subsistence ready at hand, exists independently of him, and is the universal subject of human labour" (ibid.). So, yes, there a level of "subsistence" available from nature in its "virgin state," but that isn't enough, as Smith and others before him have argued. Marx adds two kinds of the engagements with nature, the first he associates with those activities which "labour merely separates from immediate connexion [*sic*] with their environment," such as fishing, collecting water, and using timber from the forest, and the second with those activities which have been "filtered through previous labour" (ibid.). Because of the inevitable labor relation of humanity with nature, he concludes this section of *Capital* by saying, "Thus Nature

becomes one of the organs of his activity, one that he annexes to his own
bodily organs, adding stature to himself in spite of the Bible" (ibid.). If we
thought that the nineteenth century references to the Bible may be subdued if
not completely disappear, here we have Marx setting his own view in contradistinction to the Bible.

There are no divine gifts given to humanity for its enjoyment and everlasting contentment, but instead nature is appropriated by humanity as part of
its "organs," as if it were an integral part of its activities and meaning. For
nature to have any human meaning it must be labored upon, it must be
interacted with, whatever the level of participation. In order to fully understand the significance of natural resources to human development, Marx
offers a comprehensive theoretical map that moves us from more primitive
modes of production to those of capitalism, allowing along the way for
human alienation from nature—in capitalist manufacturing institutions—as
well as the exploitation of workers by capitalists. If labor is the denominator
by which natural resources are measured (rather than the largesse of divine
creation or royal decree), then it becomes the Marxian yardstick according to
which all economic relations (and interpersonal ones as well) are to be measured. Adam's curse is not limited to what the Bible reports, but extends way
beyond hardship and sweat to complete exhaustion and suffering. The capitalist, in Marx's rendition, has taken God's punishment further into a systemic process of exploitation.

Marx's discussion of the notion of scarcity takes into account its ideological aspects as an analysis followed by a proposal for a solution to a situation
that is not empirically tested. Though not criticizing directly Malthus's theory of population for political and pedagogical reasons, according to Michael
Perelman, Marx does not avoid the discussion of natural scarcity. But for him
that scarcity is historically conditioned by a certain mode of production that
renders scarcity permanent. Therefore, says Perelman, "Marx was convinced
that the problems of population and scarcity, as well as environmental abuse,
could best be solved by socialism" (1987, 28). The emphasis here is on
"solving" scarcity, not merely creating an economic framework that would
prudently handle it. For Marx, then, the Malthusian issue of overpopulation
is relative to the needs of capital accumulations and not to natural conditions.
As Perelman continues, "Scarcity in this context is scarcity of employment
owing to the concentration of the means of production under the control of a
small class of capitalists operating according to the logic of profit and competition" (ibid., 31). In this respect, the notion of scarcity is intertwined with
a multitude of capitalist practices, practices that manufacture scarcity in the
form of shortages. The Marxian presumption that there is no inherent natural
scarcity is shared (contrary to Perelman) with other classical economists,
such as Smith.

Even if Perelman is correct in explaining why Marx attempts to downplay the importance of Malthus's concern with natural scarcity, there is no philosophical difference between his minimal use of the concept and the use that Smith, for example, makes of it. Marx perceives scarcity to be an ideological tool with which classical economists justify their theoretical constructions. Would it make any difference to Marx if there were relevant empirical data with which to examine scarcity? Though concerned with empirical data so that the scientific status of his critique is secured, Marx understands how the ideological game played by his predecessors (and ideological rivals) can work against them. The notion of scarcity is useful for Marx's critique of capitalism and the promotion of socialism, regardless of the empirical evidence that can be brought to bear on its significance.

VI: SOME REFERENCES IN CONTEMPORARY LITERATURE

One of the leaders of neoclassical economics, Lionel Robbins, recalls the biblical description of abundance and scarcity as mentioned above. He begins by reminding his readers that "we have been turned out of Paradise. We have neither eternal life nor unlimited means of gratification." He continues to say that "scarcity of means to satisfy ends of varying importance is an almost ubiquitous condition of human behaviour." This proposition leads him to state: "Here, then, is the unity of subject of Economic Science, the forms assumed by human behavior is disposing of scarce means" (1935, 15). According to Robbins, economists study "the disposal of scarce means." In this sense, then, "Economics is the science which studies human behavior as a relationship between ends and scarce means which have alternative uses" (ibid., 16).

Without the notion of scarcity as it applies to the means by which needs are satisfied, there is no such a thing as political economy or economics as a separate discipline. Put differently, since what is studied by political economists is human behavior, and since such behavior is studied in parallel by economists, political scientists, sociologists, and psychologists, it seems that contemporary thought cannot do without the concept of scarcity. What is scarce can be disputed, revised, and reconstituted; but that some sources must remain scarce can never be disputed. It is interesting to note that under the conditions of modern, postindustrial capitalism, one can find scarcity not as a source of concern (or manipulation), but rather something that can be easily overcome. Charles Maurice and Charles Smithson, for instance, believe that "if the marketplace is allowed to function, it will allocate scarce resources and thereby eliminate any future resource crises. A functioning marketplace will avert the resource-based Armageddon that some self-styled experts have predicted" (1984, 1). We can only guess what a functioning marketplace under *realpolitik* would look like, since it can either be unfettered or regulated and controlled so as to maximize efficiency and minimize waste from monopolistic-like behavior by large participants.

So, contemporary capitalism not only uses scarcity as an assumption to justify its theoretical framework but also in effect uses it as a tool by which scarcity can be efficiently handled so that its presence causes no crisis situations. But here Maurice and Smithson do not distinguish, as shown in the beginning of this chapter, the notions of scarcity and shortage. They say that their "faith in the marketplace is based on a simple observation: markets have dealt successfully with resource shortages for the past ten thousand years! We see no reason to expect this market system to suddenly fail today—as long as it is not suspended as it was during the 1970s" (ibid., 10). The notion of scarcity, then, remains central to neoclassical economics. But since scarcity is applied to human behavior and the human condition and not only the natural endowment of the world, and since it is not examined empirically, it seems to be ideological. Though empirical evidence is incorporated into the discussion, it is important to remember that such evidence is selectively employed, and that certain pieces of data count as evidence while others are left out. It is not as if theoretical models that are termed ideological contradict the data, but rather that they push for a certain framework regardless of additional relevant data. The choice of data is ideologically motivated insofar as it helps garner the support of allegedly scientific legitimacy. The ideology of scarcity is employed by modern neoclassical economists in order to maintain the status quo of the theoretical underpinning of advanced capitalism.

Not so, says the standard text in economics. According to its author, Paul Samuelson, there is no such thing as "the law of scarcity." This law is based on the facts that an infinite amount of every good cannot be produced and that human wants can never be fully satisfied. The study of economics and the notion of "economizing" emerge because human wants are never fully satisfied due to the fact that there is never an unlimited amount of goods. Samuelson concludes by saying: "While political economy recognized the important germ of truth in the notion that America has become an affluent society, economics must still contend with scarcity as a basic fact of life" (1973, 18–19). According to Samuelson, the concept of "economic scarcity" refers to "the basic fact of life that there exists only a finite amount of human and nonhuman resources, which the best technical knowledge is capable of using to produce only a limited maximum amount of each and every good" (ibid., 23). In contemporary economic literature, in the cannons of the field, scarcity is assumed to be an actual natural condition, not merely an assumption with heuristic value. But such an assumption is quite insensitive to the history of economic thought, the concerns of anthropologists, such as Sahlins, who dispute the facts of the matter and thereby would contest the status of law given to the above proposition.

VII: THE GAIA HYPOTHESIS

Since in this chapter we are reviewing some of the classical literature on the question of abundance and scarcity, and since so far we have noticed how abundance and scarcity are assumed in theoretical discussions, perhaps another philosophical detour is in place. What is this nature or natural resource we are talking about? Outside of the original fascination with the gifts showered on humanity by God, outside of some biblical narrative where plentiful is provided gratis, what view of nature have we been assuming in the West for the past three millennia? To begin with, as Fred Bender (a dear retired colleague) has brilliantly explained, the first thing to note is that humanity is always at the center of the narrative. Likewise, a mechanistic view of nature and its resources permeates the literature so that whatever is needed by humanity is indeed available. But James Lovejoy radically disrupted this narrative (Bender 2003, 385). Lovejoy, with the help of scientists such as Lynn Margulis, transformed our twentieth-century view of nature into what has been called "the Gaia Hypothesis." As Bender critically retells this history, what becomes evident is that "Earth behaves not so much as an inanimate sphere of rock and water sustained by geology's automatic process, but as a self-adjusting and self-regulating biological super-organism, or *planetary body*" (ibid., italics in the original).

Those converted to the Gaia Hypothesis are environmentalists and deep ecologists sensitive to the precarious condition of our Earth and the precious equilibrium with which it maintains life as we know it. The miracle, if that is the right term, is neither that the biblical God created it nor that humans were created in the image of God as theologians remind us, but instead that humanity made it at all. The odds of life coming into being and the odds that all the complex astrophysical and biological variables would line up to produce eventually humanity are indeed astounding. And because of this real miraculous occurrence the very existence of the animal world and humans among it deserves the utmost attention as the potential for disaster is just around the corner. No matter our theological beliefs or views of the plenty of natural resources, we should be cognizant, remind us the converts, not only that global warming is human-made (and therefore must be humanly stopped) but also that our own extinction isn't as far-fetched as some would like to believe. We may pray for God's forgiveness post the biblical Fall, but without the fine and extraordinary calibration of numerous variables and processes we don't stand a chance to survive. The static view of nature or earth has been transformed into a dynamic view of the ongoing environmental changes undertaken with or without humanity.

The contemporary view of nature offered here enlightens us to think in terms that extend the notion of a gift relationship between the divine and humanity. We should be mindful and grateful for the gift bestowed on us, but more importantly, we are playing an active and interactive role with this gift. We can destroy it at our own peril; and, unlike the gift given once and then given again, as the biblical story of the flood and Noah's ark seems to imply, the contemporary view has no allowance for regifting. If the equilibrium is disturbed beyond a certain point—for example, increasing Earth's temperature by more than five degrees Celsius—there is no return, no makeover, and no redemptive prayer. This way of thinking more deeply about our environment by some, and the refusal to think like this for others, shifts the theoretical construction of models from focusing on natural resources to those of technology and human ingenuity.

VIII: FROM NATURAL TO HUMAN RESOURCES

So far, we tried to focus on nature itself: not its origin story from the Big Bang or God's creation to its evolution in its current form, but more about its abundant resources to accommodate humanity over the past few thousands of years. As we conceptualize nature in political economic terms it becomes obvious that notions of abundance are replaced by notions of scarcity. The question is whether scarcity is indeed a natural phenomenon (because of inherent limits, exhaustion of resources, or overuse by humans) or a constructed reality perpetuated by those who wish to either put the fear of God in us or take advantage of this condition. This shift in conceptualization would make us agnostic about the choice between abundance and scarcity, as data points can sway us one way or the other. So, instead of arguing or trying to quantify once and for all natural resources, we are more likely to offer three alternative narratives.

The first narrative focuses on the modes of production and distribution of natural resources such that an optimal level is reached to ensure a sense of abundance even amid scarcity. The Efficient Market Theory, for example, is one such candidate that explains the use of natural resources in market terms (more on this later) and insists that this mechanism is both transparent—matching information about needs and availabilities and fair—ensuring prices reflect what people are willing to pay for what they want under conditions of equal accessibility. This narrative has been promoted from the inception of political economy since the days of Smith all the way to the present global economy, where natural resources are understood and consumed globally through chains of extraction and delivery.

A variant of this narrative claims not only that scarcity is a constructed notion but also that the issue is accessibility to resources rather than their inherent quantity. Peter Diamandis, for example, argues that the shortages we encounter are about our expectations that everyone should live under American standards, which may require five planets full of natural resources to sustain (2012, 5). The issue isn't scarcity and human expectations only, but limited accessibility to natural resources. When seen from the technological perspective, he claims that "few resources are truly scarce; they're mainly inaccessible. Yet the threat of scarcity still dominates our worldview" (ibid, 6). If accessibility can be ensured, then speaking of abundance would be more reasonable. Biblical allusions come to mind when he defines abundance as being "about creating a world of possibility: a world where everyone's days are spent dreaming and doing, not scrapping and scraping" (ibid., 13). But then Diamandis becomes more specific in his image of abundance, where the pyramid has a bottom tier that includes food, water, shelter, and other survival necessities, a middle tier devoted to "catalysts for further growth like abundant energy, ample educational opportunities, and access to ubiquitous communications and information," and a top tier reserved for freedom and health as the necessary "prerequisites enabling an individual to contribute to society" (ibid., 14). Diamandis's contribution is not another faithful adherence to the promises of technology, but a concern with the psychological hindrance to the conceptual acceptance of abundance (ibid., 35), appreciating technology as the engine that accelerates the potential for growth and global abundance. This faith, incidentally, is similar to that of the theologians, even though the language and mechanism are quite different. Some would object to the standard binary between faith on one hand and certainty on the other, since we in fact have the know-how and tools with which technology has rescued us in the past and can probably do so again in the future. To conflate "faith" with "reasonable expectation" may turn out to be a disservice to the cause of reframing the economic model. Our faith in this or that device performing as expected is indeed a reasonable expectation that is predicated on successful past experiences.

The second narrative is related to the first but is more concerned with technological developments themselves, the ones already recognized in the Industrial Revolution. Technological innovations can extend the abundance of natural resources because additional efficiency in transportation and energy, for example, can bring goods to markets more cheaply as well as ensure a more efficient agricultural and manufacturing processes. Greater agricultural efficiency in modes of planting and harvesting, not to mention later developments of more resilient and productive seeds through GMOs, eluded the likes of Malthus who worried about population growth. The faith in technology being able to supplement whatever plentiful gifted from the gods is a faith in human perfectibility and the ongoing progress humanity is capable of accomplishing. As some argue, "Scarcity is the failure of man to adequately improve technologically" (Malenbaum 1975, 72).

If only technology kept up with human needs and wants, if it was up to the task, humanity would never suffer from any scarcity whatsoever. And when technology keeps up the pace of human development—demographically and geographically—it's then only institutional organizations that may hinder its potential. These institutions include market-capitalism, where bottlenecks "create" scarcity, or political ones, such as central-power communism, where allocation of resources is dictated from the top and is poorly informed and inefficient. The main conceptual contribution here is the realization that technology doesn't operate in an organizational or conceptual vacuum, but that it can be positively or negatively harnessed to the ideological percepts of the day. The image of technology as the engine of abundance presupposes an equal distribution of its fruits rather than the consolidation of these benefits in the hands of the few at the expense and misery of the many. These additional presuppositions, as we shall see below, eventually overshadow the discussion of the potential of technological innovations to bring about abundance. Some may rephrase this to say that technology hasn't failed us, but instead we are the ones that have failed technology by "spoiling or abusing its fruits" (almost in Locke's sense).

The third narrative that emerges out of the shift from discussing natural resources to the resources offered by humans—from intelligence and hard work to inventions and cooperative modes of communal organization—is one that nowadays defines scarcity in terms of time and energy, personal resources that affect one's very existence and interaction with the social and natural environments. As Sendhil Mullainathan and Eldar Shafir convincingly argue, "By scarcity, we mean *having less than you feel you need*" (2013, 4; italics in the original). As they look for some logical string by which to pull together various strands of scarcity discussions, they admit that scarcity is not simply a psychological symptom but itself "captures the mind," so to speak; the mind "orients automatically, powerfully, toward unfulfilled needs" (ibid., 7). In pushing this line of argument, they want to distinguish the conversation about scarcity in economic terms—where "scarcity is ubiquitous. All of us have a limited amount of money; even the richest people cannot buy everything"—from the one where "the feeling of scarcity is not" ubiquitous, where it's circumscribed to some and not all (ibid., 11). For them, it is the "selective perception" of scarcity that matters, especially when we feel unhappy; there are ways in which we can overcome this kind of scarcity, even if the material kind persists.

For Mullainathan and Shafir, "scarcity is not just a physical constraint" and therefore cannot be thought of or dealt with in economic terms alone; "it is also a mindset." And this difference matters because when we "function under scarcity, we represent, manage, and deal with problems differently" (ibid., 12). Being "preoccupied by scarcity, because our minds constantly return to it, we have less mind to give to the rest of life" (ibid., 13). Thought and attention, stress and anxiety are now foregrounded as important for the rest of our interactions with the material world. There is no Cartesian mind-body distinction, but instead a unity of purpose that affects the one because of the other. While some rationalists, like Spinoza, hoped to have the mind control our bodies—our thinking controlling our emotional states of being—it becomes clear from these more recent studies that what we are dealing with here is not simply a "metaphor" about what is missing or needed; instead, they argue, we "can directly measure mental capacity or, as we call it, *bandwidth*. We can measure fluid intelligence, a key resource that affects how we process information and make decisions. We can measure executive control, which is a key resource that affects how impulsively we behave. And we find that scarcity reduces all these components of bandwidth—it makes us less insightful, less forward-thinking, less controlled" (ibid., 13). The impact of the scarcity mindset is heady.

According to Mullainathan and Shafir, there are "scarcity traps" (chapter 6) that humans can detect and avoid. Because "scarcity captures our attention," this "provides a narrow benefit: we do a better job of managing pressing needs." If we pay attention to our scarcity anxieties and are mindful of what they are doing to the rest of our thinking and decision-making processes, we may avoid neglecting "our other concerns," and ensure that we do not become "less effective in the rest of life" (ibid., 14–15). Is this view a manual for mindful living and the elimination of anxieties? Not quite. In pointing out the psychological impacts of thinking through the prism of scarcity, the authors hope we stop the vicious cycle of scarcity, offering hope that it's possible to change the psychological conditions with appropriate tricks to limit this self-perpetuating cycle of doom (ibid., 144–45). It seems, then, that if there might be a way to control or minimize the scarcity mindset if not eliminate it, then there might be also some social benefits for thinking about what is abundant around us for which we should be grateful and feel secure (ibid., 232–34).

Walter Weisskopf, for example, draws attention to the perception of individuals as "free mostly to renounce possibilities," because every choice entails a "sacrifice" of alternatives (1971, 23). At stake for political economists is, as Smith indicates, the relationship between individuals and the choices they make among alternatives that are either naturally "given" or artificially created by other individuals. The importance of the notion of scarcity in political economy is due not to the limits of resources (land as well as labor), but to the assumption of an unlimited amount of needs. Weisskopf continues: "Seen in this light of abundance is an ideal which can never, and should never, be reached; the basic assumption of scarcity of means and unlimitedness of ends prevents the possibility of ever establishing complete abundance" (ibid., 178).

The notion of scarcity, then, is not dependent on specific empirical data the way Malthus sets his argument, but is instead based on a particular psychology and ideology as understood already in Sahlins's study. Psychologically, or existentially in Weisskopf's sense, "The scarcity principle im-

plies that in the human situation means of production and need satisfaction
are always scarce in relation to needs and ends which are unlimited and can
never fully be satisfied" (ibid., 23). This situation leads to the realization that
"there is a continuous gap between means and ends, and such a gap can be
overcome, if at all, through a process of a never-ending economic growth"
(ibid.). One question mentioned above (in light of Sahlins's anthropological
study) surfaces anew at this juncture of the argument: Is this situation—a gap
between needs and their satisfaction—"historically relative and culture-
bound and represents the special orientation of industrial society toward
economic activity and material need satisfaction" or "universally valid"?
What enshrines the universality of the situation, and thereby the universal
validity of the employment of the concept of scarcity by political economists,
are "the conditions under which human beings exist" (ibid., 187). Weisskopf
argues, Existential scarcity is caused by human finitude on the one end, and
by the human ability to transcend this finitude and the given existential
condition through consciousness and thought on the other hand. This situation shows all the characteristics of the scarcity principle as applied in economic thought. The two principles can be distinguished as economic versus
existential scarcity. Both lead to an allocation problem of scarce means to
alternative ends. Both involve the sacrifice of alternative potentialities which
are the cost of any definite concrete allocation (ibid.).

It seems that the notion of scarcity is central to any economic discussion
as it explains the focus on the allocation of (scarce) resources to a multiplicity of consumer demands (and needs). It also explains the emphasis on economic activity within capitalist society as a means toward economic growth,
where growth might be the only (even if temporary) solution to the continuous gap between needs and their satisfaction. As a critic of capitalism,
Weisskopf argues against the one-dimensional treatment of the notion of
scarcity by classical and neoclassical economists. The focus on economic
scarcity fails to include the seriousness and applicability of existential scarcity that has a direct impact on allocation problems of time and energy in a
broader sense. What is missing from the standard discussion of scarcity is
some reference to the personal toll of such theorizing. The human element is
itself part of the question that is under consideration. The narrowness of the
neoclassical treatment focuses on the circumstances that enhance or impede
economic growth and overlook the psychological propensities that may
transform the marketplace itself.

David Levine is in agreement with Weisskopf's analysis of the centrality
of the notion of scarcity for neoclassical economic theory. Levine says that
property is treated as a scarce resource and provides the foundation for neoclassical economics. In neoclassical terms, the economy, or more precisely
the marketplace, is seen as "a mechanism for the allocation of scarce resources among competing ends," regardless of whether these resources are

understood as available property or in terms other than property proper (1988, 47). Levine would also agree with Weisskopf that the notion of scarcity plays an important role in justifying economic growth as a potential for decreasing (if not eliminating) the gap between needs and their satisfaction. However, economic growth can function to increase human needs (in the Marxian sense of the fetishism of commodities), and thus undermine the possibility of closing the gap generated by economic activity. If we look at the economy, at people's needs and their satisfaction, from the standpoint of wealth instead of scarcity (ibid., 48), then some of the consequences of neoclassical theory may be avoided. Such avoidance is possible, in light of Weisskopf's discussion, Levine's argument, and Sahlins's evidence, because psychological principles and evidence underlie and may undermine the theoretical foundation of neoclassical theory.

IX: FROM SCARCITY TO ABUNDANCE

At issue in contemporary literature is not the scarcity or abundance of nature—whatever was given by God or accident—but rather the human condition, human nature, and human behavior. This issue, call it existential scarcity or the human condition, is not examined; it is assumed. And as a working assumption it is the cornerstone or bedrock of any contemporary economic discussion. One need not refer to Marxist thought or other schools of economic thought critical of mainstream neoclassical theory to question the validity and therefore the role of the notion of permanent scarcity or the law of scarcity. John Maynard Keynes, for one, agrees with all contemporary thinkers that "the economic problem, the struggle for subsistence, always has been hitherto the primary, most pressing problem of the human race—not only of the human race, but of the whole biological kingdom from the beginning of life in its most primitive forms." Using Samuelson's terminology, the "basic fact of life" has not changed the past, and it is as fundamental to biology and evolution as it is for the socialization of human beings. In light of this natural condition, says Keynes, "We have been expressly evolved by nature . . . for the purpose of solving the economic problem [of scarcity]" (1930/1963, 363–67).

Though from a radically different perspective, Keynes echoes here the concerns of Sahlins, Weisskopf, and Levine about the psychological conditioning of human beings, and the impact of that conditioning on their economic behavior as well as on their acceptance or rejection of the so-called law of scarcity. However, continues Keynes, what would happen if the economic problem is solved? To begin with, following the logic of his argument about the purpose of human activity, Keynes argues that "mankind will be deprived of its traditional purpose" and this will be accompanied by "dread of the readjustment of the habits and instincts . . . bred into him for countless generations" (ibid.). Mankind, in Keynes's view, will be lost if the situation Galbraith describes as affluence does indeed occur. Keynes acknowledges quite openly the necessity of employing the concept of scarcity at the forefront of any discussion, and especially as the primary concern of economics. Paradoxically, this may mean that without scarcity there is no human purpose, no reason to live. But must this be the only logical conclusion of the shift from the notion of scarcity to abundance? Can the notion of abundance, as used in social, political, and economic theory, rescue an ideal for humanity, different from the warning of a mass "nervous breakdown" predicted by Keynes almost a century ago? Keynes himself intimates that new possibilities might dominate human activity and expand the horizon of human interaction. Once the so-called economic problem is solved, he writes, there will emerge the "permanent problem" of how to live a happy life, probably in the Greek sense: "Thus for the first time since his creation man will be faced with his real, his permanent problem—how to use his freedom from pressing economic cares, how to occupy the leisure, which science and compound interest will have won for him, to live wisely and agreeably and well" (ibid.).

Though conceding that "life in abundance and comfort . . . has created a whole new pathology," Mihailo Markovic still prefers to envision a society where "scarcity has brought about a hunger for goods, a lust for unlimited private property" (1974, 220). What has exasperated this situation and developed the mentality of *homo consumens*, according to him, is the creation of certain conditions in industrial society "for mass satisfaction of material needs" (ibid., 223). But the satisfaction of material needs loses "a good part of its meaning" under the conditions of abundance in what is called postindustrial society, because other concerns become more important (ibid., 224). Among other concerns valued more highly are education and traveling, for example, since material scarcity is no longer of primary concern. In his position on human nature, on the potential stored for it in future generations, Markovic finds himself not only in the company of his ideological rival, Keynes, but also in the company of one of Keynes's predecessors, John Stuart Mill. Mill is as concerned as Hume and Smith with the vices associated with greed and the accumulation of wealth: "I confess I am not charmed with the ideal of life held out by those who think that the normal state of human beings is that of struggling to get on; that the trampling, crushing, elbowing, and treading on each other's heals, which form the existing type of social life, are the most desirable lot of human kind, or anything but the disagreeable symptoms of one of the phases of industrial progress" (1848/ 1965, 754).

Under conditions of abundance, Markovic would agree at least with this much of Mill's and Keynes's predictions, that the purpose of life and the notion of happiness would be transformed. How that transformation will take place, and what will be its secondary effects, one cannot know for certain. Yet there is no reason to believe that there will not arise, as Levin attempts to show, a new theory of political economy more concerned with the psychological well-being of society as a whole, returning in effect to classical political economy: political economy must be understood philosophically and psychologically. The theory of political economy must also be understood in psycho-social and moral terms, and not only in political and economic terms. As such, the traditional boundaries of the discipline will be blurred and expand beyond the narrow confines imposed by an appeal to scientific rigor.

X: UTOPIAN VISIONS

The image of the Garden of Eden is one of the bookends at the beginning of life, while at its zenith or end an image of heaven, just as fantastic and abundant, is the other bookend. What becomes evident from our brief survey is that notions of abundance and scarcity are as much constructed as simply assumed. This means that in order to socially and politically justify or explain a certain mode of institutional organization we must add "value" to whatever we are assessing by claiming a certain level of scarcity, as is even done in cases of cultural wealth (Bair 2011). An appreciation of our surroundings is intermixed with images or construction of abundance and scarcity as the two extremes of a spectrum of ways to value anything, from having little or no value (because abundant) to valuable (because scarce). Theological images of heaven are utopian, promising freedom from want and suffering. These utopian visions have been offered over the years, with some hope of bringing them into fruition in the here and now. Christopher Jennings brings this narrative of utopian abundance and peaceful coexistence into the American context of the nineteenth century. He reports that "countless people on both sides of the Atlantic believed that a new and wondrous society was about to take form in the American wilderness. It was a time when the imminence of paradise seemed reasonable to reasonable people" (2016, 3).

One need not be a devout religious person or a delusional idealist to appreciate and even accept the reasonableness of a paradise on Earth. Two ideas were brought together, in Jennings's mind: the ancient and mystical "Judeo-Christian proposition that history is bookended by golden ages" and the modern, rational one, "that the human race is advancing ineluctably toward a perfection of our own making" (ibid., 4). Between divine beneficence and modern excellence (human perfectibility), what can stop our progress toward this nirvana? There were five communalist movements in nineteenth-century America with at least one hundred "experimental communities" who agreed that "men and women are more or less equal, that financial competition is morally corrosive, and that material equality is a precondition of a just society," and as such shared at least one "basic premise of utopianism: that the society in which they lived required a total overhaul. Utopianism may be a species of optimism, but it is always born of discontent" (ibid., 7–10). The Industrial Revolution didn't bring about the prosperity it promised, and when it did, it was left in the hands of the few rather than spread around fairly if not equally.

The five groups of utopians in the United States consisted of the Shakers, Owenites, Fourierists, Icarians, and Oneida Perfectionists who "all labored under the very specific belief that small communistic societies could trigger a new and perfected existence across the entire globe" (ibid., 11). The reason to bring up this episode in American history is not for the sake of nostalgia for the good old days when utopian thinking was practiced in small communities around the country, but in order to observe that these attempts were not technologically driven. The faith in humanity to change and reform, to transform its modes of thinking and working, was just as profound as the faith our forefathers had millennia ago. It should also be noted here, as we shall repeatedly do in other chapters, that "in utopia, size makes all the difference." As Jennings explains: "When Brook Farm collectivized agriculture and sent the intellectuals out to mow wheat, the results were goofy and edifying. When Mao Tse-tung tried the same trick, forty million starved" (ibid., 19). Likewise, it should be noted that all of these utopian experiments failed, abandoning their communities and returning to the urban centers from which many of them came. And the residues from these failures resonate with us today: "Calling a proposal 'utopian' is among the more routine slurs on Capitol Hill" (ibid., 17). And finally, we must admit with scholars of these episodes in human development that "many of the darkest episodes of the twentieth century—the Thousand-Year Reich, Soviet Gulags, the Khmer killing fields—were born of utopian and millenarian ideologies" (ibid., 18).

Despite all the doom and gloom associated with these failed utopian experiments, they made some philosophical contributions to awaken us to reconsider some fundamental framing questions of our social and moral institutions. Here is a laundry list of questions that were addressed by these utopian communities, however differently: "Must the family be the base unit of civilization? How does diversity affect a highly socialized society? Can citizens really be transformed by the institutions within which they live? Is monogamy required for a stable, prosperous society? Is private property? How much must theory bend in the face of circumstances? How does spiritual authority interact with political authority? Does social progress flow from the initiative of self-advancing individuals or from broad, collectivist reforms? Is competition the ideal motor of innovation and prosperity? Can social solidarity be stimulated or must it arise spontaneously?" (ibid., 20) And as Jennings concludes: "Hovering above all of these questions is the overarching dialectic that defines civil society: the back-and-forth between individual liberty and mutual aid, between the freedom to do as you please and the freedom from being cold, hungry, and alone" (ibid.). The moral lesson we can learn from even raising these questions is that it's not only reasonable but also essential that there was something utopian thinkers and practitioners reacted to, some moral refusal to accept the given. In his words: "They demanded more fellowship, more pleasure, more learning, more time, more dignity, and more equality" (ibid., 381). As such, their outlook is reminiscent of biblical prophets and intellectual critics of all generations that remain steadfast in their objections to what is happening around them and beseech political leaders to reform their domains of power.

The utopian thinking of the nineteenth century seems naïve or even misguided to some because it shied away from the technological advances of the urban industrialized centers of America and went to work the land. Yet the accompanying optimism remains evident among contemporary utopian thinkers who are infatuated by digital technologies and use them as a means toward a utopian end. Among them is Jeremy Rifkin, whose vision is summarized briefly in these terms: "A zero marginal society, in which scarcity has been replaced by abundance, is a far different world than the one we're accustomed to" (2014, 109). For him, this is a broad historical perspective that remains promising, almost inevitable: "If the steam engine freed human beings from feudal bondage to pursue material self-interest in the capitalist marketplace, the Internet of Things frees human beings from the market economy to pursue nonmaterial shared interests on the Collaborative Commons" (ibid., 132). "The Networked Commons" isn't to be found in a faraway agrarian community but in the midst of urban centers, where one can expect "a new collaborative economic paradigm" (ibid., 151). His voice is added to many others who believe that digital technologies offer abundant resources with little costs or waste of infrastructure (already explained by Benkler 2006). A new and emerging model of human activity at the peer-to-peer level has convinced many contemporary economists that "crowd-based" capitalism offers more abundance than ever before. Add to this the notion of a "sharing economy," as Arun Sundararajan does (2016), and one might claim that indeed we have reached paradise here and now.

These theorists have in common a view of how old-fashioned capitalist organizations that are hierarchical and benefit only some and not all can be transformed into more leveled or horizontal ones where cooperation and social networks are based on trust rather than competition and exploitation. Rifkin, for his part, suggests that our mindset should change to thinking about the triple bottom line of "people and planet before profit" (ibid., 264). The big picture is envisioned in terms of hybrid partnerships so that the "near zero marginal cost society can take the human race from an economy of scarcity to an economy of sustainable abundance over the course of the first half of the twenty-first century." To ensure that this view merges his faith in technology with faith in human transformation, he concludes by saying that his "hope rests not with technology alone, but with the history of the human narrative," seeing a shift of consciousness from mythological to theological to ideological to psychological to an empathic one (ibid., 298–302). In order not to be dismissed as yet another utopian crank whose predictions sound lofty but hallow, Rifkin explains that "often people mistake empathic consciousness with utopianism when in fact, it is the very opposite . . . There is no need of empathy in heave and no place for it in utopia because in these otherworldly realms there is no pain and suffering, no frailties and flaws, but only perfection and immortality" (ibid., 301). Contemporary ideas about abundance and scarcity have come full circle: from an abundant beginning to a scarcity and strife back to ways in which abundance can be reintroduced. If this may seem idle speculation, there are those like Sundararajan who insists that simple cellphone applications prove how we can more fully utilize the resources that are at hand, from cars that are used only infrequently to empty bedrooms (2016).

XI: A BRIDGE

One direction that a theory about the well-being of society may adopt can be distilled from the work of feminists, such as Michael Gross and Mary Beth Averill. Concerned with the "patriarchal image of nature" and with substituting it with a feminist one, Gross and Averill suggest that "nature may be better understood in terms of plentitude and cooperation" as opposed to "scarcity and competition" (1983, 71). The theoretical and experimental apparatus supporting the theory of evolution that focuses on scarcity and competition (and their intimate logical and practical connection) can be transformed without thereby creating an epistemological void. The ideological matrices set by Gross and Averill take the notion of scarcity and its attendant notion of cooperation, and once they substitute one set of concepts for another, nature can be restructured differently.

However, one may object to the logical validity of the conceptual "coupling" offered above. Is scarcity responsible exclusively for a competitive environment? Is it not possible that under conditions of scarcity, say diminishing energy resources, people are more likely to cooperate? Would the horror of some scarce resource not force marketplace participants to think more broadly about the consequences of such scarcity and attempt collectively to avoid the disasters that may come about if competition alone were to rule the marketplace? In a similar fashion, one may argue that abundance need not lead to cooperation but may foster competition, even if of a different kind associated with the neoclassical marketplace. For example, even among those who live in abundance, there is a sense of urgency in trying to create hierarchies and compete for ever-higher positions, ranging from prestige and esteemed social status to power and glamour. In this respect, then, the feminist critique mentioned above may not be able to overcome the problems accompanying the notions of scarcity and abundance. Yet a feminist critique may broaden the discussion to include ideological questions as components and not simply consequences of the discussion.

At stake is an ideological commitment that must be addressed directly and without pretense that it is merely secondary or irrelevant. Once ideology itself is admitted into the discourses, once its role is given legitimacy rendered to any other so-called empirical variable, theoretical discourses will change. Theorists will be more accommodating to the force of persuasion with which one framework is debunked and another is admitted. By changing allegedly scientific discourses into discourses that include ideological principles, platforms, and agendas, one can expect competing theories to be examined not only for their internal consistency or their correspondence to external empirical data. Instead, competing theories would be exposed to a thorough and explicit examination of their ideological rhetoric as well (McCloskey 1998).

Does this imply that choices be made in accordance with one's ideological sentiment alone? Not necessarily. Rather than hiding the ideological behind an alleged scientific veil, ideological commitments must be acknowledged as important components of the choice one makes among incommensurable theories (Sassower 1988). But would this mean that empirical evidence and what is considered unsubstantiated beliefs will be blurred? If ideology is understood not only in terms that ignore empirical evidence but also in terms that influence data choices and that influence what is to be counted as empirical evidence, then indeed there is a blurring of the differences between data and ideology. And here, from yet another perspective, epistemological questions are linked to metaphysical issues that must be considered in the examination of any discipline. The blurring of differences (between the empirical and ideological) does not mean that there are no differences, only that the differences are themselves informed by certain commitments, positivist, phenomenological, or postmodern. Such commitments should not be left at the threshold, before the discourse begins, but should be incorporated into the discourse as an important component.

In this chapter our main concern was to elucidate, with numerous historical references, the basic assumptions we are still using today in regard to abundance and scarcity. Whether the abundance of nature is related to divine gifts or to the peculiarity of complex variables that brought about life on our planet is irrelevant. What does matter, though, is under what conditions we are supposed to live, those of abundance or those of scarcity? It becomes quite clear that some level of plenty is presupposed. It is also quite obvious that perception of that abundance is skewed in time and space according to whatever is the reigning ideology of the authors we briefly examined. While for the likes of Aristotle the issue is sufficient natural subsistence to allow for moral conduct, for others, like Marx, the issue is the sinful ways in which humanity strayed away from its natural paradise into industrial centers where scarcity has been constructed, both physically and mentally. And as we closed the chapter, the promises of utopian thinking have been anchored in a strong faith that technological innovation could transform real or perceived scarcity into plentitude.

Recent iterations of the technological faith supersede the promise of productivity achieved by the brute force of mechanization and automation. In paying attention to underutilized resources, from cars and homes to tools and labor power, the so-called crowd-based capitalism or sharing economy offers higher levels of efficiency. Despite its reliance on market-capitalism, there is a promise not only of greater reach and scalability of peer-to-peer exchanges but also more importantly a new level of trust that can be verified and promoted by digital platforms and devices. Just as the talk of natural resources moved toward an appreciation of human resources, so has the talk of abundance and scarcity moved toward a discussion of building new communities of peers. This parallel shift can push the discussion toward a more concrete appreciation of human relations rather than staying at the abstract philosophical or theological level of nature.

As we move to the next chapter, we should keep in mind that the discussion about abundance and scarcity is reintroduced in the views and images of the "state of nature," but with a different emphasis: How does the bounty of natural resources influence the relationship among humans? What kind of starting point do we assume in order to explain and justify current political arrangements? How should human relations be regulated, if at all, to ensure peaceful coexistence, if not complete trust?

Chapter Two

The State of Nature and the Social Contract

The heuristic notion of the state of nature, speculative for some, idealized for others, has played an important role in suggesting why we need political arrangements to organize society and coordinate its economic transactions. From Thomas Hobbes, John Locke, and Jean-Jacques Rousseau we have a long and rich tradition in which the specter of humans living (in reality or hypothetically) in a natural state has been the backdrop against which to make arguments that justify social and economic mechanisms. If we are "brutish," then we need laws and the police; if we are "compassionate," we can be trusted to cooperate with each other. The genealogy of this frame of reference is important to outline so as to explain why certain ways of thinking have been bred into our discourse about human behavior and interaction. Sure enough, if our natural state is also abundant, it would lead to different arguments than if it were limited by scarcity.

This transitional chapter pulls together some of the threads already offered in the previous chapter—where idealized notions of abundance were evident in a conceptual or virtual space and time—but here the emphasis isn't so much on natural endowments as such, but on the interactions among people in that natural state. What becomes obvious is that some presuppositions in regard to human nature come into play. But we'll devote a separate chapter for this notion or philosophical conviction, even though the overlaps are obvious already at this stage. Rather than enumerate, as we did in the previous chapter, all the different views of historical figures, we'll instead set up the two main divergent views on how humans must have behaved in a state without government or laws, where natural law was the sole guide. This chapter ends with a brief sketch of the argument for the social contract as a means by which to understand civil society and the interactions of individuals in a community.

If Plato gave us one of the first prototypes of what a State should look like (the *Republic*), then every subsequent political philosopher was hard at work to figure out what the ideal (utopian) State could look like. Though a prominent contributor to the discussion of a social contract, Rousseau was not alone in rationalizing the ways by which individuals form communities. Unlike Hegel's notion of the family unit leading to civil society and then to a State, there are those, like Yuval Harari (2015), who outline a different developmental trajectory for how *sapiens* organized themselves and survived in the process of human evolution. The nation-state has become ubiquitous in our global discussions, despite ongoing critiques that date back to the likes of Louis Althusser (2014), who have argued about the ideological apparatuses that insidiously control and influence our thinking and behavior in a repressive environment. This frame of reference, like those discussed above, is linked to questions about the state of nature, human nature, and the scarcity or abundance we suffer or enjoy. Even if references were hypothetical or speculative in these cases, they provided the fuel that moved the argument about the need for and the legitimacy of the State into contemporary debates.

I: UNTENABLE STATE OF WAR

We are familiar with the standard negative view of the state of nature as Hobbes described it: "the life of man, solitary, poore [*sic*], nasty, brutish, and short" (1651/1968, 186). To reach this conclusion, Hobbes makes a three-stage argument. First and foremost, "Nature has made men so equall [*sic*], in the faculties of body, and mind" (ibid., 183). The first premise is problematic since we all know that people have different natural physical and mental endowments so that some are stronger than others, while others are smarter than others. Equality is not straightforward; instead, it's an equality of the threat each one has over another, so that "the weakest has strength enough to kill the strongest, either by secret machination, or by confederacy with others" (ibid.). We are therefore all equally in danger of being killed by our fellow humans. The second premise is about how human "equality of ability" gives rise to "equality of hope in the attaining of our ends" (ibid., 184). The notion of attainment is not manifest in the exertion of power over natural resources or over other humans in the vicinity, those who might hamper one's ability to attain one's goals. The third premise relates to human nature and how it figures into the conditions under which humanity finds itself in the state of nature. For Hobbes, there are three main reasons why people "quarrell" [*sic*] with each other: "First, Competition; Secondly, Diffidence; Thirdly, Glory" (ibid., 185). These traits of human nature move people to behave in the following ways: "The first, maketh men invade for Gain; the second, for Safety; and the third, for Reputation" (ibid.). What is the conclusion, then?

As far as Hobbes is concerned, under these conditions and without the benefit of "a common Power to keep them all in awe, they are in that condition which is called Warre [*sic*]; and such a warre [*sic*], as is of every man, against every man" (ibid.). Sufficient natural resources matters little when it comes to human altercations in the state of nature. The great attribute of original equality turns out to be, once human nature is added to this conceptual concoction, a recipe for disaster: perpetual war. This circumstance inevitably leads to the conclusion with which we began the section: human life in the state of nature is indeed "solitary, poore [*sic*], nasty, brutish, and short." Who would want to live like this? Would it not make sense for reasonable people to shift to a peaceful coexistence that civil society offers with a social compact of some sort, agreeing on a central governing body that would lead this body-politics, this enormous Leviathan? As Hobbes continues, because there is no right and wrong or any notion of justice in the state of nature, there must be some reasons that move us to think about a different state of existence: "The Passions that incline men to Peace, are Fear of Death" (ibid., 188). Reason alone cannot convince humans to reach for the political structure under which peace can be guaranteed, and therefore the fear of death is brought into play. The combination of the two yields to the next stage of his argument, one that we'll pick up below.

II: POSITIVE BUT PRECARIOUS STATE

Whereas Hobbes's view of the state of nature was pessimistic if not outright dire, based as it was on the equal opportunity to kill everyone, Locke's starting point is about freedom. In Chapter II of the *Second Treatise* he describes the "state of nature" as a "state of perfect freedom to order their actions and dispose of their possessions and persons as they think fit," all "within the bounds of the laws of nature." And it is "a state of equality" (1690/1947, 122). However, unlike Hobbes's concern with the equal threat of being killed, here the notion of equality is associated with the understanding that power relations are "reciprocal, no one having more than another," where there is no "subordination or subjection," conditions more apparent much later in human development (ibid.). Locke continues to explain what this freedom and equality amount to: "being all equal and independent, no one ought to harm another in his life, health, liberty, or possessions; for men being all the workmanship of one omnipotent and infinitely wise Maker" because they are "his property whose workmanship they are" (ibid., 123). The reference to the divine, as we saw in the previous section, still dominates the discourse, and remains a frame of reference even under a secular discussion of political philosophy. The state of nature is governed by the Law of Nature (later Natural Law), which is based on reason and sanctioned by divine providence. Yet Locke, just like Hobbes, realizes that his fictional framing is conceptual only and that it requires the shift to civil society: "I easily grant that civil government is the proper remedy for the inconveniences of the state of nature" (ibid., 127).

In addition to emphasizing the natural (and divinely inspired) principles of all political philosophy, freedom and equality, Locke is also aware of the natural inclination of humans to ensure their own "preservation" and to thwart all others from harming them. He therefore concludes that "the execution of the law of nature is, in that state, put in every man's hands" (ibid., 124). This empowerment is of course problematic and not as efficient as having a centralized executive power, as we shall see shortly. The other important idea that Locke brings up is the notion of "possession" or more specifically one's "property" in the state of nature. Though "God hath given the world to men in common, hath also given them reason to make use of it to the best advantage of life and convenience" (ibid., 134). For him, anyone who "hath mixed his labour with, and joined to it something that is his own thereby makes it his property" (ibid.). The point here is twofold: though given in common, nature's fruits become one's own with the addition of labor, but this process is undertaken for the sake of satisfying human needs and wants and should not exceed a certain level of what Aristotle called subsistence. Moreover, Locke insists that "there is enough and as good left in common for others" (ibid.).

The law of nature that grants everyone portions of the bounty should prevent hoarding and ensure that enough is left for others, and is thus turned into "law of reason." And here a passing reference is made to the Indian who kills the deer in a hunt (ibid., 135). This arrangement makes sense to Locke because everyone is forbidden from letting the fruit of labor "spoil" or taking more than "might serve for his use." If each person in this state has enough, "there could be then little room for quarrels or contentions about property so established" (ibid., 136). Given the two conditions of abundance and initial common access to this abundance, Locke is sensitive to the fact that the result would be communally advantageous: "He who appropriates land to himself by his labour does not lessen but increase the common stock of mankind" (ibid., 139). In light of this reasoning we eventually find ourselves in a social contract that ensures the protection of the principles of freedom, equality, and private property. The imperfections of the state of nature, however political its character, bring about the need for the legislative, administrative, and judiciary powers of the State.

In answering "Has the Restoration of the Arts and Sciences Had a Purifying Effect upon Mortals?" in his *Discourse on the Arts and Sciences*, Rousseau refers to "those savages in America" as "those happy nations" who are unacquainted with the "vices" of his day. Their "simple and natural regulations" are much more honorable and morally sound than what is known in Geneva of his day (1750/1964, 42). Humans exemplified "the happy ignorance in which eternal wisdom had placed us" (ibid., 46). Nature's protection is understood as protecting humanity from knowledge (ibid., 47). He goes so far as to pray to God to "give back to us ignorance, innocence, and poverty, the only goods that can give us happiness and are precious in thy sight" (ibid., 62).

In his essay "On the Origin and Foundations of Inequality among Men," Rousseau brings up the idea of "the equality nature established among men" in the state of nature (1754/1964, 78, 92). In the most self-conscious and reflective tone so far displayed, Rousseau explains why the state of nature ought to be posited: "for it is no light undertaking to separate what is original from what is artificial in the present nature of man, and to know correctly a state which no longer exists, which perhaps never existed, which probably never will exist, and about which it is nevertheless necessary to have precise notions in order to judge our present state correctly" (ibid., 92–93). Rousseau's own notion of the "noble savage" is clearly understood in the natural terms of primitive, yet noble behavior (prior to the introduction of reason): "self-preservation" (as seen in Hobbes and Locke) and the "natural repugnance to see any sensitive being perish or suffer, principally our fellow-men" (ibid., 95; see also 130–31). Human interaction isn't exclusively understood in one's survival against all the odds but is supplemented by the notion of compassion or pity toward others. This moves us much closer to the notion of moral sentiments as explicated by Smith in 1759.

It's also noteworthy that Rousseau mentions Hobbes's view of the state of nature and that according to him, "man is naturally intrepid and seeks only to attack and fight"; but then he contrasts this view with those of Cumberland and Pufendorf that "nothing is so timid as man . . . he is always trembling and ready to flee at the slightest noise he hears" (ibid., 107). From these two alternative views, Rousseau concedes that when humans compare themselves to each other and to other animals, they distinguish themselves because of their sense of "self-perfection" (ibid., 114–15). When Rousseau pulls together natural pity and the notion of the perfectibility of humanity, it's no wonder that he transcends Hobbes and Locke and suggests that principles such as "*Do what is good for you with the least possible harm to others*," found in the state of nature, give way to the most "sublime maxim of reasoned justice, *Do unto others as you would have them do unto to you*" (ibid., 133, italics in the original). As Rousseau suggests from the start, the speculative moment in the argument about the state of nature is supposed to lead us toward an inquiry under what conditions and for what reasons we should embrace civil society and the authority of governments as the legitimate expression of the sovereign, the people. We should mention in this context that there were some clear agnostic voices on the postulates of the state of nature, such as Hume's, who claimed it was "a mere fiction," or "idle fiction" (1978, 493–94). But inasmuch as he dismissed this conceptual exercise, he still admitted that it was necessary in order to postulate and eventually fully appreciate the need for morality and justice (ibid., 494–95).

The final and perhaps most significant argument used by Rousseau on behalf of the social contract is that on balance every individual is better off giving up some natural freedoms because in return individual rights are given back to everyone with the authority and the sanction of the State. Perhaps some freedoms are given up, but in their place rights are now protected by the State in ways that ensure greater freedoms rather than anything less than was originally granted in the state of nature (1762/1978).

III: NATIVE AMERICANS

Because some philosophers have mentioned "savages" and "Indians," it may behoove us to make a short detour and consider their views of nature and how humans should behave within its confines. Alvin Josephy suggests that "many" of the Native Americans have always felt "a sacred attachment to the land and a reverence for nature that is incomprehensible to most whites" (1968, 7). This is not a conceptual apparatus that is empirically contested, as Rousseau posits, but an ongoing feeling and attachment that has lasted to this day. "Many, though Christians, find repugnance in the idea that man possess dominion over the birds and beasts, and believe still man is brother to all else that is living" (ibid.). The Christians may have forced them to convert, even decimated their numbers once arriving on the American shores, but the biblical narrative of "dominion" never stuck, and a level of sharing and brotherhood continues to characterize their relationship with nature. From this general sense of nature's abundance and its gifts to humans, Native Americans also have a sense of communal ownership or stewardship that never transformed, even under Western influence, to the level of private ownership of property. Instead of conquest, their attitude is that of keeping the natural balance in which they found themselves.

In more specific ways, Indians, as Josephy calls them, believe that in the spring the "earth is pregnant and they must not harm her body," and therefore they take off their horses' shoes and walk themselves in "soft-soled shoes" (ibid., 26). Likewise, the Taos Indians "avoid the use of modern agricultural implements, such as steel-bladed plows, which would slice open the breast of their earth-mother" (ibid.). The imagery is reminiscent of Hobbes's notion of the bounty coming from nature's "breasts," and requires a different approach to human interactions with nature and by extension with each other. The maintenance of "harmony" and balance with nature is a prerequisite of life, and if it were disturbed, as Euro-Americans have, "illness, pain, death, or other misfortunes would result" (ibid.). Interestingly, only more recently has there been some recognition of this viewpoint (e.g., Udall in 1963), one that replaces notions of conquest with those of "learning to live in harmony with nature" (ibid., 32). Though most European references to Indians were to their happy savagery, there was never a full realization of their own views of nature and how they ought to behave. Their exotic status, in the "orientalism" sense of Edward Said (1978), is all too often overshadowing a serious engagement with their traditions and thoughtfulness. And as some might argue, their own harmonious coexistence with other species was fraught with perilous conditions, some of which brought their entire tribes to a point of extinction even before the invasion of the Europeans.

IV: SOCIAL CONTRACT THEORY

The presuppositions that underlie the notion of a state of nature relate and to a great extent explain the notion about abundance and scarcity examined in the previous chapter. In the same sense, any discussion of the state of nature and the inevitable move to civil society brings out another set of assumptions about human interaction in that state and the ways by which it's possible to counter their disastrous consequences. The main point here is that uncertainty (or the notion of risk assessment so familiar to business people today) is being invoked time and again. It's not that humans couldn't survive or even flourish in their natural habitat, but their success and progress were impeded by levels of fear from death and suffering that their attention was diverted from their potential perfectibility. Under conditions of uncertainty, any proposal for some modicum of predictability is welcome. Before we move to examine some of the classical arguments for this shift—historical or conceptually ad hoc—we should mention that this argument rests on additional assumptions about human nature, some simply invoked, others implicitly assumed (and these views will be examined in the next chapter).

Instead of plodding through the intricacies of the arguments provided by all of those who used the state of nature device to get to the social contract that legitimates the State, some general comments are in order. Ernest Barker, for example, credits Thomas Aquinas as formulating the theory of contract in 1250, basing it on the Bible, Roman Law, and the principles of Aristotle's *Politics* (1960/1947, viii), at least to the extent that the authority of the "contract" depends to some extent on God's authority. In this sense, there is an intimate argumentative move to formulate a connection between social contract and Natural Law, thereby adding the naturalness and reasonableness of such arrangement and not simply appealing to divine providence (ibid., x, xvi). Overall, the social contract is based on two ideas: first, "that the State, *in the sense of the government*, is based on a contract between ruler and subjects," and second, that "the State, *in the sense of a political community, and as an organized society*, is based on a social contract—or rather on myriads of such contracts—between each and every member of that community or society" (ibid., xii, italics in the original). Admittedly, different thinkers in formulating their arguments in favor of the move from the state of nature to civil society—and the need for a social contract—had different notions of what constituted a "community." For Rousseau, it was a self-governing society, for Locke it was a fiduciary government that can be dismissed, and for Hobbes the community relinquishes its rights once forming a governing board (ibid., xiii).

Rousseau's own words are important to quote so as to appreciate the conceptual underpinnings of his argument on behalf of the social contract. For him, it's essential that "*each of us puts his person and all his power in common under the supreme direction of the general will; and in a body we receive each member as an indivisible part of the whole*" (1978/1762, 53; italics in the original). His insistence on the "general will" is not simply the collection of individual wills canceling effects of contradictory self-interests of participants. He also argues that when each person enters this contract, "each gives himself to all," but in point of fact "he gives himself to no one" (ibid.). This means that what seems to be a loss of one's independence or the exertion of one's power, practical, political, or intellectual understood as one's "natural power" is gained through the social contract as "civil freedom" protected by and enforced through the governing body of the now constituted State (ibid., 56). Leaving aside the notion of the "lawgiver" whose supreme wisdom is assumed by Rousseau, and leaving aside the problematic vision he has of what democratic institutions of governance will look like, we clearly get a sense of the rationale for moving toward or even imposing a social contract on members of a community. Of special interest is also the language used by Rousseau to explain the long-term benefits of this set up. In his words: "A convention that is *legitimate* because it has the social contract as a basis; *equitable* because it is common to all; *useful* because it can have no other object than the general will; and *solid*, because it has the public force and the supreme power as guarantee" (ibid., 63; italics added). Here Rousseau seems to cover all his bases, from legitimacy and equitability to usefulness and solidity to convince the faint hearted that his proposal is worthy of anyone who wishes to transform their daily life from the dangers of the state of nature, however noble it may appear, to a state of civil society where one's freedoms and fair distribution of possessions are guaranteed by the entire community.

Though it seems that the social contract is among equals who have the same rights and duties and therefore the ultimate power to enter or exit the contract, Barker is adamant in arguing that in fact the "contract" in this case isn't among equals, because the trustee has duties but no rights and the beneficiary has rights but no duties (ibid., xxiv). This lopsided arrangement comes about because a third party is introduced into the equation, the government or governing boards, may they be of the monarchical kinds advocated by Hobbes or the democratic ones advocated by Rousseau. For Rousseau, the social contract is first and foremost progressive insofar as it lifts humans from their original state, second is the basis for a reasonable and legitimate State that represents the "general will," and third that this "general will" is about the attainment of general good and not the aggregate of the self-interests of individuals (ibid., xxxii–iii). If Hobbes, Locke, and Rousseau, in their own ways, found it reasonable to use the social contract as a means by which to legitimate the State and its governing apparatus, we are reminded that Hume remained a critic of social contract theory and its logic, because such device assumes the tacit consent of the people who may not have perfect information on which to base their consent (ibid., xli). As a critic, Hume invokes his view of human nature as loving oneself more than others and therefore expanding one's acquisitions regardless of the well-being of the community as a whole or the available natural resources (ibid., 160), and thereof for him the social contract ploy is both unrealistic and internally contradictory (ibid., 165).

More recent commentators, like Charly Coleman, suggest that for Rousseau the shift from the state of nature to civil society was accompanied by a radical transformation of human nature as a break from the past into the necessities of the future (2014, 222). This change of heart, rather than just a change of mind, is illustrated in Rousseau being the most notable advocate of the forceful denial of individual possessiveness in the service of social community building (ibid., 229). "According to Rousseau, the act of voluntary self-surrender gives rise to a collective moral being that absorbs all particular motives in public life into its own totalizing force" (ibid., 236). This develops the notion that when one gives oneself up to all, it is like giving oneself to no one (in particular). And "as the repository of rights surrendered in common, it is everything. As a particular entity that stands apart from the whole, it is nothing" (ibid., 237). Therefore individuals do not possess property rights either naturally or through labor, but only as part of a social convention and legal framework that determine them as far as they are conducive to the common good (ibid., 238–39).

As Barker reminds us, the notion of behaving "as if" there was a social contract is also understood in terms of historic continuity, religious belief, and legal argument (1960/1947, vii). As we mentioned above, Aquinas is credited with the formulation of the theory of contract, but under what conditions can it persist into modernity? Just as Locke and Hobbes had a sense that one's acquisitions should not detract from the general well-being of others, there is a more focused argument here about the contingent status of private property rights; namely, that they can and should be sanctioned only under the condition that it is better for society as a whole. Incidentally, this way of thinking, according to Coleman, is what distinguishes the American Constitution and its French counterpart: the former insists on individual rights while the latter sanctions individual rights in conjunction with (and for the indirect fulfillment of) the rights and benefits of the community as a whole.

V: RATIONAL STARTING POINT

By the time we come to the Enlightenment, the notion of the reasonableness of moving from a state of nature to civil society with a social contract in place becomes standardized. In his political writings, Immanuel Kant (1724–1804) makes reference to the works of his predecessors about the social contract as a "basic postulate of reason" (1970, 83). He is dismissive of their own speculations about it being "something which must have taken place in *reality*," even though "there is no document to show that any contract was actually submitted to the commonwealth, accepted by the head of State, and sanctioned by both parties" (ibid.; italics in the original). For him, though, what remains at the heart of this false belief is the reasonableness of the notion of a social contract as the basis for the relationship among individuals who were removed from the state of nature. This contractual transformation is brought about when one's natural inclinations, however aggressive and noncooperative, are brought into a state of individual rights recognized by the State. In language reminiscent of Rousseau, Kant argues that "the mechanism of nature by which selfish inclinations are naturally opposed to one another in their external relations can be used by reason to facilitate the attainment of its own end, the reign of established right" (ibid., 113). Opposing inclinations are transformed into rights that can now be adjudicated by reason, reducing conflict and strife, and ensuring, as the title of this particular essay says, "perpetual peace."

Kant's presumption of what it was like in the state of nature comes closer to Hobbes than to Locke and Rousseau. He speaks of the "warlike state of nature" among people and that the rational avoidance of this circumstance isn't limited to individual inclinations and rights but also to those of their "public" relations, how they are situated as members of the State (ibid., 121). The famous Categorical Imperative that binds everyone to unconditionally and universally adhere to a moral maxim in regard to one's behavior is an outcome of Kant's understanding of the central role played by the social contract. When it comes to the "principle of publicness in the questions of rights"; that is, how individual rights are understood in the public domain, it's crucial for Kant to invoke the "civil contract" according to which one's rights are now sanctioned publicly (ibid., 126). The point here, as elsewhere in Kant's writings, is the rational recognition that only under contractual conditions of membership in a State can one make reasonable claims about one's rights, both privately and publicly.

One of the most Kantian of political and moral thinkers of the twentieth century is John Rawls (1921–2002), who attempts in his theoretical construction of "justice as fairness" to bring about a reasonable way of thinking about the crucial and rational role of a social contract. In his words: "The guiding idea is that the principles of justice for the basic structure of society are the object of the original agreement." And these principles, he continues, are those of "free and rational persons concerned to further their own interests," but who "would accept in an initial position of equality as defining the fundamental terms of their association" (1971, 11). In a short sentence, Rawls pulls together the notions of freedom, equality, and rationality as applied to an initial or original (hypothetical) position where people can make choices about the just foundations of their State. Instead of continuing to develop the particularities of the Rawlsian theory of justice, we should note that, like Kant and others before him, the basis of agreement or consent is rationality. Human reason will compel individuals whose differences are usually foregrounded to see what minimal conditions can be satisfied to ensure peaceful coexistence if not prosperity. Incidentally, Rawls is most sensitive to the economic consequences of the initial position in which individuals are ignorant of the outcome of their choices. We should also note these economic issues as preliminary references to our more general discussion of the quest of prosperity.

Rawls's two principles of justice in the "original position" (akin to a social contract) are as follows: "First: each person is to have an equal right to the most extensive basic liberty compatible with a similar liberty for others. Second: social and economic inequalities are to be arranged so that they are both (a) reasonably expected to be to everyone's advantage, and (b) attached to positions and offices open to all" (ibid., 60). Here, too, liberty and equality are the guiding principles, but with an additional twist to the standard "harm principle" (that one's liberty is curtailed by not infringing on someone else's liberty); namely, that whatever inequality ensues later it will be beneficial to all, rather than just to the very few (as seen in contemporary capitalist systems). This is reminiscent of Rousseau's distinction between natural and moral or artificial inequality, the former justified by natural circumstances, the latter a by-product of social relations that should not accede one's lifetime (as an argument against hereditary aristocratic titles and wealth). This line of argument brings together concerns over the legitimacy of the State with the actual workings of the legal system in protecting the rights of individuals and what conditions of freedom and equality that they can expect. There is no preconceived notion that democratic institutions will necessarily guarantee prosperity to all, but instead an agreement about the conditions under which an efficient economic system, with this liberal orientation, will ensure advantages and progress even to the most disadvantaged in the community.

Politically, there has been a long tradition where equality has been contrasted to freedom: the more freedom, the less equality, and vice versa. The argument has been based on the idea that unfettered freedom would allow individuals to pursue their interests and succeed in ways that would set them apart from others who are less talented, lucky, or industrious. Likewise, if equality were the only concern of a society—as envisioned inaccurately in regard to communist regimes—then certain liberties would have to be curtailed, those that would distinguish one person from another. Rawls's *Theory of Justice* is an attempt to square this circle, so to speak, and allow for both principles to prevail within one system. This may mean that we shift the discussion from an absolute sense of equality, for example, which is neither natural nor real, and appreciate nuances of equality—allowing for natural differences in talents and temperament—and eventually settle on a less grandiose sense of "equal opportunity." This may sound like a truncated ideal, but as long as it is fully articulated and judiciously administered it may be the way by which we hold onto equality without compromising the ideals of liberty.

Moreover, if we follow the Kantian features of Rawls, we recognize the rational and principled manner by which society can be organized: the so-called veil of ignorance undermines the potential of self-interested abuse in selecting one policy over another. Not knowing the outcome of a choice makes the choice more principled, more categorical, and universalizable. We should acknowledge that both Kant and Rawls and the many others who have been working along these lines have assumed a liberal and democratic State. They also assumed that those fully participating in the life of the community would appreciate the ways by which their own interests and concerns can be addressed rationally and publicly with levels of compromise present-day American politicians have abandoned.

VI: THE BRIDGE

As already mentioned above, one set of assumptions begets another; one conceptual apparatus invokes or is based on another. As we have seen when discussing the state of nature and the social contract, most authors either implicitly (in a side remark) or explicitly talk about human nature. To begin with, they have no problem generalizing about humans and their inherent nature, and likewise, they seem unperturbed drawing on their generalization in order to make arguments about how the political order should be organized. Though there is much to tease out from the writings of the authors we have encountered so far, we plan on dealing with human nature more generally, and only then recalling some of these references. The worry, as always, is missing the forest for the many exciting and enlightening trees we find along the Western canon. What sustains this kind of exploration for most thinkers is a sense of order, natural or divine (or a combination of the two), one that is imagined rather than observed, but one whose heuristic value is profound for the development of our thought. As Harari reminds us: "Because the Sapiens social order is imagined, humans cannot preserve the critical information for running it simply by making copies of their DNA and passing these on to their progeny. A conscious effort has to be made to sustain laws, customs, procedures and manners, otherwise the social order would quickly collapse" (2015, 120). The "conscious" effort, whether by philosophers or politicians, that can ensure some modicum of social order and civility is what these chapters in the first part of this book are all about: Is it possible? Is it sustainable once introduced? And will it ameliorate some of the negative consequences of promoting collaboration instead of self-interested competitiveness?

Chapter Three

Human Nature and the Human Condition

By now it should become more obvious how our views of human nature are interconnected with our views of the state of nature and its abundance or scarcity. Human nature, according to this historical retelling, is bound with the conditions that help manifest our best or worst characteristics. After outlining the four standard views of human nature—good, evil, neither good nor evil, and propensities for good and evil—and documenting their genesis—Bible, major religions, and ancient texts on ethics (from Aristotle to Tusi)—it appears quite logical to see their connection to the first two frames of reference insofar as those would enhance or retard some of them. Human sociality, as discussed by Matthew Lieberman (2013), for example, will be instrumental in shifting the individualistic-based framing into one where interactions are essential.

If the previous frame of references that dealt with the state of nature and the social contract are questioned, what is questioned as well is our human nature as competitive or cooperative individuals. Behavioral economists and psychologists are eager to disprove standard assumptions about human nature and the human condition, understood here in terms of the conditions of scarcity and abundance that surround us—from natural resources to human kindness and empathy—as well as in terms of what are "givens" as opposed to what we can change or transform. The human condition is as much linked in the literature to human nature as it is to the state of nature; it is also linked to the artificial situations of markets and the State into which we are born but that should not constrain us. Questions of wealth and income inequalities—much in the news since the Great Recession and Thomas Piketty's book edited in 2014—come into play in this frame of reference. The experiences of the two world wars of the twentieth century play a vital role in this discussion, illustrating how violence and brutality was exercised by armed forces while victims' behavior varied from the heroic to the beastly.

I: THE STANDARD FOUR VIEWS OF HUMAN NATURE

The schemata of the four different views of human nature is based on generalization that are either conceptually set in place or derived from empirical observations. In what follows, no distinction is made about the sources of the views and therefore of their scientific validity; instead, as has been done so far, the reason for this brief survey is to offer a conceptual landscape to tease the assumptions we commonly make when discussing questions of human exchange relations or the power relations that come about after certain state institutions are constituted. When speaking of human nature, we are examining the inherent natural qualities found in humans in terms of their psychological makeup and the mental processes through which decisions are naturally made, so to speak. The difficulty with this conceptual construction is that we imagine, just as in the case of the state of nature, what it was like before social conventions were adopted, and prior to any linguistic and cultural formations, as opposed to some other surveys where a worldview informs human behavior (Stevenson 1974). Given this setup, whatever we survey here is conjectural and speculative. But the speculations are worthy of provisional consideration because they are later used to justify a set of ideas that are the basis for rule formation and the establishment of modern institutions.

For example, Lieberman points out that "most accounts of human nature ignore our sociality altogether" (2013, 9) because they focus on people as unique and differentiated individuals. Sociality means layers of "connection" with other human beings, "mindreading" as a way to understand and even empathize with others around us, and "harmonizing," which is "the neural adaptations that allow group beliefs and values to influence our own" (ibid., 11–12). The insistence on figuring out a preexisting situation in which humans are separated and only later come together makes no sense in this critique of conceptualizing human nature. For Lieberman, *"Our brains are built to practice thinking about the social world and our place in it"* (ibid., 22, italics in the original). Criticizing the "axiom of self-interest," Lieberman argues that, given many studies, "mutual cooperation activates the reward system as an end in itself" (ibid., 86). He also argues that "the theorizing of Hobbes, Hume, and all other intellectuals who claim that self-interest is the source of all human motivation has produced a self-fulfilling prophecy" (ibid., 96). This critique should be kept in mind as we forge ahead into the hypothetical world of ideas.

(a) Good

The first view is that all humans are by nature good, that their natural inclinations are to behave well, be empathic to fellow humans, and when in need help others. As we rely more heavily on scientific research rather than the speculations of philosophers and theologians, as Adrian Ward reports (2012), our behavior is prompted either by intuitive or reflective responses. Intuitive responses correlate with what we would label natural behavior, behavior unmediated by social cues or pressure from others, and as such are more accurate representations of what we are like naturally. Ward reports from a variety of studies run in the United States that when confronted with the need to react quickly or make a quick decision, the majority of people are indeed good, cooperative, and selfless. A hint of this was already mentioned in the previous chapter when discussing Rousseau's view of human's capacity for compassion or pity, their innate propensity to identify with the hardships of others in the state of nature. This means that what makes us bad, when we behave poorly or selfishly, is outside influences, from upbringing circumstances to specific ways by which we are rewarded for putting our own interests above all others. This kind of initial goodness is what we recognize as genuine altruism when we care to do something nice for a family member or a stranger without regard to any reciprocal action.

To be sure, there have been various psychological studies to prove the "pro-social" and empathetic behavior in toddlers (e.g., Svetlova et al. 2010) so as to "prove" that babies are inclined to be good or behave in a manner that adults, given their social environment, would judge to be so. But empirical data alone cannot persuade us that this is indeed the case with all children across all geographical and generational spheres so as to make this a universal claim. Instead, we can offer a qualified nod in this direction given some empirical substantiation.

(b) Evil

Whether first formulated by St. Augustine or much earlier, the notion of Original Sin or the fall from grace with the expulsion from the Garden of Eden has dominated Western culture ever since the Catholic Church has taken center stage in our conception of humanity. This view of human nature sees humans as prone to evil deeds and corrupt by nature, with a promise for redemption with sufficient repentance. Free will is driven, according to this view, by one's instincts and emotions, from animal instincts to fear and greed, and therefore we find ourselves behaving badly. Our selfishness or self-centeredness is naturally translated into a deep sense of competitiveness to ensure our success at the expense of others in the struggle for survival. There are, of course, many consequences to this view of human nature, from a reluctance to cooperate and the ethical problem of the "free rider" of those who take advantage of others in a team, all the way to the need to set in place rules and regulations to curtail bad behavior and punish violators. The entire legal system (in addition to religious institutions) is formulated in ways that presuppose the evil nature of humans and the ways by which they can hurt each other. The State apparatus, as we have come to know it even in democratic regimes, is predicated on the need to exercise sanctioned violence in order to keep peace among members of any community. Though he doesn't elaborate on this much, Locke mentions in passing the "baseness of human nature" in regard to the potential of someone acquiring "absolute power" as if it "purifies man's blood" (1947, 166).

Just as there are numerous studies that attempt to substantiate the goodness of toddlers, there are studies that suggest that young children can be viewed as psychopaths, displaying antisocial behavior verging on cruelty because of lack of any empathy (e.g., Coid et al. 2009). The history of warfare can just as well serve as the empirical database for the ongoing evil that permeates humanity, all the way to more specific cases of genocide, the Holocaust being the most symbolically powerful and convincing case.

(c) Tabula Rasa

The third view of human nature claims that we are neither good nor evil by nature, but are a clean slate, *tabula rasa* in Latin, on which goodness and evil can be later inscribed. It is *nurture* rather than *nature* that dictates and constructs what kind of people we turn out to be. If we grow up in an environment rampant in crime, where our parents pay no attention to us and where we must participate in gang activities in order to survive, we are likely to turn out to be bad people, or at least people who do bad things. By contrast, if our home environment is loving and caring, with family, school, and church support, we are more likely to turn out to be good members of society, contributing to the welfare of others. This view of humanity was the foundation of the prison reform movement in the 1970s that believed in rehabilitation of criminals so as to offer them the kind of nurturing and educational opportunities they missed growing up. The blame or responsibility for bad behavior, when displayed, was lifted from individual actors and squarely placed on environments and institutions. According to this view, any offenders are considered not behaving out of free will or rationally, but victims of their circumstances (LexisNexis PCLaw, 2016).

Studies that examine this view sometimes refer to it as studying the influence of nature versus nurture in the development of children into young adults. There is a useful meta review of most of the twin studies in the past fifty years, which concludes that it is neither one nor the other, but rather both contribute to the mindset and behavior of adults (e.g., Polderman et al.

2015). Incidentally, in the criminal justice field such empirical studies sway the courts and criminologists about questions of rehabilitation and the treatment of prison populations. It should be also mentioned here that some, like Steven Pinker (2002), argue against this view of *tabula rasa* as it has taken hold in the social sciences.

(d) Propensities for Good and Evil

The fourth view claims that humans have good and bad propensities, and that those come into the fore or are enacted upon depending on circumstances. Unlike the third view that claims humans are neither good nor bad, this one claims they are both, and that the intermixture of these tendencies makes us who we are as humans. Sometimes our positive or good inclinations find their way to mold our behavior, and because they are fundamentally already present in our psyche we can easily tap into them (rather than be nurtured into them). At other times, our egoism or selfishness takes hold of our outlook and we behave badly, hurt others in order to further our own needs or wants. The American entomologist Edward Wilson (2012) is a proponent of this view, as he juxtaposes his observations from ants and bees to our species, showing along the way that we are genetically hardwired to have these two contradictory propensities or traits. Under different conditions we are prone to invoke or follow one set of propensities instead of the other, being highly cooperative and helpful to each other to survive (as a group) in the face of menacing predators, for example, or behaving selfishly when courting one of our own for procreation. This kind of behavior includes benevolently intended behavior (to save the colony, for example), which is unequivocally detrimental or even disastrous for the individual who perishes. As for empirical data, Wilson's work offers ample observation from different species.

II: CANONICAL REFERENCES TO HUMAN NATURE

(a) Plato (c. 428 BC–c. 348 BC) and Aristotle (384 BC–322 BC)

Some of the references to the three parts of the soul or the three souls with which humans are born are discussed by Plato in *The Republic* (436b). After separating between the body and the soul, the body understood as the encasement of the soul and therefore worthy of healthy treatment to ensure the health of the soul, Plato divides the soul into the rational, the spirited, and the appetitive. The rational soul, which is the mind or the intellect, is where discernment and judgment are undertaken, where wisdom eventually finds itself. The choices and decisions humans make come forth from this part of the soul. The second part is that associated with human will and is therefore the spirited part, the part that brings about human agency and our actions.

The emotional part is the third, where self-control is best advised as it should be within and under the control of the other parts of the soul. In the *Phaedrus* (246a–254e), Plato gives an image of a rational charioteer whose horses, desire and will, draw him in different directions, but he must maintain control so that the chariot isn't overturned. The focus is neither on the inherent goodness nor evil of the human soul, but on the sense that humans by nature must maintain a certain equilibrium, a certain level of balance and control over the various tendencies they may feel or display. The mindfulness of each and every one may come closest to the fourth view about human propensities insofar as it explains why sometimes humans err and behave poorly and at other times behave properly, as social beings ought to within their community.

The Greek notion of living in accordance with nature and of believing that nature is designed in a way to single out humans as different from other "beasts" is well articulated in Aristotle as well. He was concerned with human virtues and how they come into play in the interaction among humans, as seen in the *Nicomachean Ethics* as well as in his statements about the social nature of humans in *The Politics* (1252a–b). Not only are humans understood to be "political animals," they are also considered to prefer the company of each other for the sake of procreation or socializing, from household economics to the State. The virtuous life of individuals is measured and judged by their behavior toward or in the company of others, whether they display courage in battle or are worthy friends to their fellow citizens. Overall, one can extrapolate an adherence to the fourth view of human nature where animal instincts are subdued and brought under the guidance of rationality.

(b) Nasir ad-Din Tusi (1201–1274)

Nasir ad-Din Tusi, in his *The Nasirean Ethics*, suggests that "the human species, which is the noblest of existent beings in the universe, needs both the aid of the other species and the co-operation of its own kind to ensure the survival of the individual as well as that of the race" (1235/1964, 189). He argues that the inevitable need for cooperation among humans is obvious, as no one can provide for "his own sustenance" because "if his days were to be divided up among several occupations, he would not be capable of doing justice to any of one of them all" (ibid.). On the other hand, "When men render aid to each other, each one performing one of these important tasks that are beyond the measure of his own capacity, and observing the law of justice in transactions by giving greatly and receiving in exchange the labour of others: then the means of livelihood are realized, and the succession of the individual and the survival of the species are assured and arranged: as is the case in fact" (ibid.). The social facet of humanity isn't a Greek ideal or the telos for which nature has prepared the species, but an essential feature of human survival. This eventually develops into what Smith later calls the division of labor among people to make our work more efficient. Tusi promotes this level of cooperation among humans through the invocation of "Divine Wisdom": "There should be a disparity of aspirations and opinions, so that each desires a different occupation, some noble and others base, in the practice of which they are cheerful and content" (ibid.). Different interests and talents bring about different occupations, but instead of leading to competition, people are "cheerful and content." Does this mean that he implicitly endorses the first view of human nature that humans are by nature good?

Tusi answers this question by claiming that there are five "classes" of humans: (1) "those who are by nature good, and whose good is communicable"; (2) "those who are by nature good, but whose goodness is not communicable"; (3) "those who are by nature neither good nor evil"; (4) "those who are evil, but whose evil is not communicable"; (5) "those who are by nature evil, and whose evil is communicable" (ibid., 230–231). This division allows for the three of the four views listed above, but with a twist. Though someone may be good or evil by nature, this goodness or evil may not be "communicable." What does this mean? Perhaps Tusi appreciates the ways in which one's nature may not be discernable or may not be fully evident to others. Perhaps the point is that we can observe only subsets of good and evil people by nature, and that in general one's true nature may remain hidden because it is "not communicable." What hinders the communication of one's true nature? Is it the social and moral norms surrounding us, where behavior may or may not be sanctioned and therefore cannot be publicly expressed? Whichever way these questions are answered, the Persian version of the classification of different kinds of human nature is already codified in the thirteenth century, though it is rarely mentioned.

(c) Niccolo Machiavelli (1469–1527)

Unlike the thoughtful and meditative view offered by Socrates and Plato in regard to the human soul, when we think of Machiavelli we commonly recall his cunning advice as to how to manipulate people for the sake of the prince holding absolute power in his domain. The various side comments found in *The Prince* are informative about what Machiavelli's view of human nature must have been. He says that "it is the nature of people to be fickle," so that "to persuade them of something is easy, but to make them stand fast in that conviction is hard" (1513/1977, 18). In this sense, it's not a question of the goodness or evil of humans, but their inability to use their heads to control the emotional sway of ideas propounded by rhetoricians. He continues to say that fear and hate are the most crucial motivations for injuring other people, as if these two emotional drives or instincts are what constitute the way humans react to each other (ibid., 24). In addition to their reactions based on fear and hate, and their inherent fickleness, Machiavelli also suggests that people are lazy by nature: "Men are always wary of tasks that seem hard" (ibid., 31). If humans by nature are lazy, then their behavior is bound to neither exemplify the virtues of goodness nor the fight against the temptations of evil. If they are "simple of mind" (ibid., 50), then they are prone to manipulation, and a prince can take advantage of their fickleness and laziness. Their immediate concerns focus their attention, and "remote events" do not concern them as much (ibid., 68). But then there is a slight turn toward judging humans as being "rotten" (ibid., 48). Their rotten nature (or evil tendency) partially expresses itself in their concern for property over family relations, so that if their possessions are protected they are content (ibid., 48, 51). As for free will, he argues that "Fortune governs half of our actions, but that even so she leaves the other half more or less in our power of control" (ibid., 70). This nuanced view of what is within human control and what isn't remains a hallmark of the both/and way of phrasing or accounting for human behavior rather than the either/or view that condemns or condones with little regard to the subtleties facing human action and decision-making processes.

George Akerlof and Robert Shiller, in the context of discussing how free we are to make choices within markets, echo some of Machiavelli's judgments about how easy it is to fool or trick people and prey on their weaknesses. For them, human nature in fact denotes "human weaknesses" such that "people are less than perfect"; this translates into market realities wherein people can "potentially, be tricked and fooled" (2015, 164). For Machiavelli, the context of denigrating human nature as lazy and fickle, as prone to manipulation by the prince, was the political sphere; for Akerlof and Shiller, the context is economics or the goods and services sold to consumers in the marketplace. They claim that "modern economics inherently fails to grapple with deception and trickery," and that "competitive markets by their very nature spawn deception and trickery, as a result of the same profit motives that give us our prosperity" (ibid., 164–165). What was true of leaders of the past (Machiavelli's princes) remains true of today's corporate leaders who are prone to use the entire psychological arsenal at their disposal to take advantage of the naïve reception of ordinary customers. A decent marketing professional would then be well advised to follow as much of Machiavelli's list of tricks and methods of treating his own people or enemies so as to maximize submission and the consumptive acquiescence so apparent in consumer behavior of modern economies. The expert devices of contemporary advertisement simply follow some basic principles of human deception already articulated centuries ago.

III: CLASSICAL VIEWS OF HUMAN REASON AND RATIONALITY

By the time we move to the modern age of the seventeenth century and the Enlightenment in the eighteenth century, the very notion of the self is revisited. No longer is human identity intertwined with divine design and the offerings of nature, but instead it is understood in more social and psycho-dynamic terms. This means, for example, as Coleman reminds us, the possibility of a new social order based on "collective rather than individualistic principles" (to some extent under Spinoza's influence), so that we see the emergence of "selflessness as an ethical ideal" (2014, 6). This aligns also with Rousseau's notion of a social contract where the limits on the exercise of individual will is predicated on the consent of the body politics as a whole (ibid., 7). Most leaders of the Enlightenment fully appreciated nuanced approaches to individualism as the foundation of a social order, because by now the individual is contextualized within a community of others (and not only understood in relation to God or to Nature). But this doesn't mean that by the eighteenth century the divine is completely ignored or cast aside from the discussions of the social conditions of a political order; instead, the divine was marshaled when needed to retain the stability of the collective whole and to ensure the legitimacy of state powers (ibid., 12). Since this is also the Age of Reason, arguments about the interactions among humans are based on rational principles and the overall authority reason should have in the affairs of the state.

In explaining the approach French thinkers were adopting in relation to human rights as opposed to their American counterparts, Coleman also points out that for Rousseau the shift from the state of nature to civil society was accompanied by a radical transformation of human nature as a break from the past into the necessities of the future (ibid., 222). This meant, among other things, that a static view of human nature was untenable, that indeed the notion of human perfectibility incorporated a transformation of the very essence of humanity, not merely a change of their social institutions. Incidentally, this Enlightenment view of the potential transformation of human nature is echoed in the twentieth century by economists like of Joseph Schumpeter, who says that "human nature is certainly malleable to some extent particularly in groups whose composition may be changed" (1942/1975, 203). As we already noted in chapter 2, Rousseau's argument on behalf of entering the social contract was not only in political and legal terms of rights and duties but also suggested a preconception of the position of the individual within a society—being part of a greater whole where one may seem to get lost, but in fact remains free and equal to all. In this light, individuals do not possess property rights either naturally or through labor, but only as part of social conventions and legal frameworks that determine these rights as conducive to the common good (ibid., 238–239). Subordinating one's interest or natural inclinations in the service of the collective whole is reminiscent of the way the ancient Greeks and the Persian thinkers of the thirteenth century have.

If the imagery of the state of nature and the conceptual acrobatics of the social contract could be dismissed, there is a recognition at least by some philosophers that human nature is implicitly part of every treatise, every manuscript that deals with human affairs or political institutions. In his *A Treatise of Human Nature*, Hume says, "Tis evident, that all the sciences have a relation, greater or less, to human nature; and that however wide any of them may seem to run from it, they still return back by one passage or another" (1738–1740/1978, xix). Hume, who is considered a critic rather than a promoter of the Enlightenment ideals, perhaps a skeptic of the great advantages reason has to offer humanity, is still driven to pontificate on human happiness as a goal worthy of achieving. In his words: "Human happiness, according to the most received notions, seems to consist in three ingredients: action, pleasure, and indolence: And though these ingredients ought to be mixed in different proportions, according to particular disposition of the person; yet no one ingredient can be entirely wanting, without destroying, in some measure, the relish of the whole composition" (1752–1758/ 1970, 21). Here, too, we see a philosopher struggling to articulate not only the composition of human nature or the human psyche as we saw with Plato and Aristotle but also prescribe the proper admixture that each facet of humanity should contribute toward being content, if not happy.

Eugene Rotwein explains that Hume understood that "the cohesive moral forces which preserve mutually satisfactory relationships in society are themselves largely a product of society's influence," quite like Rousseau's appreciation of the transformation of human nature (ibid., xcix). He continues to say that "Hume defines 'sympathy' as an associative mechanism through which the mind, primarily on the basis of resemblance, infuses the 'idea' of the emotions of others with the 'liveliness' intrinsic to the impression of 'self.'" This means that as humanity evolves, a "more closely knit society may be traced to its influence in widening the basis for the association of 'self' with others, or in deepening the sympathetic process through which we participate in the immediacy of our experience" (ibid., xcix–c). Rousseau's notion of "pity" or "compassion" comes to mind just as Smith's more elaborate discourse on "moral sentiments." But one must also admit that Hume remained agnostic on what human nature was like, when he says that "human nature is too inconstant to admit of any such regularity. Changeableness is essential to it" (Hume 1978, 283). Not knowing what human nature is like in terms of its origins is no excuse, then, for offering some ideas of the ways in which humans have coped with each other over time and learned to cultivate their sentiments. Some may think about this in terms of how "happiness" is nothing but a ratio of what the individual learns to expect over time and how social reality frames this expectation. In short, society informs individual expectations.

The opening lines of *The Theory of Moral Sentiments* are explicitly devoted to what Smith considers to be human nature. In his words: "How selfish soever [*sic*] man may be supposed, there are evidently some principles in his nature, which interest him in the fortune of others, and render their happiness necessary to him, though he derives nothing from it, except the pleasure of seeing it" (1759/2010, 47). He starts with the common presupposition about human selfishness, the kind of inherent self-preservation that induces self-interested behavior, but contrasts this view right away with the evidence of human altruism. Though humans gain no personal benefit from seeing the benefits others enjoy, they still seem happy from such observations. This deep emotion he calls "pity or compassion," just the terms used by Rousseau around the same time, and classifies them as a "sentiment" (ibid.). He appreciates how situational this kind of "sympathy" is bound to remain, but then reverts to talking about "one of the most important principles of human nature, the dread of death" (ibid., 53). This dread, to be sure, isn't invoked as a reason for "self-love" (about which he subsequently talks) but rather in order to remind his readers that this is a "great restraint upon the injustice of mankind; which, while it afflicts and mortifies the individual, guards and protects the society" (ibid.).

Right away, in the first chapter of this treatise, Smith moves the individual into a relation with others, thus explaining our human nature in social and not individualistic terms. He implores us to recall that "nature teaches the spectator to assume the circumstances of the person principally concerned"; that is, put ourselves in their shoes so as to empathize with their calamities (ibid., 67). To be virtuous, then, is "to restrain our selfish, and to indulge our benevolent, affections, constitutes the perfection of human nature" (ibid., 71). Does this mean that human nature isn't "perfect" yet? Does it mean that in order to bring about the perfect illumination and foundation of human nature we ought to restrain our selfishness and indulge our benevolence? Either way, it's clear that as an Enlightenment figure, Smith believes that first, we do have natural inclinations; second, that we can modify them; and third, that striving toward perfection isn't just a Greek ideal but an accomplishment close at hand. If we aren't clear what human characteristics ought to be foregrounded and cultivated, Smith makes it clear in this passage: "Generosity, humanity, kindness, compassion, mutual friendship and esteem, all the social and benevolent affections, when expressed in the countenance or behaviour, even towards those who are not peculiarly connected with ourselves, please the indifferent spectator upon almost every occasion" (ibid., 94). The introduction of the "indifferent" or "impartial spectator" in various places in this text has been interpreted either as an appeal to God whose impartiality and omnipresence are self-evident or to one's conscience where rational reflection judges (or controls) one's emotional outbursts.

Not only does Smith continue the view of human nature as inextricably connected to other human beings and the community within which we find ourselves, but he also emphasizes the benefits that are bound to accumulate when everyone is worried more about being loved by others than just loving oneself. Though phrased in the third person, we can observe Smith's own commitment to some version of the first view of human nature, the one that focuses on the natural goodness to be found in humanity. In his words: "Man, it has been said, has a natural love for society, and desires that the union of mankind should be preserved for its own sake, and though he himself was to derive no benefit from it" (ibid., 169). This statement, even though sounding as if he's quoting someone else, reassures his readers that in fact society's well-being is paramount in human's hearts and minds, that it is a natural inclination to which they are drawn without any utility to themselves. This inborn altruism is sometimes difficult to associate with the one who also spoke of the "invisible hand" much later. But if we continue and note that "the orderly and flourishing state of society is agreeable to him, and he takes delight in contemplating it," then it makes sense that once this delightful situation is in place, any kind of market exchange can take place without acrimony or deceit (ibid.). He continues to say that "its disorder and confusion, on the contrary, is the object of his aversion, and he is chagrined at whatever tends to produce it" (ibid.). Here the modernist ideals of natural order in the affairs of the State come to light, and the "aversion" that is felt can only be handled through a relationship among people that are other-orientated, that attempt to fulfill the needs and wants of others as much as those of oneself. "He is sensible, too, that his own interest is connected with the prosperity of society, and that the happiness, perhaps the preservation of his existence, depends upon its preservation" (ibid.).

Just as we saw in earlier authors of the period as well as those of much earlier ages, once the individual is understood in terms of society the very conceptual exercise of separating the individual from the community makes little sense. In other words, if one's well-being, "interest" in Smith's terms, depends on society's well-being, then inevitable cooperation will ensue. If cooperation is too strong of a term here, then at the very least one's behavior must align and be coordinated in accordance with whatever is going on in society at the time. The philosophical framing of the individual versus society or the individual entering the social bond with others is dismissed here, as the individual is always already part of a greater community, a community whose "prosperity" is important, and this, as we saw earlier in Smith's own words, isn't about economic gains but the need to be loved by others and to display these emotions or sentiments in return. It is true that in his more famous and later work, *An Inquiry into the Nature and Causes of the Wealth of Nations*, he does talk about "certain propensity in human nature," or something that is "common to all men," which is "the propensity to truck, barter, and exchange one thing for another" (1776/1937, 13).

What is refreshing, though, is that Smith deals with this "propensity" directly rather than allude to it, assume it, and then deploy it as part of his argument about the division of labor and the efficiency that exchanges allow for. He admits that "whether this propensity be one of those original principles in human nature, of which no further account can be given; or whether, as seems more probable, it be the necessary consequence of the faculties of reason and speech, it belongs not to our present subject to enquire" (ibid.). Though agreeing not to explore what human nature really is, he cannot help himself from actually speaking about it. A couple of pages later he says: "The difference between the most dissimilar characters, between a philosopher and a common street porter, for example, seems to arise not so much from nature, as from habit, custom, and education" (ibid., 15). This seems to align with the third view of human nature outlined above that suggests humans are a clean slate at birth, and that nurture, in the form of "habit, custom, and education," is what distinguishes us from each other. But just because we are different or have innately different talents does not mean we should be fighting with each other or descending to the second view of human nature, the one that claims that we are evil by nature and therefore are out to get each other. Instead, this line of argument about different talents is reminiscent of Tusi's notion of the inevitable cooperation among humans: "Among men, on the contrary, the most dissimilar geniuses are of use to one another; the different produces of their respective talents, by the general disposition to truck, barter, and exchange, being brought, as it were, into a common stock, where every man may purchase whatever part of the produce of other men's talents he has occasion for" (ibid., 16).

IV: CONTEMPORARY REFERENCES

C. E. Ayres, the Institutional or heterodox economist, reminds us that when classical economics was formed the intellectual climate favored "natural order"; namely, a way to organize ourselves in self-evident and natural ways that accomplish two feats at the same time: appeal to the natural, hence universal and legitimate, way things ought to be, and a quest for order as manifested either by divine wisdom of natural laws or the explanatory and predictable powers that such an order conveys (1944/1978, 62). In his words: "Science has eliminated the guiding hand of Providence but not the conception of a providentially well-ordered universe" (ibid., 71). Human affairs, in this light, should mirror the orderliness of nature, and therefore "a valid way of thinking in economics must derive from a valid conception of human nature." But he continues, "What is a valid conception of human nature?" His answer: "As it is presented to the student of economics, this problem is complicated not only by parochial disputes among contemporary psychologists but by issues which go beyond psychology proper and involve the whole roster of biological sciences on the one hand and on the other the whole roster of social sciences, all of which are in some sense or other sciences of 'man.' Is psychology a physical science or a social science? Is human behavior to be explained in terms of minute currents of electricity conducted by nerve fibers, or is it to be explained in terms of the configuration of social situations? Or are these absolute alternatives?" (ibid., 90) What Ayres points to is the utter confusion, and perhaps this explains the refusal to deal with human nature as such in the literature, and the oblique references economists and other social scientists make about human nature, exploring it with experiments and observational data, but still ending up supporting one of the four views with which we began this chapter. Should we simply remain with leftist critics, such as the Noble Laureate Joseph Stiglitz, who glibly suggests that "greed may be an inherent part of human nature" (2013, 100)? Or, should we demand that he and every other social scientist actually unpack this notion or at the very least posit it explicitly before offering a well-argued treatise on economic relations and the relations of political power that affect income and wealth inequalities (as Stiglitz does)? Perhaps one way to think about this is that greed need not necessarily be understood in individual terms, but that the tacit endorsement of greed becomes communal or societal.

Then there are those who don't fully subscribe to the greed element in human nature that is exacerbated under conditions of competitive capitalist markets, but instead promote more of the features of the first view of human nature, that we are by nature good. Another Noble Laureate in economics, Edmund Phelps, argues that indeed there is such a thing as universal and everlasting "human nature," one that "at the highest level" includes the following features: "a desire to express creativity, a relish for challenge, an enjoyment of problem solving, a delight in novelty, and a restless need to explore and tinker" (2013, 297). The urge to bring to fulfillments all of these traits is what distinguishes us as humans, according to this view, and what eventually brings about what Phelps terms "mass flourishing." But what if this kind of fulfillment of human nature was different from and even overlooked what he calls "different human nature," one associated with traditional values of caregivers and God worshippers? This line of inquiry leads Phelps to question what kind of justice one could expect from the Rawlsian position as discussed in chapter 2 (ibid., 297ff). So, even the optimistic and flourishing kinds of human nature associated with artists and scientists, as we see in this example, pose some concerns for rational and equitable economic arrangements in the modern state.

Contemporary thinkers who deign to discuss or mention human nature at all fall neatly into three groups: first, those who suggest that there is a problem here and that we should really explore more fully this concept; second, those who assume the second view of the evil nature of humans (in terms of greed and unbridled competitiveness); and third, those who assume the first view of the natural goodness of humanity and therefore its creativity and industriousness. The two last groups are reluctant to set their arguments in the form of "if human nature is x, then it follows that we should do y." Instead, we are left to carefully search for their presumptions, the initial conditions they attribute to humanity before they fully describe what ought to be their socio-political framework for economic exchanges.

V: THE HUMAN CONDITION

When we talk about the human condition we commonly mean the conditions under which the human species has coped with environmental changes, or the methods by which humanity has learned to deal with a set of circumstances not necessarily of its own design. Existentialists since the nineteenth century have emphasized the lack of meaning in human life, the futility of our existence, and offered a variety of ways by which we can confront our eventual demise. Unlike the postulates of human nature and the organizational arguments emanating from them, in the case of the human condition, we attempt to think through and collect as much observational data about what ails us and how we should respond in the face of these circumstances. Most interesting in this conversation is the recognition that though we may face our quandaries all alone, they may have come about from a social and political setting that encompasses our community or even the entire globe. Since we speak of the human condition in the present tense, since we are concerned to make decisions now that may improve our future, our approach is radically different from the hypothetical past of the state of nature where certain conditions may or may not have ever held. In other words, the luxury of the conceptual exercise deployed by those invoking human nature are not available to those concerned with solving immediate problems and fully appreciating what humans can or cannot do in light of environmental changes.

Before articulating some obvious material changes in our contemporary environments, we should mention that there are traditionally two ways in which responses can be processed. There are those who believe, like Spinoza, that we can control our emotions with our thinking minds. In short, the mind can control the body; we can talk ourselves out of pain or at the very least follow the Epicurean mantra that we can only control our reaction to what happens to us, not the causes that bring about this or that calamity. This is a powerful position in which training our minds to reason through a situation and learn to control our reaction to what happens gives us a level of tranquility we could never achieve if we were to fight against natural phenomena or attempt to control that which we can never control. Whether we accomplish this feat of control through meditation or reflective thinking is not as important as the focus on the coping mechanism itself. Realizing that there are some things we cannot control, and that therefore we should learn what we can control—that is, the response to those events which we cannot control—shifts the mental energy in a positive and pragmatic direction. If this means that reason is cultivated in order to monitor and govern our emotions or passions, then we at least can be more responsive and responsible for our behavior (Epictetus 2004, 125).

Against this view of reason regulating, managing, or even controlling the emotions, we find the likes of Hume, who suggests the opposite: reason is nothing but the handmaiden of the emotions; reason remains at the service of our passions; and they, in turn, are the real engines of our behavioral processes. In his words: "Reason is, and ought only to be the slave of the passions, and can never pretend to any other office than to serve and obey them" (Hume 1738–1740/1978, 415). This means that human passions fundamentally evade rational assessment, so that even thinking about emotions as being either rational or irrational is silly; our passions and emotions are strong "impressions" whose impulsive feel come directly from the natural environment in which we live. Under these conditions, we can appreciate Hume's notion that human reason is nothing but a by-product of custom and habit, the kinds of experiences we have endured over the years and from which we have learned only how to react after the fact (ibid., 179, 183).

So, what should we make of our human condition from these alternative postures about the power of reason to control and direct our emotional well-being and behavioral reactions? To begin with, it's obvious that unlike the postulate of human nature that was supposed to be universal and permanent, even if fictitious, the human condition is ever-changing, temporal, and diverse in its manifestations. As Harari reminds us, though we are only looking at the past seventy thousand years of human history (as opposed to the Big Bang time scale of 13.5 billion years), there have been three monumental revolutions that characterized the evolution of humanity and its culture. The first was what he terms the Cognitive Revolution about seventy thousand years ago, the Agricultural Revolution that took place some twelve thousand years ago, and the Scientific Revolution about five hundred years ago (2015, 3). Depending on the time scale, we can easily identify major changes in climate and living conditions that transformed not only how *Homo sapiens* survived and developed their communities, but also how the shift from agrarian society to an industrial-urban one affected their cognitive abilities and their capacity to interact on larger social scales. Whether he speaks of the idea that a woman would have sex with multiple men so as to increase the protection of her newborn as a coping and survival mechanism (ibid., 42), or about food surpluses as the foundation for politics, wars, and the culture we have learned to appreciate (ibid., 101), Harari offers a broad brushstroke view of the changes we have endured and brought on ourselves. If this sounds somewhat materialistic in the Marxian sense, then this approach can highlight the extent to which our immediate environment influences our behavior and thought processes.

When we think of the Digital Age, for example, it's obvious that some radical changes have taken place in a relatively brief period of time. From the inception of the Internet in its current form in the early 1990s to the smartphone and 3D printer two decades later, communication, transportation, finance, and every other facet of our daily existence has made a difference in our lives. It's therefore reasonable to find the standard two opposing conceptual and critical camps: those who endorse all the technoscientific transformations and the gadgets they offer us as harbingers of overall progress and the improvement of the human condition, and those who find the onslaught of digital devices undermining the human spirit. Here we find the technophiles and technophobes of yesteryear, the ones who focus either on the positive or the negative effects of technoscientific developments. Among the technophiles, for example, we have the promoters of the "sharing economy" or the "crowd-based capitalism," who argue about the newfound levels of trust among strangers because of platforms for car or home rentals; Airbnb and Uber are their favorite examples (Sundararajan 2016). And among the technophobes we find the likes of Jaron Lanier (2010), who worries about what he calls "cybernetic totalitarianism," where power relations and surveillance control are in the hands of either the State or large private corporations. As digital technologies are being deployed in various contexts and with different intent, can we generalize about the human condition in the twenty-first century? Must our view be informed by the differences experienced by diverse groups of participants and the different levels of their participation in the digital spheres they encounter? One could argue that technology is inherently neutral and that what is at issue is its application, and that any application is prone to succeed or become dangerous depending on human agency.

Perhaps no generalization is possible. The human condition of twenty-first-century wealthy Westerners may have little to do with that of poor people living under totalitarian rule in Sub-Sahara Africa. Likewise, even within Western democracies, rising levels of inequality of income and wealth prevent any sense of a common "human condition" shared by all; instead, we find the conditions of some being so out of line with those of others that any "social science" like stratification or classification defies empirical observations. The most we can say is that the human condition keeps on changing as the environmental and material conditions are changing as well. The Epicurean strategy of focusing solely on one's reaction to the changing circumstances makes perfect sense: we should realize what is going on around us, not hold onto some static view of our "nature," and thereby be more flexible to reconsider what is a reasonable and responsible response. Admittedly, this may not be a commonly pursued strategy among those who ignore empirical evidence or who choose to fight windmills.

VI: THE BRIDGE

As we have been arguing in the first three chapters, our assumptions about scarcity and abundance, the state of nature and the social contract, and human nature and the human condition are intertwined. When talking about one of them, you are bound to make references or even invoke another. But as they all remain hypothetical tools or heuristic devices informative for further articulation, they should be made explicit. In other words, we should refrain from vexing nostalgically about the good old days or about the way we lived in harmony with each other, because such fictions distort and even undermine a sober analysis of the ways we behave today, given the conditions under which our behavior is reasonable and responsible. As we move forward in the next chapter to discuss the standard assumptions about property rights, private or public, we cannot but recall all the assumptions brought forth in the first three chapters.

The notion of rationality attributed to humans as a distinguishing characteristic may or may not be operative at all times and under all circumstances. The attraction of this human feature was not simply to distinguish us from the rest of the animal kingdom, but also to suggest that we had a capacity to process information in a way that would yield beneficial results. Moreover, if rationality was the core of our decision-making processes, then we could also critically reexamine previous choices and correct them in the future; we could have rational criteria according to which we prefer one choice over another. And finally, if rationality were the single most relevant aspect of our behavior, then we could come together with others to form communities in what Hegel, for one, perceived to be an inevitable developmental stage in our history. But this notion of human rationality has been under attack recently, not by romantics and existentialists, but by behavioral economists who offer ample experimental evidence that we are indeed quite irrational, and predictably so. Their latest set of theoretical proposals rests on empirical and experimental data, and what they convincingly suggest is that we have gone about organizing ourselves in exchange communities and marketplaces in the wrong manner. In short, we have irrationally used the assumption of rationality, and when doing so we have failed miserably to explain and predict human behavior or the overall failure of markets.

Chapter Four

Individual versus Communal Property Rights

Though the ancient Greeks, such as Plato and Aristotle, spoke of private versus public property and the advantages and disadvantages associated with them, it was the moderns, from Locke down the line of Enlightenment figures, who focused more carefully on the essential part private property plays in establishing rights to individuals. Understood within a framework of political and legal rights, these so-called natural rights are always argued about in retrospect; that is, from the perspective of an already existing State where these rights are legitimated both philosophically and practically. The very notion of these rights is suspect, just like other frames of references and the assumptions that inform them. Admittedly, there could be situations in which such rights are useful, but to argue that without them one would lose one's very safety and sense of self as a political entity is silly. This basic assumption in the discourse of political economy is critically examined here so as to appreciate what other models and theories could be substituted. Assumptions about property and property rights are as much about economic relations and the politico-legal framework that supports them as they are about moral principles and conventions; namely, the way we implicitly add an ethical dimension to our political status.

We should also mention from the outset that though for some the notion of property and the rights associated with it relate primarily to individual ownership of things—land, equipment, home, or car—what is excluded, but was for centuries considered part of this notion, is other human beings in the form of slavery. The ancients took it for granted that various forms of slavery conferred certain rights to the master, perhaps permanently, perhaps temporarily, with caveats—as in the Bible—for Jubilee freedom. This alerts us to the fact that all relations of property are primarily for the explicit legitimation among people and States, so that what one owns is recognized as such by others, with the tacit sanction of the laws of the lands (Graeber 2011/2014, 198ff). Questions of slavery were either ignored or taken for granted, for example, by the framers of the Constitution, who had no qualms writing that "all men are created equal" while ignoring their own African and Native slaves as well as the rights of women. US economic history is relatively silent on the great personal and national wealth that was accumulated over decades because of the employment of slaves with almost negligible labor costs, not to mention the domestic breeding of slaves for sale to plantation owners. (There are some exceptions to this rule of silence on the importance of slavery for American capitalism, such as Baptist 2014.) The sanctioned slavery of yesteryears has been replaced by a similarly pernicious state of the wage laborers who live paycheck to paycheck, always in a precarious state of complete despondency, without the possibility of escaping this kind of servitude.

I: THE ANCIENTS AND NATIVE AMERICANS

As already mentioned, the Garden of Eden where abundance was guaranteed by a benevolent God relates to the notion of property. Though not explicitly articulated, it's assumed that in that utopian and perfect landscape everything was held in common, so that any notion of ownership was absent (everything was a gift from God), and secondly, that any notion of private property made no sense. How can one own privately that which is abundantly given to humanity as a whole? This is not to say that the Bible remains silent on questions of property and property rights. The most interesting element in its presentation of land cultivation by the Israelites is the Law of Jubilee that enshrines the principle of debt forgiveness every seven years. As David Graeber reminds us, the forgiveness of debts on this "Sabbath" year relates to money debts, liens on property, and even slaves (2014, 82, 95). There is here a shift from owning everything in common to private ownership of material possessions legally construed in moral terms: if someone was unable to repay a debt in seven years, one should forgive it, it's the right thing to do. Incidentally, bankruptcy provisions today resemble the spirit if not the letter of this mindset. The very idea of the Law of Jubilee is tied with freedom, the ongoing appreciation of the need to emancipate those who for whatever reason became indebted to their fellow humans. Though endorsing private property rights, it seems that in biblical times there was a presupposition that one's ownership was contextualized communally so that it was proper for the community to expect, even demand, that one forgive old debts, that one free one's slaves or those indentured because of debts.

But the Garden of Eden image also reminds us that after the Fall we lost the unique and utopian state of bliss when all of nature was collectively owned, when this was considered an ideal and not the false promise of the USSR, for example, or the disastrous Chinese experiment with the Leap Forward policy that starved and killed millions. In other words, what we have seen with assumptions about abundance in the state of nature was as much about natural resources and their communal allocation as about not needing to segregate one's land or possessions from those of everyone else. By the time we get to Locke, the very notion of property rests on one's own body and therefore denotes, in the same vein, a sense of absolute if abstract sense of freedom.

Though writing much later, Thomas Paine (1737–1809) reminds us in his "Agrarian Justice" that "it is a position not to be controverted that the earth, in its natural, cultivated state was, and ever would have continued to be, *the common property of the human race*" (1797; italics in the original). Following the image of the state of nature as the Garden of Eden, it's obvious to the enlightened Paine that the "earth" was always "common property." As he continues to explain, "In that state every man would have been born to property. He would have been a joint life proprietor with the rest in the property of the soil, and in all its natural productions, vegetable and animal" (ibid.). Not only is property to begin with commonly owned, but more specifically this means that every human has a natural right of ownership simply by being a human being living on this Earth. This blessed existence leads him to claim that "the life of an Indian is a continual holiday, compared with the poor of Europe; and, on the other hand it appears to be abject when compared to the rich" (ibid.). Right away class distinctions come into play in assessing the great life the "Indian" lives as compared to the life of Europeans. It's interesting that Paine openly and explicitly talks in envious terms about Native Americans rather than just label them "savages," as the likes of Locke and Rousseau have done.

It's also noteworthy that according to Paine, "Poverty, therefore, is a thing created by that which is called civilized life. It exists not in the natural state. On the other hand, the natural state is without those advantages which flow from agriculture, arts, science and manufactures" (ibid.). Native Americans are in the perpetual state of bliss and "holiday" because poverty is unknown to them, being as they are so close to the original and communal appropriation of property as we think of it. It's civilization that brings about poverty and scarcity in its allocation of resources. Paine doesn't want to give up on civilization or the benefits of cultivating the land and ensuring its abundance to larger and larger populations, but he warns us against its unintended consequences.

As for Native Americans, Terry Anderson suggests that "Indian land tenure systems were varied" (1997). While some were communal, others were private. "The degree of private ownership reflected the scarcity of land and the difficulty or ease of defining and enforcing rights" (ibid.). But even when tracts of land were marked as privately owned, this was "usually by families or clans rather than individuals" (ibid.). As an example he cites the Mahican Indians in the Northeast who "possessed hereditary rights to use well-defined tracts of garden land along the rivers," recognized by Europeans in terms of deeds and by other Indian tribes "by not trespassing" through them (ibid.). When some Southeastern Indians owned and cultivated the land in families, they also "contributed voluntarily to a public store which was kept in a large building in the field and was used under the direction of the town chief for public needs" (ibid.). Likewise, hunting and fishing rights were acknowledged from one generation to the next and from one tribe to its neighbor. But tribal hunting and fishing "grounds" were not understood in the same terms as those brought into the territories by the European invasion, and therefore miscommunication was rampant.

Though Native Americans's notion of what we call today environmental ethics was strong, and though they upheld a sense of the abundance bestowed on them by the deities and therefore saw themselves as custodians or guardians of the land, they had some occasions in which private property came into play. As Anderson tells it, "Personal items were nearly always privately owned. Clothes, weapons, utensils, and housing were often owned by women, for whom they provided a way to accumulate personal wealth. For the Plains Indians, the tepee offers an example of private ownership. Women collected enough hides (usually between eight and 20), tanned and scraped them, and prepared a great feast where the hides were sewn together by the participants" (ibid.). So, though temporal and personal ownership of some objects was traditionally endorsed, this was both limited in scope and unlike the land claims introduced by the Europeans.

As we move to the ancient Greeks, we find that while Plato advocates that the state should own communal property, Aristotle argues that individuals having the right to own private property is best for the State. Their two views of private property offer the extreme of a spectrum of views.

Both in The *Republic* and in the *Laws*, Plato is explicit about communal ownership of property. In his discussion of the guardians, he emphasizes that the "houses and possessions provided for them" should be set up in a manner that would not "interfere with the best performance of their own duties" (*Republic*, 416d). That means that "none must possess any private property save the indispensable," and that whatever needs they have will be provided by the State (ibid.). This is repeated later when the injunction is that "these helpers must not possess houses of their own or land or any other property" since their "support" will be coming from "other citizens" (ibid., 464b–c). It seems that for Plato property can lead its owners to distraction, and that if the city wants its guardians to fulfill their role properly, they should not own property privately without being deprived of their needs (ibid., 543b–d). Plato generalizes from his focus on the guardians to discuss the "first-best society," with the "best constitution and code of law," and asserts without qualification that "property is indeed common property" (*Laws*, 739c). He is concerned with eliminating "everything we mean by the word," so as to ensure that "even what nature has made our *own* in some sense is common property" (ibid., italics in the original). The reason for this insistence on seeing even one's own acquisition from nature's bounty as remaining common is clarified later when Plato explains that when land is divided among the citizens, that division must be made "with some such thought as this, that he to whom a lot falls is yet bound to count his portion the common property of the whole society" (ibid., 740a–b). In this manner, hopes Plato, cross-generational responsibility will persist among those who cultivate the land. What was given from father to son shall be maintained to the next generation as well, as part of the maintenance of the common well-being of society. This communal view of property is not limited to the guardians, but extended to everyone.

Aristotle, by contrast, suggests that "the territory of our state should be divided into two parts, one of which will be public property, while the other will belong to private owners" (*The Politics*, 1330a). And these two parts should in turn be divided into additional two parts: the public part should have a "section for the gods" and the other for the "common tables"; the private part should have one section on the frontiers and one close to the city. These divisions, he thinks, will have two advantages: "It satisfies the claims of equality and justice; and it produces more solidarity in the face of border wars" (ibid.). Aristotle's endorsement of the provision of private property is based on a broad view of how equality and justice, not to mention border security, can be enhanced. Earlier in the same text, Aristotle understands the notion of property—including that of slaves—as belonging to his arguments about household management that is the cornerstone of his discussion of property and exchange in the *polis*. For him, there are two forms of the appropriation of property and its workings, the one that meets with his approval because it takes care of our subsistence in accordance to nature, and the other of which he disapproves because its acquisition and accumulation "is made at the expense of other men" (ibid., 1258b). This "censured" kind of abuse of property is most notable in the "retail trade," which is "hated most" because "it makes a profit from currency itself instead of making it from the process [i.e., of exchange] which currency was meant to serve" (ibid.). This critique is as relevant today as it was in Aristotle's time, as we have seen the financial features of Western economies lead to bubbles and the Great Recession. Since a greater portion of the current Gross Domestic Product relies on the activities of large banks and hedge funds who produce nothing tangible and this in turn increases debt-related risks, Aristotle's critique still holds

true. Can we then categorically say that any society whose economy is beholden in large part to arbitrage-like trading is irrational or unreasonable? Or
does such a judgment make sense only in capitalistic settings?

There are those on the political right, like Murray Rothbard, who find in
Aristotle the beginning of arguments in favor of private property, having "set
forth a trenchant argument in favor of private property . . . deliver[ing] a
cogent attack on the communism of the ruling class called for by Plato"
(2009). For the likes of Rothbard, there are three reasons for favoring private
to communal property, and they find ways of interpreting original texts to
support their own views. The first is that "private property is more highly
productive and will therefore lead to progress" (ibid.). This means that when
everything is commonly owned, it's bound to be neglected as opposed to the
self-interested diligence shown under conditions of private ownership. The
second is that "communal property would lead to continuing and intense
conflict, since each will complain that he has worked harder and obtained
less than others who have done little and taken more from the common store"
(ibid.). This, as we have seen above, isn't exactly what Aristotle has said
when promoting "equality and justice" in reserving some parts of the land as
public property. And the third reason given by Rothbard is that "private
property is clearly implanted in man's nature: his love of self, of money, and
of property, are tied together in a natural love of exclusive ownership"
(ibid.). Now this claim is definitely not coming from Aristotle's words but
inserted *post hoc* by someone finding a small rift between Plato and Aristotle, without due recognition that Aristotle himself was more than willing to
carve out large swatches of land for communal ownership. Incidentally, this
is no different from the overall American Catholic position in favor of capitalism as opposed to the more critical view espoused recently by Pope Francis against the abuses of capitalism as we know it.

II: CLASSICAL MODERN VIEWS

Locke agrees with the biblical supposition that God has "given the world to
men in common," but in order to circumvent the problem of how one moves
from this situation to one in which individuals own property separately, he
adds the fact that God also gave "them reason to make use of it to the best
advantage of life and convenience" (1947, 134). Here he invokes the "Indian" to suggest that "the fruit or venison which nourishes the wild Indian,
who knows no enclosure and is still a tenant in common, must be his, and so
his, that is, a part of him, that another can no longer have any right to it
before it can do to him any good for the support of his life" (ibid.). This is
more of an assertion than an argument because it's unclear why the very

consumption of common natural resources is any more than a sharing of the bounty of natural resources without any claim of ownership.

Locke therefore needs to introduce the notion of property somehow, and he does so by claiming that "every man has a property in his own person" (ibid.). And from this awkward construction—that our existence is a form of ownership of our own selves—he continues to argue that "the labour of his body and the work of his hands, we may say, are properly his." Anything "mixed with his labour," on this line of argument, "makes it his property" (ibid.). And from this Locke triumphantly concludes that this is "unquestionable" and that it constitutes a "right." Given that for him this is the "law of reason," Locke is emboldened to draw three more conclusions: first, that this process of appropriation "does not depend on the express consent of all commoners" (ibid., 135); second, that God's command to humans to "subdue" nature is in fact His way to "necessarily introduces private possessions" (ibid., 138); and third, that the limits of private possessions is set by one's ability to be industrious "before it spoils" (ibid., 136). If so far the starting point of the biblical narrative had more to do with the abundance of the Garden of Eden, in Locke's interpretation the emphasis is on the divine injunction to rule rather than to cultivate and protect nature; likewise, though waste is abhorred on some benign level of parsimony, there is a quick insertion of the right to private property whether based on labor or ingenuity, instead of a continued sense that what has been given in common can be enjoyed in common, no matter who uses or consumes what part of the abundant natural resources.

Among the American thinkers who follow the main guidelines of Locke's argument is Paine who appreciates the cultivation of the land as adding value to its owners. But he worries about the moral consequences that come with claims of land ownership. He suggests that there are three sources of added value: cultivation, inheritance, or purchase. Unlike Locke, he argues that the cultivation of land eventually brings about "the landed monopoly" that in turn "has produced the greatest evil. It has dispossessed more than half the inhabitants of every nation of their natural inheritance, without providing for them, as ought to have been done, an indemnification for that loss, and has thereby created a species of poverty and wretchedness that did not exist before" (1797). Paine is aware of the negative consequences of monopoly feudalism of his day, and is identifying "poverty and wretchedness" as inevitable outcomes of property rights, the rights of some that overshadow those of others, even if legally gained. He then continues to offer the remedies he finds legally and morally justifiable, some of which have been echoed most recently by the likes of Robert Reich in regard to minimum wages and guaranteed property to every American to foster personal independence for the sake of democracy (2015, 216).

Rousseau, for his part, explains in his *Social Contract* that the right of occupancy already mentioned by Locke is dependent for its legitimation on the social contract: "The right of the first occupant, although more real than the right of the strongest, becomes a true right only after the establishment of the right of property" (1978, 56). The fact that some people have occupied a piece of land and thereby call it their private property is contingent, in Rousseau's schema, not on their physical strength but rather on the State acknowledging the very notion of property and then attributing rights to those who hold it. For him, three conditions would justify the authorization of such rights: first, that "this land not yet be inhabited by anyone"; second, that "one occupy only the amount needed to subsist"; and third, that "one take possession not by vain ceremony, but by labor and cultivation" (ibid., 57). These conditions repeat the ancient Greeks' ideals as well as those of Locke and other thinkers. Rousseau's contribution to this discussion is not just the need for the State to be the ultimate legitimation source of land claims, but that he is communal in his approach. He argues that "since the possessors are considered as trustees of the public goods" and since these rights "are respected by all the members of the State," this means that "the right of each private individual to his own resources is always subordinate to the community's right to all" (ibid., 57–58). And if anyone questions this subordination, he continues to explain in Platonic, Aristotelian, and Native American terms that without this recognition "there would be neither solidity in the social bond nor real force in the exercise of sovereignty" (ibid.). One must admit already at this juncture that the concept of communally guaranteed property for the sake of a healthy democracy is quite established.

Contemporary debates over private property rights neglect to mention these historical and conditional concerns. Private property rights are subordinated to the official State that grants, guarantees, and protects them, and when doing so, the State as well as the individual in question are mutually conscious of the fact that such warranties should benefit the collective whole. This conditional status of private property rights is missed from many debates because of its fundamental inconvenience, the kind of inconvenience that requires thinking of others as much as thinking about one's self-interest. This doesn't mean advocacy of communal or communist view of public ownership and the prohibition of any private ownership of land or other material objects. Instead, putting the burden of proof, so to speak, on the individual who must ask, "How is my claim beneficial to others?" denotes the contingency of ownership. If one can prove that productivity will be greater, then it makes sense. But if the best one can say is that inheritance rights should supersede all others, then the argument is weak, if legitimate at all. This approach bespeaks of a consideration, from the very start to its eventual conclusion, that any argument about property rights is socially determined, temporal and contingent on whatever social needs and aspiration a State has in mind.

As mentioned in earlier chapters, the American view of private property differs from the French. Coleman explains that the Declaration of the Rights of Man cites property as "a sacred and inviolable right," more exalted a status than liberty, security, and resistance to oppression (other named rights) (2014, 253). But as he continues: "The apparent triumph of self-ownership as an axiom of revolutionary political culture in fact originated in an act of collective abandon" (ibid., 254). Robespierre "relativized the status of property," favoring small and middling property holders, the purpose of which is to ensure provisions for all (ibid., 257). In this sense, the well-being of society could comfortably rest on the contributions of property rights that ensured self-preservation and contributions to all (ibid., 258). The French Revolution taught us that "the aim of political regeneration, then, must be to ensure that the virtues of the citizen triumph over the prerogatives of the individual" (ibid., 260), both recalling Rousseau's everlasting influence on the debate and coinciding later with Proudhon's so-called third way between private property and communism, where the "possession of each to the benefit of all" (ibid., 298). When we hear arguments today about gun rights, for example, the issue is characterized in personal, individualistic terms, without the appreciation that one's status as a "citizen" necessarily and inherently brings forth the consideration of society and the State apparatus that legitimates laws and rights.

III: MARXIST CRITIQUE OF CLASSICAL ECONOMICS

Since Marx's critique was primarily addressed to classical economics, it may be necessary to recall some words about what Smith says about property and slavery. In his *The Theory of Moral Sentiments*, the mention of property is in relation to the "breach of property," which is understood as "theft and robbery"; namely, taking from us "what we are possessed of," and is considered a greater crime than "breach of contract, which only disappoints us of what we expected" (1759/1976, 163). The "laws of justice," those laws that "guard his property and possessions," come right after in importance the guarding of "the life and person of our neighbor" (ibid.). "Personal rights" come last, as they are understood in terms of what is "due to him from the promises of others" (ibid.). Property rights, then, are just below the right to life, assuming that these rights were established in the past as opposed to rights about future relationship or exchanges.

In his *The Wealth of Nations*, Smith repeats the accepted convention about property, linking property to labor: "The property which every man has in his own labour, as it is the original foundation of all other property, so it is the most sacred and invaluable" (1776/1937, 121–122). Any interference in this original right of property is in fact qualified as an assault on one's liberty. The sacredness of property is again mentioned in regard to what Rousseau would have claimed is the importance of public interest. Smith completely disagrees with any priority, either philosophically or practically, given to public interests and says that the "sacred right of private property are sacrificed to the supposed interests of public revenue" in such cases (ibid., 170). His distrust of public works and the institutional inefficiencies of the State become the starting point of his argument for the significance and protection of private property rights—their "sacred" status not only theoretically (or theologically) but also practically.

We also recall that Rousseau famously starts his *On the Social Contract* with the sentence: "Man is born free, and everywhere he is in chains," and continues to say that "one who believes himself the master of others is nonetheless a greater slave than they" (1978, 46). For him, slavery was a nonstarter for any discussion of the modern State and its interactions with its citizens. Smith, writing not much later, is still speaking of slavery as an existing, even thriving, institution, one whose economic analysis is a worthy undertaking. Instead of railing against its immorality or why it's indefensible in the modern world, this moral philosopher makes an argument from efficiency. "It appears," he says, "from the experience of all ages and nations, I believe, that the work done by freemen comes cheaper in the end than that performed by slaves" (1776/1937, 81). Is this the best we can expect from a professional moral philosopher? A similar argument is repeated later in the text in regard to the motivation of freemen tenants to produce more than is needed as rent to their feudal lords, while in the case of slaves, they "can acquire but [their] maintenance," and therefore are less motivated to be industrious beyond what is due to their master (ibid., 336–337). In these comments Smith isn't discussing slaves as the private property of their master but their relationship to land as property. What can be gleaned from Smith's ideas of the sacredness of private property seems more bound with a notion of industrious individualism than an appreciation, like Rousseau, of the contingent nature of such rights and the greater well-being of society and the State. More importantly, it seems that by the time Smith writes his magnum opus he assumes that everyone agrees that private property rights are sacred and that closes the discussion. Perhaps a brief comment from an American perspective should be added here in terms of the division between "field slaves" and "house slaves," each group associated with a different relationship with its owners: the former an economic variable which is exploited and abused, while the latter still exploited and abused (sexually and otherwise) but with a greater sense of familiarity and even some level of familial care.

No wonder that when Marx embarks on his critique, he is bound to go even deeper into the meanings associated with the established relationship between human labor and private property. It's not that Marx disagrees that labor is part of the life of every person, but he asks: "What then is the power of the political state over private property?" and responds right away that "it is the power of private property itself, its essence brought into existence" (1975, 168). What is troubling to Marx is that the "will of the family and society" is replaced by the "will of a private property purified of family and society," so that private property is considered the "the highest reality of the political state, as the highest *ethical* reality" (ibid.; italics in the original). The primacy of the family and society is symbolically replaced with a notion of private property, and that replacement tosses away humanity in the name of an ethical "reality." Is private property indeed the embodiment of our reality? "Political 'independence' is interpreted to mean 'independent private property' and the 'person corresponding to that independent private property'" (ibid., 173). Personhood, either in its relation to others or its political status, is contingent on one's private property rather than the other way around. This perversity is what Marx finds offensive and unacceptable in its Hegelian original presentation. The fact that our autonomy or political independence depends on our ownership of property implies that without property, as he eventually argues about the proletariat, humans are enslaved. If property is extracted from the political equation as a qualifying variable for citizenship and self-legislation, then being propertyless is no hindrance to full membership in the State (ibid., 219).

In addition to the linkage between property and citizenship or between the power to legislate with or without private property rights, there is also a deeper concern with the relationship of property to labor. Labor has been construed as private property's "essence," whether it's Fourier's notion of agricultural labor as the "*best* form of labour" or Saint-Simon's insistence on "industrial labour" being the exemplar, but his critique is about the very nature of this labor (ibid., 345). For Marx, labor is "estranged" from the laborer and from the object of the labor; "alienated" labor works on at least three levels: alienation from what is being produced, from other workers and nonworkers, and from nature itself—at least in the sense that everything human labor encounters is both instrumentally conceived (a means to an end and never an end in itself) and is a form of servitude to those who own the means of production (ibid., 342–344). Private property on this view is nothing but the abstraction to higher conceptual form of all labor in general as it is fetishized into the pursuit and accumulation of wealth. In *The German Ideology*, Marx reminds his readers that in ancient times there was "tribal property," but along with it "real private property began with the ancients [as well], as with modern nations, with movable property," the kind we mentioned above in regard to Native Americans (1845–1846/1972, 150). Tribal property eventually evolves into "feudal landed property, corporative movable property, capital invested in manufacture—to modern capital, deter-

mined by big industry and universal competition, i.e., pure private property,"
the kind of property that has "cast off all semblance of a communal institution and has shut out the State from any influence on the development of
property" (ibid.). In his concise and historically informed summary, Marx
highlights the fact that, unlike the claims of Locke and company, the starting
point of property was communal and only later has it turned into privatized
corporate property that even defies State control. In this way, we must agree
that Marx's critique is still relevant to contemporary economic power relations that control political institutions and elected officials.

Marx's historical analysis includes also a psychological dimension. Using
the French, English, and American modern States as his exemplars, he claims
that they exist "only for the sake of private property, so that this fact has
penetrated into the consciousness of the normal man" (ibid., 151). What has
"penetrated" isn't Locke's or Smith's sacred notion of individuals owning
property privately because of the fruits of their labor, but instead a corporate
ownership whose private status is the very basis for the existence of the State
apparatus. It's not simply that the State protects corporate private ownership,
or that this kind of ownership fulfills the needs of the State; on the contrary,
as we have seen with the recent American bailout of private banks in 2008,
the sole role of the state is to secure these private rights (at all costs) regardless of the citizens' will, interest, or benefit. The "consciousness of the normal man" here stands for the given presuppositions that are not being questioned anymore, that are accepted as true regardless of logical or empirical
support for them.

Marx's critique of estranged and alienated labor and the very concept of
private property that has been transformed from the farmer who works the
land and enjoys its fruit into the corporate world that controls the State lead
him to offer a solution. For him, the classless society as described in *The
Communist Manifesto* is based on the abolition of private property for the
sake of public ownership of everything, from the means of production to land
and natural resources. As already argued in his *Economic and Philosophical
Manuscripts*, communism is the "*positive* supersession of *private property* as
human self-estrangement, and hence the true *appropriation* of the *human*
essence through and for man" (1975, 348; italics in the original). Human
essence, for Marx, is associated with humans as social beings, rather than as
enslaved workers. This notion of communism is here defined in terms of its
"naturalism" and "humanism," because it is a "*genuine* resolution of the
conflict between man and nature, and between man and man, the true resolution of the conflict between existence and being, between objectification and
self-affirmation, between freedom and necessity, between individual and
species. It is the solution to the riddle of history and knows itself to be the
solution" (ibid., italics in the original). This long quotation rings so modern
and fresh today because it offers a bridge where only gaps—of income and

wealth, of status and misery—have been talked about in popular media and even scholarly circles. Its direct language may have seemed prophetic or even messianic a century and a half ago, but it has become a rallying cry for the disenfranchised.

We know what Marx means when he speaks of communism as the resolution to estranged and exploited labor, because we know how modern capitalism has appropriated the notion of property rights into the corporate world where as legal entities, large corporations have managed to claim the status of individuals with freedom of speech, for example, commonly associated only with living humans. We also appreciate, as mentioned a couple of times above, how our understanding of property has changed in the "crowd-sourced capitalism" or the "sharing economy," where ownership as such is much less important to the new millennial generation (born after the 1980s) than access to such commodities and services as housing and cars, equipment, and professional expertise. Even if this generation has not endorsed communism as defined by Marx, its members are less indebted to or compliant with a notion of private property as either "sacred" or the goal toward which they must work. This is not to say that young people don't like their gadgets, iPhones, and tablets, but these are more of the "movable property" sanctioned already in tribal communities, the kind of possessions that encourages mobility and openness instead of the limitations necessitated by land cultivation. Some would argue that these gadgets foster community. For example, the Internet is an infinite resource if used for that capacity (as opposed to personal entertainment). If the issue is indeed accessibility, one can obviously suggest that there are abundant digital resources that are only rendered scarce by controlling or limiting such accessibility; moreover, the Internet itself is rather communal than private and its ongoing growth is enhanced by communal contributions. Have we become more communal and nomadic? The recent events of Brexit (the British vote to leave the European Union) demonstrated without doubt that the majority of young voters preferred to stay in the European Union with all its allowances for travel and work across national borders. Perhaps not quite communal, but certainly a move toward nomadic existence.

Half a century after Marx, we find some British thinkers, such as George Jacob Holyoake, who chronicle the attempts of systematic cooperation in England along the Marxian ideals of communism. For him, "The original object of Co-operation," as it was practiced in English small-scale communities, "was to establish self-supporting communities distinguished by common labour, common property, common means of intelligence and recreation" (1903/2012, 1). Their main principles were "Concord, Economy, Equity, and Self-help" (ibid., 21). It's clear that cooperation isn't simply "profit-sharing" all along the supply chain, but also an expectation "from each person the best service he is able to render, under the condition of rewarding him according to what he does" (ibid., 24). This, of course, is a variant of the famous Marxian dictum "from each according to his ability, and to each according to his needs." And as he goes on, Holyoake eventually connects these experiments with Marx's own language: "The original aim and continuous policy of Co-operation is communism, which, as the reader has seen, means a self-supporting society distinguished by common labour, common property, and common means of intelligence and education; whereas Socialism conserves class distinctions, class privileges, and class war. It would mitigate these evils but not supersede them" (ibid., 150). And as a promoter of a new level of consciousness among British workers, Holyoake is quick to claim that this form of organizing society isn't "philanthropy, nor a scheme of benevolence, nor a form of Utopian sentimentality, but a business which has to pay like any other honest business—and does it." In other words, it isn't "an emotional contrivance for enabling others to escape the responsibility of making exertions on their own behalf, but a manly advice for giving honest men an equitable opportunity of helping themselves" (ibid., 187).

These instances in which communist-like cooperation were attempted and succeeded on a small scale in Marx's adopted home of the British Isles are worth recalling. Unlike tribal relations that can be observed everywhere when parents help their children on their farms or in their homes, or when grandparents move in with their children, the cases reported above brought together strangers. What gave them the stability and feeling of belonging to a community was an explicit manifesto or rule book to which they all adhered and from which they could draw continuous inspiration. As we shall see below, there are other institutional organizations that attempt to bring together a group of strangers and make them feel and behave as if they are one family, cohesive units with similar outlook and goals in mind.

IV: INTELLECTUAL PROPERTY RIGHTS AND THE COMMONS

The tension between private property rights and their presuppositions and communal or public ownership of natural resources continues into the twenty-first century. The terminology may have changed, even the contours of what terms mean, but the schism remains as strongly entrenched in the "consciousness of normal men," as Marx suggested long ago. Nowadays we are much more worried about patent infringement, copyright protections, and intellectual property rights than about one's rights to a cultivated piece of land. Likewise, we are more concerned about the virtual commons in Internet "space." The principles and arguments, though, are still the same as those used in the seventeenth and eighteenth centuries. Do we own everything in common to begin with and then parcel out property to individuals because it's more beneficial for society? Or, by contrast, are we an amalgam of individual property owners who under some social contract constitute a community or State? The conceptual starting point matters regardless of the historical record for two reasons: first, the historical record is always a selectively fabricated reconstruction that doesn't represent reality as such, and second, the priority we give to the starting point eventually influences how we conclude our argument about who legitimately deserves these rights (in the sense of path-dependence).

Locke's view of the relationship between the government of a State and the individual property owner inspired the authors of the US Constitution. In his *Second Treatise* he argues in regard to the formation of "civil society, the chief end whereof is the preservation of property" (1947, 162). Later he repeats this sentiment when he says: "The great and chief end, therefore, of men's uniting into commonwealths and putting themselves under government is the preservation of their property. To which in the state of nature there are many things wanting" (ibid., 184). Once the motive of uniting into civil society or commonwealth is established, Locke continues to warn that "the supreme power cannot take from any man part of his property without his own consent; for the preservation of property being the end of government and for which men enter into society, it necessarily supposes and requires that the people should have property, without which they must be supposed to lose that, by entering into society, which was the end for which they entered into it—too gross an absurdity for any man to own" (ibid., 191–192). This argument begs the question by assuming its conclusion: first, all people have property, and second, that their sole motivation for entering any kind of association with others is the preservation of said property. Both assumptions may be false, and the conclusion on the limits of government would then not follow logically. The role of government is to adjudicate among competing property claims and set in place laws and regulations that ensure justice in property disputes. But once again, Locke insists that the government can "never have a power to take to themselves the whole or any part of the subject's property without their own consent; for this would be in effect to leave them no property at all" (ibid., 192). This sounds more like a cautionary argument against the arbitrary usurpation of property by monarchs rather than a government, for what does it really mean that a government, as an elected and representative body in a democracy, would "take to themselves"? Does this mean that a mayor or governor takes over my home or car for personal use? A king might have done so, but is it even conceivable to see modern public officials engage in such behavior?

The US Constitution includes specific clauses to deal with property rights, and as we shall see, it's reasonable to argue that its views have been informed by Locke's work. To begin with, it says that "Congress shall have Power to dispose of and make all needful Rules and Regulations respecting the Territory or other Property belonging to the United States; and nothing in this Constitution shall be so construed as to Prejudice any Claims of the United States, or of any particular State" (Article 4, Section 3, Clause 2). Congressional powers extend to "territory" and "other property"; namely, one's rights of private ownership are indeed subordinated to the State. Likewise, it says that "Congress shall have Power . . . To promote the Progress of Science and useful Arts, by securing for limited Times to Authors and Inventors the exclusive Right to their respective Writings and Discoveries" (Article 1, Section 8). This is the clause concerned with one's rights beyond land and possessions, extending one's rights to "writings and discoveries." Already in the eighteenth century, intellectual property is constitutionally recognized. But the context of these rights should be emphasized, since in the Preamble to the Constitution, the general well-being of the country is foregrounded: "We the People of the United States, in Order to form a more perfect Union, establish Justice, insure domestic Tranquility, provide for the common defense, promote the general Welfare, and secure the Blessings of Liberty to ourselves and our Posterity, do ordain and establish this Constitution for the United States of America." Individual rights, then, emanate from and are protected by the government to benefit society, as Plato and Aristotle argued, and not to benefit exclusively an individual. The goal is justice, tranquility, defense, and general welfare. One can rephrase this by saying that on some fundamental level, we have no rights to intellectual property if the government can show a "compelling interest" that supersedes personal gains. One famous example is the voluntary refusal to patent the polio vaccine by Jonas Salk (who spent seven years developing it). For those interested in the legal genealogy of this principle, the following cases remain relevant: *Jacobson v. Massachusetts* (1905), reaffirmed in *Zucht v. King* (1922), and in *Prince v. Massachusetts* (1944), all establishing the government's right to interfere for the greater good.

The promotion of these lofty constitutional goals recognizes the inevitable conflict that may arise when one's property, land, or discovery is needed for the common welfare. Under what conditions can the government on behalf of its citizens confiscate one's property? The Fifth Amendment to the Constitution declares in part that no person shall "be deprived of life, liberty, or property, without due process of law; nor shall private property be taken for public use, without just compensation." This sentiment of property rights protection—the proper process and procedure according to which property can be taken away—is echoed later in the Fourteenth Amendment (Section 1): "nor shall any state deprive any person of life, liberty, or property, without due process of law." The interpretation of these clauses has been historically in dispute, as claims for "eminent domain"—where public interests supersede individual ones—have been adjudicated in courts of law. Clear cases are when the widening of a road or bridge requires the condemnation of houses or property with proper "market value" compensation. Less clear are cases when a private corporation, real estate development corporation, or a large chain, such as Walmart, asks for properties to be condemned by the State so it can expand a store whose "public benefit" can be contested. This was indeed the case of *Kelo v. City of New London* (2005), in which the Supreme Court agreed with such "taking." The dissenting opinion voiced the worry that if the actual use was private rather than public, "Any property may now be taken for the benefit of another private party, but the fallout from this decision will not be random. The beneficiaries are likely to be those citizens with disproportionate influence and power in the political process, including large corporations and development firms." Is the government then working on behalf of a private corporation and against the private interests of its citizens? Is justice upheld under such circumstances?

Robert Venables reminds us in this context that during the Philadelphia Convention of 1787 a clear contrast was set in place between life and liberty on the one hand and property on the other (as opposed to the conflation of the three into one singular framework wherein they all are both intertwined and mutually supportive). The issue was how to balance life and liberty, which were well represented by the "savage state" and the notions associated with property. "Too great an emphasis on property would have smacked of the corruption which has ossified the European societies and against which the colonists rebelled" (1992, 93). But by the same token, property could also be having a stabilizing effect on the newly formed United States. So, he continues, at one point the Founding Fathers extolled the virtues of the so-called savage state, life and liberty, and at another established the kinds of checks and balances that ensured the protection of property as a right that would bring about prosperity to all (ibid.). Venables argues that there is no natural need for property as such, nor does property guard one's life and liberty. On the contrary, human behavior associated with the accumulation and protection of property may be contrary to any notion of liberty, the freedom to roam the land and enjoy its natural fruits with little or no labor, and definitely not in terms of one's life, which is unencumbered when no labor or property are required. The wording of the Constitution glosses over this conceptual divide as if there a seamless connection between life, liberty, and property. In other words, raising the question about this contrived relation is already an implicit critique: Should we make this connection? And if we do, would it stand the test of history, not to mention the test of logic?

As we moved to the Digital Age where the Internet provides global connectivity of "writing or discoveries" already mentioned in the Constitution, straightforward notions of property rights as separate from the public domain become more complex. There are those, like Yochai Benkler, who argue in a semi-Marxist fashion that the very decentralization of property (read capital) and the increase of all forms of communication ensure the reduction of "barriers to entry" commonly experienced in real markets (2006, 105–106).

This openness is evident in "open-source" platforms that share software codes and the likes of Wikipedia where millions of volunteered hours bring about encyclopedic knowledge for free. The protection of intellectual property rights in this digital environment makes little sense. Large corporations have realized that their patents, for example, are not as valuable in themselves but that the services and modification they offer customers are more important for the extraction of fees (ibid., 44–48). Benkler is among those who recognize that the foundation and development of scientific knowledge has always been and should continue to be a group effort, something that individuals cannot and should not claim ownership over (ibid., 63). Critical practices of "copy-left" emerged as open rejections of the rights associated with one's ideas or knowledge production to emphasize the common right and free access to anything produced in the information age. Benkler concludes his argument in favor of greater collaboration and the widening of the networked society with these words: "The primary obstacles to the diffusion of these desiderata [of greater free access to information and knowledge] in the required direction [of welfare, development, and growth] are the institutional framework of intellectual property and trade [Constitutional and regulatory] and the political power of the patent-dependent business models [of the past two hundred years] in the information-exporting economies" (ibid., 354).

Among those who concur with Benkler are legal scholars, like Lawrence Lessig, who address intellectual property rights in broader cultural terms. For him the issue of the "remix culture" is a radical transformation since the 1990s of what is expected to be "fair use" of others' "writings and discoveries" mentioned in the Constitution. The millennial generation takes it for granted that they are entitled to download for free music and other artistic creations, enjoy them, and remix them in whatever fashion suits their divergent tastes. They find nothing sacred nor legally binding in the inspiration they receive from global sources, and treat their own work in the same manner. This has changed, for example, the music industry so that musicians are more than happy to post their songs for free consumption on the Internet and social media, knowing full well that their own compensation may come from concert tickets, increased reputation translatable into merchandise, or paid appearances in televised networks (Lessig 2008). Perhaps like Benkler's scientists, Lessig's artists see themselves as members of a larger cultural community where any sort of "property rights"—intellectual or material— are subordinated to the welfare of others. Perhaps there is a lingering subconscious appreciation of their role as the new Platonic "guardians" of our community, trusting the public to provide for their needs. We should note here that changes in long-standing commercial practices in the music industry have experienced some pushbacks in how musicians want to be treated and properly compensated for their work.

Other leftist thinkers, like David Berry, push this reconceptualization of the rights associated with private intellectual property both historically and politically. Historically this means revisiting notions of liberty and democracy as they are being challenged by the strictures of capitalism; and politically this can mean that new digital formations can offer new forms of resistance. His is an attempt to "uncover the way in which the open source and free software groups are challenging our existing liberal categories (around cultural production, knowledge ownership and authorship) both in economic terms (that is, as a new form of commons-based peer production) and in terms of political liberties (for example, the question of free speech in a democracy)" (Berry 2008, x). He is part of a movement labeled "digital environmentalism" that is concerned with the basic protection of the "commons" in a similar way that deep ecologists are concerned with pollution and climate change as public matters rather than corporate deal making. As such, Berry focuses on the "global intellectual property regime" that transcends national borders and whose regulation might be differently applied (ibid., 31). For him, "Ownership of copyrights and other intellectual property rights will be a site of power *and* resistance in the twenty-first century" (ibid., 32). Power relations will revolve around old-fashioned protection of copyrights and patents so that "corporations increasingly seek to own and profit from creative copyrights in perpetuity, in effect owning and controlling culture . . . By controlling the use of trademarked phrases, brands or copyright claims, code is able to act as a gate-keeper to knowledge and police the ability to use and disseminate it—through code-enforced intellectual property rights (such as digital rights management). Computer code has the potential to have a chilling effect on democratic debate" (ibid., 37). These warnings must be heeded in an age that is seduced by the openness of the Internet without realizing its "chilling effects," its potential for silencing critical voices and controlling the outcomes of political debates.

More significantly, the likes of Benkler, Lessig, and Berry alert us to what is at stake when property is considered. This is not your grandfather's plot of land, nor is it the possessions you can transport easily from one place to another in order to conduct your daily business. Instead, the intrusion of government on behalf of these corporate interests may be monumental and unstoppable; it may overwhelm the very notion of individual property right on the one hand, and undermine any sense of communal ownership of knowledge and ideas (or any semblance of common land in the form of parks, roads, and rivers). Asking questions about the relationship of property and our political health isn't as far-fetched as it may sound at first. To this we may add a dose of utopianism (seen above) from the likes of Rifkin and Sundararajan. Rifkin, for one, cites the Free Software Movement "whose aim was to create a global Collaborative Commons" (2014, 100) as an effort to transcend intellectual property rights and establish a global framework for the free exchange of software codes and information. He recalls also the Free Software Foundation of 1985 and its four principles: "The freedom to run the program, for any purpose . . . the freedom to study how the program works, and change it . . . The freedom to redistribute copies . . . the freedom to distribute copies of your modified version" (ibid., 174–175). Likewise, there are other forms of what Berry might call "resistance," such as the Free Culture Movement and the Open Source Initiative of 1998. If the connection between technological innovations, property rights, and democratic politics are to be examined, they should be in light of the potential to overcome the rigid constraints imposed by one form of capitalism or another. According to Rifkin: "The global democratization of culture is made possible by an Internet communication medium whose operating logic is distributed, collaborative, and laterally scaled. That operating logic favors an open Commons form of democratic self-management" (ibid., 177). This is reminiscent of what we already said earlier in relation to "crowd-sourced capitalism" and the "sharing economy."

V: THE BRIDGE

Rifkin quotes Gandhi's statement that "the earth provides enough to satisfy every man's need but not every man's greed" (2014, 274). This is an important reminder to contextualize many of the assumptions we are examining in these chapters. Are the views mentioned above utopian because they are presupposing human needs rather than human greed? Are they useful assumptions nonetheless because we can easily distinguish between human needs and greed? Our concern in this chapter about property and the ways in which it has been understood philosophically, practically, and politically depends to a large degree on our view of society: Is it merely the collection of individuals entering some social contract to protect themselves from each other? Or is it instead first and foremost a community of people whose own interests and needs are subordinated to the welfare of the community? As problematic as these questions may appear, and as differently interpreted by the anthropological data—were we hunters and gatherers in groups? Or did we individually evolve after struggling with each other?—they keep on informing us how we see ourselves in moral terms and how we think we should be legally regulated. Utopian or idealized, we should admit that our policy decisions and the frameworks we fight to maintain or change are of our making. Therefore, any reexamination of these frames of references and their underlying presuppositions are worth undertaking.

Chapter Five

Markets

Most political economists of the Enlightenment period provide a narrative of the natural development of markets from antiquity to the present, highlighting along the way, as Smith famously framed it, our natural inclination to barter and trade, to exchange goods and services with other people in our community. There are some, like Graeber (2014), who dispute this naturalistic genealogy and suggest instead that markets are artificial constructs that came into being under specific conditions of warfare and state building. Others, like Karl Polanyi (1944/1957), explain that changing cultural and political conditions transform the contours of economic markets; as such, markets are contextualized, they do not emerge naturally out of thin air. As with other frames of reference, this one is interlinked with other assumptions about human nature and our natural inclinations to own property or accumulate wealth.

It's quite reasonable to talk about markets in all their different guises. We have a market for food, a housing market, and a stock market. We can segment these markets further and show how they are related to each other. We can even speak metaphorically about the marketplace of ideas, where ideas "compete" for our attention, where we "buy" some and let others languish, and where their "price" is weighed in nonmonetary terms (prestige or the status of their originators). But no matter how we speak in contemporary culture about markets, there are some presuppositions attached to their deployment, metaphorically or otherwise. Some presuppositions are associated with their features, such as the rational behavior of market participants that eventually become ingrained in our collective consciousness. In other words, shorthand descriptions of these presumed features transcend empirical evidence and inform our ideas about ourselves and those with whom we interact.

I: DIFFERENT MARKETS

There are three different views of the market itself, some informed by classical economists and most debated by contemporary thinkers who realize that market failures should give rise to a reevaluation of what markets are, under what conditions they come to be, and what allows them to persist over time.

(a) As Smith already suggested, because of the innate human inclination to exchange goods among themselves (1776/1937, 13), there is a natural tendency among humans to engage in a *division of labor* as the most efficient use of the labor of the community. It is the "surplus part of the produce of his own labour, which is over and above his own consumption" that turns him to "live by exchanging" and thus he "becomes in some measure a merchant," and the community in general "grows to be what is properly a commercial society" (ibid., 22). At this juncture, the appeal of this view is that all participants come to the marketplace—even though Smith doesn't use the term—as equals, and they do so voluntarily. The Enlightenment ideals of equality and freedom are therefore neatly preserved, or more precisely, the marketplace brings to practical light the philosophical commitments of moral philosophers. The last feature of Smith's market is that prices are determined by the dynamic relationship between supply and demand as if guided by an "invisible hand."

Milton and Rose Friedman follow this classic rendition of market forces and suggest that the market has the power to ensure cooperative exchanges among individuals. They insist on the simplicity and truthfulness of Smith's maxim about market exchanges: they must benefit all parties for their completion. Cooperation is voluntary and satisfies separate self-interests, but when they come into play under one roof, so to speak, they do not conflict but bring about the improvement of the conditions of all the agents (1979, 13). With this running assumption of seamless free cooperative exchanges, any government intervention is superfluous if not damaging, and therefore no laws or regulations should impede the freedom of market exchanges. This reformulation of the classic view becomes the standard neoclassical view of the Chicago School. With this in mind, all markets are by definition the only means by which the distribution of any product should be handled, from bread and beer to international trade and "cap-and-trade" agreements in regard to environmental protection from industrial pollution.

The appeal of markets is threefold: individual freedom to enter or exit the market, the equal opportunity everyone has in entering or exiting the market (even for the sale of one's labor power), and the unfettered efficiency of markets to process information about goods and services without outside intervention (regulatory agencies or foreign powers). These are the fundamental principles to which both defenders and critics of the market ideology revert in one form or another. What is fascinating about this view is how romantic or even fantastic it is, since we cannot really claim for it the nostalgia of the past in a pristine form. Perhaps in Smith's imagination the small village and its market could be a model; perhaps his naïve view of how people should or would exchange their goods and services in barterlike conditions makes sense. But if we are speaking today of global markets or the financial markets after the Great Recession, then the "village" has disappeared and with it the justification for Smith's imaginary market. It does make sense to have the villagers in a small hamlet in England during the eighteenth century behaving morally with the oversight of an "impartial spectator" (1759). It also makes perfect sense to see these sympathetic and friendly neighbors interact freely in an emerging marketplace. And then it makes perfect sense to conclude that even in a market they will continue to behave morally as if guided by an "invisible hand" (1776) because the "impartial spectator" has not left the stage. Indeed, if we all know each other and are bound to encounter each other for a long time (and cross generationally), then we will trade fairly and justly with each other, never cheat or steal, never behave immorally; we are already accustomed to behave properly and the only reason for us to cease such moral behavior is when the system breaks down.

Even those who are critical of capitalist markets and their ongoing impact on inequality grudgingly accept the centrality of market economies as the bedrock of our current economic reality. Among them we find John Ehrenreich, in his description of what he calls "third-wave capitalism," as a period that follows the industrial capitalism of the nineteenth century and the corporate capitalism of two-thirds of the twentieth century. He explains that his choice of this label is preferable to the alternatives: global capitalism (pretense of integrated global economy), finance capitalism (finance can't explain everything), late capitalism (too vague), and neoliberal capitalism (misuses the liberal designation) (2016, 18–19). He characterizes this latest phase of capitalism as featuring "free market, individualistic ideologies flourished, promoted by a well-financed and self-conscious propaganda barrage from conservative business leaders and media. The relationship between government and business became more intimate, and, correspondingly, the protection that the federal, state, and local governments offered the poor and the middle class began to fray" (ibid., 17). The reliance on markets isn't limited to corporate interests but extends to the ideologues of the day who promote a level of narcissism never seen before: "Third Wave Capitalism is characterized by greater narcissism and unrealistically high self-appraisal" (ibid., 158). This means that increased levels of anxiety and depression (because of unmet unrealistic goals) and the fixation on immediate gratification have brought about an age of anxiety without the support of community that was available decades ago. This view supports the claim that markets cannot operate as Smith envisioned them even with underlying "moral sentiments" of the community of participants.

(b) The Marxian critique of Smith's markets comes to mind right away, as the very notions of freedom and equal opportunity, fairness and moral conduct, evaporate like the morning mist. In his *Capital* (Volume I), Marx reminds his readers that "commodities cannot themselves go to the market and perform exchanges in their own right. We must, therefore, have recourse to their guardians, who are the possessors of commodities" (1867/1976, 178). Using Plato's notion of guardians, Marx is clear that there are very visible hands; namely, the hands of the "possessors of commodities" who actually bring items to the market, who actively pursue the economic relation of exchange that for him is also a "juridical relation" (ibid.). This economic and juridical relation is one where "the persons exist for one another merely as representatives and hence owners of commodities" (ibid., 178–179). The alienation of these "owners" from their product is compounded by their treatment of each other as means for an exchange and not in the benevolent manner in which Smith considered his villagers to be bartering among themselves as sympathetic neighbors. And finally, Marx continues to explain that the commodities themselves lose their original "use-value" and in their "exchange-value" find an equivalent value in order to be exchanged. In his own words: "The natural form of this commodity thereby becomes the socially recognized equivalent form. Through the agency of the social process it becomes the specific social function of the commodity which has been set apart to be the universal equivalent. It thus becomes—money" (ibid., 180–181). Two important features of market exchange are brought forth here: first, there must be a society or social organization within which to make sense of commodity exchanges, a forum and framework, both legal and economic, to sanction and protect such exchanges; and second, the rise of money as the form of equivalence is introduced and it, too, eventually becomes a commodity to be traded, loaned, and accumulated (regardless of its actual use value).

The second line of critique of Smith's fictitious image of the rise of the markets as if by natural powers comes more directly from Polanyi. Here is an explicit example of what this book is about: someone refuses to accept certain presuppositions about human propensities or the inevitable formation of an exchange market. Not only does Polanyi charge Smith and his disciples of the "self-adjusting market" as a "stark utopia," he also argues that markets were by-products of other institutional developments, much more social and political in nature than strictly economic (1944/1957, 3–4). What markets need are "market laws," and only after a whole "transformation" of an *a prior* social system is in place is the very notion of "self-regulation" or an "invisible hand" a relevant category. The transformation "resembles more the metamorphosis of the caterpillar than any alteration that can be expressed in terms of continuous growth and development" (ibid., 38–42). In a generous but ironic turn of phrase, Polanyi says that Smith's move from the division of labor and human propensities to a full-fledged marketplace can be characterized as "no misreading of the past" but instead a "prophetic [view] of the future" (ibid., 43). Smith's narrative is dismissed as "apocryphal," given a more robust anthropological data collection about human behavior that was primarily related to reciprocity, redistribution, and household management in Aristotle's sense (ibid., chapter 4). So, concludes Polanyi, once markets come into existence, human behavior adjusts to them and is transformed from its initial concern with extra-economic relations. And as he says, "The economic system was submerged in general social relations; markets were merely an accessory feature of an institutional setting controlled and regulated more than ever by social authority" (ibid., 67). And as these markets emerged, with their national and international institutional customs and laws, "a deep seated movement sprang into being to resist the pernicious effects of a market-controlled economy" (ibid., 76). Society learned that it had to protect itself, perhaps in the Marxian sense of uniting the workers of the world, or in more modest local terms that dealt with the ruinous and devastating consequences of dehumanizing human labor and humans themselves (ibid., 163, 177). Though his language differs from Marx, Polanyi is clear about his critique of Smith's assumptions and the ensuing arguments that have persisted into the twentieth century about the effectiveness and moral stature of market economies.

In more recent years, David Harvey, for one, maintains Marx's relevance today because of his insistence that there is an inherent violence in the domination of capital over labor both in the marketplace and in the process of production and consumption: "We are daily witnessing the systematic dehumanization of disposable people. Ruthless oligarchic power is now being exercised through a totalitarian democracy directed to immediately disrupt, fragment and suppress any coherent anti-wealth political movement (such as Occupy)" (2014, 292). The bogus idea that laborers and capitalists enter the same market under the same conditions is ludicrous; in fact, it is a set up to lure unsuspecting laborers who may think they have a chance to negotiate, to sell their labor power for fair wages and benefits and without being exploited. Capitalists pretend to negotiate in good faith with this or that group of workers, always concerned with national union formation, but in fact they threaten to close factories and take them elsewhere, where labor is cheaper or less demanding (what has been euphemistically called "outsourcing"). Marx's call for the proletariat to unite and revolt wasn't an idle dream but a necessary step in their struggle to become equal partners in the production of goods. Polanyi argued for the same need of society to protect itself from unfettered or unregulated markets and the dire consequences to laborers and citizens alike. In this context, we should mention that the utopian visions of the likes of Sundararajan always admit on the margins that our contemporary and highly alluring "gig economy" or the "on-demand" workforce is bound to leave workers with only unstable part-time jobs without benefits. The appeal of liberation and self-initiated labor time turns into a nightmare when regular work isn't available or when one falls ill.

Then there are those, like Simon Griffiths, who examine a different set of values presupposed by the British liberal and neoliberal insistence that the Enlightenment ideals of liberty and equality should be kept in mind when critically evaluating the merits of market-capitalism. What he contributes to the debate is his ability to pull together the ideas of the likes of Friedrich Hayek and John Maynard Keynes and those of David Miller and the New Labour Party in the UK. For him, the tradeoff between equality and liberty (the increase in one is at the expense of the other) should be rethought in the sense that the one is needed to accomplish the other: more equality offers more freedom, and more freedom will allow greater equality. He explains that the Austrian economists, such as Hayek and von Mises, argued that "the free market was not only efficient economically, but it was also indispensable for a free society" (2014, 7). Assumptions about values and ideals translated into economic strategies that could enhance or accomplish political goals. Referring to John Rawls and Robert Nozick for moral fortification, what was at stake in this argument on behalf of markets was how they promote moral principles, such as fairness and justice (ibid., 33). Griffiths includes Andrew Gamble as agreeing with the role of markets in teasing out the needs, wants, aspirations, and novel forms of coordination of individuals that are freely allowed in markets (ibid., 105). Unlike market-socialists, for example, who attempt to bring together social ownership with the efficiencies of market mechanisms, there is an argument to be made about how to increase individual commitments and responsibilities under market conditions. Would this be a better strategy than the Marxian collectivization of property and labor under the auspices of the State? Is it possible, likewise, to transform the very question about the superiority of market efficiency into a question about its moral potential? Or even to suggest using the tax system as a mechanism by which to reward moral behavior and punish offenders?

Another way of approaching the persistence of assumptions about markets and their natural outgrowth from human propensities has been to inquire what effects they have on humans. We already saw what Polanyi says about how markets have confined human socializing into economic frameworks (dominated by markets), and now we can push this point further. According to Steve Fraser, "What is . . . most pernicious about the recent ascendancy of free market thinking is perhaps not so much the triumph of its public policies. Rather, it is how its spirit of self-seeking has exiled forms of communal consciousness, rendered them foolish, naïve, wooly-hearted, or, on the contrary, sinful and seditious" (2015, 370). Having people think of themselves as separate from others has grave psychological consequences, as we have seen already in Ehrenreich's listing of new cultural pathologies; here we see a sense of shame or irresponsibility if one thinks in terms of the community rather than exclusively in personal terms of self-motivated and self-seeking gratification and greater wealth. This turns into a cultural atmosphere within which any communal organizations are suspect and even downright unpatriotic, as we have seen in recent years with the response to Occupy Wall Street. It wasn't only the police that harassed its members, but political leaders were quick to bar its ongoing protests and public displays of resentment and resistance (citing zone restrictions on sleeping overnight in public parks).

(c) A third response or attitude toward markets and the presuppositions that inform their formation can be seen in Graeber's historical account of debt. He argues that while contemporary views put the State and the market as opposing forces, "they were born together and have always been intertwined" (2011/2014, 19), so that only "stateless societies tend also to be without markets" (ibid., 50). Not only has money been introduced because of warfare and the need to pay soldiers, but historically "States create Markets. Markets require States" (ibid., 71). The classical myth of individuals entering markets without debts while owing allegiance to their respective national States is false; it sets up a false dichotomy between the freedom of the former framework and the subordination to the latter. Just like Polanyi, he, too, is the slayer of Smith's myths. According to Graeber, there was never barter in the economic sense of markets, except among strangers, and that led to warfare as one side thought it was taken advantage of by the other (ibid., 30). The division of human activities that allows for economic exchange to be separate and the barter that ensues from it cannot be found in the historical records. Instead, there were credit systems dating back thousands of years and gift economies rather than markets (ibid., 33, 36–38). In this context, Graeber argues that while Hobbes insisted on the contractual relations of individuals with the State, Smith envisioned a utopian market so as to deal with the theological presuppositions of the day and the need to contain greed under State control (ibid., 335–336). Smith's utopian world is a "vision of an imaginary world almost entirely free of debt and credit, and therefore, free of guilt and sin; a world where men and women were free to simply calculate their interests in full knowledge that everything had been prearranged by God to ensure that it will serve the greater good" (ibid., 253–254). Exchange has always been theological as well as moral rather than simply economic. Smith needed to construct his imaginary marketplace to take care of a set of concerns, just as social contract theorists had done as well.

Though more concerned with notions of debt than markets, it's worth quoting Graeber's own demystification: "Our two origin stories—the myth of barter and the myth of primordial debt—may appear to be about as far apart as they could be, but in their own way, they are also two sides of the same coin. One assumes the other. It's only once we can imagine human life as a series of commercial transactions that we're capable of seeing our relations to the universe in terms of debt" (ibid., 75). And here a strong Marxian notion comes into play, both in terms of the dehumanization that follows any kind of financial transaction and in terms of slavery (discussed above in relation to property). When human life is considered in terms of currencies and exchange, certain violence enters the equation or the transaction, and that's where slavery is introduced (ibid., 158ff). Such transactions extract the person from the community to be able to deal with them as a commodity that was sold and bought, according to the logic of debt (ibid., 162–164). Power relations among people are expressed by the use of money as a form of degradation in line with the slave trade, so that "the notion of absolute private property is really derived from slavery" (ibid., 189, 199). To bring us up to date, he comments about contemporary "wage labor, which is, effectively, the renting of our freedom in the same way that slavery can be conceived as its sale" (ibid., 206). Even today we find so-called debtors' prisoners whose only crime has been not to be able to pay a fine or come up with bail money until their trial date.

We should close this section recalling first the important distinction about the rationale for the division of labor (which leads or doesn't lead to market exchanges): for Smith, it was reduced to our "natural propensity to truck and barter" while for Tusi it was an extension of mutual aid. The point is that while for the former it's a utilitarian principle, for the latter there is a moral dimension as well (ibid., 279–280). There are therefore different moral implications and opposing worldviews that underlie markets. The spread of Islam and its support for markets separate from the State meant that handshakes were important, and that one's moral obligation was more profound than the one displayed in Western culture. Second, we should note that there are some "commodities," such as blood, that defy the market-exchange rationale and operate on the premodern basis of "gift relationship" both in kin relations and even among strangers (Titmuss, 1970). As we shall see later, market-socialism offers a compromise between the benefits of information about efficient resource allocation and the drawbacks of the abuses by large participants who monopolize power and extract unjustifiable high prices. Third, as more current observers and critics note, the marketplace of commodities and labor that was the standard for the past two centuries has radically changed into information, communication, and networks of digitized exchanges. In such markets, many of the presupposition that informed the classical models of market behavior may be obsolete: examples of open-source and nonexclusionary practices appear everywhere, and collaborative phenomena, such as Wikipedia, confound the old principles of personal self-interest, competition, and the maximization of one's utility. Perhaps Smith's original notion of one's need for the love and approval of others (1759) may come into fruition much more than his subsequent discussion of the propensities to truck, barter, and exchange (1776). And if we are concerned with the tradeoff between personal gratification and happiness on the one hand, and one's personal cost of cooperating with others on the other, Benkler suggests that "social production systems—both peer production of information, knowledge, and culture and sharing of material resources—can be more efficient than market-based systems to motivate and allocate both human creative effort and excess computation, storage, and communications capacity that typify the networked information economy" (2006, 115). One wonders how long it will take until economists and politicians appreciate the transformation not only of the markets but also the mindset of their participants. Is the transformation only apparent in the high-tech sector of the economy? Is it only true for millennials who have given up on their predecessor's infatuation with property ownership and the personal rewards they claim to deserve?

II: SCALE, RATIONALITY, AND THE FAIRNESS OF PRICES

Though never specified by Smith, it seems that small-scale markets, the ones found in villages and cities even today, could perform well for the exchange of goods and services. Once the scale is global rather than local, would the same mechanisms and attitudes prevail? Does the direct involvement of those participating in the immediate exchanges transfer into the indirect chain of exchanges that are truly invisible? Will the personal attachment and loyalty of those meeting daily or weekly in the marketplace be possible when linguistic barriers and geographical distances are standard? Since the market is supposed to process information about the supply of goods and services and the demand that matches them, prices are determined by this confrontation: too much supply relative to demand, and prices go down; too much demand relative to the available supply, and prices go up as more people are willing to pay more than before for the same goods and services. This phenomenon is described as if it emerges naturally and therefore is justified practically and more profoundly, morally. Questions of scale, however relevant and important because of our assumption that what works in one context is scalable to another, seem irrelevant in light of this immutable law of nature: prices are always already justified. But this may not be the case. What about controlling the supply? What about "cornering the market" and pretending there is less supply so as to artificially increase prices? It's no secret that retail giants, like Walmart, dictate the price at which they'll purchase their merchandise and that their competitive discounting advantage (because of their sheer size) puts out of business smaller retailers when they enter the market.

Moreover, the scale of markets also dictates the institutional framing of individual exchanges such that some semblance of cooperative exchanges is sustainable over a long time with a broad spectrum of choices expressed in various markets. As Douglass North argues, several assumptions about markets and market behavior come into play in the classical and neoclassical microeconomic model of markets: scarcity of resources, competition, rational behavior of consumers, transparent information about all market conditions, and the equilibrium of supply and demand (1990, 3–26). What is important to keep in mind is that "institutions basically alter the price individuals pay and hence lead to ideas, ideologies, and dogmas frequently playing a major role in the choices individuals make," such as the complexity and incompleteness of information that eventually also has the power to undermine the very neoclassical model of market performance (ibid., 22–23). The emphasis in this view of markets is not on their natural or divine emergence, but instead on the institutional settings that ensure that the exchange process is measured and enforced, and that these are part of "transaction costs" that aren't accounted for in the neoclassical model (ibid., 27, 31, 68–69). In his words: "How well institutions solve the problems of coordination and production is determined by the motivation of the players (their utility function), the complexity of the environment, and the ability of the players to decipher and order the environment (measurement and enforcement)" (ibid., 34). This level of regulatory oversight, even if internal to markets and without the visible interference of the long hand of the law, is still a precondition for markets functioning the way they are supposed to, guaranteeing that prices are determined by the supply and demand curves of each good and service.

Contemporary economists are more willing to admit that classical exchange relations exist in the abstract drawing boards of theorists. There are at least three kinds of exchanges that may be observed in markets: first, personal exchanges that require little oversight if any; second, impersonal exchanges that require religious or ritualistic supervision; and third, impersonal exchange with third-party enforcement of the State (ibid., 34–35). It makes perfect sense to think of these three kinds of exchange in evolutionary terms, moving from tribal and kinship to more anonymous exchanges; but in fact, as Graeber already mentioned, these different kinds of exchanges were historically operative all along. What has become more pronounced and as such sanctioned in more recent times is the impersonal nature of exchanges that cannot function without the State. Of course, "no institutions are necessary in a world of complete information. With incomplete information, however, cooperative solutions will break down unless institutions are created that provide sufficient information for individuals to police deviation" (ibid., 57). What neighbors know of each other's needs and wants is lost in the gigantic global marketplace where "needs" are fabricated from unknown "wants," where advertisement manipulates us to think of gadgets we didn't even realize exist as necessities. Instead of borrowing a neighbor's tool, for example, we are prone to buy a better one, to show off that we have the latest and the best money can buy.

The notion of "rational economic man" has been one of the main pillars of the classical and neoclassical model. Admittedly, Smith's language in this regard couches human's rationality in their emotional or psychological pre-dispositions so that they reasonably behave in a particular market-oriented manner. By the time the neoclassical model evolves, its dependence on and reference to the rationality of our behavior is fully entrenched. As the authors of the standard critical text on this issue, Martin Hollis and Edward Nell, explain, the impetus for the neoclassical notion of rational human behavior originated in the Enlightenment ideals of humanity. If humans are inherently a "bundle of desires," all of which are rational, so would their behavior attempt to meet and satisfy these desires in the most efficient, utilitarian manner. Just as each individual could calculate this utility, so could an entire marketplace that is made up of these individual utility maximizers. "Society," according to this line of argument, "becomes a construct out of individual behaviour and the individual is defined schematically in terms of choices made rational by prosocial desires for self-evident goals" (1975, 50). This view of marketplace behavior is of course fraught with problems. Marx already warned against the fetishism of commodity consumption, alerting us to the very problem of how and under what conditions desires come into being and how and why they are satisfied. Likewise, the ability to rationalize nonrational or even irrational desires has come under attack by the likes of Thorsten Veblen in his coinage of the term *conspicuous consumption* (1899/ 1953) (keeping up with the Joneses, showing off a pretense of wealth, and the herd mentality of buying into the fabrications of marketing agencies). And scale does matter, as Hollis and Nell concede (1975, 51), so that one's environment and the behavior perceived around us influence how we behave, what we react to, and how we have incorporated consumer behavior as an expression of our inner psyche, with its highs and lows.

The assumption of human rationality is so sacrosanct with economic analysis and the potential for predicting market forces that it took half a century to bring its conclusions into critical reconsideration. Behavioral economists have posited the alternative "irrational" human behavior as more consistent with the actual behavior observed in the marketplace, and even found a means by which to estimate and predict outcomes (Levitt and Dubner 2005; Ariely 2008). The fact that the neoclassical view had human behavior be both an average and an abstract ideal lent it scientific credibility difficult to challenge. And when challenged, auxiliary hypotheses could be added to ameliorate concerns, such as elastic substitutions among commodities or the elasticity one could find in consumer demand (Hollis and Nell 1975, 54ff). Would consumers indeed maximize the utility of their purchases to fully satisfy their desires? Or, by contrast, would they be content to partially satisfy said desires? The very notion of maximization is both assumed and promoted under abstract human behavior so that eventually we consider those who work just enough to meet their needs as lazy if not outright less than rational. We speak of ski bums as those earning just enough to enjoy boarding in the winter and hiking in the Rocky Mountains with a joint in hand. What's wrong with them, we ask rhetorically; and most often their "less than rational" behavior is explained in terms of Rocky High, a state of ongoing hallucinating stupor. Only in the past few decades a different, more complex image of human behavior has been on display in theoretical economics, one that also explains volunteer work and collaboration, the willingness to contribute hours of time and work without attribution or credit for publicly available projects like Wikipedia. Such behavior, of course, defies the standard neoclassical and neoliberal models, and highlights the assumption we should or shouldn't be using anymore. Instead of judging behavior as rational, we may want to question its contribution to the well-being of individuals and their community.

III: EFFICIENCY, EQUILIBRIUM, AND THE MORALITY OF MARKETS

The notion of utility maximization has been challenged and replaced by what some would consider a more stable state of affairs, where optimality is the idealized target. Allen Buchanan defines the state of a given system as Pareto Optimal "if and only if there is no feasible alternative state of that system in which at least one person is better off and no one is worse off." A state is Pareto Superior to another if and only if there is at least one person who is better off in this state and no one is worse off (1985, 4). The debate over the optimality of market forces relates to market efficiency; that is, under what conditions will the flow of information and of goods and services guarantee the best outcomes for all participants, suppliers, and consumers who come together to exchange what they have or need. Buchanan alerts us that "for the same reason that productivity is inadequate for overall efficiency assessments, neither the growth rate, nor the rate of capital accumulation is by itself a satisfactory measure of a system's efficiency, unless we divorce the concept of efficiency from that of well-being" (ibid., 6). But what if optimality is reached and everyone is not worse off than before but there are still glaring injustices and inequalities among participants? Will the efficiency of the market achieve moral goals as well? Even if we move to a Pareto Superior state where more people have improved their position, there is no guarantee for an accompanying improved moral condition (ibid., 9–12); nor is there any guarantee that the position then remains static: American market exceptionalism, for example, remains without sufficient empirical support.

The case for the existence and soundness of markets is usually made on efficiency grounds: "exchanges in the ideal market reach an equilibrium state that is Pareto Optimal" and the assumption that "actual markets sufficiently approximate the efficiency of the ideal market to make them preferable to nonmarket arrangements," such as feudal power relations of exchange or other inequities (ibid., 14). The five conditions for market efficiency are full information, costs of enforcing contracts and property rights are zero, individuals are rational, transaction costs are zero, there is perfect competition, and finally, products are undifferentiated so that they allow for easy substitution (ibid., 14–15). If all conditions are satisfied, Pareto Optimal outcomes can be expected. If all conditions are met, there is no need for government intervention as a corrective agency. But what is also clear from this list is that to begin with, we are still idealizing human behavior, and second, that such conditions prevail if and only if some state institutions are already in place. As Graeber reminds us, the State is indeed a precondition for the market and not the other way around.

The likes of Buchanan shift the discussion of market efficiency and the equilibrium that ensues when Pareto Optimality reigns to suggest that even moral arguments can be articulated on behalf of these exchange relationships. The first argument is the one espoused by the Social Darwinists who believe in applying "natural selection" and the "survival of the fittest" to individual participants in markets. This argument is based on natural phenomena with divine sanction and it translates into morality. The second argument is about one's desert; namely, market outcomes for losers and winners alike reflect their just desert, and so it's a moral argument on behalf of unregulated markets. There is a subtle caveat here, and that is to distinguish between what people deserve and what they are entitled to (ibid., 49–53). A third set of arguments originates from utilitarianism, the theory that calculates the greatest benefit for the greatest number of people. But here, too, one must distinguish between maximizing utility overall and the potential for a mutually advantageous state of affairs where everyone benefits even if not as much as everyone else. Likewise, there is a distinction between Act and Rule Utilitarianism, whether "rightness" is defined in terms of acts and their consequences or in terms of the rules that inform these acts regardless of results. In Buchanan's words: "According to the utilitarian argument, the justification of the market is that general compliance with the rules that constitute the social and legal framework of the market maximizes social utility" (ibid., 55). With all of these arguments for the morality of markets, there is a wide agreement that however large the role of the market in our social relations, "safety nets" must be guaranteed as well (ibid., 59). The fourth set of arguments are libertarian in Nozick's sense (1974), and it assumes the fundamental right to private property as both the starting point and the end goal of market exchanges (ibid., 64–65). This approach also claims that the market offers the best protection of civil and political liberties: "A market system is best because there is a strong correlation between the existence of markets and the flourishing of individual liberty in general, not just civil and political liberty" (ibid., 79). And the fifth and final argument on behalf of the moral attributes and consequences of markets is that markets provide the conditions for the development of human personality, ambition, creativity, and ingenuity (ibid., 80).

More contemporary supporters and advocates of the markets even claim that they have evolved into an inexorable set of values embedded both in what gets exchanged in markets and the social and cultural relations displayed there. In other words, one need neither assume a set of values that predate or undergird the market, as Smith has done, nor attempt to *post hoc* argue for the morality of such exchanges. Instead, markets have become "morally coded" because all the culturally sanctioned (and therefore expected) moral principles and ideals are already an "integral part of modern exchange relations" (Stehr 2008, 213). This indicates a level of prosperity, knowledge, and power each individual brings into the marketplace, itself an overly optimistic presumption since most participants may be reluctantly there, each operating under radically different sets of conditions. Even when market liberties are common and exercised by most, this alone doesn't guarantee the elimination of inequalities. Perhaps only institutional procedures and state regulations can offer some solace and protection from potential abuse of seemingly voluntary market exchanges. Can we eliminate the gross abuses of markets, constraining discrepancies to ensure the exercise of freedoms and equal opportunity to all?

Marx and his disciples scoff at such preposterous suggestions, reminding us that exploitation and alienation are the two pillars on which market-capitalism operates, with its insistence on private property rights. Non-Marxists critics, such as George Akerlof and Robert Shiller, have more recently argued about market manipulation and deception that even when optimal equilibrium is reached in markets, it's really not in terms of what people want but rather "in terms of our monkey-on-the-shoulder tastes [things we are told to want] . . . Standard economics has ignored this difference because most economists have thought that, for the most part, people do know what they want" (2015, 6). The notion of "free to choose," heralded by the likes of Freedman, suffers from both psychological and informational "dysfunctional decisions" as there is a disjointed process of what people think they want and what they actually want when outside influence is powerfully exerted on them. They continue to suggest that the myth about unregulated free markets presents markets that are bound to "yield the best of all possible worlds. Just let everyone be 'free to choose,' says the mantra, and we will have an earthly paradise, as close to the Garden of Eden as our existing technology, our human capabilities, and the distribution of income will allow" (ibid., 150). But in fact, this is a two-edged sword that can either benefit everyone or hurt most participants, because without some controls, monopoly behavior or simple unscrupulous predatory behavior by large corporation and small con artists can sway otherwise reasonable people to part with their money to their own detriment (admittedly, even when they freely choose to be swindled). If people are "less than perfect," if they indeed can be "tricked and fooled," and if competitive markets by their very nature "spawn deception and trickery," then markets will inevitably lead to disasters (ibid., 152–164). The market myth overlooks its constituents and the conditions under which they operate to stay ahead of their competitors. There is no leisurely and friendly exchange of commodities; instead, self-interest is transformed into a competitive game where simply doing better than someone else or succeeding where someone else failed may not be enough; when success is being celebrated and rewarded disproportionately (with acclamation and financial rewards unrelated to profits), the danger of internalizing one's success and developing a heightened level of greed that wasn't there before, where more is better, may breed immoral behavior by otherwise quite decent human beings.

A more journalistic but highly informed account of contemporary market behavior is provided by Jeff Madrick, who declares from the beginning of his book that "to call economists overconfident during the modern *laissez-faire* experiment understates their hubris" (2014, 16). The ideology that supports the hands-off mentality is one in which interested parties want political entities to stay out of the business that transpires in markets. Recently, this ideology came under fire because of a "market failure" that required government intervention in the form of bailing out the large banks with the claim that it would ward off the collapse of the American (and indirectly the global) economy. When the failure became apparent, the underlying ideas that supported capitalist markets all along were questioned as well. Among them we already mentioned the "invisible hand" and the requirement to limit government intervention. But it's worth noting here Say's Law that supply creates its own demand (ibid., 45). This so-called law suggested that any commodity that came to the market will immediately or eventually create its own demand. But even if this works in many cases, as unimagined products find their way into our homes and workplaces, the real issue, as we have seen above, is the interplay between supply and demand and the disequilibrium that may ensue: Do we really need that much of this or that? Is there something else that can substitute for this product and satisfy us just as much? Is the market in fact self-adjusting enough to account for all data sets and all alternative items already in production?

Madrick reminds us of the Efficient Market Theory (EMT) as "another example of how faith in the rationality of free markets was pushed too far" (ibid., 139), because instead of examining and verifying its validity, it has become an article of ideological faith. If you reject it, then you are a conspiracy theorist who believes that nefarious forces are about to take advantage of you and the market; if you accept it, you are bound by what Daniel Kahneman calls the "there is only what I see" propensity to ignore variables that are invisible but real (2011). If people aren't "purely rational," then EMT doesn't work, nor does the belief in the Invisible Hand hold (Madrick 2014, 149). According to any observer of American markets, from stocks and bonds to housing and health care, speculations and manipulations of the markets are prevalent, even systemic, and as we scale to global markets, potential abuses are even more profound and devastating (ibid., 160ff). Can anyone imagine the potential misunderstanding and outright lies in trade cases among nations with different cultures, laws, and currencies? For example, should Western companies be outraged by the fact that Asian nations regularly copy trademarked and patented manufacturing products and mechanisms? If one doesn't believe that individuals ever fully invent anything but are simply expressing cultural knowledge in specific ways, then notions of intellectual property rights make no sense. Competitive advantage in such cases is about who brings products to market more quickly or cheaply, rather than who has an everlasting right to control these products because they "invented" them. And here not only presumptions about the scalability of markets are presupposed but also that all participants share the same set of moral and legal convictions.

   Looking at markets from a political and constitutional perspective, Timothy Kuhner reminds us that the "efficient market hypothesis" is about the rationality and efficiency of markets and the way their pricing mechanisms express accurately information about the supply and demand of goods and services and the health of corporations. In doing so, the EMT suggests that markets possess the kind of insight and wisdom individuals and other organizations do not (2014, 33). It therefore makes perfect sense that any regulation of this wisdom should be avoided, and that economic inequality may be an unintended consequence, one that admittedly translates into political inequality since absolute equality interferes with free markets (ibid., 37–45). Market liberty or the freedom expressed in market exchanges may indeed be economic in nature, but isn't it also associated with politics and political rights, as great resources overwhelm smaller ones? Here something alarming seeps into our consciousness: that the moral justification for market exchanges are applicable to any "commodities," even those of the mind. Kuhner quotes Justice Holmes from one hundred years ago to have said: "The ultimate good desired is better reached by free trade in ideas . . . the best test of truth is the power of the thought to get itself accepted in the competition of the market . . . That at any rate is the theory of our Constitution" (ibid., 54). The application of EMT to the law and the Constitution is hereby presented as if the struggle over ideas and truth, from Socrates and Gandhi to Martin Luther King, Jr., has never taken place. Though the idea of open competition for the hearts and minds of people sounds reasonable enough, there is danger in conflating the two domains of markets and laws. The danger is that the legal and political systems will eventually seem open to financial manipulation and the forces of monopoly capital. The sad part is that the trap of political markets—where ideas and their representatives can be bought and sold—is supported by neoliberals, *laissez-faire* conservatives, and neo-Keynesians, all overlooking the fact that ideas cannot be commodified and that democracy isn't a market (ibid., 140). The inherent problem is not that ideas shouldn't be tested and argued about, supported and criticized; instead, what sounds like reasonable pluralism turns into a free-play for interest and lobbying groups that are neither equal in credibility nor in financial resources (ibid., 162).

The current intermingling of politics and the economy has become apparent after the Supreme Court's decision in *Citizens United v. Federal Election Commission* (2010), when it became clear that under the consideration of freedom of speech, corporations have the same legal standing as individual citizens. As he considers this problematic intermingling and its effects on democracy, Kuhner argues that the Supreme Court uses the following theoretical principles: "deliberative insofar as moneyed interests deliberate, republican insofar as moneyed interests are virtuous, perfectionist and transformative insofar as a variety of interests use money to pursue their political goals" (ibid., 188). What informs legal scholars in regard to the separation model of capitalism and democracy is that "just as capitalism holds that politics is not an economically legitimate form of competition, democracy holds that the market is not a politically legitimate form of governance" (ibid., 283). Can we hope to retain such a separation? Can politics remain outside the influence of market ideologues?

Robert Reich, the former Secretary of Labor in the Clinton administration, echoes some of the concerns about markets already examined above. If civilization "is defined by rules" and if "rules create markets" and "governments generate the rules," then any argument about unfettered capitalist markets makes no sense (2015, 4). As a leftist critic, he is as concerned as Kuhner with the impending conflation of capitalism and democracy, where at the end democracy becomes an appendage of the market. He quotes Edward G. Ryan, Chief Justice of Wisconsin's Supreme Court in 1873: "Which shall rule—wealth or man; which shall lead—money or intellect; who shall fill public stations—educated and patriotic free men, or the feudal serfs of corporate capital?" (ibid., 45) He also reminds us in less flowery rhetoric that the Sherman Antitrust Act of 1890 attempted to curtail monopoly power, and the moral principle that apprises those who sign contracts under coercion rather than consent (ibid., 54). The moral framework of markets we explicated above should not be forgotten, as we observe not the freedom of market participants but the "redistribution upward" from the poor to the rich (ibid., 118); more generally, there is a "predistribution" of wealth and income because the rules of the game of contemporary capitalism dictate its operations. He insists that this form of predistribution is "invisible" insofar as it doesn't happen like the redistribution downward in the form of taxes and welfare policies; it's fastened to the rules of the market, from property and monopoly power to contractual relations among corporations and their workers to the laws of bankruptcy and the lack of enforcement of laws passed by Congress (ibid., 154). In his words: "Put simply, large corporations, Wall Street, and wealthy individuals have gained substantial power over market rules that generate outcomes favoring them—power that has been compounded as the additional wealth has accorded them even more influence over the rules" (ibid., 157).

In addition to enumerating the statistical facts that prove the increase in wealth and income inequality in the past few decades and the egregious manner by which corporate America lobbies Congress and writes laws that then are passed by it (either wholesale or as riders or amendments to legislation), Reich follows Kuhner in bemoaning the impact such behavior has had on the very foundation of our democracy. One way to appreciate this situation, then, is to reiterate statements made by leading jurists who understood what was at stake when unfettered capitalism was left to exert its power. For example, Supreme Court Justice Louis Brandeis said: "We can have democracy or we can have great wealth in the hands of a few, but we cannot have both" (ibid., 159). How can economic and political injustice be fought against? If Reich is correct that "in recent years, fully half of all retiring senators and 42 percent of retiring representatives have turned to lobbying, regardless of party affiliation," then any hope for the governance and regulation of markets by political powers is gone (ibid., 176). Instead, powerful market participants are the ones dictating the legal conditions under which they can retain their advantages, but now with political sanction and legal impunity. If "economic and political power have thereby been compounded," then we have been duped by the rhetoric of freedom and equal opportunity and have been left with neither freedom nor equality even as abstract concepts worth pursuing (ibid., 180). Incidentally, herein lies Plato's expectation that politicians be denied private property and wealth, because to accept public office is to accept responsibility for the State and simultaneously to expect that the State takes care of politicians so that they shall want for nothing.

Wendy Brown picks up this critical stance and focuses on the neoliberal turn in American political and economic life. She argues that "neoliberalism as an order of normative reason that, when it becomes ascendant, takes shape as a governing rationality extending a specific formulation of economic values, practices, and metrics to every dimension of human life" (2015, 30). The fact that marketlike thinking is applied to marketlike activities isn't a problem, of course. But when marketlike neoliberal thinking permeates every facet of human life, when it becomes a dogmatic mode of rational discourse, then what happens is that "neoliberal rationality disseminates the *model of the market* to all domains and activities—even where money is not the issue—and configures human beings exhaustively as market actors, always, only, and everywhere as *homo economicus*" (ibid., 31; italics in the original). Even though most professional economists shy away from a full-fledged commitment to what we have seen above in the terminology of "rational economic man," their ideological counterparts still hold onto this fictional ideal as if it has both philosophical meaning and an applicable mode of behaving across one's decision-making processes and interpersonal relationships.

Brown speaks of "economization" as a uniquely neoliberal trend with its "diffusion and multiplication," one that in its exclusivity becomes the forum for competition based on human and financial capital. In her words: "The subtle change from exchange to competition as the essence of the market means that all market actors are rendered as little capitals (rather than as owners, workers, and consumers) competing with, rather than exchanging with each other" (ibid., 36). This means that each participant or agent in addition to trying to "maximize" the value or return of such relations is also turning into a competitive machine that dehumanizes the potential for friendship or collaboration in organized unions, for example, or other forms of association. The point, though, is the dehumanization of actors and participants since they are all now considered "human capital": first, the individual internalizes this sense of self-worth and is treated as such by everyone else, other individuals and the state; second, inequality is the medium of competitive relations, and the political premium originally given to equality disappears; third, "when everything is capital, labor disappears as a category as does its collective form, class"; fourth, when the political is transformed into economic terms, notions of citizenship, public-goods, and the commons disappear as well; and fifth, "liberal democratic justice concerns recede" (ibid., 37–40), because, as is evident today, even justice can become a scarce resource when fairness (central to social stability and thus the State) is undermined or absent. Markets subsume all parts of the State so that the State itself is reduced to the calculus of markets without reference to its own goals and charge, constitutional or otherwise. "As the province and meaning of liberty and equality are recalibrated from political to economic, political power comes to be figured as their enemy, an interference with both" (ibid., 42). Under these conditions, there is an inherent conflict between political forces (representing fairness and justice) and those of the economy (representing maximization of utility and profit). No wonder that one fears for the future prospects of democracy in general or any political agency that is supposed to oversee egregious or nefarious behavior in the marketplace.

IV: UNCERTAINTY AND RISK (MARKET FAILURES)

Part of the allure for corporate lobbyists to write legislation and pay for its passage is to ensure the stability and longevity of their corporate bosses. Relevant in this context is the long-term predictability of market conditions and the guarantees that come from either federal subsidies or tax incentives. If exogenous variables, those variables external to the equilibrium that emerges from market forces, can be controlled, then planning can proceed and guaranteed profits can be expected. As invisible as the hand of the law and the marketplace may seem in Smith's idealized markets, so is it important for market participants to have visible signposts and structures that they can follow or avoid, that can reduce uncertainties. There are numerous kinds of uncertainties that increase the risk of doing business and the assessment of which must be calculated. If risk is properly addressed, its cost can be configured into the business model and eventually paid for by consumers. Keynes recognized the kind of uncertainties that affect one's psychological disposition and therefore one's behavior in the market. For example, any kind of investment includes three levels of risks: an entrepreneur's, a borrower's, and/or a lender's; their risks are associated both with the investment itself and also with an eye to the future value of money—will its value increase or decrease because of inflationary pressures? Will it be devalued by a government in order to improve its trade balance or its potential for more competitive exports? (1930/1963, 144)

Uncertainties about the future state of affairs are handled, according to Keynes, by all participants in terms of their current levels of confidence in making decisions: "the outstanding fact is the extreme precariousness of the basis of knowledge on which our estimates of prospective yield have to be made" (ibid., 149). How do they all deal with this precariousness? They use what he calls "convention," meaning the conventional wisdom of the day, one that is "assuming that the existing state of affairs will continue indefinitely, except in so far as we have specific reasons to expect a change" (ibid., 152). This is a stretch, since it's obvious that economic and political conditions aren't bound to stay identical and stable into the indefinite future, but that's a starting point. After that, any domestic or foreign instability can affect the value of one's investment.

For Gerd Gigerenzer (2002), risk assessment is interlinked with some appreciation of how to interpret statistical data and how to avoid one's own ignorance of risks when deceptive practices abound in the marketplace. Though his own concern is with the healthcare market, where patients and physicians and Big Pharma dance around the prevalent innumeracy of patients and their families, and where corporate interests overwhelm the decision-making processes of clinicians, his insights and warning are broadly applicable. It's easier to appreciate the complexity facing individual market participants, but when corporate giants deliberately perpetuate confusion the market looks much less fair and liberating than its advocates claim it to be. Indeed, it looks outright manipulative.

At this juncture, we are switching the analysis from the more theoretical underpinnings of market mechanisms and how they should be working in an ideal world to the realities of daily decision-making processes under conditions of uncertainty. John Cassidy, for one, argues that we should pursue what he calls reality-based economics as opposed to utopian economics "because the modern economy is labyrinthine and complicated, it encompasses many different theories, each applying to a particular market failure" (2010/ 2009, 9). As we mentioned above, the ideology of *laisse-faire* market-capitalism has been touted as competitive and therefore efficient, self-correcting, and establishing an equilibrium of fair prices that reflect all the information relevant for all commodities and services so that this kind of "utopian economics goes beyond a scientific doctrine: it is a political philosophy, a secular faith" (ibid., 33). And as we have already seen, such political philosophy or ideology becomes detached from the realities of market behavior and therefore can disregard any need for minimal regulation or government intervention to protect consumers, spur the investment of producers, or ensure fairness in global trading practices. Even the likes of Bertrand Russell, firm believer in the expediency of markets, still found plenty of roles for governments to fulfill, from national defense (which is a mighty factor in market-capitalism) to justice, education, and public works (1949). Cassidy reminds us of the standard three sources of market failures: first, monopoly or oligopoly power that skews prices, undermines competition, and creates barriers to entry into the market (as in the case of giant oil companies or Big Pharma); second, how to deal with public goods both in terms of government-private investments and the so-called external benefits they confer on market commodities that may not account for their costs (as is the case when energy policies benefit one segment of the industry and not all, and may require military intervention to secure extraction and shipment); and third, externalities that include the justice system and air pollution just as much as the settings for communicating information about what will eventually influence internal market conditions (as in the case of the airline or energy industries in terms of public transportation and infrastructure) (2009/2010, 126–127). Finally, Cassidy brings up the obvious problem of the Prisoner's Dilemma that "the application of rational self-interest in the marketplace leads to an inferior and socially irrational outcome"; namely, there is an incentive to not confess to a crime that was indeed committed to win the shortest possible sentence for both prisoners (ibid., 142). Put differently, there is a dissonance between one's own preferred choice in a market and the overall well-being of society, contrary to Smith's belief that the amalgam of individual choices necessarily produces the best result for everyone.

As technological innovations compound, they are not confined to the improvement of the efficiency in the production of commodities; they also transform markets themselves. The best example of this is seen in the financial markets where "frequency trading" has changed the very nature and composition of trading stocks, bonds, options, and commodities. Sal Arnuk and Joseph Saluzzi chronicle the ways by which predatory practices now overcome any pretense of fairness in financial market trading. Theirs is a scathing indictment of computer-generated trading at nanosecond speeds that allow those in the position of buying and deploying expensive computers with physical proximity to the trading floors to avert the standard practices of trading where buyers and sellers face each other and agree on prices. With powerful computers and ingenious algorithms, the offer to buy or sell stocks or bonds is changed as access to the price offered for either sale or purchase is revealed a few nanoseconds before the actual exchange or trade can take place, thereby establishing a new price before the two original parties can meet to consummate the trade. This predatory advantage is no different from "insider trading" because the computer algorithm "discovers" what the offers are before the two parties have a chance to exchange information, and by the time the two parties were supposed to agree on a price, a third party intervened and completed the trade. Though relegated to computer-generated high-frequency trading, the human element cannot be ignored: this is a breakdown of the very notion of a market where buyers and sellers meet. Or, this is taking market rationality to its very extreme of efficiency, eliminating the human factor, so to speak, and letting computer programs "make" decisions on behalf of their owners. The problem is compounded in this case because any claim for market liquidity is undermined by the great risks of market collapse, since such trades can run amok and ignore external market cues. Here, too, questions about the essential regulatory authority that is needed is commonly deflected by ideological arguments about freedom and ingenuity, the heights of the human spirit and its creative possibilities, as if the moral framing of the very activity of arbitrage is irrelevant.

The presumptions about market efficiency and its blending with political and moral principles of freedom and equality, fairness and justice, is well established in the American psyche. In its name, arguments have been launched on the appropriateness of certain inequalities in wealth and income, for example, or on behalf of the centrality of *laissez-faire* marketlike behavior in all spheres of life, not to mention the ongoing assessment of any idea, product, or behavior in monetary terms. Against this grain, we should recall again Stiglitz, who warns us not to buy too much into the market mythology of the neoliberal variety. He explains the linkage between the political and economic realms in these words: "The inequality is cause and consequence of the failure of the political system, and it contributes to the instability of our economic system, which in turn contributes to increased inequality—a vicious downward spiral into which we have descended" (2013, xxxix–xl). His argument has three related parts: first, that markets are neither efficient nor stable; second, that the political system failed to correct market failures in the recent past; and third, that both systems are fundamentally unfair. Unlike Smith in earlier times and Stehr in more recent times, Stiglitz believes that markets, no matter their enormity, have no inherent moral character and that they ought to be tamed if we want to ensure that they benefit most citizens rather than only the few at the top (ibid., xlii). His argument is that inequality is the result of political forces as much as economic ones because they dictate and enforce the rules of the "fair game," and as such any exclusive focus on markets is both empirically incorrect and pernicious (ibid., 38). But this is not true, of course, if the market has been endowed with divine authority through the various origin stories with their attendant moral values and authority.

Regardless of Stiglitz's own opinion that "greed may be an inherent part of human nature" (ibid., 100), he is quick to assure us that there is something we can do to regulate, curtail, or even tame such human instinct. Analyzing the increase in monopoly power, he says that first, without government regulation enforcing competition, consolidation ensues; second, there is even an increase in monopolizing the standards by which markets operate, what he calls "network externalities"; and third, as monopolies get larger and stronger, they erect barriers to entry by potential competitors, may they be domestic or foreign (ibid., 56). Unlike many conservative and neoliberal economists, Stiglitz finds it necessary to have government intervention in all markets to guarantee that some of their potential benefits can reach more people. Government, on this view, has a responsibility to forestall monopoly-like behavior in markets before inequalities become apparent, thus preventing rather than correcting them after the facts are clear and it might be too late to do much to rectify their deleterious effects (ibid., 96). This can mean, on the positive side of the coin, not the harsh treatment of corporate giants, but the infusion of energy into potential widely spread entrepreneurship (ibid., 115–116). Supplementing his arguments for the need of government regulation and intervention, Stiglitz offers a broader view on the importance of what this current book is trying to focus on.

Though still committed to some form of market-capitalism, as he says that "the real economic reform agenda would simultaneously increase economic efficiency, fairness, and opportunity" (ibid., 336), Stiglitz is clear that ideological debates are not simply debates over ideas but more specifically about the competence of those entities, like the State or the markets, to deliver what they promise (ibid., 193–194). The question already asked by Keynes was under what conditions the government should and could effectively intervene to balance trade, for example, or to ensure domestic full employment, regardless of the ideology of the time (1930/1963, 376–78). As we have argued all along, ideas and their underlying assumptions offer ready-made frames of reference for both theorists and practitioners. This means that instead of examining market failures as indicators of what should have been done to prevent them, we should dig one level deeper and examine critically the presuppositions on which they rest. What is being assumed about human nature? What is being assumed about human behavior and interaction with others? Are such assumptions static and bespeak of a permanent state of affairs, or do they evolve and are being transformed?

V: THE BRIDGE

Some heterodox economists, such as John Commons, follow the lines of argument about private property and their reliance on human labor, and radically transform them in the twenty-first century when explaining how markets work. He agrees that "rational labor, therefore, gives a title of ownership to whatever one takes from nature's abundance, which ownership, because the resources are abundant, does not deprive any other person of what he also may wish to take from that abundance" (1934/1990, 33). He then quotes Locke who connects one's labor to one's property as a right under conditions where "there is enough, and as good, left in common for others" (ibid.). The point of the individuation of property is not in contradistinction to other's claims of property but rather in accordance with having enough for all, as perhaps the French understood this. In this light, Commons understands Locke's political ideas as enhancing "nature's abundance" rather than creating any sense or reality of scarcity (ibid., 34). "Hence Locke's presupposition of abundance of land granted to free men in common by a beneficent creator, with the duty to work and multiply. The economic term 'abundance' is equivalent to Locke's theological term 'beneficence.' With this presupposition of abundance there could be no contradiction between material things and ownership of the things." But he is quick to explain, "Not until property means scarcity and labor means abundance does the contradiction appear" (ibid., 37). The "institutional" sense of political economy comes through with the insistence that the definition of political economy not be limited to nature and individuals but to a community of individuals who have "mutually dependent interests" within "security of expectations" that he understands as "order" (ibid., 57). Hence the notion of "transactions" among individuals that are not simply exchanges in the market but embody future-looking interactions in society (ibid., 58, 118). For Commons, there is a "shift from commodities, individuals, and exchanges to transactions and working rules of collective action that marks the transition from the classic and hedonic schools to the institutional schools of economic thinking. The shift is a change in the ultimate unit of economic investigation, from commodities and individuals to transactions between individuals" (ibid., 73).

We see in this closing analysis the lockstep movement from one set of assumptions to another, so that a shift from one framework to another can be accomplished. Any heterodox economist will be quick to observe that institutional settings matter, that what is at stake is not a reconfiguration of this or that feature of individual behavior or of how markets function most efficiently, but instead a broader understanding of the relationship that evolves among participants within various institutions. Whether one wishes to call this Marxist or leftist in the sense of appreciating the fundamental social role humans play in their economic exchanges and the ways they communicate and construct their cultural narratives is of little importance. What is at stake, though, as we move to the next chapter, is the realization that in the name of many of these assumptions conclusions have been drawn that affect the daily lives of people, that legitimate exploitive and abusive systems where the few benefit more because of their powerful positions than because of their hard work and talents.

Chapter Six

Economic Growth

Modernity and the Enlightenment have brought about future-looking perspectives on progress and growth as indispensable features of the rational process of the evolution of humanity. For capitalism to survive and succeed, already Smith and Marx admitted in their different ways, it must be growing, conquering new markets, in an ever-expanding range of all human activities. Economic growth as an article of ideological faith is part of the political economic discourse, whether we are speaking of job creation or harnessing the energy of the sun. The specter of globalization and its discontents in Stiglitz's sense (2002) has been with us for some time now. Perhaps reconsidering this framing may help us rethink whether or not we wish to pursue growth rather than adapt a more viable and sustainable set of economic practices without the threat of self-destruction.

The engine of growth has been associated with technological development from the Industrial Revolution to the Digital Age of computing power and the Internet. In its name, most political arguments have been fought, from tax policy and its impact on economic growth to government intervention in crises or cyclical downturns in the economy. We measure our personal success in terms of salary raises or increase in wealth, and that of corporate giants in terms of their quarterly sales and income growth. As we shall see in this chapter, the incessant drive for growth almost at any cost has some drawbacks. Likewise, the emphasis on growth is at times at the expense of other variables that make the economy flourish, like investments in infrastructure. And finally, we shall examine the potential for sustainability (with or without actual growth) of markets and businesses as a healthy alternative to the quest for growth.

I: PERSONAL GROWTH

Perhaps it's fitting to begin by reminding ourselves what Abraham Maslow (1943) proposes as the stages of human growth in terms of the various levels or stages of human motivation. Of the five stages, the first is associated with physiological needs, the second with safety needs, the third with love needs, the fourth with esteem needs, and the final fifth with the need for self-actualization. Maslow's "hierarchy" illustrates that more basic needs must be met before pursuing others, and that if the basic ones are not met, the others will not be met as well. In other words, we should pay attention to food and water and shelter before worrying about self-actualization. This starting point is relevant to our discussion because market-capitalism is supposed to deal well with some of these human needs but is unable to deal with others. As Walter Weisskopf, for example, has argued, not only is capitalism supposed to be perfectly suited for accommodating our basic and safety needs as we move up the Maslow hierarchy, but it can also do much more—it can take care of all our needs and desires, our wants and aspirations. In fact, it's the key for the ultimate human liberation already envisioned by the Enlightenment leaders. The so-called economic pie may be divided unequally among members of the same community, but if "the pie itself can be expanded over time, the size of each person's piece can be increased without any change in the degree of inequality, and the struggle over the division of the pie can be attenuated" (1978b, 406). This, as we shall encounter later, is sometimes called "trickle-down economics," where the largesse of the very wealthy and their expenditures eventually benefit everyone below them, increasing employment opportunities because of the spending habits of the very wealthy. The promise is not simply that this or that need can or will be taken care of, but that everyone's material well-being will improve over time, and therefore overlooking ongoing inequalities is a small price to pay. The accompanying feature of this process of material growth is that one can look forward to a better future, that the promise of tomorrow makes the pain or suffering of today palatable and even reasonable (as one sacrifices today for the sake of tomorrow, one generation suffers so their offsprings will be better off).

But are there no limits to material growth and the improvement of the material conditions of humanity? Though basic needs can be fulfilled with the growth of the economy, as growing production meets growing consumption, other nonmaterial and social needs are neglected. Put differently, to meet the increasing basic needs of humanity, market growth is undertaken at the expense of these other, (Maslow) higher needs. In Weisskopf terminology this means that there is some internal "irrationality" in the push for growth, and that two "significant contradictions" become apparent; the first is associated with growing inequities that destabilizes communities in regard to ongoing labor conflicts with capital, and the second one is associated with environmental costs borne by society rather than the corporate entities that pollute the air and waterways or dump waste without regard to its ecological impact (ibid., 406–407). The irrationality and internal contradiction of market-capitalism is most acute when growth is put forth as the solution to inherent problems (already explained in detail by Marx) when in point of fact it raises more problems. Weisskopf is prescient in his early identification of impending problems associated with the growth model despite his appreciation of the great increases in productivity that technological advances allow for; instead, he realizes that no matter how the production cycle grows and thereby also increases consumption, there are limits to the material enjoyment of the human race (perhaps not in less developed countries, but definitely so in the more developed ones where minimal levels of basic needs are met with welfare safety nets and other public policies).

Despite Marx's and Weisskopf's warnings about the limits of the material improvements both in themselves and the toll such improvements take on market participants—individuals and corporations alike—and the social and natural environments in which they are supposed to grow and flourish, there are some contemporary thinkers that are still under the spell of the growth model. Peter Diamandis and Steven Kotler, for example, suggest that the shortages we encounter are about our expectations and as such are not really shortages at all. They argue that everyone should not live under American standards that may require five planets to sustain, rather than enjoying the bounty of this one planet and adjusting our aspirations accordingly (2012, 5). But even with such adjustment, we must account for the fact that our complaints about available material resources isn't their scarcity but accessibility; that is, we have plenty to go around but we have mismanaged our distribution processes that produce levels of waste that affect some part of the global population, and therefore "when seen through the lens of technology, few resources are truly scarce; they're mainly inaccessible. Yet the threat of scarcity still dominates our worldview" (Ibid., 6). Touching on the themes already covered earlier in the first chapter of our book, they note that "abundance is about creating a world of possibility: a world where everyone's days are spent dreaming and doing, not scrapping and scraping" (ibid., 13). They follow in some sense Maslow's hierarchy of needs and (as shown before) offer their own pyramid of abundance: bottom level includes food, water, shelter, and other survival necessities, the middle is devoted to "catalysts for further growth like abundant energy, ample educational opportunities, and access to ubiquitous communications and information," while the top is reserved for freedom and health as the necessary "prerequisites enabling an individual to contribute to society" (ibid., 14). Just like Maslow, they point out the psychological hindrance or barrier to the conceptual acceptance of abundance, with an innate faith in technology as the engine that accelerates the potential for growth and global abundance (ibid., 35).

Others, like Edmund Phelps, push the idea of personal growth to include the notion of "flourishing," which means "engagement, meeting challenges, self-expression, and personal growth," a sense of personal involvement in the life of the community as well as the "broad involvement of people in the processes of innovation: the conception, development, and spread of new methods and products—indigenous innovation down to the grassroots" (2013, vii). For him, the potential for ongoing growth and the fruits it brings about aren't about science but about modern culture, so in this sense he claims to argue against Joseph Schumpeter's view that "innovations are sparked only by exogenous discoveries—and the neo-Schumpeterian corollary that innovation could be increased only by boosting scientific research," and instead argues for "indigenous innovation" that is self-directed (ibid., xi, 14). Overlooking any concerns about the deleterious effects of material growth, Phelps is an ardent believer that in the world of material comfort and even abundance the potential for innovation increases. This goes against the common grain that "necessity is the mother of invention" by suggesting the opposite: "abundance frees the mind to wander and invent." If one looks at the historical record, both options can be empirically confirmed. But since "confirmation bias" skews our vision in the direction we already find more acceptable or pleasing, we are loath to change our view with new evidence that contradicts our expectations. So, once again, our predispositions and our presupposition impact our views and behavior and exclude alternative ways of looking at ourselves and our environment and changing our behavior according to new findings.

II: THE MORALITY OF ECONOMIC GROWTH

As already mentioned, if indeed the available pie gets bigger and bigger under the promise of the growth of markets and economies, it stands to reason that one would find this both descriptively and prescriptively appealing. But here we encounter two kinds of growth, one that can be called internal and the other that can be called external. The internal or inward growth is highly dependent on what already Smith and Marx realized, which the greater productivity of the labor force is. This can come about because of better machinery, improved organization of the workplace—in the sense of Taylorism and Fordism, from more precise division of labor into miniscule and measurable tasks easily monitored and managed to the assembly line— and the improved machinery of the workplace that includes the introduction of computing power and robotics. External growth, by contrast, focuses on the incorporation of additional natural resources that are available either domestically or in foreign lands. This brings about the commercialization for

production and eventually consumption of material variables, from newly
discovered natural resources not mined before all the way to eco-tourism and
space travel. This also brings into more intimate contact the possibilities
available on foreign soil, both natural and human resources, so as to expand
local markets to the global economy. At this stage of the discussion we
should assert that both expansions are costly in human terms, dehumanizing
the workforce and threatening warfare in colonial, imperialistic, or other
overbearing senses, promoting corporate power in nation-states' militaries.
As essential as economic growth is both as a basic tenet of market-capitalism
and as a promise for future amelioration of current pain and suffering, it still
warrants a critical moral examination.

Benjamin M. Friedman reminds us that moral societies should be judged
in terms of "the benchmark for examining what difference economic growth
makes is the image held out by the Enlightenment thinkers . . . Its crucial
elements include openness of opportunity, tolerance, economic and social
mobility, fairness, and democracy" (2005, ix). Economic growth according
to these standards means not only the rising of standards of living for the
majority of the population under consideration but also other features, such
as fostering "greater opportunity, tolerance of diversity, social mobility,
commitment to fairness, and dedication to democracy" (ibid., 4). The Enlightenment ideals with which we are still implicitly operating would thereby
link the economic and the political, illustrating how progress in one area, the
economy, would inevitably bring with it an improvement in the other arena,
the political. These kinds of improvements are not measurable in market
terms alone, and therefore ought to be accounted for by supporters and promoters of market-capitalism. This means that "calling for government to
stand aside while the market determines our economic growth ignores the
vital role of public policy: the right rate of economic growth is greater than
the purely market-determined rate, and the role of government policy is to
foster it" (ibid., 15). This is an extremely important point as we aren't talking
of growth as such or growth in an abstract or absolute sense, but about
nuanced rates of growth, some of which indeed are acceptable, manageable,
and positive, while others could be dangerously low or high and undermine
the very fabric of the market, destabilizing relations among participants and
incurring grave inequalities.

Once again, we find ourselves endorsing the importance of government
intervention and the ways in which it can improve and implement public
policy. According to Friedman, there are three ways in which public policy
can be deployed: "create and deploy more resources, devise new technologies for using those resources in production, and use existing resources and
technology more efficiently" (ibid., 402). What policy to adopt will depend
on the recognition that "both physical and human capital formation contribute to an economy's productivity and thereby foster its long-term growth.

And it is in large part up to public policy to determine how much investment in these resources an economy undertakes, as well as what kind" (ibid., 405). Perhaps in the context of long-term calculation the Popperian notion of "piecemeal social engineering" comes into play as a methodology for policy implementation that favors incremental changes and reforms and the inevitable corrections to any market setbacks (Popper 1957).

Though he cites Max Weber as the one who argued that "an inner moral attitude had importantly spurred the development of capitalist economic growth" (ibid., 17), Friedman's argument is that "economic growth not only relies upon moral impetus, it also has positive moral *consequences*" (ibid., 18; italics in the original). He then continues to identify a "causal link . . . from scientific and economic progress to positive changes in the political institutions and social attitudes" (ibid., 26). This doesn't mean a change in "human nature," but instead this means that changes come about "because *conditions* were different" (ibid., 30; italics in the original). Friedman relies in his argument on the likes of Auguste Comte insofar as he claims that "all human progress, political, moral, or intellectual, is inseparable from material progression" (ibid., 31). This intimate inseparability of material and human growth is reminiscent of Stehr's argument about the intricate relationship between markets and the morally embedded commodities they produce and exchange. And as mentioned above, he is a firm believer in "technical progress" as the engine of "economic growth" (ibid., 63). There is plenty of empirical evidence to support this article of faith that economic growth can and at times indeed does bring about the progress of the human spirit. But more often, as Paul Baran and Paul Sweezy argue (1966), the costs associated with what they call "monopoly capital" are devastating to a great segment of the population. The suffering from increased productivity weighs heavily on their mind, just as the inclination to warfare to expand into foreign markets (as the history of the United States has shown time and again), from the Middle East to South and Central America.

The European Union offers a more glaring example of how the very notion of growth is wrapped up in so many other policy considerations and even promises for prosperity that may not materialize. Moreover, as was in the case of Greece defaulting on its inter-European loans, an accompanying notion of austerity is always one step behind such promises. Greece is expected to execute austerity measures to ensure the decrease in government expenditure in the hope of eventually having a balanced budget (between revenues from taxes and fees and the costs associated with governing the country). Austerity has become code word for decrease in salaries and benefits to government employees and the decrease in government services, from healthcare and transportation to education and defense. Austerity measures have regularly affected those in the greatest need of government support and subsidies, while the very wealthy corporations and individuals can still hide their wealth in tax-haven countries and islands around the word to avoid any taxation. Austerity reduces economic growth, and in fact it is the opposite policy or approach to government stimulus that spurs employment and increases the demand for goods and services (as Keynes advocated after the Great Depression period in the United States). This is what Carlos Closa says about "German ordoliberalism," which blames debtor countries of irresponsible behavior and excessive expenditures on the one hand, and on the other excessive consumption and loss of competitiveness. In "ordering" these countries into economic (which really means political) submission, the great European powers, especially the dominant German economy, can exact levels of discipline unfathomed by a nonoccupying and supposedly friendly powers in the ironic name of solidarity among members of the Eurozone (2015, 41). The austerity predicament demands structural reforms that curtail the welfare platform of poor countries and therefore undermines the possibility of any future economic growth. In addition to economic reforms, these measures are supposed to be attended to and complemented by legal and constitutional reforms as well, all of which are bundled under a moral cloud of suspicion and lack of trust by the dominant members of the European community in relation to the less affluent ones, such as Greece, Italy, Spain, and Portugal. Erik Eriksen, in the same volume of essays on the future of the European Union (2015), explains that economic crises have been interlinked with and usually accompany political shifts in loyalties and power relations.

Thinking about the rift between democracy and capitalism in terms different from those explained above by Kuhner and Reich, in the European context the fear isn't only that the State becomes subordinate to the will of large corporate interests, but that what we observe now is a "post-humiliation society" in Europe, as a "democratic supranational federation" that could embrace the best of the democratic principles tried by nation-states but could also transcend their limitations and become less democratic (ibid., 248–249). Growing national markets as was done in Europe in 1993 so as to make them continentwide was a deliberate attempt to grow the European market so that it could more plausibly compete with other large markets, such as those in the United States, China, Latin America, and India. But there are costs to such growth, as we have seen more recently in Europe. Are all nations treated equally? Will an economic agreement overshadow political agreements? Will the market dictate what policies nation-states will have to conform to? These questions have been festering among nation members so that the potential departure of one signals some deep domestic dissatisfaction, one that threatens the very union of all other European nations (Brexit). This, then, is a limit to or boundary condition for market growth, when unfettered expansion may break down the market itself, with nation-states returning to their own currencies (which they can devalue at will) instead of the mighty Euro. One may ask in this context how does one ensure that there is equal participation in and enjoyment of the fruits of economic growth? Could the concept of economic growth even be appropriate in societies that have (or wish to) organized themselves as American Natives did?

III: UNTENABLE GROWTH

Though discussing economic growth in environmental terms rather than those of the marketplace, Fred Bender reminds us that there are limits to growth. In the debate over the limits to growth, environmentalists were keen to incorporate as many variables as possible and not limit themselves to the Malthusian concern over population growth relative to the growth of food-stuff. These variables included "population and food production to industrial capital, pollution, resource depletion" and others that should be considered in analyzing the potential breaking point of the global system in which we live (2003, 328). The limits of this limited-growth model is that it remains market driven, confined ideologically to market-capitalism and the political and ideological blindness that prevents it from recognizing colonial and domestic inequalities; market-mechanisms are construed as the means by which to solve growth problems without admitting that no solution is sufficient (ibid., 329ff). At stake for deep ecologists is an ideological shift and a change of consciousness that embrace human-nature harmony that in turn would neces-sitate setting limits to growth of any sort. But even if we remain within the confines of the crisis-prone market-capitalist framework, there are some in-herent concerns that should be addressed, the kinds already mentioned by Marx and echoed here and there by concerned economists and politicians.

Satyajit Das looks at the growth patterns of the last century in these terms: "The postwar expansion collapsed under the weight of four main factors: high debt levels, large global imbalances, excessive financialization, and a buildup of future entitlements that had not been properly provided for" (2016, 33). This view is internal to market-capitalism and its own mistakes that will eventually threaten its very existence. High debt levels that leverage the future in the present and that expect great returns as economic growth seems to guarantee increased prices can be detrimental if only one miscalcu-lation collapses the tower of financial cards. Underfunded investments that rely too heavily on borrowed money become impossible to stabilize with cost overruns or a longer-than-expected timeframe for completion. Similarly, the increased reliance on financial institutions for economic growth distorts all other sectors of the economy and makes it look as if financial instruments and institutions themselves produce something when in fact they have histor-ically been the grease that oils the economic engine and never the engine itself. Global imbalance eventually brings global markets into disequilib-rium, resulting in either war or default. And finally, starving present employees in the name of a better retirement future turns out to be so costly that many large corporations and even municipalities and states have tried to declare bankruptcy to be free of such obligations. Because of all of these variables coming together at once and at this early part of the twenty-first century, Das concludes that "the central illusion of the age of capital—endless economic growth—is ending" (ibid., 93). Does this mean that the fundamental principle of market-capitalism will vanish from our collective theoretical and practical psyche? Incidentally, interest on the national debt in the United States constitutes 6 percent ($223 billion) of the federal budget in 2015; at what point does this debt (and its attendant cost) constitute an indirect theft from or levy on citizens and their children?

It's interesting to follow Das's historical review as it suggests that the infatuation with growth "is a relatively recent phenomenon" (ibid., 101). He quotes at length from the historian J. R. McNeil that up until 1500 there was only minimal global growth, and that from 1500 to 1820 "global GDP [Gross Domestic Product] increased from US $240 billion to US $695 billion (in 1990 dollars); between 1820 to 1900, the GDP almost tripled to US $1.98 trillion, and between 1900 and 1992 it increased to US $28 trillion; finally, GDP between 1992 and 2014 doubled again to US $60 trillion" (ibid., 101). One can clearly follow here the extreme acceleration of growth in the past one to two hundred years as compared to the entire recorded global history. The greatest growth periods were between 1873 and 1914 and post–World War II until the 1980s. But despite these recent spikes in growth, Das forecasts smaller growth or no growth and possible negative growth into the twenty-first century (ibid., 103ff). If this will be the case, will market-capitalism as we know it collapse? Should the classical, neoclassical, and neoliberal models be discarded? Should we move toward a more ecologically friendly sustainability rather than remain infatuated or even dazzled by potential growth models, the kind of models that promise to overcome inequalities in the name of increasing the whole pie of goods and services? According to Das, lower growth may not be a problem, as one sees in nature that growth spurts are short-lived overall instead of having an everlasting long-term momentum. Yet he admits, "The current economic, political, and social system is predicated on endless economic expansion and related improvements in living standards. Strong growth is also needed now to resolve the problem of high levels of government and private debt" (ibid., 119). If the economy grows, even if under inflationary conditions (when all prices rise, from labor costs to the costs of finished commodities and housing), today's debt is in fact paid for in cheaper (because inflationary) dollars in the future. The value of the dollar diminishes under inflationary growth realities, and so there is an inevitable interest on the part of borrowers (individuals, corporations, and government agencies) to postpone to the future the payment of current debts. Yet there are some obvious natural constraints on growth from water and food resources to cheap energy resources and climate warmings, all of which are exasperating Malthus's predictions and fall in line with critiques such as Bender's and deep ecologists' (ibid., chapter 5).

It was Smith who advocated free trade between the UK and the "New World" to expand the geographical horizons of the market and take advantage of newly found natural resources that could be imported quite cheaply from the Americas. It was of course the exploitation of slaves more than raw natural resources that made such trade so attractive to the Europeans and Americans alike. During the eighteenth and even the nineteenth century there were global markets to be opened and exploit, so that it became not simply an article of faith that growth was necessary and prudent, devoid of any moral qualms, but also a conviction that such ongoing expansions would last forever. Expectations of improvement in one's standard of living went hand in hand with growth, so that any deviation from or undermining of expanding international trade was considered inappropriate, or worse, simply the misguided policy of unsophisticated politicians. They were indeed Smith's targets in his relentless promotion of the ever-expansion of markets. But those days of pristine new lands that could be grabbed and conquered and the population of which could be militarily subdued and even enslaved are over (despite the attempt to treat poorer sovereign states as if their workers are the ready substitutes of the cheap labor of slaves). As Das argues, "The growth in trade and cross-border investment that underpinned prosperity and development is weaker, removing a key driver for economic growth" (ibid., 173). If prosperity depends on growth and if growth is slowed or reversed, domestic growth and prosperity are bound to suffer as well. This situation of domestic isolation may only work under the specific conditions of domestic growth available only to the very largest and strongest economies, such as the United States. Other smaller and less well-endowed nation-states may suffer from stagnation and even economic retrenchment, as has been the case in the Japanese economy in the past three decades.

We should end this section by emphasizing that the pretense that growth eliminates poverty despite some vestiges of inequality has been proven empirically not to be true in the United States, where post the 1980s, despite GDP per capita increase of 147 percent, poverty inched up from about 11 percent to 12 to 15 percent (ibid., 207). As Reich and other critics of market-capitalism insist, "In 2010, the wealthiest 10 percent of US households owned 70 percent of all wealth, while the top 1 percent owned 35 percent. The bottom 50 percent of households owned 5 percent" (2015, 210). So, is economic growth unsustainable? Is it immoral? Is the promise of ever-expanding markets and the ever increase of the economic pie misleading and false? As Das concludes, indeed, "Economic growth and prosperity were by-products of consumption, unsustainable resource exploitation, and serious environmental damage"; and this is of course untenable for any country in the long run (2016, 287).

IV: SUSTAINABLE GROWTH

Is there such a thing as sustainable growth? Or, are we instead discussing or speculating about new forms of sustainability that promise no growth at all? Goran Therborn suggests that "sustainable development" would have been more appropriately a by-product of socialist thought rather than the compromise between environmentalism and developmentalism of the twenty-first century; such a compromise will inevitably underrepresent the social needs of the environment and the long-term effects of such a compromise (2008, 37). If human emancipation from exploitation, oppression, and discrimination is folded into a new and hopefully sustainable mindset, then much more is at stake than reducing pollution, for example, or outlawing certain chemicals from wide usage. From a Marxist perspective, it may be the case that "neither capitalism nor its polarizations of life courses appear very likely to disappear in the foreseeable future," but this doesn't in and of itself negate any potential for critical analysis and the rethinking of economic relations under which sustainability is more valued than growth for the sake of growth alone (ibid., 110). Growth, as far as Therborn is concerned, has benefited primarily the wealthy and corporate giants, and has done little to ameliorate the suffering and poverty of the working classes: "In 1905, the fifty largest US corporations, by nominal capitalization, had assets equal to 16 percent of GNP [Gross National Product]. By 1999, the assets of the fifty largest US industrial companies amounted to 37 percent of GNP" (ibid., 13). This repeated snapshot undercuts the very promise of market-capitalist growth that is supposedly undertaken on behalf of benefitting all members of society (even if some inequalities remain). Those who still uphold the tools of Marxist critical dialectic explain that these tools are more useful in articulating the intricate relationships between workers and corporate managers, between producers and consumers, and between citizens and their government agencies. With a dialectical sophistication of analysis—namely, scrutinizing multiple variables simultaneously for their reciprocal influence—it is possible to see both progress and exploitation, rather than just a linear-like image of progress without its attendant costs (ibid., 125).

This line of argument about the direct and indirect costs of growth and progress—as they are regularly posited together—finds adherence even among those who study the historical record of economies and the claims that are being made with disregard to this record. One of the latest academic celebrities in this area is the French economist Thomas Piketty, who reminds us that "the history of the distribution of wealth has always been deeply political, and it cannot be reduced to purely economic mechanisms" (2013/ 2014, 20). This means, among other things, that "knowledge and skill diffusion is the key to overall productivity growth as well as the reduction of inequality both within and between countries" (ibid., 21), but these alone have been "largely illusory" when it gets to wealth and income inequalities (ibid., 22). With meticulous study of historical records, Piketty is able to debunk old myths and emphasize that inherited wealth has become a dominant feature in the increase of inequality regardless of any claims for economic growth (ibid., 26). Another complaint registered by Piketty and one that adheres to general Marxist critiques of market-capitalism is that whenever numerical and statistical data are offered as evidence of the positive outcome of economic growth they are commonly presented as "aggregates and averages" that mask "distributions and inequalities" (ibid., 59).

As he follows Rousseau's notion of the difference between natural and social inequality, Piketty inveighs against the conventional wisdom that economic growth is a "marvelous instrument for revealing individual talents and aptitudes" (ibid., 85), because in point of fact it turns into a mechanism by which greater and greater inequality is being fortified between the very wealthy and the rest of society. How can this ongoing increase in the wealth and income gap be bridged? What can be done except for the declarations of doom and gloom so fashionable on both the right and left of the ideological spectrum? In Piketty's view, "It is perfectly possible to imagine a society in which the growth rate is greater than the return on capital—even in the absence of state intervention. Everything depends on the one hand on technology (what is capital used for?) and on the other on attitudes toward saving and property (why do people choose to hold capital?)" (ibid., 358). This means that first, there will necessarily be some surplus that could be used for the redistribution of wealth and income, and second, that with proper policies such a possibility could be implemented. As Piketty makes clear, there must be political will to control and divert economic practices as they have become accepted norms of the capitalist system. Market-capitalism can be sustained under his view into the long-run if and only if it will accommodate some policy changes so that neither crisis will be inevitable nor a civil rebellion against the concentration of wealth and income in the hands of the very few.

Marx's analysis of market-capitalism rested on class struggle and the impending potential for a revolution so that the means of production would be communally owned. Piketty continues to explain how the classes aren't the old proletariat and bourgeoisie but instead those with inherited wealth and all the rest. Others, like Fraser, still hold onto the belief that economic growth and progress could have and was supposed to dissolve some of the antagonism in the ever-rising standard of living into the twentieth century (2015, 197). But as this process has been unfolding in the past century or so, "one consequence of that achievement was to blur the boundaries of class identity . . . blending of styles of consumption helped dissolve a consciousness of class into the amorphous universe of the middle class: the class that wasn't one" (ibid., 199). Because of the amazing adaptability of capitalism, says Paul Mason (2015), we may have missed the opportunity of collapse predicted by Marx. Likewise, the notion of class has been transformed as well, as we speak nowadays about the employed and unemployed and the underemployed regardless of their identification with so-called manual labor or the "cognitive" sector of the economy. Moreover, class boundaries aren't simply blurred because of consumption patterns and the availability of most gadgets on credit, but are cleverly disguised by a neoliberal ideology and rhetoric that portrays even the underemployed as free to choose when and where to work, in the ever-increasing pool of workers who are "crowd-sourced" (Sundararajan 2016; see also Fraser 2015). The point here is that in order to "sustain" the main features of markets, human labor has been transformed and recategorized: you aren't suffering from the instability of your work prospects but instead are the beneficiary of ample opportunities to thrive and prosper on your own. But this, of course, is a sham. Perhaps the only sustainability we can speak of is that of maintaining the status quo without any promise for or illusion about growth. Though sustainability can be a promising outcome of market analysis and a way to prevent failures and crises, it still remains an open question if such sustainability improves the lives of market participants or is still geared toward the exclusive enrichment of the few at the expense of the many.

V: THE BRIDGE

Growth as a basic assumption of the potential benefits of markets and as a means by which greater inequalities become more explicit is no different in kind from all the other assumptions and myths we have examined in previous chapters. The underlying question of this book is not whether there are assumptions and what they are, but instead what is the conceptual framing these assumptions bring about. With conceptual framing, such as the legitimation of market-capitalism and the belief that resources can always be understood in terms of scarcity and abundance (rather than in light of how they can or cannot improve the human condition), economic theories and principles find their way into public policies endorsed by political power players and the public. The endorsement is bound to come under scrutiny and disaffection as the results of these policies have aggravated the economic landscape and not turned it into a more pleasant place for everyone's prosperity. We have witnessed 2016 as a year of political acrimony and distrust, when candidates for the presidency have portrayed not only each other but also the economic environment in toxic terms rather than as a set of reasonable debates over basic assumptions about economic relations and best policy recommendation for human prosperity.

All other things being equal, the American economy has fared relatively well in the post–Great Recession period when unemployment has been decreasing steadily and when more people enter the job market. Yet dissatisfaction remains high as both left- and right-leaning citizens protest loudly about their levels of disenfranchisement. Occupy Wall Street members and their supporters share the same attitudes as the Tea Party and its members and supporters, even though their targets may differ: big banks for the former and big government that bailed out the big banks for the latter. What they share is a feeling of being left out of the political-economic system, of having no access to the great benefits promised to all. They see the "insiders"—economic and political—as having gamed the system and disproportionately benefitted from economic growth. Big banks get bigger and richer; large corporations get larger and wealthier; and the 1 percent remain aloof from daily worries and continue to accumulate wealth in greater speed than ever imagined. Is it then those with access to decision makers versus those without such access who now replace the standard antagonism of the proletariat and the bourgeoisie? And if this is indeed the case, what assumptions should we discard and what should we reconsider as we move forward? Should we promote growth anymore? Or should we focus instead on the reformulation of market- rules to ensure fair distribution of income and wealth? These questions will be answered in the next part of this book. As for economic growth, we must also be prepared to discuss, as a society, what price are we willing to pay for it.

Part II

Framing Theories

Theories are not invented from thin air, nor are they fanciful outcomes of imaginative minds. Instead, they offer a complex combination of perceived observations about what happens in the environment that surrounds us and some ideas about how things work in the world. Human imagination has a role to play here, of course, and undoubtedly the mindset or prejudice of the modeler comes into play when a theory or model of the economy is proposed, with or without the quantitative data to support it. Following the scientific method, as many political economists have done in the past, it is expected that once a theory is fabricated it should be tested against empirical evidence to ensure that its predictive powers match its explanatory powers; that is, that it withstands the unforgiving encounter with reality. This is true of physics and of political economy, we are told; but we are also aware that the variables associated with human behavior are more complex if not impossible to model as accurately as those in physics or chemistry. The ascendency of behavioral economics in the past few decades has signaled the demise of the classical notion of "rational economic man," replacing it with the predictable irrational behavior of observed people who interact with each other in the marketplace and everywhere else in their environments. This kind of shift, just as the shift from classical to neoclassical economic theories and the eventual mathematization of all that can be conceived of in economic terms, reminds us how important it is to pay close attention to the assumptions we use, the presuppositions we may be taking for granted as we try to explain or predict the economic behavior of people. Because of this realization, we should spend some time thinking through these issues.

Chapter Seven

Dangerous Assumptions

In an age that is fast paced and wants us to get to the point right away, the "bottom line," it's clear that long meditations or detailed argumentation are unwelcome. We are asked to get to our conclusion first and not bother with how we got there. It's the kind of bottom-line mentality that looks for a shorthand one-liner to summarize everything; perhaps it's a socialization process afflicting young kids already in K–12 when the teacher just wants to see the work done and not the method or process by which it was accomplished. This is a dangerous trend that should be slowed down or even reversed. The point is not to know where one wants to eventually go but how one plans to get there, and when we think slowly, as Kahneman reminds us (2011), we use our rational faculties more thoroughly to overcome false quick responses that are only useful under specific circumstances (when reacting instinctively to the danger of predators). First and foremost, then, we must make explicit and pay attention to the assumptions that we use, the ones that undergird our theoretical frameworks. Some of these assumptions are benign and some contestable; it's the theoretician or philosopher who must choose which is which, and under what conditions seemingly benign assumptions can become contestable or even dangerous. Assumptions understood to be dangerous are qualified as such because of the dire or even catastrophic intellectual and practical consequences to which they lead. For example, assuming scarcity and promoting this assumption as one worthy of public attention and alarm might lead to a general attitude and behavior of the "survival of the fittest" where people will literally fight for what may not really be limited resources, as Malthus's case teaches us. Was there indeed a scarcity of "foodstuff," or was it only a fictionalized image formulated to ensure the decrease in population growth, and more specifically to curtail sexual activity? In other words, suggesting that assumptions reflect empirical states of affairs (rather than admit they are conceptual propositions worthy of investigation) is a dangerous, even if common, move.

Likewise, assuming abundance of natural resources can lead to wasteful behavior both personally and by State authorities. This kind of unintended consequence can be viewed almost everywhere around the globe where water is not preserved for draught conditions or where the consumption of beef, for example, requires, according to some estimates, 2,500 gallons of water per one pound of beef (http://www.cowspiracy.com/facts). If we believe that there is abundance of water and that we shall never suffer from any water shortage, waste is not understood as such but rather as a way to continue our way of life. And this vision of an American lifestyle of large herds and big steak dinners is considered natural, acceptable, almost sacred in the eyes of parts of American culture. If the air we breathe is considered a God-given gift that is abundantly available we may forget that pollution must be regulated if not stopped completely. The question isn't whether or not the air is divinely given or a necessary element in our species' existence, but what kind of air we should or should not breathe, and under what conditions we can ensure the health of our and related species. How the rain forests participate in this ecological balance becomes then part of a larger economic discussion that may be missing its targets if framed too narrowly—that is, if framed in terms of short-term goals or the geographically circumscribed regions under study. Separating one set of assumptions from others just because they may only be tangentially relevant is problematic as well. A certain large-picture perspective is required, as deep ecologists and environmentalists remind us: what happens in one corner of the planet affects the rest of it. These are dangerous assumptions; assumptions that are ignored or overly hyped up insofar as they might be leading to grave situations or bringing about a situation where human extinction is possible (as in the case of global climate change).

As we know from logic, assumptions or premises can be either true or false but not dangerous or useful. But the point of logical analysis, once we allow assumptions to be either true or false, is to ascertain if a deductive argument is valid or invalid; it's valid if all its premises are true and it leads, necessarily, to a true conclusion. This implies a sound argument. An argument can be valid and hopelessly misguided. A valid argument can have a false premise and lead to a false conclusion, as we all know from our introductory logic course; if false assumptions aren't detected, there is the danger of holding onto the validity of the argument and ending up with a false conclusion. Our concern here is less with analysis of economic or political arguments or the consistency that theories ought to be upholding to be logical, let alone scientific; instead, the concern here is to make explicit the linkage between assumptions and the theoretical framework that they uphold. This means that assumptions, whether true or false, can still be dangerous rather than erroneous. Their danger lies both in what they reveal and conceal as well as in what they lead to once accepted without any scrutiny. It's one thing to allow for a special relationship between humanity and divine powers as most religious traditions profess, and quite another to argue, from a policy standpoint, that this or that portion of the population has been divinely condemned to suffer poverty and poor health (as some religious leaders and their political mouthpieces have done in different parts of the world: the Untouchables in India and victims of hurricane Katrina in New Orleans). The danger lies not only in the unexamined life we lead following unexamined assumptions but also the full acceptance of specific ways of thinking about our relationships with natural resources and each other. One need not be an ardent Marxist or environmentalist to be appalled by certain economic conditions and offer alternative ways of reorganizing human affairs; all that is required is an open and reasonable mind that can reflect on the facts and the evidence that is provided by competing narratives of who we are, where we came from, and where we are going. The obstacles, when they become apparent, are as much cognitive, intellectual, conceptual, and ideological as economic or political. And when social and moral worldviews are added to the conversation, we must admit that it becomes a richer and even more reasonable way of looking at ourselves in relation to others and our global environment. Admittedly, *richer* and *reasonable* are terms that are predicated on an epistemological (and moral) commitment to facts and empiricism, which may not be the case for everyone. As we have seen with debates over climate change and GMOs, we are prone to trade facts for moral judgments and values based on our lifestyles. It's a difficult epistemological battle to ensure that intrinsic value judgments should be considered alongside empirical and instrumental ones.

If competition is highlighted as part of human nature or if humans are considered evil by nature, then we begin to think in these terms, and what we think becomes a self-fulfilling prophecy in Popper's sense (1957). This means that we gear policies to account for human meanness, their dislike of each other, the suspicion that follows their every move, and the overall tenor of the social settings in which they interact. Surveillance, under such circumstances, makes perfect sense, as no one can be trusted and everyone is out to get someone in one way or the other. No, this doesn't mean that we are all necessarily criminals, but we are all considered criminals-in-the-making, always one step away from committing a crime of one sort or another. The alleged crime, even if it ends up being minimal, is still worthy of surveillance and precautionary means of avoidance, according to this approach; if our presupposition begins on such a negative, or some would say realistic, tone, it stands to reason that we should protect ourselves from each other. Instead of trusting others, we coil into our little protective cages, insulating ourselves as much as possible from exposure to other people or their products. *Caveat*

emptor (buyer beware) is an often repeated trope of market exchanges, reminding us that we should be worried, very worried, some would argue,
about the products we buy. If they weren't intentionally produced to hurt us,
they were still produced with an understanding that they cannot be trusted to
function well or safely and that we ought to watch out for hazards. The
Occupational Safety and Health Administration as well as the Environmental
Protection Agency, to name just two significant American governmental
agencies, have been in place to ensure that we are not in harm's way when
we exchange goods and services, when we join the workforce, or when we
use public transportation. The criteria by which we assess risks and dangers
relate more to the consequences, intended or not, of the kinds of practices
and policies that follow our assumptions about human nature or about our
natural resources. If not explicitly examined from the very start, they may
lead to a so-called chain reaction of models and theories, organizations and
institutions, policies and regulations that may guard or harm society as a
whole.

Dangerous assumptions in the sense of risks and costs, potential harms
and hazards, are not dangerous in themselves, of course. As mentioned
above, assumptions are neither good or bad but only true or false; as such,
they are value neutral. But even if we agree that empirical data are neither
good nor evil on their own but begin to have a moral dimension when used
and deployed in different contexts under various circumstances, the dangers
we are discussing aren't about their empirical status. What remains problematic is the manipulative or malicious use of assumptions in the sense that
we prompt people to behave in certain ways—say, be more competitive—
because we socialize them into such behavior based on the assumptions that
humans are by nature competitive. We can set incentives and motivate people to deal with this assumption, or we can shift all the way to the other
extreme of this spectrum of behavioral nudges and suggest that one is a loser
or will never amount to anything if one doesn't become more aggressive in
confronting market interactions. Only when you show real and threatening
power, this extreme view suggests, will you receive the respect you deserve
and the kind of benefits from what you do or produce. As becomes clear from
this perspective, we may turn people into hungry individuals whose "me
first" motto and "only the fittest (in what sense?) survive" can turn a community into a dysfunctional sociopathic group of people. And this is dangerous,
extremely dangerous when police officers, as we have seen in the past year in
the United States, become more military like in their approach to any peaceful demonstration, assuming the crowd is there to hurt them and damage
whatever property, private and public, it encounters in the process. This form
of anger and violence escalation is based on how we perceive other people,
what we assume about their nature and their behavior, about the economic
conditions under which they were brought up, all because they are not part of

our immediate circle of friends. This concern over white officers policing in black neighborhoods is as much about them not knowing the landscape and the local culture as not having grown up with those they are supposed to protect.

As we reconsider the assumptions and presuppositions outlined in part I, any number of them would lend themselves to be exploited within an economic system that will benefit some at the expense of others. Some could argue that there is nothing new in this argument, that in fact the few always benefitted more from whatever institutional setup than the many, and that in this respect feudal lords exploiting their serfs is replicated perhaps with nicer rhetorical veneer when capitalists and captains of digital industry still exploit the population by exacting rents albeit now for the use of smartphones or other Internet-related services. This empirical fact is easily verifiable in wealthy countries like the United States and some in Western Europe and other parts of the world where the driving force for economic growth is still assumed to be necessarily accompanied by the enrichment of the population as a whole: "the rising tides raise all boats!" But is this assumption, regardless of its empirical veracity, dangerous as well? What can be dangerous about the propensity to grow businesses and projects, company sales and the workforce? How can economic expansion be problematic? While some sustainable growth might be reasonable and even desirable, there is an overwhelming corporate (which filters into nonprofit and government organizations as well) attitude that embraces growth for its own sake. Such embrace brings with it an obsession with quarterly reports that reflect growth, that show an increase in revenues (sales) even if it doesn't reflect an increase in profits. This kind of obsessive and short-term thinking encourages accounting fraud when future sales are recorded as if they already took place, all in the hope of maintaining an ever-growing enterprise (and its attendant stock price if the company is publicly traded) or the valuation of the company (if it's held privately). Cases of fraud are routinely exposed, and rare cases of suicide by corporate heads and midlevel management because of failure to keep up the appearance of growth are unfortunately part of the economic landscape in the twenty-first century. (Note the report of an executive at Abbott Laboratories in India who committed suicide, *New York Times*, August 11, 2016.)

To be clear, it's not the contention here that all assumptions outlined in part I will necessarily lead to negative or dangerous consequences. This would be empirically false and would undermine our ability to ever discuss rationally what assumptions should be used in building economic models. Instead, what is being suggested here is that when assumptions are not carefully treated and critically examined within and outside any proposed model, economic, political, social, and moral, we may be blind-sided to what we indirectly endorse. This means, for example, that we should be aware that when exalting growth as the bedrock of economic activity and the prospects of any political economy, we should also account for what we are encouraging ourselves to do: grow no matter what. Growth isn't evil by itself, but unfettered, unexamined, or unbridled growth that decimates natural resources for future generations or that pollutes the environment irreversibly is growth not worth pursuing. Is there a more productive and careful way of thinking about growth? Under what conditions of sustainability is this growth preferable to that growth? What means serve us better as we pursue the prosperity of our community? So, it's not growth as such, but *qualified growth* that we should explore, and then also the very question of the advisability of growth. For example, the resort community of Breckenridge decided decades ago, in contradistinction to Vail and Aspen (the two other large ski resorts in the Colorado Rockies), to abandon its small airstrip so as not to attract wealthy outsiders with private planes. Vail and Aspen have grown much faster, have earned a global reputation as the playgrounds of the very rich international jet-setters, and by now cannot accommodate their workforce (because real estate has become so expensive). Whose growth patterns are more sensible? Which mountain village has ensured a more controlled or sustainable growth that maintains a relative protection of those who work in its hospitality industry? Given that tourism is such a large part of the state and local economy, these are important questions to contextualize in terms of our presuppositions about the essential role growth plays in market-capitalism.

Likewise, questions about the presumptions we have about private versus public property have grave consequences in the lives of individuals and the community at large. The notion of how essential private property is to the well-being of every individual and the community skews our views and policies toward a way of thinking that may put undue pressure on people to acquire a car or an apartment. This, in turn, may put undue pressure to commit to debts that may never be paid off, that become worthy of bankruptcy courts when losing a job or when getting ill. What's at stake with this presumption of the preference of private over public ownership of housing, for example, is that alternative living arrangements may not be considered. It's interesting to note that after the mortgage bubble burst in 2008, questions of ownership versus accessibility have resurfaced in the approach and behavior patterns of millennials: Why should I buy if I can rent? Why should I pay for "my" room in a hotel when I can stay on the couch of someone else for the night and get to know them? Here, too, presumptions of privacy come into play and are being challenged. The temporary violation of privacy aspirations is of course different from the kind we worry about in the digital environments where our very moves and purchases are being monitored, stored, and reused for marketing purposes (or other security purposes). We expect the Internet to be "public" in a manner understood centuries ago just as the "commons" was to take care of farmers who didn't own the tracts of land the gentry controlled. We also expect this "network commons" to be free of charge, and in exchange we are willing to endure the annoying advertisements that pop up on our screens. Deeper questions about ownership, private or public, surface indirectly and demand we account for our implicit assumptions not only about private property but also about the rights associated with such ownership: Am I justified—economically and/or morally— to charge "rent" for my creations? Should they be "open source" for anyone else because my own contribution is nothing but an instantiation or expansion of the ideas and knowledge of past generations and other people living in my community? Likewise, when it gets to higher education, should corporations (indirectly) limit access to subsidized public education by lobbying for low taxes when that in turn results in the difficulty of finding qualified workers?

These questions have been discussed by the likes of Lessig (2008) and many others because they test the legal limits of contemporary digital society; they also bring up what this book attempts to do: questioning the assumptions on which these tests are based. Danger looms around when these questions are not being asked at all, or when they are being asked and are swept quickly under the proverbial legal rug instead of becoming a public debate over rights and duties, expectations and responsibilities. This means, as in the case of the music industry, that an entire business model is being revamped: instead of earning a commission off every vinyl or disk or download from popular songs, artists are expected to give their music for free and then recoup their "losses" (or contributions, as some would say) in concert performances and receive a percentage of ticket sales. The same can be said of academic authors and inventors whose salaries compensate for their books and poems, inventions and ideas, and they give them for free to the public. One could make here a more nuanced argument about public and private colleges and universities, about those with and without government subsidies, with or without large endowments. But still, the issue at hand is the private ownership of one's product rather than the right to one's body and soul, as we saw above, and then by extension this right has shifted from one's person to one's land. Just because our bodies are our own and just because we have certain "inalienable rights" doesn't necessarily mean that we should have a right to a piece of land in the countryside or an apartment in downtown New Yok City. The danger looms large when we confuse our assumptions or substitute some for others in constructing simple or sophisticated arguments, the sole purpose of which is to support an ideology, whether capitalist in spirit or more socialist.

When we debate the efficiency of markets in general and the particular ways in which their allocation of resources is superior to any government planning, we assume quite a bit about the competitive nature of those involved in market exchanges as well as the truth of this assumption about market efficiency. It's easy to dispute the veracity or empirical support that seem to be accepted by neoliberals, for one, without closely examining the entire record. Rather than outline the cases in which market efficiency is untenable, or even if it is, may come at the social and moral cost to society (as when efficiency is pursued at the expense of human health and safety, or when environmental issues are set aside in the name of efficiency), what makes this way of thinking dangerous is the ideological hazards associated with it (Mirowski 2011; Brown 2015). The mantra of outsourcing as a means to make government more efficient or to unburden it from the shackles of bureaucracy is dangerous on many counts (even when some cost saving is accomplished). First, the shift from one (public) bureaucracy to another (private) makes those involved in providing the services less rather than more accountable (and incentivizes them to hide any errors since profits and bonuses are at stake). This means that the transparency expected of government agencies (because of the social contract) will be surrounded by veils of secrecy (under the guise of proprietary knowledge), and any personal concern will be dismissed. Second, services provided now by private corporations that pursue profits will suffer from shortcuts that themselves are dangerous, as is the case in the treatment of prisoners in privately owned facilities around the United States. Third, while public services for which taxes are paid and are highly important may call for certain redundancies (extra safety measures or additional oversight), they will be scoffed at for their inherent inefficiencies by private corporations undertaking such services. And fourth, on a more global scale, if public services are outsourced overseas, there could be national security questions that could endanger American citizens (or for that matter citizens of any nation-state that contracts with private corporations). So, the proposition that market mechanisms by themselves are always preferable to other mechanisms deserves closer scrutiny.

The list of cases where danger looms large for anyone overlooking or merely gesturing toward the basic assumptions with which we build political-economic models and the policies that emanate from them is extensive. Yet the brevity of this survey should alert us to paying close attention to what we call here dangerous assumptions, for lack of a better term. Admittedly, the alarm has been sounded before, and there are some excellent books that have been dedicated in one form or another to addressing these concerns. One worth mentioning here is Mariana Mazzucato's *The Entrepreneurial State* (2014), in which she carefully documents the ways in which the US government has taken serious financial risks in order to underwrite new technological developments. Once undertaken, through the Department of Defense or the Department of Energy research arms, these technoscientific insights have been harvested by American corporations that cheaply licensed these patented ideas and techniques, from the by now infamous case of the Global Positioning System to the touchscreen used in smartphones. Incidentally, Mazzucato devotes a whole chapter to the fact that Apple—heralded around the world as the high-tech innovative darling with its even more famous guru Steve Jobs—has not created any of the technologies it has licensed from the government and other companies, and that it spends more money on litigation than on basic research and development. Assumptions about government waste and incompetence in relation to corporate ingenuity are debunked; assumptions about the preference of private to private production and distribution are debunked as well; and most importantly, the very role governments can and should play in economic matters is being reformulated (to expand the limited focus on national security).

The other book was written by two of behavioral economics' founders and leaders, Richard Thaler and Cass Sunstein, *Nudge: Improving Decisions about Health, Wealth, and Happiness* (2008). In this book, they basically take the third view of human nature (*tabula rasa*) to its experimental extremes and figure out how to "nudge" people to behave in ways that meet their own rational self-interest even though they may be neither aware of what this means nor figure out how to act on it. They use cases from school cafeterias and retirement saving to health and wealth management to illustrate that people aren't making the best choices in life, and that seeming irrational behavior can be changed, nudged away from bad to better choices. This includes convincing students, given the choices provided by schools, how to improve their diets and reduce youth obesity, as well as ensuring that saving for retirement becomes a default position rather than a conscious decision to put aside an extra few dollars every month out of one's paycheck. The fascinating part in this book isn't the paternalistic outlook of its authors (they know best what's good for us), but the fact that they are interested in what most economists for centuries took for granted rather than carefully examined: What can we know or say about human nature? And once we figure this out, what policies might best serve us as individuals and as a society (since social program are in some instances ad hoc remedies for poor choices by individuals)? And in this context, we should be alert to the fact that some existing social programs suffer from the poor choices of individuals for whom they were never designed, as is the case when lifestyle choices turn into medical concerns—lung cancer for smokers, diet in the case of obesity and diabetes, and dialysis for alcoholics.

Unfortunately, too often the focus of social research isn't on basic or fundamental presuppositions that theories and policies take for granted. The few cases when it's apparent should be celebrated and followed by the media with greater interest. We may be entertained by reality shows that expose our hypocrisy or our false sense about who we are or who are friends are, but how do we carry this through in a more serious and consequential manner? Are our academic colleagues sure-footed when they stride along a theoretical plank they didn't construct themselves? And when they do fabricate a pathway to get us over turbulent cognitive waters, are they explicit about what assumption they are using? Admittedly, model builders must enumerate their assumptions before they offer a complicated algorithm, but do they offer alternative ones as well? Do they simultaneously construct alternative models, or, as may be the case, are they satisfied with the one model that is based on already existing models or on the foundation of an ideology whose own foundations are beyond reproach? When it comes to politicians or other leaders who may employ social theories and models, if we use the market imagery some more, are they shopping only at the sanctioned stalls of reliable and trusted like-minded merchants of ideas? Do they ever veer to the left or the right in search of new and exotic ideas whose mettle hasn't been tested yet? In short, are they sure they are not on a dangerous path that will put their constituents in harm's way? As history teaches us, nudges can be used for rhetorical and inflammatory purposes as well, stirring the passions of constituents toward racist and xenophobic behavior.

Chapter Eight

Useful Assumptions

By contrast to so-called dangerous assumptions, useful assumptions are those that alert us to the potential of humanity as a collective of individuals who interact with each other and feed off each other in social, emotional, and psychological ways; these are assumptions that can provide the foundation for model building and public discourse. What makes them useful is the way in which we still refer to them as we discuss public policies; they are useful in being expressed explicitly, and once again not because they are true or false. This means, for example, that assuming some level of natural abundance—sun and wind, oceans and deserts—and assuming the goodness of humans, we may be inclined to adopt a friendly posture toward strangers; the necessity of the police state would be challenged; and police brutality would not be tolerated. What makes these assumptions or frames of reference useful rather than dangerous is that they may allow our political imagination to configure alternative modes of existence on the communal level. Offering free bicycles that anyone can use anytime and anywhere within the city limits, as has been tried in Holland, or free cars for kibbutz members in Israel, may encourage cooperation and goodwill rather than theft. In other words, theft can be prevented not only by locking bikes or positioning a police officer in every corner but also by appealing to human camaraderie and trust as ways to instill and socialize ourselves to behave in cooperative ways.

It is useful to think more carefully about what we mean when we speak of equality, or as it's more commonly introduced in policy debates in the United States about equal opportunity. Rousseau's distinction between natural and artificial inequality, where the former is related to one's natural endowment (physical and intellectual talents) and the latter related to one's position in society (the aristocracy of his days), is a useful reminder that we should carefully assess and clarify what we mean by the term. It's one thing to agree that incredible athletes, like the Olympian swimmer Michael Phelps, deserve not only to receive gold medals for his accomplishments but also large sums of money by sponsors who use his brand to sell their wares, and quite another to agree that someone inheriting the family crest or million dollars is similarly deserving. For Rousseau, as should be the case for all of us today, artificially constructed inequalities that become encased in a legal and political framework (think of the British House of Lords) are not morally justified the way one's talents and hard work are, even when they both bring about some wealth inequality. We should be wary of hampering the ambitions of naturally gifted individuals, we are reminded, while offering complex tax policies for those whose only claim to superior social position is the work of ancestors or the largesse of royal families. In this context, the American experience in the nineteenth century in regard to the conquest of Western territories and the opportunities after World War II for postsecondary education tells an interesting story. It was the Homestead Act of 1862, signed into law by President Lincoln, that encouraged individuals to settle parts of the United States by granting them 160 acres if they paid a small filing fee and proved to reside there for a period of time. Likewise, the Servicemen's Readjustment Act of 1944 (GI Bill) offered returning military personnel a range of government-subsidized opportunities to start their own businesses or go to universities. Both cases illustrate government intervention that offers "equal opportunity" not available otherwise. More recently, legislative work under the general label of "affirmative action" has been undertaken to overcome the devastating long-term effects of American slavery and offer various ways of assisting traditionally discriminated against minorities to have the opportunities that others already enjoy.

What these cases illustrate is the meaning American society is willing to attribute to the presumed notion of equality and its application. Assumptions about equality and freedom are as problematic in their policy implementations as those about human nature, as seen in the previous chapter. It is therefore both useful and morally imperative to dig deep into our historical record and see under what conditions these assumptions were examined, if at all, and what specific expressions have been legislated. In economic terms, this is relevant in how we think about markets as the sites where individuals enter and exit freely and as equals. Can any individual get a bank loan to start a business and compete with already established ones? Is one free to choose what job to pursue, what profession to enter into, and where to purchase a home? If these freedoms aren't absolute, as they are not, but always already circumscribed, then any claim about equality or even equal opportunity becomes philosophical musing. To actualize what these assumptions suggest requires a careful construction of policies and institutions that foster opportunities, that view blacks and Hispanics, women and LGBTQ people, as part and parcel of the American fabric of society worthy of all that an economic system can offer. It would be a sad day if the only time we are treated equally is when those among us try to get a driver's license at the Department of Motor Vehicles (itself not available for every member of society) or when we are called to register for the draft (which happens rarely in a country with a voluntary military). Is it only in the face of large bureaucracies that we are reduced to our lonely and powerless selves? Is it only at the trail of a hurricane or flood, the kind of natural disasters that disregard one's status and class affiliation, that all our homes are indiscriminately affected (even though some are insured while others are not)?

These questions bring us to another presupposition that isn't discussed enough but deserves our attention: the social contract. As mentioned in part I, this notion is as old as Western philosophy, with Socrates reminding his friends that he cannot agree to their offer to help him flee since he remains a citizen of Athens: having enjoyed its laws and benefits his entire life, he cannot escape his fate because he disagrees with its judgment of guilt. Eventually more robust accounts of the social contract find their way into European political philosophy from the sixteenth to the nineteenth centuries, agreeing that such a "contract" (however implicit) offers superior security to that of the "state of nature," and that it protects and furthers the interests of all participants. The framework of a social contract reminds us that we have rights only when we also have duties, that what we think we deserve from our society is related to what we think it deserves to receive from us. It is useful to discuss the social contract when examining tax policies or national security, or more generally, when asking what public goods should be part of an enlightened democracy: Should roads be public or have tolls? Should parks be open to the public only for a fee? Are gated communities preferable to police patrols? Should education be funded communally, or should we only establish charter and private schools? These aren't idle philosophical questions as they have been vociferously argued in print and from podiums across the political spectrum. Neoliberal extremists who follow the likes of Ayn Rand quote her words about the coercive nature of public education, while followers of Marx quote the ten ideal policies in his *Communist Manifesto*. It's not that anyone is entitled to their opinion, as many students are fond of telling their instructors; it's that some opinions are based on a specific interpretation of the notion of a social contract, and as such ought to be admitted into the court of public opinion.

Similarly, if we remain agnostic about natural and human resources and not assume scarcity for the former and abundance for the latter, we may find that our imaginative horizons expand. This might lead to a different appreciation of what we can and should do about markets for resource allocation. If we consider that natural resources are plentiful and that we should be their custodians, as Native Americans and environmentalists insist we do, then perhaps we'll never run out of anything needed for population growth. Once again, there are empirical facts that ought to guide our deliberations; yet those deliberations will be framed or pitched differently if the goal isn't to maximize use but to ensure moderate usage. We can think about creative ways of using water and sunlight to have plenty for generations to come without the scare tactics of a looming disaster. Similarly, if we prudently use whatever we produce—without the mantra of "planned obsolescence" so dear to the hearts of twentieth century manufacturers who wanted us to buy new cars and new gadgets as often as possible—and keep using whatever we have access to for longer periods of time, and also learn to share it with others, perhaps the very notion of needs and wants will change. We can see how we move from basic assumptions, like scarcity and abundance, to other presumptions, like needs and wants, all the way to economic concepts, such as marginal utility (the more you have of something the less you enjoy it or the less it satisfies your needs and wants), to economic frameworks, such as efficient markets and growth. Without exploring every conceptual and factual link in this long chain of economic connections, we are bound to miss important issues that may derail us to confusion and panic. Policies based on fear and panic will serve us economically only in the short term, and are quite likely to cause major political and social problems in the long term. One need only observe the decision-making process of the European Union to realize how some policies that have not been democratically undertaken (no consultation with the relevant populations of member states) have backfired as Greece keeps threatening to leave the EU while the UK voted in 2016 to exit the EU.

As we move along these long chains of conceptual and factual connections, as we examine more carefully assumptions and what the consequences are of holding certain views, we should notice how these assumptions are interrelated. Private property as a divine right or as a natural phenomenon that everyone must agree on plays into questions of social contracts: Is the debate over Second Amendment rights (to own guns privately) about gun ownership, one's property rights, or how this right fits into the larger context of one's personal security being protected by the State? Simply arguing about guns as private property outside the context of a social contract makes no sense, no matter what your personal opinion may be. Moreover, we should be curious if the thirst for gun ownership in the United States emanates from the fear of lack of government protection or rather from one's sense of entitlement to own anything under the sun, including guns. But if such an entitlement is pushed to its logical limits, why not have a right to own privately a nuclear missile? When the debate deals more explicitly with our assumptions and frames of reference rather than this or that particular policy implementation, we find out what we really care about and believe in: it may have nothing to do with guns per se and much more to do with our sense of insecurity (whose origins we must carefully examine). We could also learn from other nation-states where police work isn't undertaken in paramilitary fashion and much more in the sense of public service and the bridges that are built between government agents and their constituents.

Continuing this line of questioning, we should be mindful under what conditions public ownership of land, knowledge, academic and research institutions, healthcare platforms, and the defense forces that protect us all are sanctioned. Without a commitment to the principles associated with a social contract there can never be a full appreciation of our personal responsibilities to the State and its reciprocal duties to us. While American culture is more prone to speak of individual rights, it may want to learn a lesson or two from European and other countries where one's rights are subordinate and constitutive of the well-being of the community. This is not to say that rights in themselves are under attack, as may seem to be the case when listening to some popular political pundits, but rather that we ought to recognize—yes, in a normative sense of the term *ought*—how our own behavior and actions affect those around us, just as the behavior and actions of others inform our own mode of thinking. It is important to stress that whatever ideology one may endorse, from anarchism to socialism and capitalism, none of these ever inferred freedom from responsibility; freedom was always first and foremost in their theoretical minds and from it certain responsibilities "naturally" followed.

Rarely do we find political philosophers and theoretical sociologists who are so keen on preserving the individual in complete isolation from the community; seldom do we find theoretical frameworks that assume our lives to be completely insulated from civilization. In the interaction and exchange relations that evolve among people a delicate balance is struck among participants to ensure the sustainable and long-term well-being of the community. The loyalty we were supposed to render to the monarch in the works of Machiavelli and Locke, for example, has been replaced with a trust we should be granting democratic institutions. When they fail us, as they surely do historically, the solution isn't withdrawal, as some cessationists recommend when they move to remote areas and live off the grid; instead, a devoted sense of urgency to reform or if needed revolutionize the mechanisms that undergird democratic levers of power is recommended. If the power of the sovereign isn't heard, once again referring to the assumption that the sovereign is the citizen (and not some governmental agency or position, like that of the president or prime minister), there must be change. Will the change be peaceful? Are demonstrations needed? Should these demonstrations become violent, it's the superior power of the police and military forces that must show restraint in the face of angry mobs (even at their own peril). How far should mob dissatisfaction be allowed free expression? This must be contextualized, as in some cases this is a newly emerging grievance, while in other cases it may have festered for years. However flawed it is both structurally and in person, democracy remains one of the only political frameworks where power can change hands peacefully, where political discontent can be expressed in the voting booth, and where the voice of the majority (however manipulated and ill advised) decides the future.

It is useful, then, to argue about and reconsider those often neglected assumptions about humanity and its institutional setting, our rationality or reasonableness, our natural equality that should mean something even if in specific social settings some do better than others, and our fundamental freedoms as licensed and guaranteed by the community in which we live. Though we may choose to reform our current social contract, finding it too restrictive or liberal, we cannot forget that indeed there is such a thing as a social contract that binds us together and that informs the very methods by which we express ourselves and must listen to others. Perhaps only the very rich, the so-called 1 percent, can afford to ignore their surroundings and create their own islands of gated luxury separated from the daily concerns of their fellow citizens; perhaps they can insulate themselves from the financial troubles of the rest of the country and even buy politicians who will protect their interests. This was true of monarchs and feudal lords, and this is still true today of billionaires. But even if the brute facts support this reality, should we condone this?

Socrates reminded his fellow Athenians of their military duties and their responsibilities to the city-state even when demanding the right to speak his mind and be a gadfly, an outright annoyance to some in position of authority. His right was contingent on his duty, and his behavior had to conform on some level to what a responsible citizen should be doing. The trial that cost him his life was not about freedom of speech as such, but much more about the degree to which this freedom can be exercised. In hindsight we condemn the Athenians for their poor judgment (though in a mock trial carried out in Chicago in 2013 contemporary professionals found him guilty as well) but forget to think through the assumptions both parties brought to the trial: Was it about rights or duties? Was it about inciting political disorder or the expression of views by an eccentric loner? When these questions are answered, we may have a useful discussion about what laws should regulate what behaviors if at all, as some like H. L. A. Hart suggest (1963). We may find your behavior despicable, even downright disgusting, but should we enact a law about it? American legal history has plenty examples of senseless notions and their attendant laws, from slavery and probation to segregation and mixed-race marriages. In retrospect, one must wonder how wise were our politicians and judges, how historically blinded and prejudiced their views and the assumptions on which they rested. We find that duties and rights are in fact not different issues, but different sides of the same coin; inexorable from each other and meaningless unless conjoined. Martin Luther King, Jr.

famously voiced this sentiment by stating "you have a moral obligation to obey just laws; conversely, you have a moral obligation to disobey unjust laws" (*Letter from Birmingham Jail*, 1963), thereby admonishing his followers to be clear about the fundamental principle that the right to live in a lawful society comes with the duty to maintain its moral integrity.

When we speak of the usefulness of certain assumptions, we are speaking of how we can deploy them when thinking through public debates and policies; we are also speaking of how reminding ourselves that they are still ingrained in our minds and collective histories influences how we view ourselves and others, and how we view our relationship with government agencies that govern or regulate markets. We seem to forget in some of these heated political debates that all markets are regulated in one form or another, that no market can really function exclusively by an Invisible Hand; that indeed the hand may be invisible but it's still there, to help and protect, guide and guarantee compliance, tip the scales toward fairness and justice instead of greed and cruelty. Likewise, markets also operate as if there were an Impartial Spectator who observes what we do and how we behave, one that remembers our failures and successes, and steers us away from fraud and theft because our conscience or the image of God brings out the best in us: honesty, trust, and integrity. The presumption that markets rise out of nowhere and that they continue to operate independently of human will and intention is simply wrong. What may be closer to the truth is the fact that some people dislike some regulatory policies some of the time. When they generalize from those occasions to all cases and offer a categorical statement about "free markets," their candor must be questioned as well as the data they bring to bear.

Would self-styled antigovernment critics expect no legal support for contracts they voluntary sign? Will they have their personal police force to protect their possessions? What do they assume when they argue against the "government"? Do they truly feel that all governments are totalitarian and out to get the fictional little guy? Why not reformulate the question and ask instead what role should government agencies play in a democracy? Why not direct the question to a productive reassessment of frameworks? Perhaps we should begin the conversation with reminding ourselves what responsibilities we should have toward the family and community that brought us up, that socialized and educated us in particular ways, and that protected us from potential harm. This phrasing embodies an assumption about the wonderful things that were done to all of us in our childhood. But what about whole swatches of the population that have suffered from discrimination and abandonment, from police harassment and the cruelties of poverty, that have never felt part and parcel of the social contract we all assume has been here since at least the formation of the union? This takes us to another fruitful discussion, one still concerned with how we frame conversations and what assumption we implicitly bring to them.

Some more general comments about assumptions, model building, and frames of reference are in order. To begin with, there is no harm in assuming almost anything one wants and conjuring a theory out of it as long as this is a logical exercise that says that if we assume this then that is what might come about. This is what most economists believe they are doing when they propose highly questionable assumptions or assumptions whose empirical value is neither made explicit nor tested. In these cases, the only danger is that we forget what assumptions were used and treat the model as if its own validity depends on how well it will work in practice, as some like George Stigler have argued: "A science is successful in the measure that it explains in general terms the behavior of the phenomena within its self-imposed boundaries" (1982, 15). In this case, the favored assumption was about *laissez-faire*. Whenever economic theory does not conform to the realities that it is supposed to explain or predict, other social variables may either reverse, annul, or contradict the conclusions drawn from said theories or models.

So here a second observation must be made, one already figuring prominently in Marx's critiques of the economists of his day, one repeated by Stigler, a Noble Laureate in economics, in regard to the fact that economists are content to "base their goals upon the ruling views of the educated classes" (ibid., 21), or more specifically, in terms of the political and economic elites whose perspective is given priority in the name of scientific objectivity and value neutrality. Unlike investigations into the secrets of the universe or subatomic structures, social studies are about human behavior and the conditions under which this behavior can be manipulated or improved. The fact that people in positions of power can influence one's study is more prone to happen in the social sciences where funding opportunities for research not only favor one area of research over the other, say, the benefits of tax cuts, but also influence the kind of results expected from them, as we regularly observe in think tanks whose policy recommendations prefigure in what data they select to present.

A third observation relating to the first two is that at times presumptions are knowingly imported into economic thinking that are patently false or that defy common sense and empirical data, such as the one about all transactions being "free of fraud and coercion" (ibid., 23). Should such a presumption even be granted a place in a mathematically sophisticated model? Shouldn't a thorough examination of its very veracity make any further investigation suspect if not abandoned? The standard excuse is that anything can be considered in a certain cognitive vacuum until its results are implemented, thereby insulating mathematical models from their relation to reality. But what is likely to happen is that such "thought experiments" eventually take hold of our imagination and are used as if they were true, as if they had a validity regardless of empirical testing. In fact, the danger of this process is greater than is admitted by well-meaning theorists who claim to merely present alternative models: they become the central talking points of politicians (recent cases of free trade agreements) and frame the ensuing debate.

A fourth observation is that whether we like it or not, all economic ideas and assumptions, all models and theories can be understood to be inherently or at their core ethical in the broad sense of the term. This means, for example, that speaking of competition or rationality is already speaking favorably about how people should behave, what normative principles they ought to uphold or follow. The notion of doing as one wishes in an equally free manner, as a *laissez-faire* attitude suggests to us, is tantamount to approving a form of disorganized human order where everyone can equally be trusted to do no harm to another and therefore let the world be without guidance or governance, as the expression goes: *Laissez-faire et laissez passer, le monde va de lui même!* ("Let do and let pass, the world goes on by itself!"). There are numerous moral features to this so-called economic doctrine, from the reliance on individuality and inevitable personal responsibility all the way to the Kantian Categorical Imperative that recalls the biblical Golden Rule. These are no idle and provisional economic assumptions and principles, but moral and social injunctions that evoke a universal belief in how humans should behave in this world.

A fifth observation is that whenever policy concerns dominate public discourse they are intended to resolve specific social and economic problems. Only some concerns make it to the agenda, and who puts them there and who is dealing with them in what priority is already a political move, one fraught with its own biases and prejudices, with a preset power relation whose own interests become clear. Poverty was neglected as a topic of public debate in the 2016 American presidential debates because the poor are underrepresented in the halls of government, they are less likely to be registered to vote, and even when they are, they are less likely to vote because of work and family obligations. Is it surprising, therefore, that we have less policies dedicated to eradicate poverty and many more concerned with tax policies and subsidies for large corporations?

Finally, these observations are meant to remind us why part I was a necessary prelude to examining how historically informed assumptions, principles, and frames of reference are used or abused over time. What is considered a reasonable view at some point given the historical contingencies of the period and its geographical boundaries becomes the "new normal," understood later as a standard and starting point from which to begin an economic discussion. And this new normal becomes naturalized to seem as if it's "natural" to be an economic agent with specific sets of values and innate attributes, natural in the divine sense our predecessors took for granted. And herein lies the crux of the matter: just because some idea or view was considered normal or acceptable at some point doesn't justify the legitimation of this idea or view as either divine or natural in any sense of the terms. On the contrary, when anyone tells us that it's obvious that something is the case or that everyone agrees that we all share certain characteristics, we should be on guard to remain skeptical and refuse universalizing anything about us or the economy. Our intellectual vigilance may protect us from condoning or condemning that which should not be condoned or condemned.

Chapter Nine

Alternative Models and the Question of Scale

This chapter examines some of the experiments with organizing society differently from democratic capitalism. The presumption here is that we are primarily dealing with market-capitalism in its *neoliberal* guise of the past few decades. There are other variants, but for the sake of simplicity we will contrast the other alternative models or theories of economic organization primarily with this neoliberal variant. It's important to reiterate that no matter the model, its sources, and its implementation, one overriding goal is always claimed to be paramount and that is *prosperity for all*. The notion of prosperity is problematic from a philosophical standpoint because it simultaneously captures material and nonmaterial features, culminating in a sense of happiness that the utilitarian model tried to quantify. How can we quantify and measure intangible features, such as peaceful coexistence and job satisfaction? Reductionist experiments attempted to do just that, asking questions and fitting their answers into matrices that could then be compared to others. Qualitative self-reporting, we have learned from psychologists, is notoriously unreliable, and our self-deception is probably more pervasive than we are willing to admit to our interrogators. So, to speak about prosperity in terms other than monetary ones is quite tricky if not impossible. The best we can do here is to suggest that the goal of personal prosperity amid the prosperity of others has been traditionally accepted and explicitly pursued. This has been true of First People's battle with neighboring tribes over resources as well of contemporary schemes to ensure the welfare of the most disadvantaged. Prosperity, however defined and qualified, is a worthy goal that can enrich one's soul as much as one's belly. Marx correctly insisted that with an empty belly our spirituality suffers, too; that our material conditions must be sufficiently good and nourishing that we will have the opportunity to do whatever we want (even if considered to be ironically phrased): "to hunt in the morning, to fish in the afternoon, rear cattle in the evening, criticize after dinner, just as I have in mind, without ever becoming hunter, fisherman, shepherd or critic" (Marx, *The German Ideology*). This is prosperity!

Those who think about prosperity may claim that it must be measured by how much we earn, have accumulated, and can afford to spend. Beyond a certain level of satisfying the necessities of food, shelter, and clothing, the rest may become wants rather than needs and be measured in terms of entertainment and travel, for some, or the ability to work less and meditate more (Livingston 2016). Though seemingly personal in their articulation, these are of course opinions we adopt from the social environments in which we live, being socialized into what does and does not count as being prosperous. In some cultures, it's about accumulation, in others it's about generosity, while still in others it's whether one has found the path to divine bliss and an afterlife. But regardless of the definitions of prosperity or well-being, all economic models and political institutions are designed, except for few abusive totalitarian regimes, as means by which to reach that goal. The debates over means are crucial, for they expose the potential for achieving the goal—will it be for the few or the many? Can everyone expect to achieve prosperity even if differently interpreted? This also brings up the point that what may be a happy moment for one, say watching a sports event with friends and plenty of pizza and beer, may not satisfy those who prefer musical performances or theater. We are not concerned, then, to choose among notions of happiness and prosperity, only to agree at this stage that prosperity is the watchword used by politicians and economists alike when proposing public policy, when relying on theoretical constructs.

Most models of political economy have appeared as a critique of previous ones, as was the case when capitalism was institutionalized in response to and as an outgrowth of feudalism. Capitalism as an economic system was promoted because it overthrew the unfair and exploitive agrarian arrangements of the past and could fit better the urbanized industrial revolutions that followed. It should be noted here that we are more concerned with economic and not political organizations, even though in some cases they get conflated or are a better "fit" with a particular political arrangement. This means, for example, that capitalist economies can do well under democratic regimes (United States, most of Europe, and parts of Asia), under military dictatorships (Chile), or under a totalitarian (one-party) regime (China). Likewise, socialist economies have existed under totalitarian regimes (USSR, China under Mao, and Cuba) and parliamentary democracies (parts of Scandinavia and Israel with their welfare variants). To confuse the economic with the political is to go down a slippery slope that condemns socialism and communism, as we have done since the Cold War, because of the utter failure of the Soviet Union. The failure was twofold and has little to do with socialism as such: first, Tsarist Russia leaped from its feudal status to a socialist one without the benefits of going through the capitalist stage that would have provided the surpluses with which to develop the welfare state; and second, under Stalinism state control was dictatorial and not open to the democratic mechanisms by which to adjust planning and reformulate production and consumption targets. Clarifying this confusion, we can move to discuss briefly the main differences among the five models and the presuppositions or principles on which they are based: *market-capitalism, socialism (and communism), market-socialism, communitarianism, and institutionalism.* The following are purposefully only brief sketches, as many forests have been used to publish thousands of books and leaflets, articles and essays that articulate the details of each one of them. In the name of brevity and environmental responsibility we should keep our survey short. Each case outlines the main principles and ideas associated with them.

1. Market-Capitalism

    a. Private property (material and intellectual rights)
    b. *Laissez-faire* ("invisible hand" or no government intervention)
    c. Competition (fair; equal opportunity to all; no monopolies)
    d. Market (no barriers to entry; efficient information flows; supply and demand determine prices)
    e. Division of labor (productivity; specialization)
    f. Money as the measure of all relations
    g. "Creative destruction" as a symbol and method of economic progress and growth
    h. Freedom of choice (individual initiatives and entrepreneurship)
    i. Rule of law and trust (The Golden Rule)

2. Socialism (and Communism)

    a. "From each according to his ability, to each according to his needs"
    b. Public property (state ownership, optional leases to individuals, strong commitment to the Commons)
    c. Cooperation (collaboration in the workplaces and other public spheres)
    d. Central planning (from minimal guidelines to specific quotas)
    e. Freedom of choice (profession, education, work)
    f. Equality (right to work; opportunities to all)

g. Welfare safety nets (government subsidies for the needy)
h. Individual initiatives subordinated to collective goals

3. Market-Socialism

a. Collective ownership of property (land and means of production)
b. Selective use of markets (resource allocation, efficiency regulations)
c. Central planning of long-term goals (implementation through markets, the state as employer of last resort)
d. Labor management of the economy
e. Freedom of choice (profession, education, work)
f. Equality (right to work, opportunities to all)
g. Welfare safety nets (government subsidies for the needy)
h. Individual initiatives subordinated to collective well-being

4. Communitarianism

a. Individuals are socially constituted, and therefore communal interests take precedence over individual choice (without paternalism)
b. Markets remain central but heavily regulated (policy directives)
c. Balancing free market entrepreneurship and social good
d. Corporatism as voluntary "team" enterprises parallel communitarian ideals
e. "Soft" and "Strong" versions give government varying roles in setting social standards and ensuring communal norms of conduct
f. More social and political than economic, but clear effects on how the economy should be structured

5. Institutionalism

a. Markets remain central (with state regulation)
b. Institutions shaping market and individual behavior
c. Evolutionary process of economic life (technological innovations)
d. Heterodox variants as critiques of neoclassical economics (from neo-Marxism, neo-Keynsianism, law and economics, and behavioral economics)

e. Institutional ("ceremonial") features are endogenous to economic analysis (and not exogenous)
f. Concern with "conspicuous consumption" and "absentee ownership"
g. Overall closer to socialism (and communism) than to capitalism

Even though these are shorthand descriptions of the various economic systems, it's worth commenting on their difference primarily in terms of what is foregrounded in their modeling. For example, the question of the balance between the individual and the State becomes clear in how each model tips its hand one way or the other, in some cases making the individual more important than anything the community or the State might need or prefer that it's unclear why that individual is even considered a member of that community. This is the sound of unbridled private property rights that defy any sense of collegiality as understood by John Stuart Mill, for example, who invoked the Harm Principle according to which our rights are circumscribed by the violation of others' rights (1859/1956). Admittedly, in Mill's age what constituted "harm" was considerably more straightforward than nowadays when indirect physical harm (water or air pollution) and other, even more intangible harms (invasion of privacy by drones or National Security Agency meta-data harvesting and cyberbullying). On the other hand, some believe that society or the State takes precedence over the individual, either in the extreme sense that the State has the right to order individuals what to do or coerce them into doing something they prefer not to do, or in a more benign sense that communal and social conventions and traditions guide the ways in which progress is planned and promoted (as in the case of healthcare policies banning smoking in public spaces). What becomes evident along this trajectory is the fact that even under socialism there is no prohibition of the use of market mechanisms when appropriate. The convenience of markets, even if only as "shadow" markets, to collect information and indicate appropriate prices is indisputable. As long as markets aren't abusive or exploitive, as long as they are highly regulated, and as long as they benefit society as a whole, there is nothing objectionable about them. This is true because under these conditions markets are not the final arbiters of wealth accumulation, if all participants share proportionally the means of production and profits (in light of their respective contributions), and therefore there shouldn't be a principled (as opposed to an emotional) rejection of their utility. Similarly, there should be no reason to object to some form of planning, central or somewhat decentralized, when it comes to long-term public projects such as railways and energy plants, military installations, and healthcare facilities.

As we can see from the above sketches, communitarianism as well as institutionalism could be understood as variants of socialism (and communism), while market-socialism is a compromise between socialism and capitalism. We could have added welfare economics as yet another variant of market-socialism where social safety nets are either quite widely spread or minimally available. What is not considered here are forms of utopianism on their own, since these models or theoretical proposals are indeed utopian insofar as they present their principles in the most ideal fashion as if no interferences would require compromises. Similarly, there are no actual exemplars of these models. Instead, it's more apparent that certain nation-states adopt some and not all the principles associated with these models to suit their circumstances, may it be the United States in one fashion (still recovering ideologically from its own slave-market economy of one hundred years) or China in another (still remaking itself from its dynastic empires to a communist regime endorsing capitalist principles). It's not surprising, then, to find the wealthy US economy offering numerous welfare programs that saddle its national budget into recurring deficits, while China is embracing market-capitalism in its march to rapid industrialization while concerned with centrally planning the fight against pollution. These mixed-models or hybrid economies are in fact experiments that try to bring the best features of the models listed above in order to provide that elusive sense of prosperity every political leader promises in order to get elected.

There have been a few attempts to conceptualize this hybrid economic model under the label of postcapitalism. Originally proposed by Peter Drucker (1993), "post-capitalist society" was designated as information-driven production economy that required a new kind of management. In his case, the most important novelty is the shift from industrial manufacturing to a more service-oriented economy in which computers would not only replace labor but also offer new methods of measurement to enhance management practices. A management guru, Drucker isn't interested in the theoretical underpinning of this concept but with its practical application. My own contribution (2009) was in response to the financial crisis of 2008 and was informed by postmodernism as much as by the desire to find the best of capitalism and socialism without endorsing either model wholesale. The postmodern influence is important because it allows for a plurality of approaches that are deployed case by case and without any preestablished hierarchy where one model is ideologically or empirically superior to another. It therefore allows for the selective choice of principles where appropriate without thereby violating one's fidelity to morality. In a sense, this postideological approach to solving economic problems accommodates the insights of libertarians, such as Popper and his piecemeal social engineering, and Marxist thinkers who worry about exploitation and alienation. The solutions don't conform in any predictable manner to preconceived economic institutions, but therefore offer a broader imaginative spectrum of options. And finally, there is the latest attempt by Paul Mason (2015), which suggests a postcapitalist system where the innovations of the Digital Age (as practiced in the shared economy) are prominent. Teasing out the best features of collaboration and open source, for example, of the information age, he emphasizes peer-to-peer exchanges and the ways in which we should organize the economy to safeguard for and bring about environmental sustainability. All three attempts move along the lines of the present book insofar as they emphasize the centrality of the economy (as Smith and Marx and their disciples do) and the ways in which philosophical thinking (or what social scientists call Theory) can contribute not to amplify disagreement but instead formulate ways of solving urgent social problems.

Another attempt to engage the "right" and "left" of the economic spectrum is evident in the work of Simon Griffiths. Instead of continuing the debates along Cold War rhetoric, he selects major leftist thinkers, such as David Miller, Raymond Plant, Hilary Wainwright, and Andrew Gamble, who seriously engaged with Friedrich Hayek. Hayek, as some recall, was Margaret Thatcher's conservative darling and an Austrian School economist turned Chicago School mainstay. Though the context is thoroughly British, the lessons from this study range far beyond its geographical confines: Should the left engage the right? Is such an engagement politically and philosophically fruitful? Both questions are answered in the affirmative. The left's engagement with the right isn't simply a conversation about the preference of socialism over capitalism and vice versa, but under what conditions can the market replace the role of the State. In the process, conceptual categories, such as socialism, the state, the market, equality, and liberty, are reexamined and at times redefined. According to Griffiths, the New Labour party revised its stance on socialism as an ideology and political platform that "values equality, but as a means to achieve greater freedom, rather than as an end in itself" (2014, 67). As we have seen before from this approach to model selection, we are empowered not to limit ourselves to one alleged superior model; we can mix and match different aspects of alternative models in a piecemeal fashion. This also means moving the discussion from one about socialism *versus* capitalism to parts of socialism *and* parts of capitalism.

The standard view of the relationship between equality (with socialism) and liberty (with capitalism) has been one of a trade-off: the more freedom, the less equality, and vice versa. In Griffiths's analysis, the relationship has been transformed into one where the one has become a condition for the other: more equality offers more freedom, and more freedom will allow greater equality. This indeed is a case of reworking basic assumptions underlying theoretical models in light of the British realities of the Thatcher neoliberal and draconian policies of divesting the government from its traditional roles, and the collapse of the Soviet Union and its satellite states in Eastern

Europe. Hayek was a worthy adversary for his leftist interlocutors because of his dogged consistency and his deep belief that markets weren't simply efficient mechanisms for resource allocations but the bedrock of any semblance of freedom. In Griffiths's words, Hayek's definition of the term *socialism* carried the day after World War II and primarily focused on its "abolition of private enterprise, of private ownership of the means of production, and the creation of a system of 'planned economy' in which the entrepreneur working for profit is replaced by a central planning body" (ibid., 23). This definition held true for proponents as well as opponents of socialism. One response to this characterization was the introduction of market-socialism, as mentioned above, because it offered both the social and public ownership of the means of production and the deliberate and selective usage of market tools, thereby freeing itself from any accusation of reverting to Soviet-like state control and poorly executed centralized planning. Market-socialism in its British formulation could claim adherence to the moral high ground of fairness and justice as articulated by the philosophers Rawls and Nozick.

Is market-socialism the hybrid solution to the contentious quarrels between socialists and capitalists? Market-socialism received some traction because it paid attention to individual freedom of choice not only of goods and services but also of work and self-expression, while retaining worker's cooperatives that are run like small enterprises, where compensation for work is shared by all the workers (ibid,. 36–37). Such formulations remained sensitive to the two main critiques of capitalism by socialists; namely, the concern with the "distributive inadequacies of capital" (as seen today in the increased inequalities of wealth and income portrayed by the 1 percent versus 99 percent), and the "quality of life in capitalist society" (as already expressed in Veblen's famous "conspicuous consumption" view of the "leisure class") (ibid., 39; 127). While realizing the fundamental dangers of market-capitalism, advocates of market-socialism had to be careful in finding what would make their proposals feasible: Can markets tease out the needs, wants, aspirations, and novel forms of coordination of free individuals? Will some limited form of private property increase individual and social responsibility? Will greater engagement through markets bring about a more cohesive society? By contrast, does state ownership necessarily lead to paternalism? And what does self-governance look like when consensus cannot be reached? In order to answer these questions, the role of government—with or without outright ownership of the means of production—comes into play as well. In this context, Griffiths cleverly reminds us of Daniel Bell's famous quip: "The nation state is becoming too small for the big problems of life, and too big for the small problems of life" (ibid., 126). The seesaw of individuals on the one end and the State on the other has been tipping very much in favor of rabid individualism because of the horrible experiences of fascism before and during World War II. But when the State is understood as the enemy, the coercive force that is inefficient and malevolent, then any sense of collective ownership and decision making is suspect.

An interesting set of questions is informed by Griffiths's analysis, some of which he covers himself, and some are left for others to pursue. Should economic models be exclusively devoted to the means of markets (equal opportunity and freedom of choice), for example, or should they also be concerned with ends (values that must be achieved by the end of the process)? Will it be enough if markets somehow took care of the least advantaged, the poor, and the uneducated? Are people trustworthy when it gets to their self-interested choices? Aren't they susceptible to manipulation and self-deception? Should markets themselves be responsible for social transformation, as we have seen above? Will any economic exchange, market bound or not, inevitably be and lead to differential power relations? Without responding to each of these questions, suffice it here to say that first, they hinge on the question of means versus ends when it gets to economic models (because the political ideologies that set them in motion must be discussed as well); and second, that three threats of political and legal framing of economic activities come to light: mistrust, coercion, and efficiency. Without trust that the government is indeed working on our behalf and has our best interest in mind, would we be more inclined to favor market solutions to all our problems, as if nature itself is offering its services?

Likewise, if we believe that the State is by definition a coercive force with the legitimate right to use violence as a punishment tool, will anything undertaken in its name appear benevolent or just? Even safety nets might be understood as self-serving and crowd controlling, ensuring that docile poor people don't riot in the streets and demand even more. Any regulation will be deemed inappropriate even when its purpose is to protect us, because we would claim our right to be free from any advice, oppressive or paternalistic, allowed to make our mistakes. And finally, when the State is always perceived to be inefficient and ill informed, using outdated technologies and insisting on arcane rules and procedures, people would resist following State planning. This is commonly understood as the inherent and inevitable waste of government bureaucracies, the ones that cost us time and money in order to conform to mandates we have never voted for. All three perennial critiques of the State can be answered, as Mazzucato (2014) has done in regard to the "entrepreneurial state," claiming that the United States has been more aggressive in risk taking than any corporation, and that the research it has underwritten for decades makes it possible for Silicon Valley to be the beacon of technological prowess. Similarly, one can explain that bureaucracies are also found in large corporations and that therefore the waste found in one set can be equally found in the other. And finally, trust is a social phenomenon rather than a personal choice, so that we see Europeans overall more trusting of their government's respective policies and agendas than Americans (even when populist movements take over there).

Political and intellectual leaders (not necessarily overlapping classes of people) are supposed to see the big picture of their societies and lead in a direction that can improve the human condition for the majority or their constituents. As such, they must be more concerned with large-scale economic issues, from the stability of the currency to decent employment and international trade agreements, and not focus on specific partisan economic issues brought to their attention by wealthy donors. In their economic platforms, they are called upon to deal with the infrastructure of the economy and the frameworks that will promote the success of all market sectors. Public goods (and not only what neoclassical economists called utilities) require resources that go beyond the capability of any single corporation to fund because of the timeframe and the resources that are required; moreover, this process is based on information about communities' expansion plans to accommodate corporate relocation. Developmental economist Paul Rosenstein-Rodan, who coined the term *big push* (1943) to describe the multifaceted approach to economic development, already envisioned infrastructure planning. Unlike his colleague, E. F. Schumacher, who lauded "small is beautiful" (1973) in the incremental development of businesses and sectors of the economy, Rosenstein-Rodan understood that a bird's-eye view was essential to develop and sustain an economy and its various markets. This is not to say that Schumacher's concern for how development affects people is overlooked by Rosenstein-Rodan, but rather that the latter's concern for people is more comprehensive in terms of the infrastructure that they need to thrive economically. What good is it to build a factory in a distressed area where jobs are needed if there are no utilities to ensure energy supplies? What benefit would a community receive when a new service center is built in its midst if there are no roads, trains, or buses to transport the workforce to and from their homes? One of the issues that plagues models or ways of (economic) thinking is that the complexity of organizing a group of people to exchange and to interact, to live and prosper, isn't limited or cannot exclusively rely on Smith's claim about the propensity of people to barter and trade. Perhaps a small village of twenty families can rely on this "natural" propensity (which is then theoretically understood as common sense or as normal). What happens on a larger scale?

A BRIDGE

At this juncture, having shown how economic models betray a commitment to certain assumptions or frames of reference, and having illustrated some of the differences among the economic models most common in the debates of political philosophers, and before moving to part III, one additional variable ought to be mentioned. This is scale. Is one economic model more appropriate than another just because of its scale? Put differently, given that models by definition are theoretical constructs that we'd like to apply to real societies, are they equally scalable? We mentioned this variable briefly in relation to the social contract, where it seemed quite reasonable that every Athenian citizen should know the rules of the city-state and participate in its operation, from military service and legislative responsibilities to its judicial functions. Can the same be said of a country the size of China with over one billion population? Can one's affinity with one's community and one's tolerance for difference among its members seamlessly translate into solidarity? One wonders who exactly is referred to when the likes of Richard Rorty speak of solidarity (1989). Is it limited to upper-middle-class white males of privilege or society with its various minorities, not to mention the very disenfranchised unregistered or undocumented poor? Questions of scale, the size of the population, the size of the market, and the size of States have been brought up in the context of expanding globalization. Principles of fairness and equal opportunity may resonate in your village square and factory floor, but can they be exercised on the global stage? Cultural differences and the customs to which some traditions still adhere may cause levels of consternation unseen in the halls of Wall Street, where Ivy League degrees abound and where wealth is a prerequisite for future success. Implying that markets in and of themselves are mere conduits for economic exchange necessarily lead to misguided and unfortunate expectations. To expect that everyone will behave like us, and that we can categorically extend our set of beliefs to every continent around the globe, reeks of traditional colonialism. We should know better by now how to distinguish among people and cultures, and how to more carefully navigate exchange relations so as to avoid offending or harming others even though we have the financial power to do so. Recalling the treatment of Native Americans and the American history of slavery, we should admit that some have been so profoundly harmed that no degree of so-called respect or reparation would ever undo the cruelty and injustice of the past. We must also concede that some would reject any model (or hybrid model) because they'd be suspicious of taking part in exchanges that declare themselves to be based on mutual respect and solidarity when none can be detected, or when detected, may not be genuine, or when previous injustices are forgotten.

It was scale, too, which was the pivot around which the critique of socialist planning was conducted, assuming that no central committee could ever fully apprehend the complex and diverse tastes and preferences of millions of individuals. But is this true in the age of digital computing, when smartphone applications can interact in real time on a huge platform with millions of others? Aren't our modes of computing and analysis so much more sophisticated that we can account for scales much larger than ever envisioned? Aren't we daily participating in various incredibly large markets for available transportation (Uber and Lyft) or for sleeping accommodations (Airbnb)? As we shall see in the next part, the advantages and disadvantages of several alternative economic arrangements and organizations are tested along these lines as well, so that the idealized modeling we have glimpsed at so far are recalibrated. In teasing out the principle and values that we'd like to maintain in our economic relationships with others, it becomes apparent that models are not exclusively economic but social and political, communicative and moral. As such, assumptions about people and their nature, their natural and social conditions, will continue to reemerge in every debate and critique, always relevant when we make choices about how we should live. And how we should live will never be reducible to some material measure of prosperity, but will include a level of satisfaction and happiness that bespeaks of the integrity and spirituality of humanity. Smith and his neoliberal disciples claimed to seek the Marxian ideals of humans free from exploitation and alienation. If we remember this along our journey, we may be more open to consider the different methods they prefer and why they think their preference indeed leads to an ideal life for all.

Part III

Current Models

Having underlined the basic presuppositions of market-capitalism in part I, and having teased out some of the dangerous and useful assumptions we carry into the twenty-first century in part II, it's time to critically examine some of the current theories and platforms that are paraded around as if they offer the solutions to all that plagues market-capitalism. As will become clear from these separate but related expositions, most of the promises to cure the ills of market-capitalism end up challenging some but not all of their underlying principles.

In chapter 10, some forms of contemporary capitalism (or variants of market-capitalism) are briefly examined, such as philanthrocapitalism that promises that the fruits of the game played in the marketplace find their way, admittedly indirectly, into the hands of the needy. Let us make billions and then we'll make sufficient donations to worthwhile causes and draw attention to our good deeds rather than to the means by which profits were acquired. This is an old narrative that dates back to the so-called robber barons of the nineteenth century whose names now grace palaces of philanthropy—Rockefeller, Carnegie, Mellon, and many others. They eventually inspire twentieth century billionaires, such as Bill Gates, to follow suit. In the *age of distraction*, we look with amazement at the latest shiny object wealthy donors show off in public—treating malaria in Africa, helping flood victims in Haiti—and overlook how that wealth was obtained. The point here is not to denigrate the generosity of donors, but only to ensure we don't thereby give credence to the morally objectionable principle of *the means justify the ends* or argue that if only capitalism were revised here and there it would be as moral as envisioned by its founders.

In chapter 11, when we inquire about the promises of globalization as the panacea for all our regional failures, we may discover that when unequal partners trade, the strong will benefit at the expense of the weak. This may be true in financial as well as ecological terms. So instead we assume that the benefits envisioned by Smith in the eighteenth century (when parts of the world were loosely connected if at all) will be the same in the twenty-first century when we are *overconnected* or connected in precarious ways (as the financial meltdown and the Great Recession illustrated with global failures).

In chapter 12, those who wish to point out that Intellectual Property Rights are outdated capitalist ideals (though enshrined in the US Constitution) by pointing out the success of the Knockoff Economy may focus their attention too narrowly. In other words, is their critique scalable to all market sectors? Can we extrapolate from this case to other market principles, such as profit maximizing and exploitation? Will the alienation of the workforce be eliminated by the Knockoff Economy as well?

And finally, in chapter 13, when examining the latest arrival of the Sharing Economy, what ideals are being challenged? When they are, in terms of access instead of ownership (of cars and houses, tools and equipment), does this really entail a departure from market-capitalism? In other words, are we merely shifting the conversation to the digital platform while still incorporating all the vices of monetizing human relations? Have exchanges transformed from market-profiteering and greed to more nuanced and morally acceptable principles of sharing for the sake of sharing, of trusting because humans are good by nature? These are the questions that inform the following four chapters.

Chapter Ten

Contemporary Capitalisms and Their Faults

In this chapter various forms of contemporary market-capitalism will be examined so as to ascertain whether or not they can bring us closer to the "quest for prosperity," which is the title of our book. As we move from one formulation to the other, we intend to offer a brief critical evaluation of its prospects in terms of the previous two parts of the book. We should note that as we briefly survey some of these positively phrased labels, they seem to implicitly accept or broadly understand that the advantages of market-capitalism, locally and globally, rely on the motto: "The rising tide lifts all the boats." This aphorism states that any improvement in one sector of the economy (or even of one company among many) will eventually and indirectly benefit the rest of the economy. It is attributed to President Kennedy, who used it in a 1963 speech to defend his interventionist policies in regard to public works, such as roads and dams. Instead of them being perceived as "pork-barrel" projects that are considered paybacks for political endorsement of legislators, they should be understood in the Keynesian sense of overall stimulus projects to get the economy going again. More importantly in this chapter are the ways in which market-capitalism is reconfigured so that its latest negative press—in regard to the financial crisis of 2008 and the global meltdown of the banking sector and the bailout intervention of the State— may be corrected if not forgotten. In other words, looking to address public outrage over the mishandling of the global economy and the obvious fault lines of market-capitalism has brought about a resurgence of new ideas for what capitalism in the twenty-first century should look like. The background critique that accompanies this brief survey is that if only the packaging has changed, then the basic assumptions and frameworks of the market model, what some would call its rotten core, have not been sufficiently addressed or changed since the Industrial Revolution.

I: INCLUSIVE CAPITALISM

When Winnie Byanyima, the executive director of Oxfam International, suggests that the "richest 1 percent will own more than all the rest by 2016," and when she is also the cochair of the annual World Economic Forum in Davos, Switzerland, the rest of the world's leaders may listen. What is fascinating, though, and what goes to the heart of the argument of the present book, is the fact that she admits that "extreme inequality isn't just a moral wrong. We know that it hampers economic growth and it threatens the private sector's bottom line" (2015). The rub isn't that there is some unfairness in the distribution of wealth across the global stage, but that this inequality will eventually "hamper economic growth" since poor people cannot participate in the consumption process that brings about production. The outrageous fact that "1 in 9 people do not have enough to eat and more than a billion people still live on less than $1.25-a-day" is only part of the problem (the moral side of the coin); the other part of the problem is that poor people spend all their income on basic commodities, and when they have nothing to spend, the general economy suffers (the economic side of the same coin). Oxfam's research has shown that "the richest 1 percent have seen their share of global wealth increase from 44 percent in 2009 to 48 percent in 2014 and at this rate will be more than 50 percent in 2016" (ibid.). This, of course, leaves the rest of the global population in either dire poverty straits or in such a disadvantaged economic position that they hardly contribute to world consumption.

In case the dual character of Byanyima's comments was obscured, she has made it apparent: "Business as usual for the elite isn't a cost free option—failure to tackle inequality will set the fight against poverty back decades. The poor are hurt twice by rising inequality—they get a smaller share of the economic pie and because extreme inequality hurts growth, there is less pie to be shared around" (ibid.). The point is that it becomes in the best interest of the wealthy to "include" the poor in the economy, as they tend to spend all their incomes and thereby become important contributors to overall economic activity. She continues: "All those gathering at Davos who want a stable and prosperous world should make tackling inequality a top priority" (ibid.). This comes on the heels of Oxfam making headlines at Davos in 2014 "with the revelation that the 85 richest people on the planet have the same wealth as the poorest 50 percent (3.5 billion people)" (ibid.). Perhaps what is alluded to here is the fact that 1 percent may be noticing that they, too, are reaching a tipping point of wealth inequality, because they'll find themselves in a position where such inequality is detrimental to sustaining their position.

Without the spending of the 99 percent, their income and wealth will inevitably shrink.

The international agency was calling on governments across the globe to adopt seven policy principles: first, "clamp down on tax dodging by corporations and rich individuals"; second, "invest in universal, free public services such as health and education"; third, "share the tax burden fairly, shifting taxation from labour and consumption towards capital and wealth"; fourth, "introduce minimum wages and move towards a living wage for all workers"; fifth, "introduce equal pay legislation and promote economic policies to give women a fair deal"; sixth, "ensure adequate safety-nets for the poorest, including a minimum income guarantee"; and seventh, "agree to a global goal to tackle inequality" (ibid.). Incidentally, Nafeez Ahmed, in his "Inclusive Capitalism Initiative Is Trojan Horse to Quell Coming Global Revolt," explains that this new terminology is meant primarily as a public relations stunt by the very wealthy British conglomerates worried about the capitalist model after the 2008 financial crisis (2014). Is this about those left out of the markets or a pernicious concern with avoiding greater government scrutiny and the ensuing regulations that might clamp down on the excesses of the very rich?

The academic support for this way of thinking about Inclusive Capitalism has been established with C. K. Prahalad's *The Fortune at the Bottom of the Pyramid* (2005), who argues that we should first focus on the bottom of the market pyramid (the poor), and then appreciate those at the bottom of the wealth scale as consumers who contribute to the stability and growth of this market pyramid. Another early academic publication that explains the need of caring about the poor as potential consumers vital to the survival of market-capitalism is Allen Hammond (2001), who argues that privatizing public services is helpful for the inclusion of the poor in the market. As far as he is concerned, government policies have failed the poor, and only nongovernment organizations and the private sector can restore the inclusion of the poor in markets for their eventual prosperity. What becomes evident, along the lines of the argument proposed by Oxfam, is that the "world's poor—families with an annual household income of less than $6,000—is enormous. The 18 largest emerging and transition countries include 680 million such households, with a total annual income of $1.7 trillion—roughly equal to Germany's annual gross domestic product" (Hammond and Prahalad 2004, 32). More broadly speaking, we can safely say that European governments, by comparison to the United States and certainly the so-called emerging markets, have done relatively well to combat poverty, so that critics like Hammond and Prahalad are projecting American experiences.

As we can tell from this brief summary, the inclusion of a larger portion of the global population in market-capitalism ends up being self-serving. This public relations move aims to protect market-capitalism as we know it.

It's obvious that if wealth is concentrated at the very top, no matter how much the rich spend, they'll never spend as much as the poor , both in terms of the percentage allocated to consumption as well as in the actual total expenditures. When poor people participate in the markets, markets grow; when they are excluded or only included indirectly through government sub-sidies, economic growth is slow if not reversed. So, this notion of Inclusive Capitalism is not an alternative to market-capitalism as observed globally, but a mere trope in a marketing offensive to buttress the frail neoclassical and neoliberal model of capitalism. We might give credence to another interpre-tation about the 1 percent (if we choose to treat them as a singular sentient entity) as a group or class of people whose supreme goal may no longer be unlimited wealth, but power and control. Some channel their money into change (philanthropy) and others to paranoid control (political candidates and parties).

II: POPULAR/CONSUMER CAPITALISM

According to the *Oxford English Dictionary*, Popular Capitalism is defined as "a type of capitalism in which the public are encouraged to own shares, property, small businesses, etc.; the theory or practice of this." This is in line with the previously examined notion of Inclusive Capitalism wherein the public is encouraged to join markets, but here not merely as consumers but as owners. Incidentally, this is already happening to a large extent through employees's pension funds that are invested in the stock or bond markets. In doing so, these pension funds have directly taken ownership positions in large publicly traded corporations and thereby indirectly made their members owners of those companies. In case one wonders what magnitude of money we are discussing here, one should note a conservative estimate: "In January 2008, *The Economist* reported that Morgan Stanley estimates that pension funds worldwide hold over US \$20 trillion in assets, the largest for any category of investor ahead of mutual funds, insurance companies, currency reserves, sovereign wealth funds, hedge funds, or private equity" (Wikipe-dia). Putting this in perspective, the US Gross Domestic Product in 2015 was \$18.5 trillion. So, the very idea that more of the public could and should participate in market-capitalism as owners rather than simply as consumers or workers is hereby highlighted and encouraged with the notion of Popular Capitalism.

We should also note that this notion of Popular rather than Consumer Capitalism underscores the positive connotation associated with markets. We can recall that in the immediate aftermath of the 9/11 attack on the Twin Towers in New York City, President Bush entreated Americans to go on shopping trips, travel to Disneyland, and promote economic prosperity. This is, of course, not as cynical as it may sound, since about 70 percent of the national GDP comes from consumer spending. But unlike the upbeat presidential promotion of consumption, Consumer Capitalism has had also a negative connotation associated with it. In this context, Veblen's notion of "conspicuous consumption" explored in *The Theory of the Leisure Class* (1899) and R. H. Tawney's concerns in *The Acquisitive Society* (1920) must be recalled. As the Gilded Age of the late nineteenth century and the beginning of the twentieth century brought with it more ubiquitous marketing and advertisement outlets, and thereby also became part of the popular media, it overwhelmed the airwaves and print media. The negative aspects come about with the idea that consumption is manipulated by large corporations so that we end up consuming not necessarily what we need or even want, but rather what these corporations produce for sale. One feature that is introduced along this trajectory is "planned obsolescence": whatever we produce becomes useless or defective sooner rather than later and thereby forces consumers to replace more often the same product, may it be cars whose exterior look and features are changed from year to year (rather than the five-year span originally thought to be appropriate for technological innovations related to car manufacturing) all the way to personal computers later in the twentieth century and the ever-present iPhone that Apple brings to the market with greater frequency than is either technologically required or expected by users.

Raymond Williams's warnings in *The Long Revolution* (1961) that there has been a cultural revolution afoot alongside the political and industrial revolutions are prescient; the very language we use to describe social roles has transformed our views of those roles. As we have become "consumers" rather than citizens or workers, for example, it has become clear that we are perceived by market forces and corporate giants as defining ourselves in these terms, terms that seem popular and almost enticing—we are the consumers who choose what to buy—but in fact we are being manipulated to think that we are in charge. Instead of thinking of ourselves as consumers, Williams recommends that we think of ourselves as "users" who actually make judgments about what to use and how to use what we might purchase, thereby granting us more powers of discernment as well as humanizing our participation in the marketplace. Lastly, if understood in consumption terms exclusively, there is a tendency to think of our activities as short rather than long term, as if all our market engagements are consumptive in the here and now. As part of the Cultural Studies movement he helped usher into existence during the 1960s and 1970s in the UK, Williams turned the notion of Consumer Capitalism on its moral head, teasing out its manipulative aspects as a warning against turning culture as a whole into a form of consumption, popular or not.

Similarly, the French Jean Baudrillard also offers a full-fledged postmodern and sociological critique of mass consumption and the capitalist trappings in which we are caught as we move to mass production and hyperbole mass communication. For him, "Consumption is a system which secures the ordering of signs and the integration of the group: it is therefore both a morality (a system of ideological values) and a communication system, a structure of exchange" (1998, 78). In this manner, consumer culture surpasses individuals as a locus of enjoyment and happiness, and imposes itself "upon them by way of an unconscious social constraint" (ibid.). The nature of the constraint, the subconscious control it has on all of us, turns its positive effects into negative ones, where we are bound to consume even if we are reticent to do so. Baudrillard continues to argue that "the whole discourse on consumption aims to make the consumer Universal Man, to make him the general, ideal and definitive embodiment of the Human Race and to turn consumption into the beginnings of a 'human liberation' that is to be achieved instead of, and in spite of, the failure of political and social liberation" (ibid., 85). According to this view, Consumer Capitalism takes over the social and political domains and in doing so empties them from any significance as counterparts to the vicious cycle of incessant production and consumption. What is at stake when consumption alone is foregrounded in the life of individuals, when their socio-political and their moral lives are taken over by material conveniences and objects of consumption, then, is nothing less than "a potential for deep crises and new contradictions" (ibid.). What crises and contradictions does Baudrillard have in mind as early as 1970? His prescient analysis points to the business cycle as a form of impending crisis where consumers are hurt by overextending their credit and by buying more than they can afford, and consuming beyond their means, especially when these means are regulated by a labor market that is divorced from the cycle of overconsumption. What happens to the individual? How do individuals perceive their identity? Are they citizens first and consumers next, or is it the reverse? How do we judge our fellow humans if not by their modes of consumption? With these questions in mind, we can appreciate the Marxist-postmodern critique that lurks behind the temptations of Consumer Capitalism.

Returning to Popular Capitalism, Paul Keitheley reminds us that when British political leaders speak of "socially responsible and genuinely popular capitalism," they are indeed projecting their wishes more than describing what happens in market-capitalism. As Keitheley asks: "Can Britain, in Cameron's words, 'improve [the] market by making it fair and free where many more people have a stake in the economy and a share in the rewards of success' and still adhere to the components of a capitalist economy?" (2015) The key words are *have a stake in the economy*, even when other words, such as *fair*, *free*, and *success* are intermingled to paint a rosy picture of "capitalist economy." In this positive "wishful thinking" of the British prime minister at the time, a sense of Inclusive Capitalism is introduced to bring more market participants to feel that their ownership, direct or indirect, is accompanied by a way of having a stake in the future success of the market as a whole. What is being sold alongside greater involvement is an ideological sense of freedom from government regulation and perhaps a sense of fairness that was lost after the financial crash of 2008. And at the heart of the political plea, as Keitheley correctly sees it, there is implicitly much more: "Mr. Cameron may be attempting to straddle too great a divide—calling for a friendlier, fuzzier capitalism which does right by the collective while avoiding a challenge to the basic principles of competition and individual achievement. Popular capitalism's vision to 'spread wealth, spread freedom, and spread opportunity,' while good rhetoric, may remain simply that" (ibid.).

As we reconsider the appeal of Popular Capitalism as a call to arms for all participants in the marketplace, a call for greater involvement through some form of ownership, what may be missing is the inherent inability of such a promise to ever be accomplished. Is it possible for everyone to own part of the market? And even if we created the mechanisms by which we became owners of some sort, would this change overnight our positions within the market? Would our wealth be necessarily increased? Or, would the rich still be so much richer than the poor, no matter the miniscule sense of ownership imbued in their daily lives? Would exploitation and alienation disappear? What is at issue here are the power-relations that ensue when one has more than the other not simply on the margins but at the extreme, the kind of extremes alluded to above in the Oxfam report. You can tell people all day long that by simply buying a refrigerator or personal computer they have become owners of LG or Dell, respectively, but this would be laughable in real terms, no different than if you told factory workers that their pension fund is the largest shareholder of GM or Apple: What difference does this make? How could they ever translate this long-term investment into a short-term pay raise or improved healthcare provision they need right now?

III: RESPONSIBLE/CONSCIOUS CAPITALISM

Without getting into the thickest of British New Labour politics, the notion of Responsible Capitalism has been at the center of some debates, where Ed Miliband's use of the term has been challenged as either "doublespeak" or a contradiction in terms (Panitch 2014). Those promoting the term claim that despite the evidence of irresponsibility displayed in the 2008 financial crisis—where large banks squandered billions of dollars and failed to adhere to their own capitalist goals of profit maximizing and caring for the interests of their shareholders—there is a way in which capitalism can be redeemed: using market efficiencies, governments can guarantee that welfare policies are protected. Critics, on the other hand, claim that market-capitalism, as we have recently experienced it, is skewed on behalf of the few at the expense of the many, and that government intervention is primarily to bail failed enterprises under the rubric of "too big to fail." In this debate, the very mention of capitalism with any moral commitment to responsibility is dismissed: if your goal is to maximize profits and leave exogenous costs (environmental pollution and healthcare, to name just two variables) to be borne by the State (and its taxpaying citizens), then of course any talk of being responsible is simply rhetorical. In other words, to claim moral fortitude to the faceless marketplace and its corporate handlers is to make a claim that is neither empirically nor legally substantiated. As we have seen with the irresponsibility of the financial industry between 2008 and 2012, banks may have been fined for maleficence, but no bankers have been found guilty and no officers have gone to prison. CNBC reported on October 30, 2015, that about $204 billion have been paid in penalties in 175 settlements since 2009, and the clock is still ticking with more cases and fines. But despite this staggering amount, with whom does responsibility lie in this context? Is it with individual leaders of Big Business or with all of the employees, from engineers at VW to bank tellers at Wells Fargo?

Dal LaMagna lumps together the notion of Responsible Capitalism with the notion, more commonly understood, of Corporate Social Responsibility. But he explains that "Corporate Social Responsibility is a term with no universally established definition. Conceptualization of CSR varies by company size, type and culture as well as social and economic context." But despite this, "Here, we'll define it as the voluntary integration of social, environmental and stakeholder concerns in the enterprises' daily business operations—or, as the European Commission defined it in 2011: 'the responsibility of enterprises for their impacts on society'" (2016). Whether quantified in terms of carbon footprint or the amount of air or water pollution, corporations both in Europe and the United States have been under pressure by environmentalists, government regulators, and even their own shareholders to treat the environment more carefully, paying for the damage that they have caused. But one may ask, is it reasonable first to cause harm and then to offer to pay for its consequences? Why not be proactive and plan on minimal invasive or detrimental effects from the very start, and thereby prove how responsible one is to begin with? Standard Business Ethics texts from the 1970s and 1980s have raised these questions within the context of environmental disasters, such as Three Mile Island of 1979 in the United States and the Bhopal disaster of 1984 in India. Should CEOs be put on trial? Are corporations to be treated, legally speaking, as individuals? It's fascinating that in the US legal system the *Citizens United v. Federal Election Commission* (2010) was more concerned with freedom of speech rights accorded to corporations as if they were individual citizens, while ignoring the implications of malfeasance and fraud. It should be emphasized, then, that regardless of how the rich or large multinational corporations see themselves as separate from the rest of the world—because they feel they control it—they nevertheless remain bound to the fate of their customers and the 99 percent, because what we call "externalities" affect us all, from poisoned water to polluted air, from neglected roadways to battered train stations and airports.

LaMagna continues to explain that corporate responsibility "spreads beyond the scope of sustainability," since corporations are powerful agents of change. Their self-motivation is based on the fact that socially responsible actions "can bring forth improved financial performance, reduced operating costs, enhanced brand image reputation, increased sales and customer loyalty, increased productivity and quality, increased ability to attract and retain employees, reduced regulatory oversight, access to capital, and finally lower human resource costs" (ibid.). With all of these potential and practical advantages, when *branding* has become such a catchword for anything worthy to remember about a company and its products, why not claim to be engaged in a long process of morally being "responsible"? (ibid.) According to this presentation, it's in the best interest of corporations to become more rather than less responsible. And if this is the case, can one speak honestly about Responsible Capitalism? Is the responsible behavior of one or many corporations in the market qualify the market as a whole to be labeled *Responsible*? Our logic students are familiar with the fallacy of composition: the mistaken belief that what is true of one member of the group is true of the group as a whole. But the moral problem is amplified when utilitarian-like principles are invoked: Monsanto, for example, is simultaneously charged with improving food conditions for millions in the developing countries and in draught-ridden developed countries while wresting control from local communities and farmers and exerting (rent) prices that a free and competitive grain market would not tolerate. In the face of misleading or overbearing public relation campaigns, how can we assess corporate responsibility?

Similarly, suggesting that capitalism as a system is either responsible for or conscious of its market activities is committing the fallacy associated with anthropomorphism, the attribution of human characteristics or behavior to an inanimate economic system. But perhaps this is only loose talk, one that grounds capitalism morally, the kind we have already seen in Smith's *The Theory of Moral Sentiments* (1759), where human affection for others and the happiness derived from seeing others thrive is considered a foundation for exchanges in markets. Perhaps what we are left with is more of an advertisement campaign, as is the case with Hermes, an Investment Management company that offered in October 2015 a report on "Responsible Capitalism and Diversity." These kinds of reporting, even if genuine, have primarily a public relation interest in mind: wishing to portray themselves in a positive light in the face of growing cynicism by the public at large. When you meet someone and the first thing that comes out of their mouth is that they are moral, how do you react? When vendors begin negotiations by proclaiming their Christianity, are you more likely to trust them?

In case one wonders how institutionalized the notion of Responsible Capitalism has become, you can check First: The Forum for Decision Makers, and observe that in addition to government regulations that hold corporations accountable for their behavior in the marketplace, there are other means by which this approach is promoted. In its website, First makes the following claim for its international awards: "The concept of the Award for Responsible Capitalism is based on the belief that whilst commercial success can be measured in terms of standard criteria, social responsibility involves a far greater sense of the needs of the wider community, in the areas of in which business operates, as well as environmental initiatives and support for the arts and culture." Continuing to read in the website: "When making the Award the judges are looking for a business leader who has consistently demonstrated social responsibility as an integral part of commercial success, examining in particular the manner in which their business interacts both with the environment and the communities in which they operate; someone who has run a company in a clearly responsible way" (2016). Here we can appreciate the insistence that this responsible behavior be an "integral part of commercial success," one that is measured by growth and profitability. The question arises, What if it's impossible to be both profitable and responsible at the same time? What if there is an inevitable price to be paid for greater responsibility so that not everyone can afford this moral luxury? The assumption here is that there is no trade-off between "commercial success" and "responsibility." Is this indeed true for all cases in market-capitalism? Does the reward system, associated with market-capitalism, account for one's responsibility or only for the bottom line? Do corporate boards care about the moral compass according to which corporate officers operate? And if they do, how have they instituted such focus in corporate policies?

If one were to subsume Conscious Capitalism under the general rubric of Responsible Capitalism, there is a nonprofit organization that calls itself Conscious Capitalism, Inc., which is exclusively dedicated to educate entrepreneurs and nonprofit organizations to further the four principles that guide its mission. Its credo says on its website: "We believe that business is good because it creates value, it is ethical because it is based on voluntary exchange, it is noble because it can elevate our existence and it is heroic because it lifts people out of poverty and creates prosperity. Free enterprise capitalism is the most powerful system for social cooperation and human progress ever conceived." It then continues to outline guiding principles according to which every business ought to be organized. The four principles are Higher Purpose, Stakeholder Orientation, Conscious Leadership, and Conscious Culture. As for Higher Purpose, the website claims that "while making money is essential for the vitality and sustainability of a business, it is not the only or even the most important reason a business exists. Conscious businesses focus on their purpose beyond profit" (2016). It continues to say that "we all need meaning and purpose in our lives. It is one of the things that separates us from other animals. Purpose activates us and motivates us . . . By focusing on its deeper Purpose, a conscious business inspires, engages and energizes its stakeholders. Employees, customers and others trust and even love companies that have an inspiring purpose." As for Stakeholder Orientation, "unlike some businesses that believe they only exist to maximize return on investment for their shareholders, Conscious Businesses focus on their whole business ecosystem, creating and optimizing value for all of their stakeholders, understanding that strong and engaged stakeholders lead to a healthy, sustainable, resilient business. They recognize that, without employees, customers, suppliers, funders, supportive communities and a life-sustaining ecosystem, there is no business. Conscious Business is a win-win-win proposition, which includes a healthy return to shareholders." The third principle, Conscious Leadership, claims that "Conscious Leaders focus on 'we,' rather than 'me.' They inspire, foster transformation and bring out the best in those around them. They understand that their role is to serve the purpose of the organization, to support the people within the organization and to create value for all of the organization's stakeholders. They recognize the integral role of culture and purposefully cultivate a Conscious Culture of trust and care." And finally, the principle of Conscious Culture means: "Culture is the embodied values, principles and practices underlying the social fabric of a business, which permeate its actions and connects the stakeholders to each other and to the company's purpose, people and processes. A Conscious Culture fosters love and care and builds trust between a company's team members and its other stakeholders. Conscious Culture is an energizing and unifying force, that truly brings a Conscious Business to life" (ibid.).

The approach to business transactions in and out of the marketplace is not limited to one group of promoters who are self-serving in offering their workshops and literature but has been picked up by academics as well. John Mackey and Raj Sisodia argue, "Ultimately conscious businesses create lasting value as the world evolves to even greater levels of prosperity, helping billions of people flourish and lead lives infused with passion, purpose, love and creativity—a world of freedom, harmony, prosperity and compassion" (2014). Dan Schawbel echoes this way of thinking in more popular media (*Forbes*) when stating that "conscious capitalism can help rebuild corporate reputations, companies can give back to the community while still making a profit, the key pillars for conscious capitalism, and more" (2013). Does this mean that this new label, Conscious Capitalism, is mere packaging or a
· public relations stunt to cover up for capitalist maleficence? He claims otherwise. For him, it seems that "this is a way of thinking about business: to ensure that it is grounded in a higher purpose to enhance its positive impact

on the world. When reinvented in this way, capitalism is an extraordinarily powerful system of value creation mutually benefiting all stakeholders" (ibid.). The notion of reinvention can be interpreted in either positive or negative ways, appreciating the need to redirect the focus of the business, but in case capitalism were to lose its luster, we are left with the notion of "value creation," whatever it means in this context. We can reinvent capitalism all we want, but unless we discount, however mildly or completely, the profit motive, all we are talking about is what's a reasonable profit margin given the operating context. To be sure, the goal could remain to garner some profit, only this time within a new framework that assigns monetary value to intangibles and material objects where there were none before (replacing the maxim of "profit at all costs"). Perhaps the new maxim will not change much, except that it will incorporate more variables, such as political stability and moral values.

Putting these principles together, it seems that Conscious Capitalism takes a step further along the Responsible Capitalism trajectory in reorienting its followers to look at the big picture, so to speak, and worry as much about the meaning of their businesses as well as the culture within which they are operating. Though pushing ahead with a more comprehensive and even self-reflective moment in their overall strategy, it's unclear how much this movement deviates from market-capitalism. Is it willing to undo a business plan, for example, because it might not have a "higher purpose"? Is it willing to eschew the whole profit motive in the name of caring about "stakeholders"? In other words, how much can one expect of a "conscious leader" outside of being more aware about treating employees with respect and care about their personal concerns and family life? As mentioned before, perhaps this movement is a step ahead of Inclusive Capitalism and Responsible Capitalism, but it seems still framed and operationally beholden to market-capitalism. As such, this (loosely labeled) movement wants to change, but it should acknowledge that social justice progress was not handed out to those needing it but was fought for by generations of activists and unions, local cooperatives, and leftist intellectuals.

VI: PHILANTHROCAPITALISM

There are at least two ways of explaining philanthrocapitalism: it is understood as either a new way entrepreneurs tackle social problems, seeing themselves as social investors who bring market-capitalism principles to ensure efficiency and market discipline, or as a goal assumed by businesses that all or part of their profits will be donated to charitable organizations and causes. The second interpretation of philanthrocapitalism is of little interest here as it follows generations of wealthy entrepreneurs who set up family foundations through which to fund charity: once profits are amassed, a portion of them is given away. This way of behaving doesn't touch the very foundation and principles of market-capitalism, and in fact could be used, morally speaking, to be in line with the idea that the end (funding charities) justifies the means (aggressive and even brutal accumulation of wealth at the expense of workers and competitors alike). This variant is morally problematic if not outright immoral. The other variant, by contrast, is more benign on the face of it, but it in fact assumes all the moral weaknesses of market-capitalism, importing the for-profit mentality and practice into the nonprofit world. The argument here is that greater good could be achieved with greater emphasis on the bottom line and on overcoming endemic inefficiencies that plague the non-profit world.

Thinking that market-capitalism can be a model for any organization, including those dedicated to philanthropy, younger entrepreneurs emphasize three elements that ought to be followed: first, the target should be thought of in terms of an investment of sorts that yields results; second, an infrastructure should be set in place so that the investment will be part of a greater whole; and third, philanthropists themselves ought to behave like social investors who allocate resources effectively and expect returns on their so-called in-vestment (*The Economist* 2006). Without analyzing the history of founda-tions and their successes over the past two centuries, one can immediately have a sense of what is defensible in the application of market methods into this nonprofit arena. James Surowiecki, in his defense of philanthrocapital-ism, argues that what distinguishes philanthrocapitalists, the billionaires who now undertake to eradicate malaria or HIV/AIDS in Africa, is their long-term vision and the patience they bring to their charitable endeavors: "Projects like eradicating malaria or providing universal Internet access (one of Zuck-erberg's ambitions) also require investment that may not produce results for decades to come. Politicians have to worry about being reelected every few years. And global problems are inherently distant from the life of the average voter" (2015). In some very strategic way, then, the so-called investments of philanthrocapitalists cannot be measured by the same yardstick other corpo-rate investments are measured: they neither require profits nor must they comply with quarterly reports for the likes of the New York Stock Exchange. As he continues: "It's reasonable to lament the fact that a small number of billionaires have so much power over which problems get dealt with and which do not. But they have that power precisely because they are spending so much of their money to solve global problems. We, as a country, are not" (ibid.). The argument here is itself quite neoliberal: we vote with our pocket-books. Billionaires choose what they care about and then have the right to dedicate their fortunes to solve social ills they deem worthwhile solving, regardless of public opinion or the policies of the State. What made them financially successful before is making them successful now as well (no matter the methods by which they first acquired their wealth).

Critics of philanthrocapitalism have various ways to tackle the novel juxtaposition of market-capitalism on the nonmarket environment of charities: human misery isn't a commodity to buy and sell, and the eradication of diseases, for example, requires a more holistic view of the socio-political and environmental conditions under which they infect millions of residents. Moreover, funding a free hotline for those contemplating suicide or underwriting a shelter for domestic abuse victims cannot be approached with a quantifiable or monetized strategy, since the very idea of measuring one's misery or accounting for the saving of one life is anathema to this activity. Advocating more efficiency of bloated charitable bureaucracies is one (admirable) thing, but turning foundations into businesses may miss the point for which they came into existence in the first place: to help those who fall outside markets and the safety nets governments have set in place (or cannot afford to put in place). Measuring success or failure is much more precarious in the charity world than in the marketplace, and one's long-term impact can be judged at times only a century after initial engagement because what is at stake is a cultural transformation as much as immediate behavioral changes. A second line of criticism is related to the immense power given to billionaires that decide what initiatives ought to be undertaken across the globe; this is no longer your grandmother's bake sale for the Red Cross, but it has a national scale that changes the balance of powers and foregrounds certain international developments at the expense of others. Would we like to have the very rich dictate what is globally important to all of us in the social and environmental arenas? Have we lost any semblance of democracy when a small elite directs our attention to what it cares about? And the third line of critique reverts back to classical arguments about colonialism when outside foreign powers decide and dictate to local authorities what and how they should change regardless of local interest or opposition (Ramdas et al. 2011).

Even if we overlook the problematic ways in which market methods of assessments and implementation are being imposed on charitable work, we must still worry about the intent of philanthrocapitalists. Their hearts might be pure, the intentions lofty, but what they may miss is that the very roots of what they attempt to eradicate or solve—namely, abject poverty—remains untouched. They may fix this or that problem after the fact, they may change something on the margins of society, but as long as their fortunes were made within the confines of market-capitalism they have not really dealt with the incessant inequality that is the natural and inevitable outcome of market relations. In other words, breaking someone's leg along the way and then offering a Band Aid will never solve the initial calamity; but making sure no one gets hurt along the way may require fundamental reshuffling of the deck. Philanthrocapitalism expands the reach of market-capitalism by offering assistance after the dust has settled; but it doesn't change the means by which their largesse has been acquired. For those defending billionaires not in terms of how they made their money but in terms of what they choose to spend it on, we should mention one advantage they have over state-controlled and democratically run agencies: while overlooking their own damages, they can focus on esoteric or unpopular issues that the rest of us will ignore. And this freedom of choice may at times provide support for worthwhile endeavors that the State may never get to resolve.

V: CARING ECONOMICS

In addition to a book with this title, there is also a website whose mission statement is dedicated to moving us "from Homo Economicus towards a Caring Economy." Partially funded and co-organized by the Institute of New Economic Thinking, Kiel's Institute for the World Economy, and the Max Planck Institute, this movement intends to "explore new avenues of how psychological and neuroscientific knowledge about human motivation, emotion and social cognition can inform models of economic decision making in addressing global economic problems. In particular, the program seeks to generate a new generation of economic models that explore the opportunities for more cooperative, pro-social and sustainable economic behaviors. This research aims at providing a new vision of a 'caring economics'" (2016). Questioning the basic assumptions used in standard economic models, this movement attempts to examine human behavior in terms of the "external and internal conditions [that] can activate different, discrete motivational systems that can in turn prime different sets of behavior patterns" (ibid.). This means that the exploration is both behavioristic and neurological. What is interesting is that evolutionary changes are considered as well: "We also focus on studying the plasticity of motivational systems in exploring possibilities for changing preferences through mental training" (ibid.). It seems that adding a socio-psychological dimension to this approach can provide useful data from diverse sources: "Additionally, the research explores the interdependence and sociality of humans. We suggest that the traditional conception of homo Economicus needs to be replaced by a new conception of homo relation, namely, individuals who are linked to one another through personal relationships and their capacity for empathy and compassion. This new conception suggests that people are capable of intrinsically pro-social behaviors, enabling them to cooperate in ways that standard economic theories ignore. Finally, we are also interested in working on new micro- as well as macro-economic models of cooperation including also the perspective of biological evolution" (ibid.). If empathy is added to the mix, the kind of sentiment already studied by Smith, then notions of collaboration make sense (even in the age of globalization).

It should be noted that this approach seems to be the most unusual and therefore promising alternative to market-capitalism found in the literature. Admittedly it's still not completely free from the strictures of market mechanisms, but it opens the door to different modes of thinking about human exchanges in and out of markets. In a book, *Caring Economics: Conversations on Altruism and Compassion, Between Scientists, Economists, and the Dalai Lama* (2015), by Tania Singer, we are asked to rethink some of the presuppositions brought up in part I of the present book. Recognizing how capitalism has brought about prosperity to the world, the Dalai Lama explains, "It has also exacerbated the growing gap between rich and poor, not only between nations but also within nations themselves" (ibid., ix). And right away the Dalai Lama questions whether or not the "the market's invisible hand will ensure self-sustaining efficiency" (ibid.). Focusing on recent research, Tania Singer, Ricard Matthieu, and Diego Hangartner suggest that "each of us possesses a great capacity—maybe even a biological proclivity— for compassion, cooperation, and altruism" (ibid., 5). The view of self-interested individuals who are inherently selfish and the argument that therefore the very notion of altruism is untenable (altruistic acts are self-serving at their core) are being challenged here. With this in mind, these three researchers are willing to pose the question: "So how do we create a system in which people directly and regularly contribute to the well-being of others?" (ibid., 6) The experimental social psychologist Daniel Batson concludes from his research that "we need to take empathy-induced altruism into account in our understanding of human behavior, even in economic systems" (ibid., 21). The neuroscientist Singer agrees with this stance and explains that "empathy alone is not enough to create pro-social motivation and behavior; it needs to be transformed into compassion or emphatic concern" (ibid., 29). This means that simply feeling empathy isn't enough; it needs to be externally directed toward actions that express and embody this feeling. In other words, empathy has to be built into the system and not viewed as an afterthought.

Distinguishing between "negative valence empathy" (in reaction to the suffering of others), "positive valence empathy" (as a means of alleviating other's pain), and "sympathetic joy" (experiencing feelings of joy in response to others' happiness), the psychologist and psychiatrist Richard Davidson explains that with just a little training we can all participate in more positive emotional exchanges in society. This comports with what a Buddhist economics would look like, as a way of safeguarding that we attend to our individual and social emotional states to further the goodwill of which we all take part. John Dunne quotes from the Santideva that "all those who are unhappy in the world are so because they desire their own happiness. All those who are happy in the world are so because they desire others to be happy" (ibid., 90). This sentiment is at the heart of Smith's own thinking in his *The Theory of Moral Sentiments* (1959), where he implores his readers to appreciate the happiness accrued to those who see the happiness of others. Following this insight, Dunne suggests that if we consider economics not to be about external resources (that ought to be allocated efficiently) but about internal resources, then we are faced with resources that "can be limitlessly cultivated by other-centered attitudes." He continues to argue that "economics can thus be shifted so that internal resources become central to our calculations." In practical sense this would force us to "see these internal resources as relevant to our external economic exchanges, to our cost-benefit analyses" (ibid., 92). This, indeed, would bring together the early Smith with the later Smith, guaranteeing that as we calculate the desirability of our market exchanges we would also take into account how we feel about the exchange, how happy or unhappy it has made us in seeing that our interlocutor is also enjoying a level of greater happiness than before the exchange. This may sound outlandish in neoliberal circles, but a quick glance at current literature of business success would reveal that such consideration is in fact in place, even if its technical label may be more of the "developing relations of trust." Incidentally, the Dalai Lama wants to change *Buddhist economics* to *internal economics*, while Dunne suggests *holistic economics* as the more appropriate designation or the *caring economics* of the book's title.

The economist Richard Layard is adding his insights to this discussion about the fundamental transformation of economic theory and practice toward a more emotionally based exchange relationship in terms of the two different levels at which the market operates. For him, the competition that holds among firms in the market was never meant to hold in the relationship among people and their communities where cooperation and good will were supposed to be paramount. The fact that competition has been understood to be prevalent in all market relations has skewed the analysis and has pitted one individual against another, contrary to Smith's own ideas (ibid., 97–100). Layard continues to explain that "an individual becomes happier as he becomes richer, but over time the whole country does not become happier as it becomes richer" (ibid., 102). This is the case because our happiness is commonly measured in relative terms; that is, we compare ourselves to others when we claim to have become happier than before. But when it comes to countries as a whole, he finds that among the OECD countries (Organization for Economic Co-Operation and Development), those where income and wealth inequalities are the smallest are also those that report greater overall national happiness. "The less equal the country, the lower the level of trust" (ibid., 108). This observation leads him to speculate that there must be a way to build trust and happiness among people under conditions where greater economic stability and equality can be guaranteed, as can be more readily seen in the Nordic countries. Another economist, William Harbaugh, points out that in the United States some 68 percent of families "give something to charitable causes of all kinds . . . giving about 2 percent of their income away" (ibid., 117). This level of generosity cannot be explained away as "warm-glow altruism," which is more egoistic than "pure altruism" because it does indicate a level of social generosity that is culturally embedded (ibid., 122). Ernest Fehr extends this insight to argue that in order to foster a level of social cooperation we need institutions that both encourage such behavior (with proper social norms and education) as well as punish those who violate such goodwill (laws and the police) (ibid., 125–134). One may question if charity is more directly related to one's culture, as some would argue, so that levels of disenfranchisement are as relevant to rates of generosity than any tax code (Eaves 2008).

The last part of the conversation between the scientists and economists and the Dalai Lama moves to a level of implementation: How can we organize an economic system that will be sustainable and based on human relations? Among the examples that are mentioned is micro-financing, which has become quite popular in poor countries where minimal amounts of a few dollars can start a chain of events that usher local prosperity to a family or a village. As a former Credit Suisse executive explains, "there are 155 million microcredit clients in the world," so this is not a fringe phenomenon but a widespread one, inspired by Muhammad Yunus already decades ago (ibid., 151). The success of this *selfless economy* need not be justified, as it continues to operate in many countries around the world. Likewise, the Barfoot College in India has been successful in incorporating local customs and knowledge into Western knowledge and expertise and avoids many of the pitfalls associated with colonialism of the last two centuries (ibid., chapter 13). It's interesting how the insights of the East are juxtaposed with those of the West. From the East (the Dalai Lama) we get: "Compassion is not a luxury. It is a necessity in order for the human being to survive," while from the West (FDR) we get: "We have always known that heedless self-interest was bad morals. Now we know that it is bad economics" (ibid., 186). If we agree that "there is even some evidence that hints that behaving altruistically may make us happier," then we might have come here with a recipe of how to transform economic thinking from profit maximization to happiness maximization (ibid., 197).

VI: A BRIDGE

To some extent, the notion of Selfless Economics or Caring Economics brings out the best that all the other labels have in mind, forcing us to rethink exchange relations that take place in markets. It makes perfect sense to think about people first and their happiness and then think about how we can formulate and regulate a framework of exchanges that would not hurt anyone and maximize the happiness of all. But even the last section on Caring Economics is still caught up in the frenzy of profit making if not maximizing. Why model micro financing of the very poor, where $10 can make all the difference in the world for a poor farmer, as a credit in the financial sense of the term? Why exact interest and expect to profit from the feeble attempt of anyone to survive or improve one's life a little? What fundamental institutional changes must take place as well? If the institutional structure of market-capitalism doesn't change and if it's supported by laws that the political establishment enjoys, will the poor ever cease being poor? Will the rich ever give up their privileged positions in order to come closer to their brothers and sisters? Or, are all of these promises for inclusiveness and caring just hollow words uttered in an echo chamber of like-minded well-wishers? Are these, in short, false promises? Are they meant as a feel-good veneer on the horrific and brutal consequences of market-capitalism? Even the Dalai Lama, a religious leader whose integrity and credibility may seem beyond reproach, still uses the language of market-capitalism, trying to convert and reform rather than radically transform the economic landscape. If there are, in fact, hints that humans are not as selfish as some assume them to be in part I, and if these hints also suggest a great deal about our inherent altruistic propensities, why not exploit these propensities and set up institutions where we voluntary contribute to the welfare of all and get rewarded with the love and affection of fellow humans? Is it too outlandish to assume that we can judge each other with tools other than money? Or that we can find some common ground of being sensible and reasonable so as to avoid the extremes of the spectrum that runs from greed to caring? Perhaps we are lacking at this time the proper vocabulary with which to handle, let alone assess, our happiness in terms other than money.

Chapter Eleven

The Perils of Globalization

If globalization and foreign trade were supposed to ease the pains of political economy and draw on the resources of the entire planet and thereby ensure uninterrupted growth (according to Smith), it has in fact come short of its original intentions and promises. It was Marx who ended *The Communist Manifesto* by calling on the workers of the world (or working men of all countries) to unite! Perhaps he was prescient in foreseeing that by the twentieth century multinational corporations would be looking to outsource their production to regions with the cheapest labor costs anywhere in the world. Has development economics of the post–World War II years and globalization in more recent decades been a boon or a bust? And for whom? As we review some of the literature, we might note that economic globalization isn't only about expanding markets for the sake of enjoying the natural abundance of the globe, but that it might be bringing about unsustainable labor and environmental conditions of increased poverty and misery. The two presuppositions we revisit here are growth (rather than the viability of a system, as Piero Sraffa explained in 1960, or sustainability in the environmental sense) and competition (among nation-states rather than individuals). As we shall see, these presuppositions (already discussed in parts I and II) are challenged under conditions of global development and turn out to be less helpful in understanding the economic and cultural strains of this approach. In their stead, some level of international cooperation is needed among donor and recipient States, not to mention a vigorous regulatory intervention of governments and international institutions to guarantee fair trade. If the ultimate goal is to eradicate poverty and ensure the prosperity of the entire globe, mechanisms other than market-capitalism may be more effective.

I: DEVELOPMENT MODELS

The general definition of development economics suggests that it is "a branch of economics that focuses on improving the economies of developing countries. Development economics considers how to promote economic growth by improving factors such as health, education, working conditions, domestic and international policies, and market conditions in developing countries. It examines both macroeconomic and microeconomic factors relating to the structure of a developing economy and how that economy can create effective domestic and international growth" (*Investopedia* 2016). The notion of growth that comes out of this way of thinking is linked with a provisional division of the world into "underdeveloped" or more recently "developing" countries and the "developed" ones. The division is contestable because the criteria by which such a designation comes about can no longer rely on earlier ones that saw the developing world stuck in an agricultural economy beset by traditional techniques of production that barely met subsistence levels, while the developed countries were highly industrialized. With a colonial if not imperialist mindset, developed countries sought to extract valuable natural resources from the developing countries and along the way offer some financial aid for infrastructure, healthcare, and even direct food supplies when needed.

(a) Standard Models

It's no wonder that the so-called standard models of development were predominantly concerned with the technological innovations already deployed in the developed countries, northern America, Europe, and parts of the Pacific Rim. This meant both a concern with methods of land cultivation, from seeds to pesticides, and guarding water sources, from watering canals to hydro plants for energy production. In addition to establishing international financial institutions through which loans and grants can be distributed (World Bank, International Fund for Agricultural Development [IFAD], European Investment Bank [EIB], Islamic Development Bank [IsDB], Asian Development Bank [ADB], European Bank for Reconstruction and Development [EBRD], Development Bank of Latin America [CAF], and International Monetary Fund), direct loans and grants are at times secured directly by nation-states, not to mention private foundations, such as the Melinda and Bill Gates Foundation. Most of developmental models assume that with foreign aid, loans, or grants, developing countries can achieve similar prosperity as their developed counterparts. Education, for example, is mentioned in many of these models because it can offer the gateway toward a healthier society with greater control over birthrates. There is no consensus among those proposing models of development, since some ignore political factors and cultural habits, while others include them as essential variables in any investment strategy so as to minimize corruption, for one, or kinship nepotism that is endemic in tribal relations. The great challenge and promise of development, as Sudhir Sen claims, is "how to rescue two-thirds of mankind from the age-old grip of dehumanizing poverty compounded by a population upsurge; and how, with that end in view, to harness modern science and technology in the underdeveloped countries to produce enough food, to curb the runaway population growth, and to produce other essential goods and services to meet the minimal needs of civilized life" (1974, 3). As far as Sen is concerned, these objectives can be reached because of the "amazing progress" modern science is making and the fact that problems can be solved by technical means. And more importantly still, the fact that "the industrially advanced nations are enjoying record-breaking prosperity," which grants them a "vast reservoir of wealth" with which "to build a better and brighter world to the lasting benefit of all" (ibid.). The conditions for aid were in the form of capital and science, and now the issue is to convince the "wealthy countries" that it's in their best interest to help "two-thirds of mankind," at least in the sense of greater overall geopolitical stability if not the more cynical view that this aid will eventually open new markets (with numerous consumers), as we saw in the case of Inclusive Capitalism.

   Originally development models or economic models that emphasized economic development were primarily focused on domestic industries or some sectors of the economy, and only in the twentieth century have they been more concerned with international affairs or the encouragement of previously colonized countries to become not only politically but also economically independent. Growth therefore was the prime mover, motivation, and goal of both the earlier and the later models. Smith already recognized a relationship between trade and civilization, arguing that the more cultivated the land, the more internationally minded the people, the greater the growth of the economy and the prosperity of its people (1937, 19–21). Just as the "commerce of the towns contributed to the improvement of the country" (ibid., 384), so trade and treaties can bring about the "prosperity of new colonies" (ibid., 531) and eventually ensure the growth of the world as a whole. As Noble Laurate in economics Paul Krugman explains, the heyday of development economics spans the period of the early 1940s into the late 1950s. It rested on the belief that "development is a virtuous circle driven by external economies—that is, that modernization breeds modernization" (1993, 40). The idea was that in order to propel greater domestic growth, developing countries should adopt a modernization process on a large enough scale that would eventually become self-sustaining. The concern with economies of scale where efficiencies are best exploited was intertwined with the promise of ongoing growth so that when efficiencies didn't materialize, the whole development model collapsed, according to Krugman. The problem wasn't an ideological dispute over (imperialistically) exporting Western ideals to other regions of the world, but the methodological obstacles that appeared once applications of the models were attempted around the world. When midcentury economists developed highly abstract mathematical models, they discovered how difficult if not impossible it was to implement them under different political, social, and cultural conditions.

(b) Small Is Beautiful

Similar in orientation to what we saw above in the case of Caring Economics, Schumacher reminds us in *Small Is Beautiful: Economics as if People Mattered* that "economic growth, which viewed from the point of view of economics, physics, chemistry and technology, has no discernable limit, must necessarily run into decisive bottlenecks when viewed from the point of view of the environmental sciences" (1973, 29). One of the first economists to challenge the unbridled promise of growth (and therefore its global application among developing countries), Schumacher's critique resonates today (especially when he brings up environmental variables that were always considered exogenous to economic modeling). The sensitivity to both scale and to how developmental models affect the environment are Schumacher's greatest contributions to this discursive arena of developmental economics. Moreover, development economics is understood by some to be welfare economics, a field of economic research where the rich are helping the poor not simply on a personal level but nationally and internationally. Schumacher explains that when we attempt to "solve" one problem (an economic one), we might be causing numerous additional problems (environmental) that in turn require additional solutions. Questions of growth, therefore, ought to be examined in terms of the available resources and the impact such growth has on the environment (ibid., 30ff). He quotes in this context Gandhi, who welcomed the introduction of new technologies and machinery into India, but who also warned that there "should be no place for machines that concentrate power in a few hands and turn the masses into mere machine minders, if indeed they do not make them unemployed" (ibid., 34–35). And here another economic trade-off comes to light: What balance should there be between technologically driven growth and full employment? In other words, what balance are we to strike to guarantee human flourishing rather than dehumanizing technological interventions?

Schumacher offers us another perspective on what developmental economics should be concerned with: the people who are being affected and not a model formulated in a far-away developed country. He is not alone in challenging the more standard models offered after World War II; the names of John Kenneth Galbraith (1962) and Gunnar Myrdal (1970) are prominent in voicing concerns over the application of the neoclassical model to less-developed countries whose own histories and political structures do not resemble Western capitalist democracies. They all warn against an overly hasty rush to develop the entire globe as if there are no costs associated with such development. They question not the successes of market-capitalism but the ways in which they may not be favored elsewhere because of their threats to traditional modes of production, distribution, and consumption. As we saw in the previous chapter about Caring Economics, Barefoot College was mentioned as an exemplar of an educational institution that values and maintains traditional production techniques in a modern setting of developing countries. The push for jettisoning the old ways, the ways of our grandmothers and grandfathers who have lived in this land for centuries, may sound paternalistic at some level, because these economists are balking at what the establishment among developmental economists sees fit; but their critiques are on another level against the colonial attitude displayed by their interlocutors: Have the developing countries asked for a structural change or just for some temporary relief? Have these countries licensed an outright overtake by market-capitalism in the name of humanitarian aid? And finally, what of the power relations that will ensue once intervention is permitted? Will they indeed free the "masses" as Gandhi calls his fellow citizens, or will they simply make them superfluous, unemployed welfare recipients? Perhaps this binary is unfair and there are conditions under which aid enhances rather than retards freedom.

(c) Big Push

Paul Rosenstein-Rodan has become famous not only for the decades he has spent in the (economic) development sphere, from Italy in the post–World War II period to Latin America in later years, but also because he put forward propositions that the standard models overlooked. But before we move to explain his theoretical and practical insights, it's incumbent on me to be transparent: he was one of my doctoral advisers for about three years before passing away just before my oral examination. He was generous with his knowledge and time, and his philosophical sensitivity informed his economic ideas and theories. Because of this sensitivity, he understood that in order to speak of developing countries and the means by which they could become more "like us, developed countries," an entire infrastructure was needed. In other words, any piecemeal development of this or that sector of the economy, or of this or that particular factory or agricultural center, had to incorporate all the domestic variables relevant to the infusion of money as an investment. In more technical terms, Rosenstein-Rodan insisted that four dimensions of the development model should be simultaneously considered: first, disguised unemployment in agrarian regions; second, simultaneous planning of various industries to guarantee economies of scale; third, the need to start with infrastructure development before developing plants and factories; and fourth, technological external economies that include training and education should be part of the model (1943, Rosenstein-Rodan and Avramovic 1984).

Though credited originally to Rosenstein-Rodan, the idea that when approaching an underdeveloped or developing country one should consider all the relevant variables has become more accepted in the 1950s and into the contemporary context. The problem, of course, is what variables to include in one's analysis: the availability of natural resources, the health of the population, the roads and bridges that are in place, the energy sources on which to rely or that need to be installed, the social relation among tribes and villagers that may or may not hinder entry into the workforce, attitudes toward women and children and the basic education to which they have access, political structures and potential for corruption, national security, civil wars, and the climate conditions under which all human interaction and exchanges take place. His insight was to start by not excluding all but economic variables, and slowly allowing the information flow among the various interested parties—foreign investors, international aid organization, domestic businesses and politicians, bankers and military experts—to exchange as much information as is necessary to ensure development success. This approach flies in the face of the more secretive and competitive approach of market-capitalism where asymmetries of information may give one side a commercial advantage over another (to develop a mine or outsource assembly-line production). As such, there has been wide intellectual acceptance of Rosenstein-Rodan's ideas (with little attribution) without a full-fledged commitment to their implementation. This has meant, as we saw in the case of Schumacher, Galbraith, and Myrdal, that there has always been an uneven development across national borders, where more often than not we find failures rather than successes.

(d) Micro-Financing

The latest arrival in this trajectory of developmental economics has been the guru of micro-financing, Muhammad Yunus (already mentioned in passing). Yunus, a recipient of the Noble Prize for Peace, argues in his book that "unfettered markets in their current form are not meant to solve social problems and instead may actually exacerbate poverty, disease, pollution, corruption, crime, and inequality" (2007, 5). Despite this critique of market-capitalism, Yunus supports the "idea of globalization," which for him means "that free markets should expand beyond national borders, allowing trade among nations and a continuing flow of capital," considering markets as models that "can bring more benefits to the poor than any alternative." But he continues to warn that "without proper oversight and guidelines, globalization has the potential to be highly destructive" (ibid.). There is reason, then, to sandwich

Yunus's notion of micro-financing between the various views of market-capitalism and globalization: he claims to provide a bridge, on the micro, individual level, with a hint of government oversight and legal framework. Because governments may not be able to fill the poverty void that haunts the developing countries, nongovernmental organizations (NGOs) have sprouted around the nexus of development activities. For him, Corporate Social Responsibility (mentioned above in relation to Responsible Capitalism) is a means toward his end of eliminating poverty around the world, one person at a time. And his push for global micro-financing is based on the ideal of a Social Business that pays no dividends to its shareholders even when profitable; instead, investors are paid back and when profits accumulate they are used for expansion and self-sustainability rather than being divided among the original investors (ibid., xvi). The point, then, is to recalibrate market-capitalism in order to focus on social reforms and alleviate poverty without making the recipients of these loans beholden forever to their financial supporters. Though the market orientation of classical and neoclassical economic models is evident here, the goals are different and the treatment of the people is different (seeing their multidimensionality rather than limiting them to the one-dimensionality of the banking industry), and therefore the potential for less abuse and exploitation is possible as well. As an example, Yunus explains that his Grameen Bank in Bangladesh has loaned about $6 billion as of 2006, reaching seven million borrowers, "97 percent of whom are women, in 78,000 villages . . . repayment rate is currently 98.6 percent," which allows the bank to expand and remain self-sustaining (ibid., 51). But we have to submit that what may seem a benevolent and even chartable imposition of capitalist-like methods of economic sustainability (if not progress) may still be perceived by the local population as imperialistic and overbearing (even when they benefit from these methods).

According to Yunus, "Microcredit turns on the economic engines among the rejected population of society. Once a large number of these tiny engines start working, the stage is set for big things" (ibid., 56). The reason for including this nonprofit, almost philanthropic approach to economic development in the underdeveloped, less-developed, or developing countries is that it offers an alternative way of thinking about economic prosperity. First, it approaches the individual on the lowest common level possible, the farmer with a cow, the prospector with only a tool in hand, the local farmer who needs seeds for cultivation. Second, this approach, though sanctioned by government agencies, is supposed to play a parallel role and avoid the political quagmire so lamented by donor countries. And third, this approach attempts to promote self-help, moving from charity to offering a small nudge, with an eye on social justice. Perhaps what's at stake is what is captured by the old Chinese proverb: "Give a man a fish and you feed him for a day. Teach a man to fish and you feed him for a lifetime." One wonders if the promise of micro-financing is indeed fully in line with the cultural settings in which it is applied or whether this is an indirect indoctrination process of making the entire globe dependent on loans and debt, paying interest as if there is no other way to lend or borrow money, as if only financial institutions can solve the social ills of poverty. Perhaps this is why some would argue that the starting point must be reason and sensibility rather than charity and empathy so as to ensure a greater level of self-actualization and perhaps even a modicum of self-dignity.

II: THE PROMISE OF GLOBALIZATION

After World War II, most of Europe and Japan were in economic ruin, leaving millions to fend for themselves in war-torn devastation. The Marshall Plan (officially the European Recovery Program, ERP) committed the United States to help primarily the western part of Europe (since the eastern part was taken over by the USSR). The United States gave about $12 billion in aid for infrastructure development (equivalent to about $120 billion in 2016 dollars). This massive rebuilding of the parts of Europe was self-serving, of course, from two perspectives: first, it would promote American commercial interests in that part of the world, from export of goods and services to favorable trade agreements in the future; and second, it was understood that this "soft diplomacy" would guarantee American geopolitical influence in the area against the overwhelming power of the Soviet Union (in what eventually came to be known as the Cold War). Though much smaller in financial scope (about $92 million), the United States was instrumental in bringing about the so-called Japanese Miracle after World War II by remaining involved in the economic restructuring of the country, warding off the potential dominant influence of the Soviet Union and China. As John Jackson chronicles, there were three main reasons, after the Bretton Woods Conference in 1944, that motivated the United States to invest billions of dollars in foreign countries: first, "the prevention of another war"; second, "economic betterment of the whole world"; and third, "managing economic interdependence" (2000, 372). We should recall that part of the Bretton Woods accord also replaced gold with the American dollar as the international standard currency for trade, a position that put America at the center of the international community, replacing the dominance of among others the United Kingdom, whose empire was slowly falling apart. With global commercial interdependence and with the establishment of some international institutions that would guarantee a fair and competitive environment, it was believed the world could peacefully trade and maintain political stability. With this in mind, the United Nations was established in 1945, the General Agreement on Tariffs and Trade in 1947 (replaced by the World Trade Organization in 1995), and the

International Bank for Reconstruction and Development in 1944. As Jackson explains, there was a dire need to monitor that international relations followed certain agreed-upon rules, from accepting a general system of trade to the ways by which disputes would be settled. Guaranteeing international participation and expecting transparency and the legitimacy of these "regulatory" organizations was paramount in the face of national sovereignty and even paranoia after the world wars (ibid., 376–379). Incidentally, the post–World War II experience wasn't repeated in the cases of Afghanistan and Iraq, where a process of rebuilding has yielded more strife and less economic development.

As we shift from post–World War II thinking and international policies toward the actual developmental policies that ensued (as mentioned above), we begin to observe a trend toward a uniform economic model of global market-capitalism, where competition for natural resources becomes important and where labor-market advantages are apparent among the less-developed countries where poverty is rampant. All of this happens before Yunus's model of microcredit and before the Digital Revolution takes place. While the Industrial Revolution that modernized the world started in some regions and then was partially exported to others (because of infrastructure needs and technical educational expertise not equally distributed around the globe), digital connections moved swiftly from their countries of origin to every corner of the world. The promise of low infrastructure and energy costs, as argued by Benkler (2006), and the speed with which the world became "overconnected," according to William Davidow (2011), fostered a level of development and growth that would have fulfilled every dream of earlier generations of development economists. Digital networks could "leapfrog" the drudgery of building an infrastructure: instead of digging millions of miles of ditches for telephone and electric cables, one could more cheaply offer antennas and satellite connections for cellphones serving as credit devices as much as telephones. Though this path to growth and development sounds radically different from any of its predecessors, it remains neatly tucked within the market framework of neoclassical capitalism. There are the owners of capital, the distribution networks controlled by state-sanctioned monopolies, and billions of consumers who remain dependent on the goodwill of large corporations and the regulatory power of their governments. When we see pictures of women trekking for miles to collect water from a communal well while proudly holding a cellphone, we wonder if this is indeed "progress" in its fullest economic sense. No running water, no sewage treatment techniques, but a creeping introduction of the latest gadgets; is this a technological leapfrog or a backflip?

One of the main advocates of globalization and its potential for success is Jeffrey Sachs. According to him, market-capitalism could hypothetically lead to global development, since open markets and no barriers to entry are part and parcel of the theoretical model of classical and neoclassical economics. However, we should be aware that "at every stage of development, and for every sector of development, the public sector and the private sector have mutually supportive roles. Public sector capital—roads, clinics, schools, ports, nature reserves, utilities, and much more—are essential if private capital in the form of factories, machinery, and skilled-labor are to be productive. Economic development is a complex interplay of market forces and public-sector plans and investments" (2008, 219). This realization is along the traditional developmental economic models, from the Standard to the Big Push: infrastructure isn't a simple exogenous variable but an integral part of the planning for any new development of any sector of the economy. So, what is left of the competitive model of the mainstream? Sachs is optimistic in suggesting its replacement with a more cooperative one. In his words, "Global cooperation will have to come to the fore. The very idea of competing nation-states that scramble for markets, power, and resources will become passé . . . humanity shares a *common fate on a crowded planet* . . . Our challenge is not so much to invent global cooperation as it is to rejuvenate, modernize, and extend it . . . A new approach to global problem solving based on cooperation among nations and the dynamism and creativity of the nongovernmental sector" (ibid., 3–7; italics in the original). This means that our divided globe has no choice but to cooperate: we are already fairly integrated in economic terms, so now we must be more forthcoming with our political and ideological cooperation, ensuring the progress and growth that are needed to provide, as the title of his book says, "common wealth." Completely in agreement with old-fashioned ideals of economic development, Sachs argues that long-term investments may not be measured in the short term, and that applying this kind of financial assessment misses the point of realizing prosperity for the entire globe (ibid., 46ff). If we called the post–World War II economists developmental economists, we can label their modern descendants as globalist economists, those dedicated to see how market-capitalism can expand and bring with it the benefits already enjoyed by the developed countries (Sassower 2009, chapter 3).

Some current reports support this positive view of the benefits of globalization. As the World Bank reports, according to Shawn Donnan, "Despite popular belief, the world became a more equal place in the years after the global financial crisis, with twice as many countries seeing declines in inequality as increases" (2016). The World Bank also found that there has been a steady decrease in what it terms "extreme poverty," living on less than $1.90 per day (the number has declined from 881 million to 767 million in just two years). It's interesting to note that "the consensus has been that the growth over the past 30 years of emerging economies such as Brazil, China, and India has led to the biggest decrease in inequality between countries since the Industrial Revolution" (ibid.). But this decrease has been accompanied by "an increase in inequality within countries" (ibid.), especially in the more developed ones where competition for low-labor costs has caused major layoffs in manufacturing. Donnan quotes Francisco Ferreira, who oversees the World Bank's poverty research, to say that the report was "myth-breaking." The "myth," of course, is that greater development necessarily leads to greater inequality (since there is a concentration of industrial financial power); and if the data show that indeed there is less "severe poverty," the promise of development or globalization is fulfilled. We should note, though, that Ferreira does admit that some of the reported changes are due to "methodological changes," developmental calculations that manipulate data (ibid.). This way of thinking about economic growth, in Benjamin Friedman's view, has always linked it with "a rising standard of living for the clear majority of citizens—[it] more often than not fosters greater opportunity, tolerance of diversity, social mobility, commitment to fairness, and dedication to democracy" (2005, 4). This means that there are benefits not captured by the market calculus, since they are moral and social, the kind of consequences that at times filter upward into the political arena, when beneficiaries expect greater say in their future (ibid., 15ff).

Even critics of globalization, like Stiglitz, still believe that at some fundamental level "globalization itself is neither good nor bad" (2002, 20). The assessment of development or globalization, in this light, shouldn't be at the ideological level but rather at the ways in which it has been undertaken. Just as Sachs entreats his readers to think of converting old-fashioned competition with cooperation, so does Stiglitz focus on how to safeguard that the promises of globalization come true. He claims to believe that globalization, which he defines as "the removal of barriers to free trade and the closer integration of national economies," can indeed be a "force for good and that it has the *potential* to enrich everyone in the world, particularly the poor" (ibid., ix; italics in the original). What's at stake, then, is how to convert the "potential" into an actualized economic vibrancy, how to make these promises of freedom, prosperity, and international integration into a reality enjoyed by the very poor around the globe. The promise, to continue with Stiglitz, is as much economic as it is ideological, but here ideology is understood not in the terms deployed during the Cold War—the Soviet oppression of human rights in comparison to the Western enlightened liberties—but in the terms deployed by Smith; namely, the betterment of every individual while the well-being of the community is improved as well. Though individual motivation to participate in markets vary, the overall result is beneficial for all concerned, and therefore market-capitalism continues to be lauded as the best available economic system. If this is the case, even critics of globalization seem to agree, why not spread the good word, as evangelical Christians proclaim, to every corner of the world? If we found the key to prosperity, who are we to keep it hidden from the rest of the world? In other words, if we are serious about caring for the poor and eradicating poverty once and for all, why not use the only system that can accomplish this? This approach is reminiscent of the zeal and fervent belief of religious missionary work, sharing the promises of market-capitalism as heaven on earth in the here and now.

III: THE PERILS OF GLOBALIZATION

Just as Sachs was hoping for an integrated approach to globalization, replacing unfettered (and perhaps even counterproductive) competition with cooperation among nongovernment organizations and their host states, so does Stiglitz insists on government intervention to guarantee the success of global development. Instead of Kennedy's image of all the boats enjoying the rising tides, he brings forth the following image: "Small developing countries are like small boats." "Rapid capital market liberalization, in the manner pushed by the IMF, amounted to setting them off on a voyage on a rough sea, before the holes in their hulls have been repaired, before the captain has received training, before life vests have been put on board." And this has meant that "even in the best of circumstances, there was a high likelihood that they would be overturned when they were hit broadside by a big wave" (2002, 17). Stiglitz's skepticism about the survival of these tiny boats reveals his concern that intentions may have been pure, but results disastrous. From unequal negotiating power to asymmetries of information (about natural resources needs or the financial burdens on borrowers in weak positions), it has become clear that poor countries cannot participate on equal footing with wealthy countries whose corporate dominance is evident at every exchange. Though Stiglitz's ire is primarily leveled against the IMF and its manipulation by powerful state members as well as its own mistreatment of recipient states (with conditions that disable them), his overall critique of what has come to be globalization is broad based. His critical assessment extends to the Euro and the ways in which the stronger partners of the Eurozone have treated weaker ones (Stiglitz 2016). Incidentally, Jackson has the same critical lamentation about the WTO as too inept to deal with the complexities of contemporary trade agreements and their violations. If that international institution is flawed, as indeed it is from all the evidence he has gathered, and if its credibility is questioned, there are dangerous consequences that would increase the "problems for the working of markets in our globalized world" (2000, 382). A recent example of this, one that also falls in line with the warning of Davidow's "overconnected" world, has been the financial crisis that began in 2008 in the US mortgage sector and spilled into the rest of the world is short order.

Suzanne Bergeron argues from a feminist perspective that the positive accounts of globalization are in fact "globalocentric" insofar as they contend that global capital structurally dominates all other forms of global engagement (2001, 983). The logic of advanced capitalism is not only ideological but also informs our way of thinking about national boundaries, personal relations, and our culture. Her critical perspectives on globalization focuses on neoliberal rhetoric and the instabilities and inequalities of this new world order (ibid., 985ff). What is at stake here is not only the precarious economic position into which poorer countries are put, but the restructuring of cultures and societies so that indigenous people have to convert their identities into terms acceptable to the hegemonic narrative of financial success or failure. The presumption here is not that indoctrination will necessarily lead to full integration, but that a reasonable approach would ensure safeguards against such a process when it is not welcomed by the recipients of the largesse of other cultures. This means that national interests are at times guided by the constraints imposed by international banking authorities dictating policy priorities regardless of endemic domestic needs (ibid., 1000ff). It's one thing to offer aid, as Sachs and Stiglitz would concede, and quite another to dictate what national priorities should be undertaken with this aid. US foreign aid in 2015 amounted to around $35 billion, and it decreed how this aid was to be spent, from grains to guns. One can reasonably argue that this aid is in fact a domestic subsidy for American agricultural and manufacturing interests. Recipient countries receive credits to be spent on US goods, not as was the case in the Iraq and Afghanistan wars where billions were actually handed over in cash (to be spent however the recipients found fit). When credits for wheat— as a clear form of food assistance—are accorded to foreign countries, and when this credit can only be used on US soil, it's the farmers in Iowa and Kansas that benefit from this indirect subsidy—increasing, as it were, the demand for wheat (or any other agricultural commodity). No wonder that congressional delegates, however xenophobic, line up to support foreign aid vouchers that favor their constituents' production. This is similar to the Marshall Plan where American self-interest rather than altruism reigned supreme.

One way to enumerate the problems associated with globalization is in the following format offered by Gail Tverberg. In a 2015 posting on the website Our Finite World, she lists the following: "1. Globalization uses up finite resources more quickly; 2. Globalization increases world carbon dioxide emissions; 3. Globalization makes it virtually impossible for regulators in one country to foresee the worldwide implications of their actions; 4. Globalization acts to increase world oil prices; 5. Globalization transfers consumption of limited oil supply from developed countries to developing countries; 6. Globalization transfers jobs from developed countries to less developed countries; 7. Globalization transfers investment spending from developed countries to less developed countries; 8. With the dollar as the world's reserve currency, globalization leads to a huge US balance of trade deficits and other imbalances; 9. Globalization tends to move taxation away from corporations, and onto individual citizens; 10. Globalization sets up a currency "race to the bottom," with each country trying to get an export advantage by dropping the value of its currency; 11. Globalization encourages dependence on other countries for essential goods and services; 12. Globalization ties countries together, so that if one country collapses, the collapse is likely to ripple through the system, pulling many other countries with it" (2016). This isn't an exhaustive list, but one that alerts us to the kind of information and trade imbalances that are decried by economists and environmentalists alike. One can take issue with any of these twelve points, but the overwhelming evidence provided on this website and many other scholarly works indicates that indeed the tradeoffs have not been fully foreseen by economists. Perhaps, as Rawi Abdelal and Adam Segal contend, globalization has "reached its peak" and ought to be reassessed in sober terms, accounting for a number of variables that have hurt both developing and developed countries (2007).

In a research paper for the Federal Reserve Bank of St. Louis—a more conservative and hawkish institution than the liberal-minded institutions that decry the follies of international trade—Richard Anderson and Charles Gascon have studied the veracity of the political outcry about "globalization and economic insecurity." Though the context is the congressional elections of that year, one can transpose this concern to the debates in the 2016 American presidential election when trade agreements came under renewed scrutiny with the specter of a jobless recovery. The authors concede that "postwar globalization was founded on the principle that the federal government would provide economic security, while free international markets would provide the best aggregate outcomes" (2007, 1). This division of labor, as they illustrate, has not come to fruition. Add to this principle the fact that "traditionally, trade is thought of as exchanging different goods across nations, not the shifting of production from one country to another, followed by return shipments back to the original country" (ibid., 2), and what you have instead is "offshoring" (now called "outsourcing"), where jobs are moved from more developed countries (where labor costs are high) to developing countries (where they are lower at times by a factor of ten). Instead of the obvious benefits that were promised (cheaper goods from poor countries), what we find is that "workers in tradable industries and occupations express higher levels of economic insecurity; additionally, workers expressing higher levels of insecurity demand greater social insurance" (ibid., 3). Because "offshoring increases labor-demand elasticities," and these elasticities include "greater wage and employment volatilities in the labor market," we can now expect as a nation "greater economic insecurity" (ibid., 5). Economic insecurity doesn't happen in a political vacuum, as the 2016 election cycle has made clear; when workers "demand that government provide increased funds for health, education, and social security programs" (ibid., 17), what you have is a political recipe that favors one party over another or one populist candidate over another.

Thinking about global development in terms of costs and benefits not only asks us to evaluate the balance in dollars and cents (itself an exercise that foreshadows the ideological leanings of those who do the calculation) but is also sensitive to how benefits and costs are apportioned across the population. As Binyamin Applebaum argues, "The benefits of globalization have accrued disproportionately to upper-income households [that can buy goods more cheaply], while the costs have fallen heavily on the less affluent [because their low-skill jobs are being exported overseas], contributing to the rise of economic inequality" (2015, 1). What happened to "all" the boats rising with the rising tide? According to this analysis, some benefit while others lose, and simply calculating aggregates doesn't give an accurate picture of who benefits from overall national growth. Americans who see their factories close don't think about cheap products from China. And foreign beneficiaries, like China, don't think about American markets as such, but about their own ability to have taken some seven hundred million citizens out of poverty. And when more sophisticated national interests clamp down on certain imports and impose high tariffs on them in order to protect their domestic industries, international trade is in fact partially implemented, and in this partial implementation the strength or weakness of individual nation-states comes to light. China has the power to dictate some terms, while the United States has others; the EU can close its frontiers to certain imports or set regulatory barriers that others cannot overcome (GMO restrictions on beef), while the United States can subsidize its agricultural sector to the tune of about $24 billion annually.

Globalization, then, isn't exclusively an economic issue but a political one as well; and when economic inequalities are exacerbated, it also becomes a moral issue—should we be responsible to those adversely affected by trade agreements? (Rattner 2016) As Dani Rodrik explains, there is an interesting complementary relation between State and market institutions, especially when the boundary conditions are blurred in international affairs. The transaction costs of global trade are borne by nation-states while private corporations demand support, tariffs, and the rule of law to enforce trade agreements, all in the name of free trade and the reluctance to have any government intervention (2011, 22–23). Because there are three variables to consider simultaneously, claims Rodrik, "We cannot have hyper globalization, democracy, and national self-determination all at once. We can have at most two of three" (ibid., 200). As he explains elsewhere, only if trade agreements and global engagement are selectively and strategically applied can we hope to minimize if not completely eliminate the negative consequences of globalization. According to him, globalization should never be understood as an end in itself, but as a means to democratic ends (2016, 1–2). As far as Rodrik is concerned, different countries have their own paths toward prosperity, so that any prefigured and superimposed policy is inherently misguided. Like-wise, different countries have their own institutional arrangements that require reforms or complete restructuring. And finally, if the goal of economic prosperity is the enhancement of democratic principles and the protection of human rights (understood broadly), then we should recall that trade alone cannot be the arbiter of engagement with dictatorships. As already explained in part I of this book, the principles and ideals that guided economists since Smith were always intertwined with philosophical ideals of freedom and equality, of the perfectibility of humanity and the progress civilization has made and is bound to continue making. Selfishness and greed, for example, were rarely touted as virtues worth cultivating; likewise, enrichment for its own sake was frowned upon; instead, the virtues of self-help and camarade-rie were part of the narrative told about capitalism, as we noted in part II about the usefulness of implicit presuppositions in economic narratives and model building.

One issue that remains in the leftist cathedrals of economic scholarship has been the role of multinational corporations whose size and impact became evident already in the 1970s. There were some who decried their increasing power, both economic and political, and who saw their ascendency as an imperialistic move that may not be stopped (MacEwan 1978, Hymer 1978, and Weisskopf 1971). Those early treatises on the move from development to imperialism, the shift from benign aid to an intrusion that undermines local power relations, have been relatively out of sight of the mainstream of economic theory, but their insights and accurate predictions are almost generally accepted today. The power and ubiquitous presence of giant multinational corporations are understood nowadays in terms of their annual sales that in some cases are larger than the budgets of most nation-states. Vincent Trivett examined twenty-five US corporations to see where they would rank among the world's nation-states, and found that "if Wal-Mart were a country, its revenues would make it on par with the GDP of the 25th largest economy in the world, surpassing 157 smaller countries" (2011). He continues to say, "We've found 25 major American corporations whose 2010 revenues surpass the 2010 Gross Domestic Product of entire countries, often with a few billion to spare. Even some major countries like Norway, Thailand, and New Zealand can be bested by certain U.S. firms" (ibid.). Sophie Hobson similarly argues that "Apple's record value is bigger than all but 19 countries' GDP" (2015). The latest scandals are about Apple (US company) keeping its billions offshore in the tax haven that Ireland has become, and the EU demanding Apple pay back taxes in the order of $14 billion because of the unfair advantage it has claimed for itself in parking its fortunes in Ireland. Apple is an interesting corporation to study: benefitting from US Intellectual

Property laws, licensing most of its patents from US government research (see Mazzucato 2014, chapter 5), producing primarily in China, banking in Ireland, and selling in the United States as much or more than in the rest of the world. What kind of a company is it? What does it mean nowadays to be multinational? It may mean, as Halliburton has illustrated during the Iraq war, that it is entitled to receive single-source (and noncompetitive) bids from the US military (because its previous CEO happened to be the vice president during that period), and adding a headquarter in Dubai (the original is still in Houston, Texas) so that its tax liability may be lowered. Multinational corporate behavior isn't motivated by the lofty ideals proposed by the international community post–World War II and reinforced whenever a natural disaster hits a country across the globe. Instead, these corporations demand to be free of national regulatory agencies, exemplifying the faith in unfettered capitalism. Even if we remain suspicious of the ulterior motives behind US aid packages, we can still appreciate a national or domestic interest that is being assumed and that hopefully would benefit an entire population. The same cannot be said about multinational giants whose allegiance to their countries of origins is flimsy at best, and self-serving at worst (bidding for federal contracts and expecting military protection when under siege).

IV: A BRIDGE

In this chapter the connection between developmental economics of the post–World War II period and contemporary debates about globalization has been established. If yesteryear's concerns over paternalism and colonial exploitation seem to have gone away in light of greater national independence and sophistication, we have observed that globalization even under the best of circumstances may be accompanied by more problems than the ones it attempted to solve. From environmental costs to the costs of labor dislocation and increased economic inequality, we have seen that so-called economic models and the issues they address are political and moral ones as well. To isolate economic variables or to set some variables as endogenous and some as exogenous is both arbitrary (methodologically speaking) and morally inappropriate; what affects the most vulnerable in both developing and developed countries ought to be foregrounded even when aggregate accounting makes the benefits of globalization seem greater than its costs. When thinking about globalization and its discontents in political and moral terms we can augment the economic arguments and clearly see that market-capitalism is inherently ill suited to confront poverty around the world or the misallocation of natural resources (primarily energy) because thinking only in terms of low costs overlooks geopolitical instability, for example, or long-term health costs from pollution and the ever-present climate change that results from overdependence on fossil energy sources. Perhaps Stiglitz's comment that globalization in itself is neither good nor bad is still true; but this truism should alert us to become more vigilant in the face of bad policies or good policies implemented poorly, or bad intentions that have the appearance of benign or benevolent ones. Sachs's plea for international cooperation and the overcoming of the private-public divide should be heeded as well: by challenging the dominance of market-capitalism we hope to achieve any of the promises for prosperity globalization has been making for a century.

Chapter Twelve

Remixing and the Knockoff Economy

The Knockoff Economy has presented a ray of hope in the fight against the neoliberal intrusion into all exchange relationships found in the economy and the restriction on opportunities in the name of protecting the private interests of inventors. Though limited to only some sectors of the economy, the fundamental challenge to patent, copyright, and intellectual property rights goes a long way in exposing the frailty and even weak practical foundation of one of the presuppositions that shores up market-capitalism. Are humans by nature competitive? If they are, are they exclusively motivated by pecuniary rewards? Or, as some would have it, are they satisfied to see their creations and ingenuity come to life regardless of financial remuneration? In other words, in this chapter we plan to reconsider one of the presuppositions that informs market-capitalism and that has been lauded as the bedrock of human activity: incentive-driven human behavior. In this context, the protection of intellectual property rights, especially when undertaken by large corporations and not individuals, in fact shifts our economic activities into the realm of "rent seeking," where the few exact a high price from their ideas or inventions from the many. Even though the Knockoff Economy seems to offer an alternative, its potential scope remains limited because of other frames of reference.

I: COPYRIGHT BACKGROUND

Adam Smith, whose treatise is supposedly the model for classical and neo-classical economic theories, explains in passing that joint-stock companies set up by merchants at great risk and expense ought to have a temporary monopoly over their routes and the goods they import from foreign countries. He says that a "temporary monopoly of this kind may be vindicated upon the

201

same principles upon which a like monopoly of a new machine is granted to its inventor, and that of a new book to its author" (1937, 712); the same argument, in greater detail, is made in his *Lectures on Jurisprudence* (1978, 83–85). But he hastens to say there, "By a perpetual monopoly, all the other subjects of the state are taxed very absurdly in two different ways: first, by a high price of goods, which, in the case of a free trade, they could buy much cheaper; and, secondly, by their total exclusion from a branch of business, which it might be both convenient and profitable for many of them to carry on" (ibid.). The obvious point here is that even when monopoly behavior is justified—hence the notion of copyright or patent—it must be temporary and not "perpetual." If it doesn't expire soon enough, the burden on society as a whole is akin to taxation, or what contemporary economists call "rent seeking," a mode of extracting extra fees for the use of an asset, such as land, housing, or intellectual property, using government regulations that benefit some entity beyond what a competitive market would expect (unfairly sanctioning an advantage to an entity beyond reasonable fees). One could quibble what "temporary" and "monopoly" mean in this context: Is there a natural timeline justifying restrictions and then relinquishing them? How long is long enough to be compensated for risks and to recoup their original costs? And does monopoly mean that no one is allowed to copy any part of the item or technique? Some contemporary answers to these questions have been in the form of "fair use," where a certain percentage (in some cases 10 percent) of one's creation or innovation or intellectual property can be reused by anyone (Lessig 2008).

It seems that the founding fathers of the United States took to heart Smith's maxim or recommendation about inventions and authors (as we saw earlier). Article I, Section 8, Clause 8 of the US Constitution empowers Congress: "To promote the Progress of Science and useful Arts, by securing for limited Times to Authors and Inventors the exclusive Right to their respective Writings and Discoveries." In this wording and intent, we can see how Smith's sentiment (no more than a couple of sentences) has become enshrined in the American economy and legal system. Over time, disputes over "limited Times" have erupted, as well as the more fundamental questions already asked in the two earlier parts of this book: Is the "promotion of the progress in the Science and useful Arts" indeed contingent on "securing" some exclusive rights? In other words, is this security the only or primary means by which to induce reluctant inventors and authors to invent and write? This approach harkens back to certain presuppositions about human behavior and human nature, discounting our innate human curiosity and the delight we feel when we invent or write, when we come up with a new idea and share it. But there is a secondary, and perhaps even more interesting, question that ought to be asked: Can one's invention or creation be credited to an individual? Put differently, does anyone ever deserve exclusive credit for inventions or creations? For some, these questions may seem bizarre, as we are accustomed since modern philosophy and the Enlightenment to think in individualistic terms, to envision the lone genius coming up with incredible ideas and novel theories. The US Constitution is uniquely structured and worded to highlight individual rights rather than social and communal obligations, taking the notion of the social contract, as we saw in part I, to be focused on the individual rather than on the individual within the community of other individuals. The question, then, is not so much about discounting individual contributions and the ways in which they make a difference in our worldview and lives, but rather if we are entitled to claim personal authorship for them to begin with.

What's the alternative? There are cultures, like the Chinese and Japanese, where knowledge is accumulated and developed communally, so that individual ownership is nonsensical. This explains why copyright violations are so rampant in that part of the world, where reverse engineering of American technologies and products—from cars to televisions—has been common, and where the American legal arm has been thwarted. If we appreciate that our cultural heritage offers us the wisdom of previous generations, and that our educational system serves as a conduit from one generation to the next, the adage attributed to Isaac Newton that we can see so far because we "stand on the shoulders of giants" comes into play. Assuming our vision depends on others, and assuming that our contributions owe much if not all to our predecessors, then the novelty of our insights should be much more circumspect. The most we can do is add something to what was already known, or use a different prism through which to explain or explore that which was fairly well established; our contributions, however great, are fundamentally based on the hard work of many others. This level of humility, incidentally, would go a long way in setting in motion a more collegial and cooperative society, where we acknowledge others as equally important in bringing to fruition a new process, product, or invention. If this sounds somewhat unconvincing, you may want to wade into the postmodern pool and appreciate Jean-Francoise Lyotard's brilliant report that there is really nothing new in this world, that we are all making some small moves in a very large chess game (1984, 66). When postmodernists say this, their intention is not to minimize individual contributions but instead highlight our indebtedness to others—the books we have read, the movies we have seen, the products we have used in our lifetime. We are always already situated in a culture saturated with material, intellectual, and spiritual wealth. We aren't born on islands, nor do we have to reinvent the wheel or the computer; we are blessed with a variety of experiences that inform us from birth to death, and it's our responsibility to publicly admit that we borrow ideas all day and give credit where credit is due. This admission can increase communal understanding about the contention that no one has the right of ownership of our publicly funded, culturally transmitted, and openly consumed knowledge.

According to the Legal Information Institute at Cornell University,

> The U.S. Copyright Act, 17 U.S.C. §§ 101-810, is Federal legislation enacted by Congress under its Constitutional grant of authority to protect the writings of authors. *See* U.S. Constitution, Article I, Section 8. Changing technology has led to an ever expanding understanding of the word "writings." The Copyright Act now reaches architectural design, software, the graphic arts, motion pictures, and sound recordings and more. *See* § 106. As of January 1, 1978, all works of authorship fixed in a tangible medium of expression and within the subject matter of copyright were deemed to fall within the exclusive jurisdiction of the Copyright Act regardless of whether the work was created before or after that date and whether published or unpublished. *See* § 301. See also preemption.
>
> The owner of a copyright has the exclusive right to reproduce, distribute, perform, display, license, and to prepare derivative works based on the copyrighted work. *See* § 106. The exclusive rights of the copyright owner are subject to limitation by the doctrine of "fair use." *See* § 107. Fair use of a copyrighted work for purposes such as criticism, comment, news reporting, teaching, scholarship, or research is not copyright infringement. To determine whether or not a particular use qualifies as fair use, courts apply a multi-factor balancing test. See § 107.
>
> Copyright protection subsists in original works of authorship fixed in any tangible medium of expression from which they can be perceived, reproduced, or otherwise communicated, either directly or with the aid of a machine or device. *See* § 102. Copyright protection does not extend to any idea, procedure, process, system, method of operation, concept, principle, or discovery. For example, if a book is written describing a new system of bookkeeping, copyright protection only extends to the author's description of the bookkeeping system; it does not protect the system itself. See *Baker v. Selden* , 101 U.S. 99 (1879).
>
> To qualify for copyright protection a work must also exhibit a minimum of originality. In *Feist Publications v. Rural Telephone Service* the Supreme Court stated that a work must have "some minimal degree of creativity." Thus, a mere alphabetical list of data is not protected, but other original aspects of the work (page layout, design, format, or even the specific selection of data points) might be. This underscores the idea that information itself is not copyrightable, only the specific arrangements or presentations of it. (Slade 2016)

Three features are noteworthy in this brief "overview": first, the constitutional sense of "writings" has expanded and transformed in the past few decades as digital technologies have overtaken our creative world, where computer programs are considered as valuable as books; second, the notion of "fair use" remains open to interpretation and at times is so expansive that it covers a variety of activities by amateurs and professionals alike; and third, that there is a threshold that must be crossed in order to qualify for copyright protection. In short, what Smith and the authors of the US Constitution had in mind has been radically reconstructed by the twenty-first century.

The profundity of the Digital Revolution is measured and tested in terms of its breaking down and reconstituting old norms and conventions about what we count as knowledge, knowledge exchanges, and the development of knowledge regimes that make access easier or more difficult, from Internet websites all the way to social media platforms. When thinking about human behavior in the social realm and the different ways in which we interact with each other, there will always be technophiles and technophobes: those who love anything to do with technoscience and those who are fearful of the downside of embracing all too cavalierly its promises (Sassower 2013). It should be recalled that the 1790 Supreme Court decision to protect one's copyright to fourteen years was extended to twenty-eight years in 1831. The National Commission on New Technological Uses of Copyrighted Works (CONTU) was appointed by Congress to establish guidelines for the "minimum standards of educational fair use" under the 1976 act, which meant that when nonprofit organizations used materials, they could freely do it, because no profit was exacted from such an activity. The latest reiteration of the US Copyright Law took place in 2011, when "The World Intellectual Property Organization (WIPO) Standing Committee on Copyright and Related Rights (SCCR) has discussed limitations and exceptions for libraries and archives since 2008 along with limitations and exceptions for persons with print disabilities and for educational and research institutions" (*Association of Research Libraries* 2016). What remains true in the twenty-first century as it was in the eighteenth is that "content" is protected because it has value: it can be sold and bought, one can "consume" it even when it is transmitted by digitally configured devices. The value of the content—shows and books, videos and images, songs and performances—differs from valuing the digital means by which the transmission is made; but digital means are protected as well and can be patented separately.

Tricky questions come to light when genetic sequencing is patented, because it's clear from numerous lawsuits that "nature" cannot be patented; we cannot reserve a copyright for something produced naturally. However, clever attempts to patent the techniques of isolating genes, for example, or slicing and pasting strings of genes, have been contested. Given the political inclination of the Supreme Court, business interests may be awarded such copyrights and patents despite some protests from the scientific community. As the US National Library of Medicine explains in its website, "On June 13, 2013, in the case of the Association for *Molecular Pathology v. Myriad Genetics, Inc.*, the Supreme Court of the United States ruled that human genes cannot be patented in the U.S. because DNA is a 'product of nature.' The Court decided that because nothing new is created when discovering a gene, there is no intellectual property to protect, so patents cannot be granted.

Prior to this ruling, more than 4,300 human genes were patented. The Supreme Court's decision invalidated those gene patents, making the genes accessible for research and for commercial genetic testing" (*Genetics Home Reference* 2017). In short, though the thirst for patenting and copyrighting remains insatiable, there has been some legal pushback to distinguish between human-made processes that can be patented and those occurring in nature.

II: DIGITAL REMIXING

Lawrence Lessig follows some of the insights already outlined by Benkler (2006) in regard to the seismic shift that digital technologies brought about, from relatively inexpensive Internet connectivity to the "wealth of networks" that improves human interaction in the Digital Age. One of the guiding questions in Lessig's book is: "Assuming we want the market to work well, is the copyright system designed to enable that?" (2008, 265) This means for him retaining the contours of market-capitalism but carving a niche, perhaps a large one, that he calls the Creative Commons where our "Creative Culture" flourishes and distributes its wares in a profoundly more pervasive and global manner than ever before. This is true of digital production, which can be now undertaken relatively inexpensively anywhere, and distribution through the Internet with websites and social media as free conduits for circulation and consumption. Two parallel concerns inform Lessig's analysis: on the one hand, the radical changes that digital technologies have brought about to the culture of creativity, and on the other hand, the legal regulations that copyright laws have imposed given their reference to older technologies. For him, a mismatch has become apparent, one that would criminalize a whole generation of users who casually participate in the Creative Culture without any expectation of monetary rewards. Yet the starting point for Lessig remains markets: "Copyright is, in my view at least, critically important to a healthy culture. Properly balanced, it is essential to inspiring certain forms of creativity. Without it, we would have a much poorer culture. With it, at least properly balanced, we create the incentive to produce great new works that otherwise would not be produced" (ibid., xvi). Market forces still dictate the balanced ways in which copyright regulations will continue to incentivize creative minds.

In the "culture of creativity," Lessig identifies two periods or two modes of public interaction: "Read/Write," where we read and copy, remix, and re-create in different modes; and a "Read/Only," one that is more comfortable in the passive consumption of culture (ibid., 28). When thinking about "amateur creativity" and the limits of copyright regulation on it (ibid., 33), the issue is the increased level and scope of "control" granted to copyright regulation (ibid., 99). What happens then is that "by default, RW use violates copyright law, RW culture is thus presumptively illegal" (ibid., 100); what's at issue here is the blurring of the difference between the professional and amateur use of the materials covered by the law, while previously the target was exclusively that professional advantage produced profits (ibid., 103). Digital changes in technology have transformed the culture, understood as the "content industry" (ibid., 38–39), into a democratizing process that allows anyone to become an artist (ibid., 54). The creative digital culture is defined as a set of activities that are not bound by the economic models and barriers to entry known before (ibid., 83); it is a remixing culture that underwrites "creative freedom that in a broad range of contexts, no free society should restrict" (ibid., 56). Remix, for Lessig, "is a collage . . . it succeeds by leveraging the meaning created by the reference to build something new" (ibid., 76). This is the case because the Read/Write culture "invites a response. In a culture in which it is common, its citizens develop a kind of knowledge that empowers as much as it informs or entertains" (ibid., 85). Even if we agree with everything Lessig says here, we might keep in mind the economic language he's comfortable with, using "leveraging" as if it were appropriate for a group of people who are engaged and entertained, challenged and expressive, without financial incentives. Personal expressions within a communal discourse grab our attention when a clever idea or image is shared freely among the entire culture.

With this economic framework, Lessig's recommendation not to abolish copyright laws but to reform or change them enough that they don't target amateur use of creative works is designed to eliminate the criminalization of an entire generation of cultural users. Differentiation between amateur and professional use, the opt-out default option when copyright expires so that the presumption is that it will then be used freely by anyone, and deemphasizing the control and responsibility to pursue presumed violators of the copyright law are recommended by Lessig. Only when it's economically worthwhile to protect copyrights will there be an incentive to control other's use, which in his mind would complement market forces and not undermine them (ibid., chapter 9). He is right to argue that "criminalizing an entire generation is too high a price to pay for almost any end. It is certainly too high a price to pay for a copyright system crafted more than a generation ago" (ibid., xviii). But in following this trajectory that presumes the supremacy and dominance of market-capitalism and the cultural artifacts it produces as commodities that should be bought and sold, he forgets his own claim that culture is inherently communal. As such, monetizing creations and submitting them to a copyright regime is fundamentally wrong-headed. Lessig himself quotes the artist Candice Breitz, who argues that "no artist works in a vacuum. Every artist reflects—consciously or not—on what has come before and what is happening parallel to his or her practice" (ibid., 8). Why not follow this sentiment and dispose of the whole argument of the unnecessary and deleterious impact of criminalizing a whole generation? His own answer is clear: "If copyright regulates copies, and copying is as common as breathing, then a law that triggers federal regulation on copying is a law that regulates too far" (269). Assuming that breathing should not be regulated (except to regulate those polluting what we might be breathing), why concede so much to the regulatory apparatus, even when reformed and modified to account for digital technology?

These lingering questions have informed a whole movement in the digital world that refuses to play by these market rules, a movement associated with "copyleft" and "open-source." Since Lessig mentions the notion of Creative Commons, understood within the broader context of the Commons (originally coined for the UK context and eventually migrated to the United States under the guise of "public goods"), we should take note of the Creative Commons website and its mission statements from 2001. According to its formulation, "The global commons is a platform for cooperation. The size of the commons is not as important as how (and if) the works it contains are used. Adding the CC license suite is just the first step in joining a vast global network of creators, companies, and institutions who are working to build context, gratitude, and other mechanisms for collaboration into the commons. We work with platforms who share our values to design tools and services that light up this universe of content and creators. Part of this is working to increase cross-platform mobility of content; another part is tracking growth and use of the content itself and reporting on major trends in our annual State of the Commons report" (http://creativecommon.org/).

The promise of a worldwide Commons that provides an alternative mode of protection and disseminating of knowledge is clear; and so is the mission of "improved search, curation, meta-tagging, and content analytics to better support creators and users of the commons, providing data for a feature in our annual State of the Commons report, development of tools and services that build context, gratitude, and other mechanisms for collaboration into the commons, [setting up] Salons and related events exploring the topics of gratitude, cooperation, and its expression in social networks, [and] other collaborations that facilitate greater cooperation and engagement in the commons" (ibid.). The inclusive nature of this website and the means by which it hopes to cope with a creative culture that transcends market-capitalist principles is encouraging. Nicolas Suzor argues that "free software licenses can be divided into two broad categories: copyleft licenses (like the GPL), which require derivatives of the software to be licensed under the same terms; and permissive licenses (like the MIT/X11 license), which allow the software to be reused in any project, even closed-source projects. There are variations, of course—the LGPL, for example, is a "weak copyleft," allowing licensed works to be used in closed-source works, but requiring improvements to the work itself to be released under a copyleft license (https://opensource.com/ 2013). Linux is a remarkable example because of its origins as an entirely open source and community built platform, and filling a void none of the software giants have been able or interested to satisfy. Linux has continued uninterrupted since 1991, a quarter of a century at this point, of open-source programming that is also used by programmers in established software companies.

Two issues that arise even under these conditions is the worry about "free-riding," when users benefit from the work of others without exerting any effort on their own, and some modicum of "user rights" associated with so-called downstream users who benefit as well from the work of others, but who contribute something to the general effort of code writing for data sets and search engines. The copyleft movement has been established to "increase the free software commons and safeguard the freedom of future users." And this means that "the licenses also reflect a particular view about fairness: a sense that it is wrongful for others to take from the commons without sharing in turn." This is ensured when "permissive licenses . . . do not treat free-riding as harmful; instead, they reflect a particular view which seeks to maximise the utility of software by refusing to restrict free-riders from appropriating its benefits" (ibid.). These are heady philosophical and ethical issues that go to the heart of our conception of human creation as well as human behavior within a community: What is fair? What rights and duties do we owe to others? And even if we believe in licensing, in this context the purpose is to protect and give credit when due rather than exact fees and fines from future users.

Suzor continues to explain on this website that "the choice between copyleft and permissive free software licenses illustrates two fascinating points":

1. Whether developers feel harmed by free-riding may be largely a result of the norms of their social network. This could have significant ramifications, since it effects their willingness to voluntarily participate in projects in the face of free-riding.
2. The copyleft licenses are a neat hack of traditional copyright practices that enable developers to set boundary conditions that create a commons that is neither fully closed nor fully open. The GPL is nondiscriminatory—it allows any potential user to join the commons, but imposes certain rules of participation. By doing so, it articulates a set of boundary conditions that are important to the community, but stops well short of total exclusivity. (ibid.)

What this commentary makes clear, as we saw in part I of this book, is that the principles associated with a social contract or the obligations of people toward their community that already established both rights and cultural knowledge play an important role. This view isn't confined to leftist critiques of market-capitalism but instead has become part of an argument for a modern movement where participants understand that a Commons of sorts ought to be formed, protected, and enlarged (whether in the physical or the digital domain). As argued elsewhere (Sassower 2013, chapters 1 and 4), what is at stake is a different way of thinking about human nature as well, as we can attest from the case of Wikipedia, where anonymous contributors spent untold hours to pull together an online resource without any compensation. Is this free contribution altruistic? How does this example, and many others, confound or undermine the self-interested mantra of market-capitalism, whether with Smithian principles or those of contemporary neoliberals? Perhaps one can claim here a sense of "belonging" to the community of contributors, but this is more an internal rather than external acknowledgment. Likewise, websites such as Craigslist offer counterexamples to eBay as free platforms for the actual sale of goods and services. Started in 1995 by Craig Newmark to share events in the San Francisco area, it has evolved into a much more comprehensive platform of all manner of classified categories in more than seventy countries. The platform itself charges no fees from participants, but, like many other "free" Internet websites and services, there are advertisement pop-ups that pay a fee to be there. In some sense, platforms like this, as we shall see in the next chapter, exemplify some sort of Invisible Hand in digital markets, but they do have an Impartial Spectator that sets the rules and regulates violation of goodwill and fair exchange.

III: THE KNOCKOFF ECONOMY

Kal Raustiala and Christopher Sprigman, in their engaging *The Knockoff Economy*, approach the question of copyright and intellectual property from a different perspective: they report that there are several sectors of the economy where no copyright or patent regulation is available to protect ideas and products, or even when brands can be protected, "the underlying clothing designs can be copied at will" (2012, 5). They illustrate an important counterargument and a counterexample to the notion that we must incentivize creators with a temporary monopoly. What's captivating in their account is that they do not focus on the reified sector of digital technologies but instead deal with everyday merchandise we all consume: the fashion industry. In their words, the "monopoly view of innovation" insists that monopoly is essential to induce the creative crowd to bring new ideas and products to the marketplace (ibid., 6). But for them, by contrast, there is a "piracy paradox": "fashion not only survives despite copying; *it thrives due to copying* . . . copying actually spurs innovation" (ibid., 5–7; italics in the original). This is true in the fashion industry, restaurant and chefs' recipes, football strategy, stand-up comedy, and open-source programming (which we already covered above). Unlike Lessig who still wants copyright law to regulate fair use and differentiate between amateur and professional use, Raustiala and Sprigman explain that innovation continues at a fairly rapid pace in these areas without any protection or regulation. The authors implicitly accept the argument that our shared background and cultural knowledge are communal and therefore cannot be parsed out piecemeal. In their words: "Innovation is often an incremental, collective, and competitive process in which the ability to build on existing creativity is critical to the creation of new and better things" (ibid., 15). Moreover, as they recount the VCR story, especially in terms of appealing to the courts to protect the potential economic losses of the film industry from VCR copying, they remind us that "the industry feared the VCR's ability to copy, but later discovered that copying created rather than killed markets, allowing the industry to grow and fueling future creativity" (ibid., 17). Predicting the future is difficult, if not impossible; and predicting unintended (positive and negative) consequences is even harder. So, unsubstantiated fears that stymie potential creativity in complementary or supplementary markets undercut the very markets that are presumed to be protected. If market-capitalism is to thrive, say Raustiala and Sprigman, then copyright legislation should be restricted if not completely abandoned. They have no problem combining what may seem to be contradictory principles: collaboration and competition. In the sectors they identify, collaboration brings about competition and vice versa. To use a postmodern lens, this is a "both/and" process rather than an "either/or" one. The fact that we work together and draw on the same sources isn't a hindrance to our competitive inclinations as to our collaborative ones (as was the case of the fourth view of human nature in part I).

Focusing on the fashion industry, the argument is that "*legal rules that permit copying accelerate the diffusion of style.*" If this conclusion seems false, the argument continues this way: "More rapid diffusion, in turn, leads to more rapid decline"; that is, decline in sales. "And the more rapid the decline, the faster and more intense is the appetite for new designs" by the consuming public, so that "as they are copied, these new designs in turn spark the creation of new trends—and, as a consequence, new sales" (ibid., 43, italics in the original). To be sure, this is not a logician sleight of hand, but an actual report from the trenches and boardrooms of the fashion industry. Just because a style is copied does not mean that the original designers rest idly or feel defeated while their creations are being copied or that there is a threat to their jobs; on the contrary, being copied is a compliment, and designers are motivated to keep on designing and set in motion new trends where their originality is appreciated and rewarded, perhaps by reputation alone, perhaps financially as well. If you remain a copier all your life, there are consequences to this as well. And this collaborative-competitive process

"drives the fashion cycle faster" (ibid.). What remains of value—the principle that undergird this process—is the "freedom to imitate" (and not the
prohibition from imitating), and economically speaking, "copying helps to
reduce the search costs of style" (ibid., 49). There are built-in economies of
scale so that the entire industry works in unison despite its differences, regardless of rivalry and branding. Admittedly, there are some social norms
that guide this open-ended knocking-off, but these are relegated to the area of
social etiquette—unwritten rules that custom and habit have embedded in the
fashion community. These etiquette rules are voluntarily followed, yes, as if
the Invisible Hand met the Impartial Spectator and decided to leave the legal
system out of human interactions (ibid., 78ff). Though Raustiala and Sprigman focus on fashion, they also make it clear that the same holds true for the
other sectors of the economy they mention. In particular, they suggest that
French *haute cuisine* abides by the following three norms: "Accomplished
chefs expect that other chefs will not copy their recipes *exactly*; Accomplished chefs expect that chefs to whom they reveal information will not pass
that information to other chefs without *permission*; Accomplished chefs expect that chefs to whom they reveal information will *acknowledge them as a
source* (ibid., 79; italics added).

The rules of this game are reasonable and easy to follow; they make
common sense. And the community of chefs in any town or city, even in any
country or continent—especially in the age of social media and Instagram—
is relatively small no matter the geographical distance. If chefs fail to follow
these simply rules, they will be exposed, even ridiculed. What distinguishes
chefs, just like designers and football coaches, is their *reputation*; the stock
in trade is how respected they are by colleagues and fellow professionals, so
that the price of being ostracized is too high. Incidentally, this way of thinking is also true for restaurant owners who know not to steal a chef or prized
employees from another restaurant. It's one thing for a chef or a key employee to want to switch jobs, quite another to be solicited from a competitor.
Restaurants in big and small cities, despite their competition with each other,
must collaborate and offer a respectable dining-out experience to the public
at large. Even if a restaurant has a dedicated following, and even if these
people eat out four times a week, they will not come to the same restaurant
all four times. Giving a recommendation of competing restaurants is routinely done so that in some real sense restaurant owners share their customers,
recommending each other with an implicit sense that this favor will be re-
turned in due course. Competition can be evident in a cooperative atmosphere.

As friendly and cooperative as the fashion industry may seem from the
evidence that Raustiala and Sprigman have collected, there are here and there
some oddities or legal cases that refute this overall sanguine attitude among
designers. As Maura Dolan asks, "Can a color be trademarked in the fashion

industry?" In general, the answer is unequivocally, no. Yet "according to a federal appeals court, the answer is yes, though the legal protection may depend on how the color is used" (2012). The dispute between Yves Saint Laurent and Christian Louboutin, is reported by Dolan: "The New York–based 2nd Circuit Court of Appeals ruled Wednesday that Christian Louboutin may prevent other fashion houses from copying his distinct use of a red, lacquered outsole on a high-heel shoe of a different color, described by the court as 'an identifying mark firmly associated with his brand.'" The issue here is not color as such but how and where it is applied, and more importantly, if a particular technique of application is directly and intimately associated with a brand (which can be patented). The Court of Appeals said in its ruling that "we hold that the lacquered red outsole, as applied to a shoe with an 'upper' of a different color, has 'come to identify and distinguish' the Louboutin brand and is therefore a distinctive symbol that qualifies for trademark protection," overturning a lower court's decision (ibid.). If this seems too expansive, the Court immediately restricted this copyright coverage. As Dolan continues, "The appeals panel nevertheless ruled that Louboutin has no protection if the color is used on both the outsole and the rest of the shoe . . . The appeals court directed the Patent and Trade Office to limit the registration of Louboutin's 'Red Sole Mark' patent only to shoes with red, contrasting outsoles" (ibid.). So, there are some cases in which a court can bring together fashion design with brand recognition and therefore protect the rights associated with the brand as they spill over into particular features of a design unique to the brand. But this case also reminds us that ongoing innovation is built into the business model of the fashion industry, and anyone caught asleep at the wheel resorts to lawsuits.

Returning to Raustiala and Sprigman's argument, even when copying becomes counterfeiting in the fashion industry, a widely popular activity around the world, "counterfeiting had a surprisingly *positive* effect on the sales of high-end branded items" (ibid., 200; italics in the original). Though sounding counterintuitive, they found that the "tendency of counterfeiters to advertise the desirability of the branded product—what we will call the 'advertising effect'—outweighed any substitution effect" (ibid.). While "substitution effect" is hurtful to sales because the brand is being substituted for an inferior and cheaper product, in this case the "advertising effects" increases sales of both the counterfeited and the original brand, especially for high-end brands. This is not true for low-end brands where the prestige of owning the brand is absent. In addition to this phenomenon, the authors also question one other market-capitalism principle: rational human behavior. In this case, they apply it not to the consumers who calculate what fashion items to purchase or to which restaurant to go, but in relation to the inventor. They argue that unlike textbooks and old-fashioned legal reasoning about the calculations these individuals make about their future prospects, there is an inherent "optimism bias" that has been reported in many studies. This bias means that calculated prospects are overly optimistic, and that individuals believe that "they will succeed where others have not, and they heavily discount the prospect of failure" (ibid., 204ff). We can safely say that we would not have entrepreneurs in this world if they didn't believe in the future success of their venture regardless of warning signs around them; risk taking is oblivious to potential disasters, and perhaps we should all be grateful that there are those among us who are willing to take risks against all rational odds and forge ahead despite an awareness that it will end badly. So, copyright or patent protection is secondary if at all part of the impetus to create, invent, and design something new.

The reason for rehearsing in some detail the issues related to copyright and patent law in regard to the fashion industry (and other sectors of the economy that are similar) is that they first, undermine certain implicit views of human nature; second, force us to examine our notions of the social contract; third, make us realize how cooperation and competition can be mutually beneficial; and fourth, illustrate in practical terms that intellectual property rights may be an old relic from a bygone era where private property defined who we are and how the State should treat us. Even if we endorse competition as a motivating factor in the human desire to excel, we should emphasize *friendly* competition rather than a savage one. We can improve someone's design or recipe, we can learn from each other and try a new formulation, maybe show off or prove we are good enough to play the game (in this or that sector), but this behavior is neither proof of our inherent competitive nature nor our gratification from money alone. As academics, we are glad if someone takes our ideas and arguments and improves on them; we are grateful to be cited by anyone who wants to critically engage us, even when they hone their scholarly attention on the problems or deficiencies they find in our work. Perhaps an academic divide comes to light among disciplinary research with the potential for commercial application. But here, too, remedies can be set in place: allowing basic research to remain public and part of the commons, while specific applications can be licensed and brought to market. Even if none of them have monopoly protection, being "first to market" (as already acknowledged in Smith's *Lectures on Jurisprudence* above) may give innovators sufficient monetary rewards, however temporary, to recoup expenses and remain sustainable. It will also signal to all participants in the market who indeed was the original inventor or creator. Pride and personal gratification of sharing one's work may count for as much or even more than a piece of paper that certifies one's legal rights. Perhaps we should end this chapter as we began it with a deeper and perhaps more congenial and naïve view found in Smith's *Wealth of Nations*. At the end of the second chapter of Book I, he says: "Among men . . . the most dissimilar *geniuses* are of use to one another; the different produces of their respective *talents*, by the general disposition to truck, barter, and exchange, being brought, as it were, into a *common stock*, where every man may purchase whatever part of the produce of other men's *talents* he has occasion for" (1937, 16; italics added).

Here is Smith, the prototypical economist, who supposedly cares only about self-interested motives to bring us to exchange in the marketplace advocating the contributions of products that result from our "genius" and "talent" into a "common stock." Exchanges may take place and prices might be set here and there, but the fundamental concern is that these geniuses and talents will find their way to a public forum, a market. This passage express- es the collective nature of our thought and work and the benefits that will accrue to the community rather than a concern about "temporary monopoly." Why else use the notion of "common stock"? Why else would humans with "dissimilar geniuses" realize that their differences are "of use to one an- other"? The point, then, is a more humane approach to human interaction, one that is as much informed by the benefits of mutual enlightenment than by personal profit. With these examples, we are confronted with more complex images of human nature and the ways we ought to think of our fellow hu- mans. If we all remember to infuse our economic behavior with a large dose of moral fortitude, patent and copyright issues would be tossed to the dustbin of historical anachronism. Or so we hope.

IV: A BRIDGE

The Knockoff Economy that is alive and well and has no signs of diminish- ing success challenges some of the preconceived assumptions associated with market-capitalism and casts new light on other sectors of the economy where digital innovations restructure market relations. Before we move to the next chapter, we must admit that some basic principles of market-capitalism remain untouched, from profit maximization to competition. The evidence before us moves us to accept Lessig's shift to a "hybrid economy" in which some parts are completely remixed while others retain barriers to copying or sharing. As he explains, what is at stake is not a legal system that should or should not be reformed, but a whole cultural sea change that has transformed young people's minds: they expect to have access to everything on the Inter- net with ease and free of charge; they expect to participate passively and actively in the Internet of everything; and they also expect that government agencies will be there to shore up the Internet, regulate its activities, and ensure their protection from predator corporate and secret agencies's surveil- lance. In short, market participation is as political as it is economic, where rights and duties are spelled out in advance and where financial motives recede to the back. Internet fees, for example, are legitimate only when they combat monopolistic or predatory market behavior. This approach is more interesting than an acceptance or rejection of market-capitalism as such, since it expresses a different mode of thinking about one's independence, money, and career. As the Pew Research Center reports, about one half of all young adults (twenty-one to thirty-four) in Europe live with their parents, while about 32 percent of the same cohort live with their parents in the United States (the highest percentage since 1940). The reasons may vary, from the impact of the Great Recession to the increase in housing costs, but the shift in a generation's attitude is not in dispute (Desilver 2016). Patent and housing arrangements may not be obvious bedfellows, but they bespeak about questioning standard frames of references. We may speculate that in an age when the Pew Religious Landscape reports that "as of 2014, 22.8 percent of the U.S. population is religiously unaffiliated, atheists made up 3.1 percent and agnostics made up 4 percent of the U.S. population," perhaps some seismic changes are taking place in American culture. Likewise, the General Social Survey reported that 21 percent of American had no religion, with 3 percent being atheist and 5 percent being agnostic in 2014 (Wikipedia). Not that religion alone is a harbinger of change, but it illustrates that perhaps old cognitive and emotional platforms are being displaced by new ones, those associated with digital technologies and with a level of custom-made communities that are temporal, distant, cooperative, and somewhat anonymous.

Chapter Thirteen

Marketing the Sharing Economy

Just as remixing and the Knockoff Economy challenge the assumption of the necessity of protecting intellectual property in the hands of private citizens, so the Sharing Economy generates optimism of change. There is a sense that a changed view of ownership is emerging, where private ownership is replaced by access to these products and services. Yet as seen with companies like Uber and Airbnb, the immediate monetizing of behavioral changes questions the hold market-capitalism still maintains on our culture. This case is interesting first, because it undermines the frame of reference of private ownership discussed in part I, and illustrates the pliability of our human nature, the human condition, and the state of our current "nature"; second, this case also reminds us that a complete money-less cooperative sharing remains suspect; which leads to the conundrum, third, of jettisoning market-capitalist practices without giving up on profit seeking as framing human exchanges.

I: THE DIGITAL AGE

(a) Technology

We already reviewed the impact of digital technologies in earlier chapters, but here the focus is on the transformative potential for these technologies; as will be seen in the next section, how they have transformed both institutional formation and the individuals who participate in them. Benkler (2006) has argued that the relatively inexpensive infrastructure required of digital networks allows for their speedy proliferation unlike anything experienced since the Industrial Revolution and the expansion of market-capitalism. This forward-looking and optimistic viewpoint has been adopted by most commentators on the Digital Age, like Clay Shirky (2010). He, too, believes in the ever-increasing democratization of processing information and the great benefits that are bound to follow. For him, the Guttenberg printing press brought about the Reformation, which heralded the scientific revolutions, which in turn brought about the Enlightenment, and which eventually delivered the Internet. It portrays a progressive historical account much akin to the view promoted by the likes of Hegel and Condorcet. For them, every historical development was either accompanied or depended on the engines of technoscience (science *and* technology). On this view, technoscience is valued for the economic growth that necessarily accompanies it. There are numerous variations of this worldview, some more concerned with economic issues proper, as in the case of classical and neoliberal economists, and some more critical (yet still progressive in the sense of seeing a future better than the past), as in the works of Marx and his disciples. Few followed the critical stance of Rousseau, who found technoscientific and economic progress to be morally suspect and therefore prone to historical regress. The various enlightenments of the eighteenth century led to an expectation of the emancipatory powers of technoscientific and economic developments, the kinds associated with the abolition of slavery and the emergence of democracy. Separating the promises of technoscience into economic, social, political, and moral is artificial at best and worse, misses the confluence of ideas and aspirations of the time.

As we move to the twenty-first century and its numerous digital revolutions, some more monumental—the Internet—and some less fundamental— the gadgets and devices consumers enjoy—we may review Rifkin's utopian vision (already cited in chapter 1). In *The Zero Marginal Cost Society: The Internet of Things, the Collaborative Commons, and the Eclipse of Capitalism* we detect how digital technologies are wrapped within a larger context of collaboration and the demise of old-fashioned capitalism. As far as he is concerned, "The capitalist era is passing . . . not quickly, but inevitably," because a "new economic paradigm—the Collaborative Commons—is rising in its wake that will transform our way of life" (2014, 1). This means that we are "already witnessing the emergence of the hybrid economy, part capitalist market and part Collaborative Commons" (ibid.). Though the notion of a hybrid economy was mentioned before, either in the context of a remixed economy or in the context of developmental economics, in this case the primary issue is that new digital technologies are bound to break down old notions, beliefs, and assumptions about human interaction in and outside the marketplace. Is this a paradigm shift in the Kuhnian sense? Are we bound to completely transform the way we think about the economy and ourselves? One answer that Rifkin offers is that given the low marginal costs of digital technologies, so low in fact that he terms this "the zero marginal cost revolution" (ibid., 4); capitalizing on digital printers, for example, will eliminate transportation costs from manufacturing facilities. His overall view is that "as more and more of the goods and services that make up the economic life of society edge toward near zero marginal cost and become almost free, the capitalist market will continue to shrink into more narrow niches where profit-making enterprises survive only at the edges of the economy, relying on a diminishing consumer base for very specialized products and services" (ibid., 5). This is what eventually has been called the Internet of Things, which is defined in terms of the connectivity through sensors that process automatically any data (ibid., 11). To use Schumpeter's terminology from a century earlier, this is a "disruptive technology" that will lead us to a "new era" in which "we each become a node in the nervous system of the biosphere" (ibid., 14). Digitized technologies and device's reliance on an "infrastructure" is radically different from previous historical moments insofar as it requires three elements: "a communication medium, a power source, and a logistic mechanism" (ibid.). Micro transactions—financial, health, social, and security—are ubiquitous in most developed countries. One can simply observe the games that are developed for smartphones/tablets and that are "free to play" as opposed to the apps that are categorized as "pay to play." Will the advertisement that accompanies them make up for their initial costs? Is this method of offering something "free" to capture attention more nefarious than traditional forms of marketing?

Digital technologies change the way we think about markets and about our interactions as participants in these markets. Unlike earlier participation we could shut off, the recent ones maintain a merciless connection to markets and workplaces even when we think we have left them behind. For promoters, like Rifkin, this Commons is "the oldest form of institutionalized, self-managed activity in the world" (ibid., 16), but critics may complain that the old Commons was a refuge while the digital Commons is a cage (however entertaining). Rifkin pushes this notion of the Commons as a "social Commons" where good will is generated and where cultural cohesion flourishes (ibid., 17), shifting the discussion from the "tragedy of the commons" (as a place decimated by capitalist forces) to the "comedy of the commons" as a way to deal with the negative aspects and to promote the positive ones (ibid., 157). And in this context, he quotes Elinor Ostrom to say that "individuals, more often than not, put the community's interest before self-interest and the long-term preservation of the common resource above each person's immediate circumstances, even when their plight was dire" (ibid., 159). If this sounds too optimistic, just think about the ways in which we download entertainment "products" to our laptops or smartphones and how by doing so we remain somehow, perhaps more philosophically than practically, part of the social Commons, exchanging our responses, learning from each other, and never quite leaving this amorphous and digitized domain. Admittedly, friendly teasing may turn ugly when it becomes bullying. The pretense that the digital Commons is virtual and therefore beyond the deleterious effects of mean-spirited individuals is naïve and misguided.

For the technophiles, the Internet of Things (or Everything) is part and parcel of a larger sociological reality that brings about "the emerging Collaborative Commons" (ibid., 18). This way of thinking fosters collaboration unseen in either capitalist or socialist models because, as Rifkin sees it, it eliminates "the centralizing nature of both the free market and the bureaucratic state" (ibid., 19). And as we shall see below, these collaborative participants are "also sharing cars, homes, and even clothes with one another via social media sites, rentals, redistribution clubs, and cooperatives, at low or near zero marginal cost" (ibid.), opting for access over ownership (ibid., 20), which is also expressed in a new kind of incentive, one that is less concerned with financial rewards and more with a desire to "advance the social well-being of humanity" (ibid., 21). This futuristic view is based on a progressive history. Rifkin identifies three Industrial Revolutions. The first (nineteenth century) started with "steam-powered printing and telegraph," which "became the communication media for linking and managing a complex coal-powered rail and factory system, connecting densely populated urban areas across national markets." The second (twentieth century) was based on the "telephone, and later, radio and television," and then "became the communication media for managing and marketing a more geographically dispersed oil, auto, and suburban era and a mass consumer society." The third (twenty-first century) is based on the Internet and "is becoming the communication medium for managing distributed renewable energies and automated logistics and transport in an increasingly interconnected global Commons" (ibid., 22). Rifkin differentiates the first two from the third because they were centralized and "top-down command and control" systems while the third is a "distributed, collaborative, and peer-to-peer technology platform" (ibid., 23), all the way to the 3D printing process that he believes will democratize manufacturing (ibid., 92–93).

The rise of market-capitalism from Rifkin's perspective combines a "vertical integration" with a view of "private property" that Weber explains is in its ideal form "a bureaucratic organization that rationalizes every aspect of commercial life under a single roof" (ibid., 44). Critics of Rifkin would point out that he considers the first two revolutions to be ushering capitalism and claiming a level of legitimacy based on the way "nature itself is organized" (ibid., 57), the kind of legitimation we observed in many of the cases examined in part I. To bolster his argument about the novelty of the third revolution, Rifkin surveys the instances where capitalist principles of competition, private ownership, and profit maximizing have been relinquished. He mentions (as we did earlier) the Free Software Movement, the Free Software Foundation, the Free Culture Movement and the Open Source Initiative (ibid., 100ff).

As we recall, Gandhi was concerned with low-tech initiatives to alleviate the plight of farmers and decrease severe poverty in India; he was also concerned with overdevelopment and the industrialization of the countryside as if it were a European continent. Rifkin follows this concern and argues for the appropriateness of the latest revolution in terms of collaboration and following Gandhi's ideals of sustainability (ibid., 107). And here Rifkin wishes to cast the latest revolution in technoscience in utopian terms: "A zero marginal society, in which scarcity has been replaced by abundance, is a far different world than the one we're accustomed to" (ibid., 109). In his words: "If the steam engine freed human beings from feudal bondage to pursue material self-interest in the capitalist marketplace, the Internet of Things frees human beings from the market economy to pursue nonmaterial shared interests on the Collaborative Commons" (ibid., 132). And the "Networked Commons becomes the governing body for a new collaborative economic paradigm" (ibid., 151). Critics would argue that so-called nonmaterial emancipation is predicated on material emancipation, because you won't be free to think if all you can think about is food. We should applaud Rifkin's engagement with some of the assumptions and frameworks we have critically discussed in parts I and II. He speaks openly about "abundance" (ibid., 273), about collaboration as "hybrid partnership" (ibid., 297), and about "empathy" and "empathic consciousness" (ibid., 301), reminiscent of the Caring Economy we discussed in chapter 10.

(b) Institutions

As we move from the technologies themselves to the people who use them and through them participate in what Rifkin believes to be a Social Commons, we are shifting from market-capitalism's framework into a more nuanced, perhaps a hybrid platform where human relations are transformed as well. It was the concern of Veblen in regard to "conspicuous consumption," as it was Tawney's concern with the "acquisitive society" over a century ago. They were both worried not so much about the profiteering that permeated markets, but what kind of institutions evolved to accommodate this culture of consumption and acquisition. Tawney was alarmed by the fact that if we were to agree that "the end of social institutions is happiness" this would mean that "they have no common end at all," and such societies "may be called Acquisitive Societies, because their whole tendency and interest and preoccupation is to promote the acquisition of wealth" (1920/1948, 29). Following the utilitarian tendencies of an earlier generation (of Jeremy Bentham, James and John Stuart Mill, and their American counterparts), this way of thinking would make "the individual the center of his own universe" and along the way "moral principles [would dissolve] into a choice of expediencies" (ibid., 31), instead of maintaining a cohesive set of communal goals.

For Tawney, as much as was the case for Veblen in terms of higher education, ownership should be "for the service of the public" and as such would remain "on behalf of the general community" (ibid., 112–113), much like the notion of a digital commons espoused by contemporary critics of market-capitalism. John Commons, the Institutional economist, is relevant here because he argued that political economy is not limited to nature and the individuals who populate it, but extends to the community of individuals who have "mutually dependent interests" within "security of expectations" that he understands as "order" (1934/1990, 57). Commons develops his notion of "transactions" among individuals that are not simply market exchanges but future-looking ways of interacting in society (ibid., 58, 118), much like Rifkin's view. For Commons, there is a "shift from commodities, individuals, and exchanges to transactions and working rules of collective action that marks the transition from the classic and hedonic schools to the institutional schools of economic thinking." He explains a century before material conditions support him that "the shift is a change in the ultimate unit of economic investigation, from commodities and individuals to transactions between individuals" (ibid., 73). The transformation is from an attitude of classical economics of "let-alone" to the more explicit permutation of neoclassical economics in its neoliberal guises as "exploitation," all the way to the more enlightened and less problematic rubric of being "pragmatic" (ibid., 117).

A similar approach to shifting the focus of economic studies from individuals and their commodities to the intangible sphere of transactions and relations among participants is also understood by Douglass North, an Institutional economist and Noble Laureate of the late twentieth century. In his view, what helps the marketplace is the institutions that surround and protect it, that define and are defined by it insofar as they "reduce uncertainty by providing a structure to everyday life" (1990, 3, 25). What institutions and their rules help accomplish is defining the boundary conditions within which individual and communal choices can be made. His interest, therefore, is to integrate "individual choices with the constraints institutions impose on choice sets [as] a major step toward unifying social science research" (ibid., 4). North sees the process of institutional change as incremental (ibid., 6), and he adds to his observations a "game theoretical framework" to appreciate coordination and cooperation among individuals (ibid., 12). In his words: "I intend to demonstrate that institutions basically alter the price individuals pay and hence lead to ideas, ideologies, and dogmas frequently playing a major role in the choices individuals make" (ibid., 22). As examples of his approach, North cites the complexity and incompleteness of information that inevitably undermine the neoclassical model that considers such issues either as transparent (reflected in prices) or exogenous (and thus irrelevant to prices). The abolition of slavery isn't an economic factor but also one that changed its institutional legitimacy, as is the case with altruism (ibid., 23–26).

The reason to rehearse some of the Institutionalist views (mentioned above) is because they offer the conceptual foundation for what is being proposed nowadays with new digital platforms. Since exchange processes must be measured and enforced, they require regulatory institutions: "How well institutions solve the problems of coordination and production is determined by the motivation of the players (their utility function), the complexity of the environment, and the ability of the players to decipher and order the environment (measurement and enforcement)" (ibid., 34). In a highly decentralized economy of everything, when transaction costs seem minimal, there still is an essential need for enforcing some rules, perhaps not the ones associated with the legal system but at least those of etiquette (as mentioned above in connection to the Knockoff Economy). We hope that participants will self-regulate and behave in moral ways when exchanging ideas and services, goods and expertise; but can we count on the goodwill of others? Can a digital platform be based on this alone? Social media platforms have denied access to those who violate a code of decency or who use profanities to express their displeasure. There is an ongoing public (not legal) pressure on the likes of Facebook and Google to exclude and censor, to monitor and filter inappropriate behavior (either in form of cyberbullying or in the form of terrorist recruitment). The fact that we might be appealing to private rather than public institutions doesn't negate the fact that an institutional intervention is both necessary and legitimate. North already outlines different kinds of institutions: "1. Personalized exchange which requires little; 2. Impersonal exchanges that require religious or ritualistic supervision; 3. Impersonal exchange with third-party enforcement of the state" (ibid., 34–35). From this classification, informal constraints and formal rules differ only in degree from each other as well as from tribal norms and kinship ties, even as they become more codified and rigid in modern economies. How many of them are personally sanctioned and internalized remains an open question that depends on other cultural customs and habits, as Hume would call them (ibid., 36–40). North continues: "No institutions are necessary in a world of complete information. With incomplete information, however, cooperative solutions will break down unless institutions are created that provide sufficient information for individuals to police deviation" (ibid., 57). One can think of the potential and actual role played by the Federal Reserve Board before, during, and after the collapse of financial institutions that brought about the Great Recession. This august institution, the most powerful in the world, was supposed to regulate rather than deregulate financial institutions on behalf of the public, and oddly enough, in the climate of neoliberal conservatism, intervened perhaps too late and bailed out private banks with public funds (Federal Reserve chairman's account in Bernanke 2015). Likewise, Prisoner's Dilemma outcomes (as we have seen) are much better under conditions of cooperation than under conditions of individual isolation and personal choice. The incentives for two prisoners to cooperate (and never admit to the crime) ignore the truth about who committed the crime. And since individual advantages at the expense of the community are counterproductive in the long run, it behooves our institutional arrangements to encourage some level of cooperation and an even higher level of transparency and accountability of all participants in transactions. Moreover, we should align the political and economic institutional outlook to ensure compatibility and harmony instead of contentious strife at the behest of economic powerhouses.

One way to rethink capitalist frames of reference in the Digital Age is Paul Mason's view of postcapitalism. Just as North uses Darwin's theory of evolution to explain how institutions are weeded out, but then he gives ample counterexamples of inefficient technologies that have survived (ibid., 94–96), so does Mason explain that capitalism has been "*a complex, adaptive system which has reached the limits of its capacity to adapt*" (2015, xiii; italics in the original). In his analysis of the future of capitalism, and the demise of Marxism (because of its lack of adaptability), Mason argues that "mainstream economists assume that markets promote perfect competition and that imperfections—such as monopolies, patents, trade-unions, price-fixing cartels—are always temporary. They also assume that people in the marketplace have perfect information" (ibid., 118); but all of this is neither empirically the case nor does it comport with the established models. Instead, he, too, promotes a notion of "third capitalism" or "cognitive capitalism" (ibid., 139), the kind that is highly dependent on the new digital technologies and all the advantages they bring to market exchanges. For him, then, a fight between "network and hierarchy" where networked individuals will resist any institutional forms of hierarchy is inevitable (ibid., 144). Though we covered the debates between technophiles and technophobes elsewhere (Sassower 2013), perhaps we should explain once again that despite the great promises of digital platforms and the easy access they offer all newcomers, there are various subtle and not so subtle forms of control and centralized censorship that are both private and governmental and that are not limited to national security. Here one can enumerate the exploitation of freely gathered data from individuals who share their personal and private affairs (from Amazon and Google profiles to Facebook and Instagram) all the way to the kind of meta-data searches regularly undertaken by the likes of the National Security Agency. Some could argue that standard hierarchical institutions of the past at least did not pretend to care about individual privacy and democratizing the public sphere, while contemporary ones disguise their power and lure us to a greater sense of complacency. The vigilance of yesteryear has been replaced with promises of immediate gratification and continuous entertainment.

II: THE PROMISES OF THE SHARING ECONOMY

As we saw above, the linkage between specific technologies and the behavior they engender has been reconfigured in the past few decades. Unlike previous technoscientific revolutions, the digital one is spurring new speculations about how people do and will interact in a much less structured fashion so that notions of the market (or for that matter, the Commons) take on different manifestations. We no longer need to physically go to a market, because the market is accessible through our personal computers and smartphones as in the case of eBay and Craigslist, to mention just two such venues of buying and selling goods and services. Large clearinghouses are set up in the background, hardly noticeable, with credit card and PayPal (and in some cases Bitcoins) as the financial lubricants to safeguard for smooth and speedy transaction fulfillment. Our local farmer's markets are nostalgic throwbacks to a period where neighbors met each other in the village square to buy and sell their products. Arun Sundararajan's *The Sharing Economy* is the most comprehensive manifesto to date and an endorsement of what we call the "shared" or Sharing Economy. Perhaps the subtle shift from the more descriptive to the more active tense of the verb *to share* is intended to push us to engage more fully in this transformative way of human relations. To begin with, Sundararajan suggests that "the assortment of behaviors (and organizations) that many of us optimistically call 'sharing economy' are early instances of a future in which peer-to-peer exchange becomes increasingly prevalent, and the 'crowd' replaces the corporation at the center of capitalism" (2016, 2). This brings us back historically to a time when "prior to the Industrial Revolution, a significant percentage of economic exchange was peer-to-peer, embedded in community, and intertwined in different ways with social relations" (ibid., 3). Unlike Rifkin's futuristic vision, this way of defining contemporary behavior and codifying its potential is retrospective, perhaps along the lines of the retro thrift stores found in hipster culture. What's new about this kind of exchange among people?

First, new digital technologies offer an expanded community, one that transcends traditional self-imposed boundaries; second, these digital platforms have enormously scaled these exchanges across demographic and geographic horizons; and third, they offer more extensive forms of financing from a crowd of entrepreneurs who otherwise wouldn't have participated in this crowd-based and sharing economy (ibid., 5–6). As already noted elsewhere (Sassower 2013), unlike venture capital and angel investing, crowdfunding is indeed a novel way of thinking about financing new ideas and their implementation, since it appeals to a wide audience of potential contributors (who may not know the person who is asking for funding), and unlike earlier modes of funding, there are no moral ties or legal obligations. The anonymity of crowdfunding liberates the inventor from the expectations of remuneration if and when the project succeeds. It also prevents the funding crowd from either directing or derailing the project, and this definitely undermines the potential of exploitation by the funding crowd if the project succeeds. The crux of this new way of interacting will necessarily "redefine whom [sic] we trust, why we trust them, what shapes access to opportunity, and how close we feel to each other" (Sundararajan 2016, 6). If other forms of funding have been characterized by profit seeking and lack of congeniality between those who come to the table with money and those with ideas, the "peer-to-peer" approach attempts to overcome this way of doing business. What is foregrounded is a newly found trust that can be generated through systems that offer some digital cues on the reliability of people and the products they offer (ibid., 60). The downside may be that crowdfunding sites may streamline efforts of potential investors to find good ideas and just buy them outright in one manner or another.

According to Sundararajan, the five characteristics of the sharing economy are: first, it remains market based and as such isn't destabilizing market-capitalism, only revising some of its practices and parameters; second, that it has high-impact capital, which means the focus on specific technologies and platforms; third, crowd-based networks are diffused and decentralized without the financial hierarchies and bureaucratic mazes that characterize contemporary market-capitalism; fourth, this way of interacting blurs personal and professional lines so that you are just as likely to enjoy the resources of your family and friends as those of complete strangers (who may become your friends); and fifth, it blurs the lines between fully employed and part-time, on-demand work, and this disruption of labor markets allows for greater flexibility and freedom to both employers and employees (whose roles are themselves blurred depending on the situation) (ibid., 27). This kind of hybrid economy is less concerned with the remixing of intellectual property rights in the entertainment industries, as Lessig, for example, was interested in exploring; instead, it blurs the distinction between commercial (market) transactions and those exchanges considered "sharing" but which do not qualify as "gifting" (ibid., 34). The fact that sharing is not gifting is important to emphasize here as there is an economic element that remains at the heart of the Sharing Economy, so that perhaps the subtitle of Sundararajan's book is more telling: "The End of Employment and the Rise of Crowd-Based Capitalism."

We will look at the first part of this subtitle in the next section (as a critical assessment), but must explain here that "crowd-based" capitalism has a dual meaning. On the one hand, it could mean Consumer Capitalism (which we already discussed in chapter 10), or it could mean that capitalism is driven by the crowds, the consumers who determine what to buy and sell, what is fashionable here and now. The former meaning has been critically evaluated above, but the second, it seems, draws its inspiration from the notion of the "wisdom of the crowd." James Surowiecki's book (2004) explains that the collective wisdom of many people is more informative and at times more accurate than that of elite experts. This democratic populism is attractive on many levels, especially when demonstrated as a TED talk with an ox whose weight had to be guessed by the audience; the average of all the guesses was 1,792 pounds and the ox weighted 1,795 pounds. This was used as a demonstrable proof that a random crowd of people can and will guess correctly anything that is posed to it, from the weight of an ox to the future of political candidates. But as impressed as we may be by such feats, we should worry if the lowest common denominator is not the ruling principle underlying this populist appeal; this in turn may not offer the best result, as we observe when fascist leaders are democratically elected. Would you trust the crowd (or an expert) to diagnose your disease? Would you want a novice to negotiate your house sale? Or, for that matter, how reliable can a bunch of strangers be in predicting the longevity of your marriage? In other words, though there is some appeal for the idea of the "wisdom of the crowd," we are loath to relegate to popular opinion decisions that are better handled by experts within the guidelines of democratic institutions.

But there is another dimension that crowdfunding and the reluctance to abide by the wisdom of experts and power elites brings into focus: people's psychological predispositions. Perhaps this is not at the conscious or critical level discussed in the first two parts of this book, but it is present in the form of wanting to care for other people and sharing one's knowledge and material possessions. The focus on the psychology of economic interactions is central to Behavioral Economics (as we already noted above), which has made us aware that our behavior is neither fully rational nor completely driven by calculated instrumental rationality. As Sundararajan summarizes some of the data collected from surveys and experimental observations, "Hyper consumption [of the twentieth century] is defined by ownership, collaborative consumption [of the twenty-first century] by shared access" (ibid., 28). This point is crucial for understanding the psychological transformation of recent consumerism, perhaps driven by digital technologies, perhaps by the fear of the recurrent failures of market-capitalism. This is a seismic breakdown of preconception about one's behavior and the yardstick by which we measure adulthood and success. If the "baby boomers" characterized their personal ascend as climbing the ladder of achievement in terms of career and possessions, buying houses in the suburbs and replacing their cars every three to four years, the millennial generation measures itself in different terms. A house is a burden, especially in view of the housing bust of the Great Recession, and a car is a nuisance in urban centers where parking is expensive if available at all. Why buy when you can rent or lease? Why invest in material possessions whose value may decrease over time rather than increase? In other words, why not simply have access to what you need when you need it while avoiding the extra costs of keeping and maintaining it while it is not being used? In short, why not share assets—car, house, tool—with others? One's sense of self, one's self-confidence, is less determined by ownership than by what clever response you can offer to this or that social media trope or meme, even though a sense of privacy is retained for some possessions, like one's smartphone.

Sundararajan sounds at times more like a marketing director for a PR company that wants to sell us on the rise of "crowd-based capitalism" than a critical academic observer of the phenomenon under consideration. Perhaps his own involvement as a consultant and investor in some of these ventures skews his views. Perhaps he still tries to shoehorn this new phenomenon into market-capitalism as an extension rather than a transformation. A clue to this sentiment can be gleaned from a quote he gives of Michael Spence: "The truth is that the Internet-led process of exploiting under-utilized resources— be they physical and financial capital or human capital and talent—is both unstoppable and accelerating" (ibid., 204). Indeed, the story told of Uber and Lyft as alternative modes of transportation has as much to do with seeing millions of unused cars most of the day (and that can be driving non car owners to their destinations) as it has to do with finding underutilized labor (to supplement cab and bus drivers). He continues to say: "The long-term benefits consist not just in efficiency and productivity gains (large enough to show up in macro data), but also in much-needed new jobs requiring a broad range of skills. Indeed, those who fear the job-destroying and job-shifting power of automation should look upon the sharing economy and breathe a bit of a sigh of relief" (ibid.). In addition to maximizing the utility of inanimate objects, like cars and apartments, we can maximize the usefulness of under-employed people, making sure they can find new niches of employment in areas that they thought were closed to them (because a taxi medallion in New York City, for example, is too expensive and thereby becomes a barrier to entry into this market sector). But if greater productivity and efficiency are the drivers of this new approach to the economy, then digital technologies simply enhance an already hyper market-capitalist economy. Is the Sharing Economy indeed a game-changer?

Thinking about the transformative core of the Sharing Economy, moving people from owners to users, undermines some of the presuppositions we examined in part I. The notion of private property as an inherent extension of one's being and one's labor is hereby questioned. Similarly, one's propensity to own, accumulate, and compete with others is questioned as well. When these presuppositions are questioned, then we also can question the condi-

tions under which a social contract should be formulated: Is it for the preven-
tion of a war of all against all, or is it instead to set parameters for friendly
relations among community members? Is the trust of the Sharing Economy
enhanced through digital platforms? If the handshake of yesterday with eyes
locked in sincere agreement is replaced by a click of one's digit on a smartphone to see previous "ratings" (of an Uber driver or Airbnb owner), are we
really speaking of different kinds of trust? Or, have we simply substituted
one form of verification with another? If we really have a stronger sense of
trust among millennials, then why even check one's background? Perhaps
there is a radical change afoot, but its implications haven't been fully tested.
The logic of "why not tap into the millions of sometimes-empty apartments
and spare rooms around the world?" (ibid., 8) doesn't exude confidence that
the owners of these apartments are trustworthy, only that they can be exploited for their sense of greed—making money off unused bedrooms. So, changing one's attitude about ownership is a game-changer, but it may not rely so
much on trust as it does on responsibility.

Perhaps what is at issue here is that millennials have figured out that
ownership is accompanied by a responsibility to maintain one's material
possessions. Or, that they may want to settle into their careers and long-term
relationships before they buy a home (Matthews 2015). So, is the distaste for
ownership an indicator of less responsibility? One could argue, on the
contrary, that younger adults are super responsible and the fact that they are
waiting longer to commit to home ownership is a clear sign of their maturity.
Unlike their parents, they don't rush into marriages (that end up in high
divorce rates) or into buying a home with a thirty-year mortgage. Having
seen their parents separate and the housing market collapse, they are wary of
being irresponsible. If we think of the Sharing Economy as the medium
through which to navigate less commitments and ensure responsible behavior
in regard to economic issues (which may not be true of hooking-up platforms
like Tinder), then perhaps this is a hint of a game-changer, a new way of
thinking about one's role and position in society (but not in the way Sundararajan sells it).

In addition to the responsibility factor, there might be another feature of
the Sharing Economy worth examining: personal empowerment. As Sundararajan suggests, "Perhaps the flexibility and fluidity of contracting through
digital platforms rather than working a day-job can be empowering" (2016,
11). Leaving aside the labor market (which will be discussed in more detail
in the next section), we can appreciate the flexibility that is enjoyed by using
cars when needed, leasing tools needed only once (for excavating a sewer
line, for example), or trying out games you may not enjoy playing more than
once. Wouldn't you rather explore the potential of a new neighborhood by
renting a room for a month in someone's house than buy a house and only
then realize that the train, seemingly in the distance, blows its whistle so

loudly that you can't fall asleep? This fluid and flexible exchange relation necessarily puts you in touch with more people than you would have if you stayed on the buying-only trajectory. Perhaps including more people in our life, incidentally and accidentally as it were, forces us to know our community better, and may bring about stronger community identity than under the consumptive model of markets. This is a potential, not a guarantee. Social platforms have been used to share information about gallery openings, farmers' markets, new restaurants, and music venues to bring people together for a while. As a means of communication, social media can and does create communities across boundaries that weren't crossed as often before. This potential is a game-changer in a growing population whose center, whether we think of the local church or the school, has become more dispersed, fractured, and diverse. When we eschew the old model that prompted us to purchase vinyl in the local record store and instead share freely music preferences with personal commentary, does this motivate us to collaborate (rather than compete) more often? Does this illustrate to the skeptic that there is some goodness in strangers whose advice we can use free of charge? Will this change the mind of market-capitalists that other forms of exchange are just as rewarding and fulfilling? And here one wonders why greater portions of our exchange relationships aren't in fact gift relations that defy the very notion of exchange value of goods and services. In the last two chapters of this book we will examine more fully this question.

Before we turn to the critical evaluation of the promises of the Sharing Economy, we should note what Sundararajan tells about the lessons of medieval trading communities in the Middle East and elsewhere. These merchants leveraged either their reputation or shared interest to establish and maintain trust among their customers and other traders so that corruption and cheating would be punished over time (ibid., 144). The rules of the game that these merchants developed became institutionalized insofar as claiming trustworthiness turned into marketing of one's brand, where trusting the brand ensures economic longevity. Think of the scandals that have come to our attention in regard to the banking sector, from fines levied against violations of the rules of the game when issuing mortgages, derivatives, to lying about setting interbank interest rates (LIBOR); all in all, the major financial institutions, from investment banks to hedge funds, have paid over $200 billion in fines and penalties over the past eight years, more than the GDP of some countries (Cox 2015). Is this the kind of trust the Sharing Economy has in mind? With access to digital information and the exposure that inevitably uncovers corruption and fraud, what we should consider *transparency by default* (because you are bound to be caught), basic trust in our regulated and already bailed-out financial institutions is not to be expected. Perhaps they believe that paying fines after their misbehavior is the "cost of doing business," so they factor these costs as nuisances on the way to profiteering;

perhaps they calculate the odds of being caught. Is the promise of trust-worthiness limited to the person who picks us up in a private car, or the person who lets us stay in the spare room of their apartment? Has the financial sector checked out of the digital revolution except to ensure the lowering of labor costs by encouraging online banking, ATMs instead of cashiers, and performing high-frequency trading? These questions lead us to the labor market that Sundararajan claims will "end unemployment," as the subtitle of his book promises.

III: MONETIZING ALL TRANSACTIONS

Three main critical approaches confront the promises of the Sharing Economy. The first is related to the question of labor or the promise of full employment. Perhaps Sundararajan is correct that more people may find flexible work hours and contract jobs through digital platforms, when "on-demand" employment is enhanced. But as he himself admits, "The drawback of this economy is related to its workforce which will become more temporary, on-demand, and therefore less reliable with no benefits" (2016, 11). Flexibility is one thing, but not having enough work, or being always worried if another job will come one's way, is more anxiety provoking than a full-time employment in a less than desirable work environment. Steve Fraser identified the issues related to this underemployment without reliability and benefits (health insurance, sick days, vacation, or pension) as related to a broader ideological warfare that has clobbered the workforce. This isn't simply a fight against unions or depleting the power of organized labor, but a more pernicious ploy that uses the rhetoric of freedom and liberation. If we are told that our "emancipation" is based on our consumptive and employment choices, that we should take on more personal, entrepreneurial "risks," then the notion of "flexible capitalism" has taken hold of our collective consciousness (2015, 214–218). What Marx understood as the "reserve army of the unemployed" that capitalists exploited because they could offer them low wages has turned upside down into "flexible" and "temporary" labor that connotes control and choice of "free agents." And this, as we have seen more recently, has freed private and public entities alike not to "pay into Social Security, Medicare, or unemployment insurance accounts, to respect wage and hour laws, or to pay workmen's compensation" (ibid., 234–255; 327–329). This has meant that over time those who are classified as poor in the United States may be fully employed or have multiple employments, all of which exclude benefits. James Livingston's damning report on the end of full employment is relevant here, too (2016).

The second critique of the promises of the Sharing Economy is more concerned with an existential "false consciousness" for which this way of thinking is responsible. Beyond individual laborers, there is a sea of change in our attitudes toward the community as a whole, where all relations turn out to be "economized." We already see that Fraser's concern is not limited to the particulars of the labor market and its abuses, but includes a more radical and disturbing trend that undermines our sense of community: "What is therefore most pernicious about the recent ascendancy of free market thinking is perhaps not so much the triumph of its public policies. Rather, it is how its spirit of self-seeking has exiled forms of communal consciousness, rendered them foolish, naïve, wooly-hearted, or, on the contrary, sinful and seditious. A cultural atmosphere so saturated with these suspicions is a hard one in which to maintain or create movements or institutions built on oppositional foundations" (Fraser, 2015, 370). The incessant neoliberal undermining of community as an ideal and as a bond for social action has been mentioned earlier by Brown as well (2015).

As the last two chapters of this book will attempt to suggest, there must be a way to recapture the sense of community and solidarity in the economic sphere. If the economic sphere itself cannot be the model for solidarity, at least it shouldn't stand in the way. But if the Sharing Economy is bent on blurring the lines between the commercial and the personal, if it is successful in bringing the personal into the commercial, we should be wary that it doesn't do the reverse; namely, turn the personal into a commercial zone of exchanges, where money dominates all relations. As Elizabeth Popp Berman reminds us (2014), the notion of "economizing" everything, from science and technology to education and healthcare, has become the battle cry of neoliberalism. This means that unless one can put a monetary value on an activity or policy, unless one can "monetize" human interaction, it has no meaning. Put differently, just as meatpackers value human limbs and body parts in a specific financial way (with legal precedence), we have taken the commercialization and financial elements of some sectors of the economy and economized the rest of our lives. These issues were brought up earlier in this book when discussing Reich's, Kuhner's, and Brown's concern with the political domain being colonized by the neoliberal tendency to quantify the agency of citizens and put a dollar value on our decision-making processes. If we encountered earlier arguments about the evolution of capitalism and its plasticity, surviving one crisis after another to retain its most salient features, in this context we are encountering its neoliberal incarnation, itself open to changes for the sake of sustaining market-capitalism and extending its hold all the way into the Sharing Economy. Just as Fraser is concerned with the pernicious rhetoric of freedom, liberation, self-expression, and even emancipation, so is Brown concerned with the "normative reason" displayed by neoliberalism: in its dominance, it is "extending a specific formulation of economic values, practices, and metrics to every dimension of human life" (2015, 30). She continues to explain: "Neoliberal rationality disseminates the *model of the market* to all domains and activities—even where money is not the issue—and configures human beings exhaustively as market actors, always, only, and everywhere as *homo economicus*" (ibid., 31; italics in the original).

The third line of critique deals with how to think about the choices that economic variables demand of us. In other words, what policies should we pursue to promote the greatest prosperity to all? How can the Sharing Economy indeed decrease inequalities and guarantee prosperity? If Brown is correct that "market actors are rendered as little capitals (rather than as owners, workers, and consumers) competing with, rather than exchanging with each other" (ibid., 36), then they have lost the potential leverage that the Sharing Economy promised them. And if the process of dehumanization isn't reversed or at least stopped under the great promises of sharing, then what use are digital inventions and platforms? In fact, they may turn out to be even more invasive and demanding, enslaving us in the name of emancipation: we readily submit to monthly payments of hundreds of dollars to have the latest version of a smartphone and its connectivity, the kind that allows anyone to track us anywhere and expects immediate response. In short, any promise of freedom and equal opportunity is decimated by the onslaught of digital innovators who turn us into addicts, who pretend to emancipate us but instead disempower us even further than our bosses. Perhaps not quite Orwellian in its dystopian images, but the Sharing Economy isn't utopian at all. Power relations are so diffused in this new economy that in fact any powerful corporation or government agency can easily and surreptitiously take charge of our lives, directing us to acquiesce in a friendly but manipulative way. At least under market-capitalism we knew what to watch out for, what to defend ourselves from, but with the pretense of a kinder, gentler, and more sharing set of relations we have put our guard down and are no match for the likes of Steve Jobs, Mark Zuckerberg, or any other young and charming nerdy genius offering us the latest candy we should try. Admittedly, these new purveyors of entertainment and distraction aren't malicious or as solicitous as some other companies whose products we really don't need; we do enter voluntarily into the sphere of Google and Facebook as opposed to being forced somehow to use financial instruments for our most basic daily transactions or being under government surveillance.

Even economists like Stiglitz are concerned with this development and advocate a resistance to unfair rules and regulation. Unlike Berman, Fraser, and Brown, Stiglitz's critical assessment of the economic mindset of neoliberal economists is still deeply anchored in market-capitalism, but at least he wants to look for what he calls "shared prosperity." His own critique of the Sharing Economy is voiced in these terms: "The sharing economy may bring great freedom and flexibility, but certainly requires that we update a legal framework forged three-quarters of a century ago, when the National Labor

Relations Act and the labor regulations that followed assumed a more sustained employer relationship and a narrower definition of what it means to be
a worker" (2016, xii). To capitalize on the promises of the Sharing Economy
we need to reformulate the legal system that is outdated if not detrimental to
its success. It's interesting that even he, as a somewhat neoclassical Institutional economist, admits that "where there was once a balance of powers
between the private sector, labor institutions, and government, we now have
forces pulling us in the direction of greater inequality" (ibid., 15). The sensitivity to power relations so far is not as pronounced as it should be, and
therefore leads many to believe that the digital revolution undermines the
power of large, multinational corporations and their lobbyists. Here we begin
to detect how there should be a link between the negative consequences of
economic inequalities and their moral dimension. For Stiglitz, an "innovative
economy requires a *balanced* and *differentiated* intellectual property regime—combined with strong direct public support, especially for basic science and technology" (ibid., 33; italics in the original). If we are lured into
believing that the market will take care of itself—and of us—then Stiglitz
warns us that the market is rigged and can be unrigged, its rules can be
changed because they are human made. This way of thinking takes us back to
some of our earlier discussions in parts I and II where we mentioned Rousseau, who distinguishes so brilliantly between natural and artificial inequalities, those we cannot control (even in the age of plastic surgery and life-
extending methods) and therefore we should leave them alone, and those
others (hereditary titles and fortunes) that can easily be transformed to safeguard at the very least equal opportunities. The Sharing Economy has its
proponents and critics, those who swear by it as the best possible economic
arrangement we can hope for, and those who realize that digital novelties
don't transform power relations on their own.

And finally, as we think about successful platforms like Uber (with market evaluation of $68 billion at the end of 2015), we should note two of its
economic features. The first is that its profits are made off its drivers, its
independent contractors, and not its full-time administrative employees.
Even Senator Elizabeth Warren (D. MA) has been quoted as saying that "the
much-touted virtues of flexibility, independence and creativity offered by gig
work might be true for some workers under some conditions, but for many,
the gig economy is simply the next step in a losing effort to build some
economic security in a world where all the benefits are floating to the top 10
percent" (Grenoble 2016). The Sharing Economy is here relabeled the Gig
Economy, where individuals have a gig here and there, the way musicians
have talked about their performances at coffee houses or nightclubs, knowing
full well that these opportunities don't amount to a full-time job with benefits. So, the first issue is the exploitation of employees as a means of profiteering. The second issue, related to the first, is that any other "me-too"

opportunist can enter this sector of the market and threaten Uber, as Lyft tried to do before and as Juno is doing now. This means that by simply appealing to a higher percentage of compensation for drivers, a newcomer can destabilize the existing platform and take away customers (Kolhakatar 2016). The question about this second point is whether there is any loyalty and trust among the members of this platform, from the designers of the platforms and their owners to the drivers and their clients. If new forms of trust were touted above, how do they fare in this platform? The simple ranking of drivers and passengers does little to warrant future interactions and brand loyalty. One wonders if this Gig Economy is moving us forward or backward, if it enhances our sense of camaraderie or exploits our diminishing resources even more than the straightforward maligned market-capitalism.

IV: A BRIDGE

As we conclude this chapter and part III, we see that these alternatives to old-fashioned market-capitalism are in fact no alternatives at all. They sound good, they even question some presuppositions, such as property rights and private ownership, but they refrain from digging deeper into the foundations of market-capitalism. One may wonder if these foundations are too strong to ever challenge; if so, is it advisable to undermine these foundations? As seen so far, and as we propose to examine in part IV, the quest for prosperity cannot rest with whatever has already been tried, since we see greater in-equalities, suffering, and disillusionment. This is not only true of the developing countries but also in the more developed parts of the world, where pockets of poverty and wage enslavement remain the policy of democratic authorities. In what follows, we attempt to break loose from the constraints of economic analysis proper or from the economic considerations that inform the institutional organization of the economy, and venture into other regions of the State, whether military or religious. Political economy informs a mode of thinking about the broader framing of economic exchanges to include the nonmonetary ones. Perhaps the goal of a community should not be growth as such, but sustainability with a cosmopolitan identity and enhanced content-ment of all its members. The ideals of spiritual leaders may spread to other leaders, whether they run companies or agencies, educational or rehabilita-tion facilities; they may help redirect our infatuation with success as meas-ured by wealth and teach us the lesson of the Caring Economy and millenni-als who insist on balancing their work and life: let us work as little as possible to live as comfortably as possible, instead of living as stressfully as possible to work as much as possible. But when this is said, it in no way endorses religious spirituality nor the institutional settings in which they are traditionally practiced. Instead, let us never forget that the accumulation of wealth for its own sake has historically been morally frowned upon, and moreover, given a critical empirical examination, we can also conclude it is an unreasonable way to conduct one's life.

Part IV

Reframing Political Economy

As we have seen in part III, most alternatives to market-capitalism adopt many of the unexamined assumptions that underline market-capitalism. In this sense, they offer no alternatives. They are additions and revisions, ways by which the core of market-capitalism remains intact and only its peripheral extensions change, given technological and cultural transformations. Digital changes to markets haven't touched the core, the rich get richer, the poor get poorer, and the rhetoric of overcoming inequality and eradicating poverty sounds as hollow as ever before. The question, therefore, is not about changing the core but what this core is all about: Is it Smith's concern for moral sentiments, or is it the neoliberal thirst for profits at any cost?

Social scientists can select their preferred set of data to prove their claims that the economy improved or that access to democratic institutions increased. But whatever one group proves, another can just as easily disprove (not because of the rhetoric of "fake news" favored in the United States). We can cite the fact that "more than 45 million people, or 14.5 percent of all Americans, lived below the poverty line last year," as the Census Bureau reported, that "the percentage of Americans in poverty fell slightly from 15 percent in 2012," that "the level of poverty is still higher than 12.3 percent in 2006, before the recession began" (Gongloff 2014). We can also cite an alternative: "The official US poverty number is 14.5 percent. That's the percentage of the population that are below the official poverty line. However, that's not actually as useful a number as many seem to think that it is. There's a number of strangenesses [*sic*] about how that number is worked out and it might well be more accurate to say that the US poverty number is 4.5

percent" (Worstall 2015). Which data presentation should we trust? Are data points the final arbiters of the state of the economy? Besides, is poverty the only or the best yardstick with which to measure American prosperity? What about inequality? (Stiglitz 2013) Should we focus on income inequality or wealth inequality? What's the relationship between them? (Piketty 2014)

Since this book is about the quest for prosperity for all (rather than an imaginary balance between those enjoying prosperity and those who are not), we are still in search of real alternatives to the core of market-capitalism. As we move in this final part of the book to examine models that might seem unrelated to economics directly, our aim is to learn something about their institutional structures and the way they approach their decision-making processes and internal policies.

Chapter 14 examines four models, the Catholic Church, the Kibbutz movement in Israel, some communes in the United States, and the military. In each case, our only concern is to highlight certain salient features that could be informative to formulating an economic model. How informative they may be to rethink our economic relations remains an open question, but what can be said from the outset is that in all these case studies, a robust sense of community is developed and a strong sense of cooperation manifests itself. Whether these practices can be imported into an economic model remains to be seen.

Finally, chapter 15 will outline an economic model that does not conform to some of the traditional frames of references and that openly challenges some of our most cherished assumptions about humanity, such as selfishness and competitiveness. This is not to say that humans under certain conditions cannot or do not display such tendencies; but our contention is that they are by-products of specific material and social conditions. If this is the case, then there is no limit to the kindness we can and should convey to all those around us in our daily exchanges (as we saw in chapter 10). Perhaps we'll have to change the cultural cues that guide our behavior, perhaps we should give prizes for moral acts rather than to essays about morality (as Rousseau suggested). Isn't it time we shifted our attention from the acquisition of money and fame, from the vile portrayals of celebrity excesses, to a sensible portrayal of humanity, vulnerability, and humility amid communal accomplishments? These rhetorical questions may sound missionary and delusional, so let's shift back to a more sensible and reasonable language.

Some preliminary comments are in order. First, *mental disposition*. American culture is predicated on various methods of vulnerability avoidance, distracting us with entertainment and pharmaceuticals from cruel realities. Likewise, consumer culture attempts to overcome loneliness and personal responsibility with social media hype on the one end of the spectrum and a militaristic patriotism on the other. This part attempts to combat these cultural and conceptual tendencies by critically examining communal practices and the ideologies that support them. Second, *the data*. What follows below is based more on ideas than on raw numbers; empirical evidence here is more symbolic than representative. The arguments are not about who has the "correct data," but how we can rethink our relations. Thinking in terms of communes and welfare is more reasonable in human terms than in terms of efficiency and profits. Third, *the scale*. Though the examples given below range from the Catholic Church with more than a billion congregants to small kibbutzim, the point is to highlight the principles of camaraderie and fellowship rather than what is the optimal scale we should pursue. Perhaps thinking globally is necessary, after all, as national boundaries are fickle and artificial, the result of historical contingencies. Fourth, *neoliberal market-capitalism*. Indeed, this part more than earlier ones is devoted to finding alternatives to the latest version of the core of neoliberal market-capitalism. The cases cited below are always already set against the realities of this dominant economic model. Fifth and final preamble, *morality*. This part is supposed to provoke further discussion on the exact economic modeling we wish to pursue with a clear realization that not one size fits all circumstances. In some cases, national-like boundaries would identify a communal unit, and at others a different configuration will be more optimal. Likewise, the communal sense espoused here overlaps with a variety of communities, sometimes religious (transcending national and linguistic boundaries) and at others more localized. In general, the approach here focuses on the moral features of economic models.

Chapter Fourteen

Informative Case Studies

What these seemingly unrelated case studies highlight is the social and moral dimensions they endorse and perpetuate. This brief survey is not critical since the purpose here is simply to learn something about these practices without condoning or condemning them. That is, we wish to extract whatever nuggets of wisdom they display and not their inevitable failings. The concern here is to illustrate that the communal sensibilities of these organizations are exemplars of sociability and moral sensibility. Put differently, camaraderie in the military, charity and good deeds toward one's fellow congregants at church, and an overall sense of communal sharing are the very foundations of these organizations. They all instill a sense of belonging to a unit larger than one's own individuality and as such undermine the modernist-capitalist view of the solitary and heroic person—the entrepreneur—whose success against all odds is a personal achievement rather than the culmination of the efforts of the entire community. One could add here even gangs as exemplars of communal solidarity, but as willing participants in criminal activities, their moral compass should not be followed (even when they take care of their own and display "honor among thieves"). Though the contexts vary, they have one thing in common: the community comes before the individual (logically, historically, practically, and psychologically) so that interpersonal connections define who we are as individuals.

I: THE CATHOLIC CHURCH

The largest single denomination on the globe is the Catholic Church with membership in 2010 of over 1.1 billion, with about 70 million in the United States. According to the Pew Research Center, "Catholics still comprise about half (50 percent) of Christians worldwide and 16 percent of the total global population," a fairly steady proportion in the past century (2013). Global distribution has changed dramatically with more Catholics in Latin America and the Caribbean than in Europe, but its center in the Vatican City has remained the same, with a Pope (Francis as of 2013) who serves both as the Vicar of Christ and the Bishop of Rome. Three caveats ought to be foregrounded: first, the hierarchical structure of the Church or its history are of no concern here; second, we shall not examine all the scandals that have plagued the Church, from its behavior during World War II, its suppression of Liberation Theology in Latin America, its bank's financial shenanigans, and ongoing worldwide pedophilia cases; and third, though perceived in terms of charity, the focus on the poor fosters the responsibility of the better off to others in the community. What is of concern in our examination, and what has been the cornerstone of Pope Francis's papacy, is the moral responsibility of the Church to the economic well-being of its own congregations as well as that of the globe. He should be credited as well for asking forgiveness of the aggrieved victims of pedophilia and attempting to straighten financial institutions that collect funds and are supposed to redistribute them to the poor and needy. Likewise, we are concerned here, as underscored by Timothy Miller, that the Catholic Church and many of its orders "fit" the communitarian model of the American experience from the nineteenth century to the present (1998, xx).

Perhaps it would be useful to cite the biblical verses that in fact support a sense of community if not outright communist ideals. We should appreciate the profundity of the historical origins of the Church in terms of the value it has so often put on the community rather than the individual. In what follows, three New Testament verses are cited (not in a specific order of importance):

And all who believed were together and had all things in common. And they were selling their possessions and belongings and distributing the proceeds to all, as any had need. (Acts 2:44–45)

Now the full number of those who believed were of one heart and soul, and no one said that any of the things that belonged to him was his own, but they had everything in common . . . There was not a needy person among them, for as many as were owners of lands or houses sold them and brought the proceeds of what was sold and laid it at the apostles' feet, and it was distributed to each as any had need. (Acts 4:32–35)

Thus, when you give to the needy, sound no trumpet before you, as the hypocrites do in the synagogues and in the streets, that they may be praised by others . . . But when you give to the needy, do not let your left hand know what your right hand is doing, so that your giving may be in secret. (Matthew 6:2–3)

The Bible doesn't support communism outright, nor does it imply that the only form of a community must be under socialist or communist ideals. But what it does illustrate, as Judaism has done with its principles of *tithing* (giving 10 percent of the fruit of one's labor to the poor and needy, whether in the direct form of products or money, or the indirect form of not collecting 10 percent of one's land's products) and the *jubilee* (forgiving debts and freeing slaves after seven years), is that even economic transactions must adhere to moral principles. Perhaps not "communist" in a politico-economic sense, but at least in the sense of communal care for all, the Bible and the Abrahamic religions that consider it sacred foreground their moral obligations to their brothers and sisters, to those in their communities that are less fortunate. And this way of thinking is divinely commanded or sanctioned. It must be recognized, in addition to what we'll see below, that The Church of Jesus Christ of Latter-Day Saints (the Mormon Church) has practiced tithing explicitly and that this practice has enriched the community.

The 1986 Pastoral Letter of the US Bishops, "Economic Justice for All," is worthy of consideration in this context for two reasons. First, it shows the way in which the Catholic Church sees its operations within an American capitalist system, and second, because it is a useful precursor to Pope Francis's own message (examined below). The Bishops begin by explaining the motivation for the Letter: "This letter is a personal invitation to Catholics to use the resources of our faith, the strength of our economy, and the opportunities of our democracy to shape a society that better protects the dignity and basic rights of our sisters and brothers, both in this land and around the world" (1986, vi). After quoting the New Testament, they explain that "the challenge for us is to discover in our own place and time what it means to be 'poor in spirit' and 'the salt of the earth' and what it means to serve 'the least among us' and to 'hunger and thirst for righteousness'" (ibid.). Neither condemning American capitalism nor endorsing any specific economic theory or model, the Letter proposes six moral principles that should be followed: *first*, "Every economic decision and institution must be judged in light of whether it protects or undermines the dignity of the human person," so that "the economy should serve people, not the other way around"; *second*, "Human dignity can be realized and protected only in community. In our teaching, the human person is not only sacred but also social," which means asking the question: "Does economic life enhance or threaten our life together as a community?"; *third*, "All people have a right to participate in the economic life of society. Basic justice demands that people be assured a minimum level of participation in the economy"; *fourth*, "All members of society have a special obligation to the poor and vulnerable." This means that "as Christians, we are called to respond to the needs of all our brothers and sisters, but those with the greatest needs require the greatest response"; *fifth*, "Human rights are the minimum conditions for life in community"; and *sixth*, "Society as a whole, acting through public and private institutions, has the moral responsibility to enhance human dignity and protect human rights" (ibid., viii–ix). The Bishops believed these principles to be the foundation for policy recommendations and not simply an expression of faith. This means that any religious renewal is bound with a new approach to one's secular life, one's engagement in the economic life of the community.

After enumerating the various economic troubles of the 1980s—amid the Cold War and business cycles—the Bishops return to argue for the moral anchor of any policy changes: "The basis for all that the Church believes about the moral dimensions of economic life is its vision of the transcendent worth—the sacredness—of human beings. *The dignity of the human person, realized in community with others, is the criterion against which all aspects of economic life must be measured* (ibid., 8; italics in the original). Citing various examples from the Gospels, the Letter continues to argue that to fully appreciate its unique religious mission, the communal feature of the Church must be remembered and practiced: "Human life is life in community. Catholic social teaching proposes several complementary perspectives that show how moral responsibilities and duties in the economic sphere are rooted in this call to community" (ibid., 16). And contrary to capitalism's advocacy of the Invisible Hand, especially when it relates to government intervention on behalf of social welfare, the Letter continues to say: "The economy is not a machine that operates according to its own inexorable laws, and persons are not mere objects tossed about by economic forces" (ibid., 22). This means that the Church and its members are to act responsibly in the economic affairs of their state. Offering a new "American Experiment," the Bishops delve more deeply into policy matters and argue for the means by which full employment should be achieved: "*We recommend that the fiscal and monetary policies of the nation—such as federal spending, tax and interest-rate policies—should be coordinated so as to achieve the goal of full employment*" (ibid., 37; italics in the original). Instead of summarizing all the details of the Bishops' Pastoral Letter (over ninety pages), these few quotes clarify the direction and intent of the Letter, the principles in accordance to which they hope the American experiment will succeed in eliminating poverty and ensuring full employment. The focus on the communal sense of the economy (chapter IV on cooperation) and the essential role the government must play to care for all its people is paramount; the special attention that must be paid to the least advantaged in the community is also obvious. What is not obvious is whether market-capitalism can fulfill these recommendations to reach the Bishops' goals.

The Tenth Anniversary of the 1986 Letter offered a revised version of the concerns already elucidated then, but now with a measure of critical assessment. The Bishops on this occasion find that the US economy is still divided into three "nations living side by side," one that is "prospering," a second that is "squeezed by declining real incomes and global economic competition," and a third "underclass" that is "growing more discouraged and despairing" (1996, 1–2). The six original moral principles are reworked here into five: "The economy exists to serve the human person, not the other way around; Economic life should be shaped by moral principles and ethical norms; Economic choices should be measured by whether they enhance or threaten human life, human dignity and human rights; A fundamental concern must be support for the family and the well-being of children; The moral measure of any economy is how the weakest are faring" (ibid., 3). And after enumerating, yet again, some specific policies that should help alleviate poverty, the Letter concludes with this message:

> We may differ on specifics and priorities, but let us come together—across economic, ideological and ethnic lines—to work for a society and economy offering more justice and opportunity, especially for the poor. Differences over how to move forward will give rise to legitimate debate, but indifference to the need to build a more just and open economy is not an option for Catholics. Every Christian is called to follow Jesus in his mission—and ours—of bringing "good news to the poor, new sight to the blind, liberty to captives and to set the downtrodden free." That was the call of our pastoral letter almost ten years ago and still is our task today. (ibid., 7)

Before we move on to Pope Francis's message, and before we are led to believe that Catholic doctrine is only interested in the reform of market-capitalism, we should mention in passing that the opposition to the Communist oppression in Poland was inspired by the Catholic Church and Pope John Paul II as well. Perhaps this was due to the fact that the great majority of Poles are Catholics and that Lech Walesa's Solidarity movement was Catholic as much as it was political. Years later, after the fall of the Berlin Wall in 1989, the Orange Alternative Movement, while maintaining its focus on a free and democratic Poland, remained festooned to Catholic teachings. This teaches us that religious organizations can foment activism in the name of social justice, challenging the communists as much as the capitalists (even though the Catholic Church itself is not democratic). Conversely, one could cynically argue that the Church itself has vested economic interests in remaining involved in political affairs so as not to lose its own footing in the lives of its followers. Pope Francis, while dealing with a variety of issues, and in his first "Apostolic Exhortation," covers matters of faith as well as those of the environment and the economic order. One must give him credit for putting environmental concerns front and center for the largest and most powerful religious institution of the world, reminding world leaders and common folk that we are responsible for God's creation. But what is important in our context is the specific claims he makes about market-capitalism. Focusing only on his chapter 2 ("Amid the Crisis of Communal Commitment"), the Pope is clear that there is a moral equivalence between the Ten Commandments and our injunction against an "economy of exclusion and inequality. Such an economy kills" (2013, #53). The exclusion is when the news media reports on the Dow Jones Industrials' ups and downs but ignores the death of a homeless person; it's an economy of inequality when "food is thrown away while people are starving" (ibid.). He continues to say that "human beings themselves are considered consumer goods to be used and then discarded" (ibid.). This is as strong a statement as any we can find in Marx's works; and it is definitely stronger than anything said by the American Bishops. But here the Pope isn't tone deaf, and he quickly distinguishes his religious message from Marx's: "The excluded are not the 'exploited' but the outcast, the 'leftovers'" (ibid.). Though starting with the individual who is discarded and perceived as a leftover, he moves on to the entire market-capitalist model.

Pope Francis cites an economic theory that was popular in the Reagan administration, called supply-side economics (Fink 1982), arguing against its formulation (and its claims about tax reform): "Some people continue to defend trickle-down theories which assume that economic growth, encouraged by a free market, will inevitably succeed in bringing about greater justice and inclusiveness in the world" (ibid., #54). With reduced taxes on the rich, spending will necessarily increase; this will increase the overall taxes collected (and help erase the national deficit); it will also increase economic activity and create more jobs. "This opinion," he says, with a clear note that this isn't a scientific theory, "which has never been confirmed by the facts, expresses a crude and naïve trust in the goodness of those wielding economic power and in the sacralized workings of the prevailing economic system" (ibid.). What impact has this opinion had over the past decades? "Meanwhile, the excluded are still waiting" (ibid.). False promises is what the excluded are left with; and all of this because of adhering to a "selfish ideal" that benefits some at the expense of others, both locally and globally (ibid.). And then the Pope moves to explain that the Great Recession is in fact a "human crisis" that emerges from our "idolatry of money," our creation of "new idols," reminiscent of the Golden Calf (ibid., #55). This idolatry is compounded by the "dictatorship of an impersonal economy lacking a truly human purpose" (ibid.). This is a reference to the Invisible Hand that is supposedly both fair and just in economic affairs. The inequality between the rich and the poor is defended by ideologies that "defend the absolute autonomy of the marketplace and financial speculation" (ibid., #56). With this autonomy or separation no responsibility can be assumed by those who brought about this situation. He continues to exhort against this new "tyranny" and its failings, from tax evasion to desecrating the environment (ibid.). Behind this "attitude lurks a rejection of ethics and a rejection of God" (ibid., #57). But whose ethics? Must it be Catholic? The Pope's answer is surprisingly more general and therefore more generous: "Ethics—a non-ideological ethics— would make it possible to bring about balance and a more humane social order" (ibid.). In short, "Money must serve, not rule!" (ibid., #58) And "Today's economic mechanisms promote inordinate consumption, yet it is evident that unbridled consumerism combined with inequality proves doubly damaging to the social fabric. Inequality eventually engenders a violence which recourse to arms cannot and never will be able to resolve" (ibid., #60).

Perhaps this close reading of the Papal Exhortation will make it evident what is at stake when rethinking economic relations. This is as close as any world leader has come to denouncing the human failings of market-capitalism with a head-on critique of its false ideology. The status of this is doctrinal, which means that it should be followed by at least a billion inhabitants of this Earth; the Pope is speaking *ex cathedra* with God's inspiration and not simply as a religious leader or pastor. It's true that Pope Francis has said even more inflammatory things against market-capitalism elsewhere, in interviews and speeches, where he explicitly talked about the "evil" of the capitalist system and about the fact that fair distribution of wealth is not philanthropy (Huddleston 2015). Though we are no closer to finding out what specific economic model the Catholic Church advocates, we at least know that it wishes it to be moral, communal, and caring for the poor. Most fascinating is an aside that the Pope makes about the false promises of investing in education alone as if this would necessarily overcome the structural inequalities of the capitalist system. Instead, the rhetoric to reform the educational system is a distraction from completely transforming the ways wealth is divided among market participants and the power relations that never fully change even when the population becomes more educated over time. It's true that college-educated employees make more money over time, but with student loans and the prospects of the Gig Economy, the promise of prosperity is doubtful. We should be mindful that there is no pretense here to summarize the Catholic Church's two millennia of conduct or account for obvious problems of orthodoxy missionary conversions. Focusing on the communal features of the Church is informative for imagining models of communalism.

II: THE KIBBUTZ

Just as it was important to highlight the communal and moral principles that undergird the Catholic Church and its global teaching, so it might be useful to consider briefly the principles that animate the kibbutz movement in Israel. The word *kibbutz* means in Hebrew a gathering or clustering and derives from the notion of a group or community. The first kibbutz (Degania) was established in 1909 under the Ottoman Empire, which ruled the country, and numerous others were established under the British Mandate and before the establishment of the state in 1948. A century later there are about 270 *kibbut-zim* (plural for *kibbutz*) with about 125,000 members (which accounts for about 2 percent of the population). Throughout its history, the kibbutz move-ment always had more of an ideological role to play in the life of the State than an economic force, because of its appeal to a very small portion of the population that lived this way. It should also be noted that the majority of the kibbutz movement followed a hybrid of socialism and Zionism, the former in terms of the utopian vision for economic and democratic organization, and the latter in terms of enticing immigration (primarily from Europe) to buy and settle what was considered barren land; some other factions thrived as well, from the militant conservative or even religiously inspired quarters of the population. In these cases (keeping in mind that for centuries Jews were forbidden from owning land in Europe), urbanites were introduced to rural settings with agricultural labor. But regardless of the specific set of ideas around which a kibbutz formed itself, and regardless of its operations in agriculture or light industry and hospitality, several important principles guided its outlook and practices. At its heart, the kibbutz movement was indeed a "venture in Utopia," as Melford Spiro reminds us. It was based on ideals and the adherence to the purity of these ideals characterized those who joined the movement. For example, the refusal to hire labor was as much a point of pride that one can build one's life literally with one's own hands as well as a principled refusal to "exploit" others (1970, 15). Likewise, just as the principle of equality was emphasized, so was the principle of freedom insofar as members chose what to do and in which direction their commune was headed (ibid., 28ff).

The kibbutz movement saw itself dedicated to communal living, mutual aid, and social justice. Since all property was owned jointly (private property is limited to personal belongings), and since every member of the commune was expected to participate in some form in the workload (even the elderly and children contribute when they can), notions of equality and cooperation are paramount. In many ways, the kibbutz's work-ethics and the distribution of goods and services are based on Marx's principle of "from each according to his ability, to each according to his needs." Despite original subsidies to purchase land and the service the kibbutzim provided the State in being strategically located for the defense of the land and for maximization of agricultural production, most kibbutzim have become self-sufficient econom-ically, and pride themselves on being an important economic force in the country, disproportionately contributing more to the State than they are granted in special loan guarantees or direct subsidies. The population of a kibbutz ranges from a few dozens to one thousand, which is of course cru-cially important when understanding the internal dynamics of a functioning commune. So, in addition to socialist ideals, there is a strong sense of partici-patory democracy within the kibbutz: every member has a vote, every decision—from election of officers to labor allocation and the distribution of funds for any activity (buying televisions or cars, paying for college tuition or travel abroad)—is voted on and decided by the majority. New members are accepted by vote, and members who are found unfit to remain can be voted out. Decisions about expansion or new construction is likewise decided collectively, even though some day-to-day operations are left to the discretion of elected officials, who themselves are not necessarily professionals but members who assume leadership positions for set periods. This model reminds every member that no one's opinion is valued more than anyone else's, that egalitarian principles can work within a small community of like-minded individuals. One's duties and rights are symmetrically aligned, with work and service being paramount on the one side, and the benefits of equally sharing the fruits of the community on the other. And most importantly, the well-being of the commune of the whole takes precedence over the interests of the individual.

The marriage of socialist and democratic principles is important to emphasize here, as the other twentieth century examples that we usually cite, from the Soviet Union and China to Cuba and North Korea, though communists in their approach to economic affairs ended up supporting undemocratic institutions so that the Workers' Party or the Communist Party turned into a dictatorship where human rights and personal freedoms were curtailed. The kibbutz movement is unique, perhaps because of its small size, in being able to flourish both economically and politically, and ensuring the wishes of the members are carried out; when disagreements arise, some consensus can be reached amid the differing opinions of the membership. The secretary has no more sway than someone working in the fields. In case this idealized picture of the kibbutz movement sounds too good to be true, we should hasten to make the following disclaimers or critical comments. First, despite its appeal, the movement could never draw to its fold more than 2 to 3 percent of the population; the hardship of work or the strict work-ethics seems too difficult for some to handle; and because of peer pressure "free rider" cases are absent. Second, the price of collective work and education—where children live and learn separately from their parents—is sometimes too stiff insofar that, as Bruno Bettelheim has observed (1969), they fail to form strong emotional connections with others and therefore become psychologically challenged as they grow up. Third, personal aspirations that involve work outside of the confines of the kibbutz movement are more difficult to accommodate within a poor kibbutz than a rich one; when opportunities are limited, personal satisfaction can be undermined, and people tend to leave the commune. Fourth, the pioneering spirit of the first settlers is watered down by later generations, and when financial success has been established, the urgency of collective participation wanes and with it the notion of self-sacrifice for the sake of the community. Fifth, though the movement has a strong commitment to gender equality, it has become evident over time that sexism and misogyny remain. Sixth and finally, though there seems to be a veneer of collegiality and friendship among members, acrimony and disagreements erupt regularly. Even in a small commune, factions can be formed, and loyalty to some but not all the members can cause feuds that may not be resolved and that can last for years. The hardship, of course, is that members live in close proximity and therefore are bound to see each other daily. Perhaps this may suggest that larger communes might fare better than smaller ones.

What has kept the kibbutz movement in Israel as a symbol for perseverance has been its ability to foster and maintain a principled communal living arrangement that has lasted for more than a century. This is not a fleeting experiment that was appealing at one point and has become obsolete years later; instead, it's a lived experience of many people who still believe that living communally has value. Spiro's explanation for it relates much more to the secular "religious" zeal, deep faith, and personal devotion to the ideals of the kibbutz, comparable to religious communities (1970, 179). The ideology of the kibbutz has become its own religion, one that cannot be questioned or challenged, as if blasphemy is taking place among believers (ibid., 194). As is true of religious communities, any deviation is considered a betrayal, and every criticism a sign of weakness and disloyalty. The pressure to adhere and conform, not to question this or that policy because of what can of worms it may open, silences many members and takes away their sense of self-actualization and autonomy. Perhaps a personal note may highlight a particular take on these questions. I lived for more than a year in Kibbutz Hatzerim (established in 1946; in 2015 population of 786) and Mitzpe Shalem (established in 1970; in 2015 population of 173), the former near Beersheba, the latter overlooking the Dead Sea. In the former I was a trainee, working the dairy farm, milking cows twice a day, and in the latter as the secretary, which gave me a broader perspective on the workings of the commune. The former was an established kibbutz that became wealthy because of its drip-irrigation system (Netafim), exporting around the world, while the latter was a military settlement on the Jordanian border. What I recall from Hatzerim is how smoothly a wealthy commune operates: anything that was desired (way beyond needs) was easily purchased, whether it was televisions for everyone, enough vehicles anyone could use, and travel abroad. The kibbutz subsidized another, less fortunate kibbutz some miles away, and funded the care of domestic violence victims in Tel Aviv (because one of the young members was interested in this issue). The point is not so much a personal reflection on the daily life in the kibbutz, but that when a commune becomes self-sufficient or even prospers, and when it follows Marxist ideology, then its best features of social justice come to the fore. What happens to poor kibbutzim, to those who cannot afford to maintain their ideals and have to cut corners and exploit labor in order to guarantee their survival? What happens to one's ideological convictions when basic needs aren't satisfied?

It's also worth noting that the kibbutz movement, however unique in Palestine and then Israel, also operated within a broader political and cultural context. The short experience mentioned above was undergone while over 80 percent of the labor force was unionized in one form or another, when universal healthcare was taken for granted, when the leading political party was the Labor Party, and when two small communist parties had representation in the Knesset (Israeli Parliament); the two small parties were differently aligned with the Soviet Union and were at times accused of not distancing themselves sufficiently from the USSR once the atrocities of Stalin became known. So, having communal experiments around the country was not as radical or unexpected. Indeed, the one place where I resided for a year even had a member who became a cabinet-level minister. This was an example of having jobs or careers outside the commune while still maintaining the duties of membership, fulfilling kitchen shifts on the weekends, or helping the twice-annual cleanup of the chicken coops. Personal aspirations could be fulfilled alongside local obligations, with a modicum of accommodation and respect. What also becomes evident in this process of rotating both work chores and leadership positions within the commune is that some people are more qualified than others, that some have a better skill set to fulfill their roles, and that at times the price of rotation is mediocre performance. But is this a price worth paying in order to promote a sense of equitable sharing of duties and rights so that each person in fact contributes according to his or her ability? Likewise, it's easy to make compromises about the purity of ideals when a large construction project is planned: Should the commune become construction builders? Can they? Do they have the expertise? Does it not make better economic sense to hire experts but make sure to pay them fair wages? This becomes an issue as kibbutzim become larger and more prosperous, and when their own division of labor doesn't include all the professions that are needed (like car mechanics or software technicians). And finally, if the kibbutz is prosperous, as Hatzerim was, what should it do with its "profits" (or extra money that accrues from selling its products)? Should they be equally shared, invested for the collective, or spent on philanthropy?

Just as we have covered some of the moral teachings of the Catholic Church and the economic proposals it has made to combat the excesses of capitalism, so it's important to cover some of the ways in which the utopian thinking of communes is functional and thrives in democratically organized settings. In the Catholic case, perhaps the ideals of fair distribution and spiritual well-being are foregrounded, so that even if market-capitalism remains the economic model, considerations of social justice are of highest priority. In the kibbutz case, by contrast, a new model is established so that abundance and social justice are interwoven. Under conditions of abundance, fair and just distributions are more easily accomplished (especially with strong work-ethics). In both cases, we need to figure out if they work only on a small scale of a parish church and a kibbutz, or can be scalable to large swaths of the population. We should also accept that the idealized versions that are mentioned here, promoting moral and social principles as they are, are supposed to appeal to individuals rather that portray a self-righteous approach whose threshold is impossible to meet.

III: COMMUNES IN THE UNITED STATES

Though they are not thought of in terms of modern-day communes, it's fair to consider Native Americans as offering models of communal living, with shared property and the resources they either hunted or cultivated. Because we already reviewed some of their practices in part I, suffice here to remind ourselves of some salient principles; first, a very limited notion of private property, and a strong sense of shared commons among all inhabitants of Earth. This is attenuated when certain tribes are less nomadic than others, and when they either fish, hunt, or cultivate specific areas, even when they leave them temporarily. Second, politics, defined here as decision-making processes, are democratic insofar as every member of the tribe or clan has a right (if not duty) to voice an opinion, and all decisions are reached by consensus. Women and men share power equally with some deference to the clan mothers whose sanction of chiefs is essential. Third, with a custodial relationship with the land, questions of sustainability are paramount, whether this refers to water supplies or the maintenance of buffalo herds. And fourth, social standards and tribal customs inform economic transactions both within and outside the tribe. When the expectation is that we encounter each other regularly, an implicit moral code of fairness and justice rules. This does exclude exception or flagrant violations of customs and traditions. But such violations (escalating at times to warfare) are regarded as destabilizing the harmony between the sacred and the profane, between human activities and the will of the gods.

Just as Native American views and principles were already mentioned above, so we have already reviewed in part I some of the ideas and ideals promoted by nineteenth-century American commune experiments. In addition to full-fledged communes, there were several co-operative associations that came into being in the nineteenth century in England, promoting the principles of "Concord, Economy, Equity, and Self-help" (Holyoake 2012 [1903], 21). Though more concerned with financial cooperation within a company and among those participating in it to promote "truthfulness and justice" (ibid., 55), these experiments aspired to incorporate profit sharing and education, and prove that "the co-operative workshop raises a superior class of men" (ibid., 123). But unlike the kibbutz or American communes, these cooperative schemes were neither utopian nor "schemes of benevolence" or philanthropy; they were but a "manly device for giving honest men an equitable opportunity of helping themselves" (ibid., 187). Less ambitious yet practically applicable, these British counterparts illustrate that the concern for moral grounding or humane cooperation is widely spread. All of them rethink social relations and economic models, some more revolutionary about family structure and free love, some more principled about the following issues; first, the priority of self-actualizing of all members of the commune with mutual support, fulfilling spiritual and social aspirations. Second, an appreciation of the collective nature of work and prosperity so that individual contributions are valued most in light of the group's success (and thereby bracketing competition as the engine of progress). Third, a deliberate effort to create a sense of solidarity that transcends economic needs and includes social and familial relations (instilling tribal loyalty almost in Native American style but without the long tradition that anchors it). Fourth, a strong sense of personal and communal enlightenment in terms of greater learning and more pleasure time, shared by all. In this pursuit, basic notions of equality and freedom are mutually constitutive to ensure mutual respect and the dignity of all participants. Fifth and finally, there was a strong sense that in order to make the commune sustainable, every member must be on the same page, agreeing with how the commune was administered and how decisions were made. Unlike the kibbutz, most nineteenth century communes had charismatic leaders whose authority was unquestioned and to whom people flocked. This element of leadership and authority was also different from the position of a chief in a Native American tribe: while the former has absolute authority and without him or her the commune would fall apart, in the latter chiefs come and go but the tribal tradition and clan mothers hold it together.

Though most nineteenth century communes disappeared over time, a resurgence in the 1960s and 1970s brought back some of the same experimental features of the previous century. As Timothy Miller suggests, America has had a continuous history of communes even though the inspiration for their establishment changed over time. According to him, there are a few central principles that can be detected in all of the variety of communes, from the religious-spiritual to the countercultural-hippie ones. First, they all display a "sense of common purpose and of separation from the dominant society" (1999, xxii). Some level of dissatisfaction with the establishment, however conceived by those who wish to separate themselves, is obvious in the decision to leave urban centers and move to agrarian settlements. Second, a strong communitarian commitment expresses "some form and level of self-denial, of voluntary suppression of individual choice in favor of the good of the group" (ibid., xxiii). This means that the community takes precedence over the individual, and that individuals happily give up various personal desires and think of the group's needs first. The third is "geographic proximity" which means that the community isn't conceptual or virtual but in fact lives together in one place, with commonly owned and shared buildings and houses. The fourth feature or principle is "personal interaction" which includes ongoing meetings and exchanges that are deeper and more intimate than those among neighbors. The fifth is "economic sharing" which has had different expression in different communities, some more integrated than others. Some level of financial intermingling is expected, from property ownership to paying for expenses that affect all members. The sixth principle, one that responds to the idealized or utopian image communes hold in the popular mind, is that they must have "real existence" They cannot simply be drawn on a piece of paper or be understood in a brilliant manifesto; though idealized, they must exist. And the final principle is that they must have a "critical mass," one that exceeds just two or three friends deciding to live communally (ibid.). All in all, these features are important to consider as underlying not only the American communes but can also be applied to the kibbutz movement described above. As a long-lasting experiment, these communes must prove their mettle: they have to embody utopian thinking in the here and now.

As we think about communes in America, we are reminded of their *countercultural roots*—finding flaws in the dominant culture that surrounds them—and their desire to have a *proof of concept*—show in real terms what a commune would look like and how its members will behave. The point is not simply to prey on personal dissatisfaction with the status quo or with the failings of market-capitalism, but to change the outlook of participants: having people think about strangers as friends and family. For some, this was expressed in religiously rich terms; for others it meant a sexual revolution that sanctioned personal pleasure and saw heterosexual patriarchy constricted and oppressive. The right to experiment with different moral norms and social conventions transcends the critiques offered by the Catholic Church (which remained hierarchical and domineering) or the kibbutz movement (which was quite homogeneous). And in case we think that America communes of the 1960s were small and numerically insignificant, Miller claims that though exact numbers are difficult to come by, there were thousands of communes with hundreds of thousands of members. The estimates of rural and urban communes range during the 1970s from 1,000 to 50,000, all the way up to 750,000 in membership (ibid., xviii–xx). Moreover, if we commonly have an image of a small commune in isolation, Miller reminds us that there were federations of egalitarian communities, with mutual support across geographical distances. The reasons for such federations were political (to ensure ideals were reinforced), financial (to offer funding for acquisition of more land when needed), and medical (healthcare funds for medical expenses) (ibid., 89–91). If one thought that there was a limit on the size of the communal experiment (only small, insulated communities), this illustrates that a growing number of communes could mutually benefit each other and draw on each other's resources when needed (as was true of kibbutz federations). The point isn't an extraction from society, but offering an intentional and mindful alternative to the mindset of America's consumer culture.

Yet the countercultural impulses of the 1960s' communes still had to deal with their own rules and economic arrangements to survive and thrive. They couldn't just endorse a "rejection of greed, of material desire, and ultimately of individualism, at least the anticommunitarian American kind" with their psychedelic outlook, as Miller explains (ibid., 151). Their interest in "rebuilding society from the ground up" had specific ideals in mind, such as the flight from the city to the farm, appreciating the natural gifts of the land (in the sense of "rural romanticism" and "sentimental optimism") (ibid., 152–153). Miller adds that in some of these communities, the renewed interest in the land, not as an agrarian chore but as a spiritual fascination, was frequently associated with Native American tribal life (ibid., 153). Likewise, the accepted doctrine of egalitarianism extended to all members regardless of gender and race in light of the civil rights movement of the 1960s. However, Miller notes that despite the doctrinal commitment, in reality most communes were racially homogenous and that blacks were rarely found among the members (ibid., 154). Since it's impossible to generalize, Miller suggests that the variety of the egalitarian principles of the commune depended on the background and philosophical convictions of the individuals who founded the communes or took leadership roles. With strong environmental sensitivity, these communes treated their surroundings much more consciously. And as far as the day-to-day economics of the communes, no generalization will do justice to their varieties. Some were bought with the generous donation of wealthy patrons, some were leased collectively, while still others were bought with mortgage agreements that were collectively assigned. Likewise, different communes took care of their finances in creative ways, some pulling personal resources to pay for communal living and food, while others worked more like the kibbutz model with production and consumption being equally expected from every member. The profound disdain for money was both alluring and disastrous: alluring because one could avoid the ugly underbelly of monetizing all decisions and relations, disastrous because when bills weren't paid, supplies were not delivered (ibid., 158–169). What most communes found out over time is that they needed some institutional organization, some form of "government" to make decisions and to run the commune, rather than just appeal to free love and experimental drugs.

As we move into the twenty-first century, communal living takes on new forms, especially in urban and suburban settings. Not only have about 32 percent of millennials decided to live with their parents, but as Ilana Strauss notes, the return to Middle Ages communal living is on the rise. According to her, "Communal living is hardly a departure from tradition—it's a return to how humans have been making their homes for thousands of years" (2016). More specifically, she cites the Milagro Housing in Arizona's Sonoran Desert, where "families, couples, and single people live in 28 homes in a tight-knit community that shares a kitchen, laundry room, library, meeting room, playroom, and storage rooms" (ibid.). While the 1960s communes were associated with the counterculture movement, contemporary communal living may be more a result of the exigencies of post–Great Recession economic realities. Having lost their homes because the mortgage bubble burst, having lost their jobs as the economy tanked, and having realized that they would never qualify for either rental or ownership of apartments and houses (especially in expensive urban centers like New York and San Francisco), it makes sense to think of alternatives. Communal living under these conditions embodies an even wider definition than the one given in regard to the 1960s and 1970s communes. Here we find familial communities with multigenerational cohabitation and where people find themselves sharing apartments, houses, or buildings with strangers to make their lives affordable. In some cases, cohousing is by choice, in others out of necessity; the examples given here do not distinguish the two sufficiently, and because of the short time that they have been studied, long-term impact is difficult to assess.

In the United States, the Fellowship for Intentional Community, an organization that champions communities "where people live together on the basis of explicit common values," lists 1,539 cohousing communities around the country, some already formed and others in the process of forming (ibid.). As far as Strauss is concerned, "That's likely a low estimate, since plenty of shared-living communities aren't reported to any national databases. While some residents hire developers to build cohousing villages from scratch, most have turned already-existing houses and apartments into shared communities" (ibid.). The Fellowship's website lists the following principles as guiding its mission:

> To provide and facilitate access to resources that support the creation, development, and maintenance of intentional communities.
>
> To provide accurate and comprehensive information about all forms of intentional community.
>
> To make significant contributions to the articulation and promotion of cooperative culture.
>
> To create opportunities for the public to learn about and experience intentional communities and cooperative culture.
>
> To disseminate broadly what is being learned in intentional communities.
>
> To develop the network of intentional communities for the sharing of innovations, information, and other forms of mutual benefit.

To identify and import into the world of intentional communities innovations in technology, economics, governance, cooperative culture and other areas that can benefit them.

To ally with other movements and organizations that share our values, learn from them, share what we have learned, work together for mutual benefit and to raise awareness of the worldwide movement towards sustainability, cooperation, and social justice. (Fellowship for Intentional Community 2016)

These principles are similar to those expounded and endorsed by most communes, and they use the 1960s' terminology of "intentionality" and "cooperation" where support and sharing are highlighted. But unlike the fascination with rural living and a return to Native American roots, what we find now is "cohousing" as a "useful living arrangement for groups of people with all sorts of priorities" (ibid.), focused much more on technological innovations. These priorities are *intentional but nonideological*, as they revolve around similar interests, say, those of the software engineers in the Silicon Valley, where young code programmers live together to save money and may, along the way, also collaborate on their own start-up projects (but for the most part work for different, already established companies). Other communities, such as CoAbode, "link[s] single mothers who want to live and raise children together," while in Los Angeles, "about a dozen young adults live together in one large house called Synchronicity LA. There, they make art together, hold salons, divide up chores, and trade off cooking communal meals four days a week" (ibid.). So, cohousing seems to be the catchword or label given to communal living among the millennials under the latest conditions of market-capitalism. Unlike the kibbutz and earlier communes, they seem not to intentionally comingle their finances, except for sharing the burdens of rent and maybe meals; but like them, they have made a deliberate choice first, not to live alone; second, to find like-minded individuals; and third, to share their dreams and aspirations, fears and concerns with strangers who become their tribal relatives. Cohousing models, however creative, have taken the basic ideals of the commune movements of the past century and tailored them to new realities and psychological dispositions; perhaps money and consumerism aren't as evil as they were in the eyes of the 1960s hippies, but their promise has alluded them or they have realized that the promise of climbing up the economic ladder requires a whole village. Even if many of these examples suggest necessity rather than choice, exigencies rather than intentional desires to share with others, they can still be informative as to their applicability and scalability.

As Bella DePaulo explains, old models of nuclear family life, the "Leave it to Beaver" of the 1960s and 1970s, the post–World War II residential and sprawling suburban landscape, have been slowly changing, and by the twenty-first century new formulations abound. In Hope Meadows, a neighborhood near Chicago, some retired people have chosen to live together with at-risk foster kids to give meaning to their lives in retirement. In Deventer (Netherlands), college students find spaces in nursing homes with the elderly, and in return they are supposed to socialize with them and perform some menial chores (2015). DePaulo traces this cohousing (rather than communal) models to Denmark in the 1970s where some seven hundred "living" communities were more concerned about living arrangements than larger ideological or philosophical principles. Perhaps it was convenience, perhaps it was financially motivated, but regardless of the original reasons, what these communities prove (and why they are mentioned here) is that old models can be changed and that several presuppositions can be challenged along the way (such as individualism, competition, greed, ambition, and self-interested goal setting). The Dutch and Danish experiments have been replicated also in Sweden where there are "state-owned" cohousing buildings for hundreds of people to live together, subsidized, as they are, by the State (ibid.). Strauss reminds us that "Commonspace, for instance, is a company that designs and runs apartments consisting of about 20 small units around a common area occupied mostly by young and single people, sort of like a dorm for adults," and "there are now only 160 American cohousing communities built from scratch" (2016). We need not delve into the psychological details of Strauss's and DePaulo's works in order to appreciate the collegial nature of cohabitating, where the company of others is comforting, where we can vent among those who will listen because they share our views, outlook, and aspirations. This can happen when the young and the old interact in nursing homes—the young listening to the wise advice of the old and the old enjoy the tech-savvy help of the young for their gadgets—or when techies find soul mates with whom to share a frustration or a great idea—perhaps as fellow travelers, potential collaborators, and seldom as outright competitors. Even when software replaces handiwork, or where the urban setting replaces the pastoral farm, what is at stake in such cohousing communes is a sense of belonging, a sense that someone cares about us. Yes, smartphones and virtual realities bring strangers together from all over the globe, but they never quite offer the intimacy of a handshake, embrace, or kiss. They never fully replicate the experiences in close physical proximity of a community.

IV: THE MILITARY

As improbable as the Catholic Church appears in this book in relation to postcapitalist economic relations, so is the military; both are hierarchical and circumscribed by discipline and obedience to rules and regulations; but they are also large communities where the well-being of the community is valued, where camaraderie is deeply felt and practiced, and where caring for others is not simply a divine or military command but a lived reality, at times out of sheer altruism and at others for the very survival of the group. If the Catholic model is too religious for some, the kibbutz movement too colonial in its Zionist garb for others, and the 1960s commune too hippie and psychedelic for still others, perhaps the secular model of the military will have something to offer us. What is of interest here is to transcend the usual ideological categories with which we condone or condemn models, and instead see if any valuable principles or practices are replicable today. Assuming, for the moment, that we will not abandon all the practices of market-capitalism, and assuming as well that we are unable to mobilize millions the way the counterculture revolution of the 1960s prompted students and beatniks to rebel against the status quo of the dominant, consumerist culture, what new (or retooled) ideas can we offer to generate a conversation about how to change our world? In other words, what vocabulary should we choose to find alternatives to what ails our economy and therefore the people who populate it? On a personal note, my own four years of military service in the IDF inform my thinking here; it's amazing that as my own reflections are being examined here, an American Marxist openly discusses this institution as well.

Unlike the Catholic Church with over one billion members or the commune movements with several hundreds of thousands, the armed forces in the United States are expected to number in fiscal year 2017 over 1.2 million in active duty and close to one million in reserve units. There are about twenty-two million veterans alive in the United States. About 10 percent of Americans served in the military. Without accurate numbers, the Israeli military numbers less than one million active and reserve personnel out of about three million eligible people, while the general population of the state is around eight million. One can speculate that more than half of the Israeli population had direct military experience. The United States and Israel are compared here not only because of my personal experience but also because both democratic nation-states have a military ethos and rhetoric that is part of their national identity. Admittedly, Israel has mandatory conscription where everyone at the age of eighteen must register and pass a battery of tests (which is also true of many other countries with mandatory conscription, selective conscription, and national service mandates), while the United States has a voluntary army. Unlike the Israeli draft where few exceptions exist (for religious reasons, pregnancy and motherhood, and racist prohibitions against Arabs), the American model is understood to be both voluntary and professional, but not quite mercenary. While the Israeli model forces everyone to begin service at the lowest possible rank (except doctors), the American one has two points of entry, at the enlisted level and at the officer level (with college degree). As we shall see below, there are many reasons to prefer the draft model to the voluntary one, but in this context we shall only mention that the rhetorical power of the notion of "volunteerism" sounds

hollow in light of the fact that for many enlisted personnel's lack of job
opportunities pushes them into this career path, while for others who are
gainfully employed, military careers have several advantages that cannot be
attained in market-capitalism (from free healthcare and education to housing
allowances and pensions). But instead of delving into the differences between the Israeli and American military models, we wish to highlight some
of the salient social principles that we can emulate from them.

What do moral principles look like in the military context? Many, like
Major Damon Armeni, think about them in broad national terms, how to
justify the national use of force. For him, this means that "moral justifica-
tions for sending men and women to war are necessary for every governmental system. Examined through the lens of Clausewitz's Trinity, the people
grant authority and legitimacy to the government, the government extends
legitimacy and authority through the use of the military, the military represents and defends the population and government, and the population in turn
gives the military legitimacy and moral absolution" (2013). But though this
statement gives the framework of the legal and political conditions under
which nation-states declare and conduct war (there is a separate military
conduct rulebook), what it misses, and what we are interested in here, is the
communal settings under which military personnel operate. They include, for
example, a sense of camaraderie that is established in training and that is
fostered in a variety of other ways before any combat experience. What binds
these soldiers together? Is it just a sense of particular missions, such as
defeating the enemy (however defined), or is there something more foundational being cultivated? Pride in one's unit is paramount as well as pride in
the very notion of service. The social value of service on behalf of the State
is foregrounded. When you add to this pride of your unit, because it is
famous for accomplishing this or that task (at war or at peace), then pride is
added to service as a powerful elixir to motivate total strangers to collaborate
and respect each other. Whether this socializing is undertaken under conditions of stress or danger or within more casual surroundings of a support unit
makes little difference; at stake is the conscious process of community building, very much like the intentional and deliberate process commune members
feel when first initiated.

The US Army has its own list of "values," listed on its website. They are
worth repeating here at length, because they could be the game-changers as
we try to find a new way of thinking and a vocabulary with which to articulate it. When the army speaks of *Loyalty*, it has in mind those joining the
military and perhaps being confronted for the first time with this concept.
This means "bear true faith and allegiance to the U.S. Constitution, the
Army, your unit and other Soldiers. Bearing true faith and allegiance is a
matter of believing in and devoting yourself to something or someone. A
loyal Soldier is one who supports the leadership and stands up for fellow

Soldiers. By wearing the uniform of the U.S. Army you are expressing your loyalty. And by doing your share, you show your loyalty to your unit." While loyalty is expected of the Constitution, there is also the immediacy of one's "fellow Soldiers," the ones with whom you are serving, and on whom you must rely in peace and at war. When it comes to *Duty*, the website's language is also crystal clear: "Fulfill your obligations. Doing your duty means more than carrying out your assigned tasks. Duty means being able to accomplish tasks as part of a team. The work of the U.S. Army is a complex combination of missions, tasks and responsibilities—all in constant motion. Our work entails building one assignment onto another. You fulfill your obligations as a part of your unit every time you resist the temptation to take 'shortcuts' that might undermine the integrity of the final product." Here what is emphasized is "team work" and a sense of "responsibility" that transcend simply completing an assigned task. And the notion of "the integrity of the final product" comes up, the way, for example, it hadn't come up at VW when emission controls were fraudulently calibrated to work under the testing conditions of US authorities. *Respect* is next on the list of values, and here it says: "Treat people as they should be treated. In the Soldier's Code, we pledge to 'treat others with dignity and respect while expecting others to do the same.' Respect is what allows us to appreciate the best in other people. Respect is trusting that all people have done their jobs and fulfilled their duty. And self-respect is a vital ingredient with the Army value of respect, which results from knowing you have put forth your best effort. The Army is one team and each of us has something to contribute." For Christians, this sounds like the Golden Rule, and for philosophers this sounds like Kant's Categorical Imperative. Not only should people be treated as ends and not as means, not only should we expect to be treated in like manner by others, but a psychosocial dimension is added when "self-respect" is mentioned. Trust is added to the mixture of this value as a necessary ingredient in building and maintaining the "team" (https://www.army.mil/values/).

If we mentioned the notion of service above in conjunction with both voluntary and mandatory conscription as a service to the State, here the term is *Selfless Service*: "Put the welfare of the nation, the Army and your subordinates before your own. Selfless service is larger than just one person. In serving your country, you are doing your duty loyally without thought of recognition or gain. The basic building block of selfless service is the commitment of each team member to go a little further, endure a little longer, and look a little closer to see how he or she can add to the effort." What makes this service selfless is that it requires everyone to look at the big picture, the unit, the group, and even the entire country. When speaking of *Honor*, the military code says that each person should "live up to Army values. The nation's highest military award is The Medal of Honor. This award goes to Soldiers who make honor a matter of daily living—Soldiers who develop the habit of being honorable, and solidify that habit with every value choice they make. Honor is a matter of carrying out, acting, and living the values of respect, duty, loyalty, selfless service, integrity and personal courage in everything you do." Honor in this context brings together some previously stated values, but what is fascinating here is that honor should become a "habit," just like Integrity and Personal Courage, which are the last two values to be discussed. *Integrity* means "do what's right, legally and morally. Integrity is a quality you develop by adhering to moral principles. It requires that you do and say nothing that deceives others. As your integrity grows, so does the trust others place in you. The more choices you make based on integrity, the more this highly prized value will affect your relationships with family and friends, and, finally, the fundamental acceptance of yourself." And likewise, *Personal Courage* is defined as "face fear, danger or adversity (physical or moral). Personal courage has long been associated with our Army. With physical courage, it is a matter of enduring physical duress and at times risking personal safety. Facing moral fear or adversity may be a long, slow process of continuing forward on the right path, especially if taking those actions is not popular with others. You can build your personal courage by daily standing up for and acting upon the things that you know are honorable" (ibid.).

Having enumerated these values and the military's definition of them, we should hasten to explain that under certain conditions they can be manipulated to rationalize improper behavior of the kind seen by Nazi or other fascist military forces. Can loyalty as a value be sanctioned regardless of some other values, such as critical thinking and the integrity of a legitimate political system? Under what conditions will a military force maintain these values internally but abuse them when it gets to the "enemy," domestic and foreign? Can one's choice of how to apply these values become one's own undoing? One can even make the argument, as both Stanley Aronowitz and Fredric Jameson do, that in fact a voluntary army is both dangerous (because it is paid to do the bidding of the State) and undemocratic (because it is self-select and mercenary), as opposed to a national army where everyone must serve (2014). In their respective ways, they recount the history of national armies that not only fought wars but also were the backbone of bringing together different clans and tribes, various principalities and communities, into one coherent system (with a single language and payment system). If a volunteer army is indeed a mercenary army that is professionalized on the one hand, but also privatized on the other (as we have seen in the last Afghanistan and Iraq wars with outsourcing military work to Blackwater), we may reasonably worry about what is left of the values listed above. What kind of self-respect can a soldier in Iraq muster while fighting alongside a Blackwater operative who gets paid twice as much and who has half the experience? What sense of honor and integrity are brought forth when military service has been monetized in the neoliberal State? And what culture of camaraderie can be expected if only the unemployed are more likely to serve? (Aronowitz and DiFazio 2010). In other words, as much as these values are inspiring, as much as they contribute to a social setting where the community of citizens is pulled together under the goal of national security and the defense of democracy, might they not fall on deaf ears when the majority of the population in the United States (90 percent as we saw above) has never served in the armed forces and has no inclination to participate?

Perhaps it is with these questions in mind that we come to the utopian vision Jameson brings to our attention in *An American Utopia: Dual Power and the Universal Army*. The conceptual setup for Jameson's book is how to bring about a communist utopia—more specifically, what strategies have been proposed by the left in the past century? Three options have been suggested: revolution, reform (socialism), or dual power. Since the failures of the revolutionary movements in the past century (from the USSR to Cuba), and since the shortcomings of the reformist social democratic parties in Europe, Jameson has chosen dual power as the only remaining viable political strategy. As he says: "The army is a viable candidate for the emergence of dual power . . . it is not a utopian scheme but eminently practical" (2016, 20). For him, this "new army" is a "universal army" that embodies a "socioeconomic structure" and represents the "collective action" of the population (ibid., 20–21). To be clear, this universal army will not replace the State, nor will it challenge its function and power, but instead will work in parallel to offer social services not provided by the State and with its decentralized but universal reach will become a parallel force that safeguards the well-being of the people. Without following Jameson's critique of the State, both as an organizing conceptual category and as a practical power, the concept of "failed states" that has been in vogue in the past few decades (whether of the old communist variety or the more democratic ones) drives his analysis. It should be also noted that for the army to be universal and engage in "a concrete political program" it would have to conscribe the entire population, like a "glorified National Guard" (ibid., 26). This "citizen army," based on the draft, is "virtually the only institution to transcend the jurisdiction of state laws and boundaries" given our federal system (ibid., 27). And in this sense, the army can play a unique role in the federalist structure of the United States: "The single advantage of the army as a system is that it transcends that document [the Constitution] without doing away with it; it coexists with it at a different spatial level and becomes thereby a potentially extraordinary instrument in the erection of dual power" (ibid.).

Historically speaking, the United States had the draft during the Vietnam War, and when President Nixon ended it he was counting on the popular resistance to the war to end as well. In other words, Jameson is aware of the power of a national draft to bring people together and have them critically evaluate government policies, such as the declaration of war. This is doubly so when their own lives are on the line, when they are asked to participate in what they consider an illegitimate foreign policy (ibid.). In reinstituting the draft, Jameson hopes that the army will be a "popular mass force" capable of being more representative of the people's will than any of the existing political modes of democratic representations (all of which have been corrupted in the past few decades). This process will institutionalize a counterbalance to the undemocratic and nonrepresentative political system of the current State (ibid., 28). Because this army will include all those aged fifteen to sixty, because it will practically encompass the entire population, it will be both "unmanageable" and "incapable of waging foreign wars, let alone carrying out successful coups" (ibid.). As an example of successful implementation of something similar to this proposal, Aronowitz brings up the short period in the history of revolutionary China when the army had the role of redistributing land, providing free education (more accurately, indoctrination), and training. He admits that of course the army also killed millions who resisted its civilian policies or were unwilling to conform to the totalitarian strictures of the Communist Party (2014). Jameson, for his part, reminds us that in cases of natural crises, such as floods, the army is called in to offer help without thereby threatening the power of the State; on the contrary, its activities are coordinated through the State. But in addition to the more extreme cases where the National Guard is called upon for immediate and short-term intervention, it's the military in general that offers universal healthcare to its soldiers, education, professional training, and all the other social and economic benefits the rest of society lacks. To put this in perspective, the Census Bureau reports that federal, state, and local government agencies employ about twenty-two million citizens, and if we add to this the military (both active and veterans), we come to about forty-four million who are beneficiaries of several social programs unavailable to the rest of the population. Despite some grumblings about the failures of the Veterans Affairs agency, its healthcare system is a model for a full integration of physical and psychological treatments.

Jameson admits that since the army has been traditionally based on "discipline and hierarchy" it may not lend itself to being a democratically run counterbalance to the powers of the State (2016, 30). Yet he envisions the popular army as being transformed into more decentralized institution where civilian activities would transcend defense. This image of a civilian army draws from a variety of utopian texts, all of which find a more benign, even important, role for the army to play outside warfare. If the military's focus is no longer warfare, it could now use discipline to guarantee "that the functions required for society's existence be secured" (ibid., 35). Jameson brings up the reality of greater desegregation experienced in the military compared to the rest of American society, and that "collective units" could democratically and in a decentralized fashion take on the responsibilities of markets and government agencies in a more effective manner, especially when using modern computing powers (ibid., 39). It's worth emphasizing at this juncture two issues: first, that this utopian vision is already partially operational and that therefore Jameson is confident in its potential for a wider implementation: there are many things we can learn from the military in how to bring about changes without threatening the Constitution or other political functions of the State, such as foreign policy and domestic legislation. Jameson makes sure we don't forget that the militarization of our civilian life is only offered as a transitional step toward the goal of a full-fledged utopia, the kind that is thinkable and as Aronowitz reminds us (2014), practically achievable under the technoscientific conditions of the present day (and therefore not utopian in the sense of unrealistic dreams about future state of affairs). And second, Jameson insists on the fact that even today's army obliges its members "to associate with all kinds of people on an involuntary, non-selective basis," and that this "forced association" offers the best mechanism for "securing a certain collective unification and levelling," resembling a classless society (2016, 61). For someone who experienced this firsthand, Jameson's assessment is reasonable and accurate. There are few conditions in contemporary culture, perhaps getting a driver's license at the Department of Motor Vehicles, under which we are indeed treated equally and where we find ourselves in close proximity to people from different socioeconomic backgrounds. Military service may discriminate between the more and less skilled, between those with greater and less physical endurance and mental aptitude, but when it comes to the other variables that define our identities, military discipline and training remains nondiscriminatory. Moreover, appeal to one's ancestry or inheritance and titles is absent in the military context: you cannot inherit your parents' rank. The Israeli military cannot make full use of its annual conscripts, but it has refused, as a policy matter, to eliminate mandatory conscription because of the social role the military plays as a cultural melting pot.

In case the image of a civilian military force is too jarring for peaceloving and utopian thinkers of the day, Jameson softens his rhetoric and arguments by introducing Charles Fourier as "the only thinker who has thus far discovered the way for a collectivity or a multiplicity to coordinate the ineradicable individualities which make it up" (ibid., 81). Following him, Jameson suggests that the provisional dual-power institution of the future will have to overcome the inevitable repressions of "libidinal" urges and that it should provisionally be called "the Psychoanalytic Placement Bureau" (ibid.). This Bureau will use the best computer systems to mediate between the individual and the collectives to which they belong, guaranteeing full employment (the production base) along the way and the best cultural outlets (the infrastructure), creating a "kinship system" reminiscent of "primitive communism or tribal society" (ibid., 82). And unlike the "planned economy" of the failed totalitarian regimes, this one would foster "collective project, collective life, the team as social being" (ibid., 83). If we look above at some of the phrasing of the US Army's list of values, Jameson's list is similar enough. Since "money no longer plays a central role" in this utopian existence, "consumerism as passion" (and addiction) will wither away (ibid., 91). But more importantly, Jameson insists on using the current rhetorical and symbolic practices of the military as an inspiration: "The stereotypes of army life are above all relevant here, for barracks life, the life of the recruit or draftee, always involves being thrown together with people utterly unlike you, from wholly different and incompatible backgrounds, classes, ethnicities, and even sexes. This instantaneous dislikes and distasteful cultural unfamiliarities, the inescapable elbow-rubbing with people with whom you have nothing in common and would normally avoid—this is true democracy, normally concealed by the various class shelters, the professions, or the family itself . . . , and warded off by wealth in its gated communities and walled estates" (ibid., 95–96).

No matter how applicable Jameson's vision of a utopian reorganization of contemporary society, no matter how attractive the army remains as an alternative power base for reconstituting social works and settling economic differences for greater efficiency and full employment, there are those, like Slavoj Žižek, who object to the depoliticization of this utopia. What kind of an institution is the military in terms of the back and forth that ensues when political discourse is the arbiter of policy decisions? What happens to the checks and balances that democratic States ought to incorporate and cherish? (ibid., chapter 10) Since we are less concerned with politics as such as with the economic models that can supersede market-capitalism, we should make sure, as Žižek insists, that even though we live in a so-called postpolitical era of the naturalization of economy, that we refrain from the tendency that "political decisions are as a rule presented as matters of pure economic necessity" (ibid., 278). In short, Žižek's critique of Jameson is not so much about the potential use of the military ethos as a transformational possibility toward communist utopia, but that the economy deserves to be examined on its own and not simply as a means to an end, such as the current policies of European austerity. The economic imagination deserves to be critically examined, and that examination is a political process where social life is debated so as to reach a political agreement.

Some critical comments are in place before we conclude. First, mandatory conscription, however "classless" it sounds, still embodies a coercive stance on the part of the State. Must we all serve? What if we refuse? Will the State use its coercive power to imprison us? Second, if the military is a "parallel" power to the State, is it as powerful as the power of the State? Does it then have an additional power of coercion and indoctrination? In other words, are individuals now subjected to the dual oppressive powers of their community? Third, is there any danger that even if the so-called civilian army is established it may find warfare in general and specific battlegrounds worthy of its power? Will the State's power constrain foreign ambitions of the military? Fourth, how is this model of dual power logistically attainable, keeping in mind a sense of decentralized coordination? The current military is notoriously inefficient (but it can withstand public outcry in the name of redundancy and national security), so how well will an enormous military function? Fifth and finally, isn't this language of military power not too macho or plainly sexist? Since when is military service as opposed to harmonious leisure existence a utopian ideal?

V: A BRIDGE

The four case studies offered us alternative worldviews about human interaction in general and of the moral conditions for them to thrive. Along the way, as we have seen already in part III, we came across a variety of challenges to the presuppositions we examined in parts I and II. Even when the Catholic Church is heavy handed in its dictates about the belief in God and Jesus, it remains a religious institution that appreciates the need to constitute economic relations that cater to the poor, that retains the dignity of humanity, and that finds capitalist greed unacceptable. It may not offer an alternative economic model, but it clearly rejects neoliberal market-capitalism. If it more carefully adhered to some of the biblical verses quoted above, it would endorse a communal economic model as experienced in kibbutzim and communes. If Pope Francis collects as much money from the rich and distributes it to the poor, he will be emulating the role of Native American chiefs entrusted to act as the redistribution center for the tribe.

The Israeli kibbutz movement and the American communes of the past century have illustrated that communal living is a viable option, that cohousing remains an option in this highly technoscientific culture, and that exchanges can be rethought. Are these arrangements genuinely countercultural (and thereby rational critical responses to the status quo) or practical reactions to financial exigencies (of the post–Vietnam era or the post–Great Recession time)? Time will tell if these communities will proliferate, especially in the age of hyperconnectivity in virtual spaces, using the Internet as a conveyor of inspirational information and as a reminder that virtual relations do not suffice for the human spirit. Questions of scale will challenge future experimentations. The communes that continue to pepper our cultural landscape are essential reminders that alternatives to individualism are available, that money doesn't have to be the only currency with which to handle relationships, and that when minimally used for convenience's sake, money can lose its addictive allure.

The list of values put forth by the military and the idea of mandatory service help nudge our individualistic worldview to one where we are always already members of a community, where shared ideals can be embraced, and where difference is understood to be temporary and merit-based. Though the military is hierarchical and discipline driven, and though its efficiency is comparable to the marketplace, it may offer a novel way of viewing human nature, one that is "grasped not as good or evil but rather as essentially inefficient" (ibid., 49). This is an example of tinkering with the presuppositions examined earlier in this book to establish different economic models. What if humanity is by nature inefficient? This should motivate us to cooperate and have the help of others; we are better off (economically and psychologically) working in teams rather than alone. The ideals of genius and solitary creativity should have been debunked already when armies of young software engineers solved problems and invented new algorithms for smartphone applications or Internet search engines. It's not simply that "no man is an island to himself," but that every person, as a member of a community or several communities, contributes to and is a beneficiary of the contributions of others. This is true whether you live in poor or rich communities, whether these are gangster or mobsters, whether they are professors or lawyers. This is neither romantic nor utopian, but an honest report of what is happening around us all the time. And the sooner we admit to this human condition, the better off our interactions with others will become.

Chapter Fifteen

Moral Framing of Political Economy

This last chapter builds on some of the salient features already examined in parts II and III, where communal relations among individuals is the standard against which economic models should be measured. This means that we neither begin with an isolated individual nor with an individual who naturally has the tendency to barter; instead, we deeply appreciate our sociality and the fact that we are inclined to share what we have and help each other. As Martin Nowak (2011) argues, altruism is part of our evolutionary makeup, and we need each other to survive and thrive. As some behavioral economists and social psychologists illustrate more recently, without a social context, without social cues and reaffirmations, our decision-making processes cannot be understood (Kahneman 2011). In other words, this chapter begins with the social so as to understand the individual rather than the other way around.

Perhaps this last chapter can help us envision a different mode of thinking for public policy, centering the well-being of the community above the happiness of the individual. Expanding our economic imagination here is bound to be based more explicitly on moral principles rather than financial ones, and as such may shift our focus from what is the most "efficient" or "profitable" policy to what is the most "humane" or "fair" way of interaction among people, in and outside markets. When fairness and empathy are foundational components of public policy, resource allocation and collective organizing will change as well, so that we might insist on public transportation rather than private cars, on universal healthcare rather than the appeal to private insurance companies. And the sense of "caring" about each other and future generations will be foregrounded.

I: UTOPIAN AND PRAGMATIC THINKING
(OVERCOMING NEOLIBERALISM)

Instead of contrasting utopian thinking with practical applications of thought, instead of remaining beholden to the binary of theory and practice, Marxism has already offered us the notion of *praxis*, where presumably the binary is overcome. Utopian thinking itself, as Kathi Weeks (2016) reminds us, can offer alternatives, potential critiques to the existing status quo, a flight of the imagination (and in some cases an avoidance of the realities that surround us), or even a form of therapy. But as outlandish as our imagination may be at times, it does offer ideas and ideals as heuristic tools with which to bring about transformations in the here and now. Admittedly, most utopian thinking today is to be found in sci fi literature that finds its way into video games and movies; but the fact that these literary devices are realized in virtual-reality forms is already a concession that their realization elsewhere is not that far-fetched. To use Aronowitz's comments in his conversation with Jameson (2016), the utopias of yesterday can more readily be implemented today because of the great technoscientific strides we have already made. This means, for example, that visions about interstellar voyages are in fact being experimented with today when the travel to Mars is explored by commercial entities; likewise, reconfiguring food-supply chains is evident in many communities where farm-to-table mindfulness is practiced. The collapse of the divide between one's imagination and our lived reality is closer at hand in contemporary society than ever before. This is not simply the kind of communication gadgets that were first seen in films, such as *Metropolis* (1927) or *1984* (1956 and 1984), where television sets or large screens were used for two-way conversations (eventually brought to wide public use by Skype and FaceTime). Instead, what we have in mind here is more transformative, exploiting our vast technoscientific treasure trove for more equitable dissemination of goods and services. Perhaps Marx's dreamlike expression of the communist ideal can more easily be accomplished today; as famously said in *The German Ideology*, it will be a "Communist society, where nobody has one exclusive sphere of activity but each can become accomplished in any branch he wishes," because this is a society that "regulates the general production and thus makes it possible for me to do one thing today and another tomorrow, to hunt in the morning, fish in the afternoon, rear cattle in the evening, criticise after dinner, just as I have a mind, without ever becoming hunter, fisherman, herdsman or critic" (1972). With this, "full employment" may have to be rethought, because robotic productivity may allow us all to work less and have more leisure time. Perhaps even this binary of working and leisure time will be overcome as our work will be our pleasure and our pleasure will be to create, and perhaps that creation will be thought of as working as well (Livingston 2016). The forty-hour workweek may be halved, retirement may be available to all of us at fifty rather than never, and healthcare will be available universally at fairly low costs. Likewise, our notion of prosperity will expand to include not money as such or material possessions, but the enjoyment of nature and other people, the routines of cleaning our neighborhoods and caring for our neighbors' mental and physical health. All of this isn't utopian, but practical; this isn't outlandish, but within reach; and perhaps it should be called *practopia*, the practice of utopia or utopian practice; a reasonable approach to our life, a way we can incorporate all facets of what we already know and care about. What will it take?

Perhaps we should worry more about how to change our outlook than about how imaginative we should be; perhaps we should focus on some moral norms rather than on the specific policies that will bring about such transformation. Instead of worrying about feats of the imagination or how to make them come true, we should worry about our thinking. Imaginative utopias are already in place, but our collective will has to be harnessed. Perhaps we lack the vocabulary and the frameworks with which to inspire and practice this manner of thinking; the first three parts were so laborious, even plodding to get us here. We have to rethink concepts, such as competition and cooperation, social contract and the general will, in order to see where we are stuck. Redistribution of income and wealth will be less burdensome in moral terms when we put less value on money as such, and appreciate its limited usefulness for lubricating the wheels of our daily interactions. No longer shall we worship wealth and celebrities who are wealthy (as if they earned their success alone), but replace them with a normalized view of members of our communities who contribute to our physical and mental health, who care to make sure that our brief presence on this planet is as enjoyable as possible. We should hasten to agree that perhaps this kind of psychosocial transformation is more readily available among those who do not starve or crave the necessities of life, but already enjoy a certain level of comfort and economic security. This is obviously true. So, the premise here is that the kind of prosperity we are envisioning should be available as a starting point for everyone, with a minimum wage or income or wealth that will allow for physical and mental health, the kind of prosperity we can reasonably expect in a flourishing and technoscientifically advanced world.

When we discussed globalization as having been initiated by developmental economics, it was made clear that the ideals of aiding less fortunate people around the world were understood as a moral imperative. What was at stake wasn't the neoliberal expansionist motive, but instead a humane approach that, if applied properly, would enhance the potential of less-developed or developing countries to become self-sufficient. The fact that asymmetries of information and trade turned globalization into the mess it is today is both a tribute to the power of ideas, as already mentioned by Keynes, and the power of the neoliberal ideology to exploit labor in poor nations and enjoy untapped natural resources of countries who needed Western technology for optimal extraction. Even those more interested in rewriting the Poor Laws in the UK at the end of the nineteenth century, like Henry Fawcett, appreciated the need to collapse the binary between labor and capital, between those who work and those who own the means of production (1871, 119–20), and to envision "copartnership" (ibid., 169). With this partnership in mind, Fawcett continues to explain that "it is essential to accompany each addition to material prosperity with a corresponding moral improvement," the kind that should evolve "from national education" (ibid., 121). Not only Marx and Engels were concerned to interweave the economic and moral dimensions, as observed in the case of pauperism. To find "sympathy" among market participants, it's "essential" to think about "moral improvement," and such moral improvement will only come about with national education. The success of neoliberal ideology to erect a theoretical wedge between the economy and all other aspects of society, between the market and the State, between what is expedient and what is moral, takes us back to feudal models.

Naomi Klein's brilliant and scathing critique of neoliberal thinking provides ample empirical evidence for the disastrous consequences of this theoretical wedge. For her, neoliberals (the Chicago School is singled out) go about changing the world with a "shock treatment," where sweeping market-oriented programs decimate state-run programs in the name of improvement, greater efficiency, and moral purity (2007, 6–7). Exploiting natural and national disasters, this approach imposes an economic model that ends up benefitting the few with the pretense of saving the many; a "corporatist" approach that brings about "huge transfers of public wealth to private hands, often accompanied by exploding debt, an ever-widening chasm between the dazzling rich and the disposable poor and an aggressive nationalism that justifies bottomless spending on security" (ibid., 15). As Klein scours the global economy, she finds examples of this approach that distrusts governments, heralds the efficiency of markets, and celebrates the wealth created by multinationals without acknowledging that along the way the public sphere, the Commons, has been eviscerated and plundered in ways reminiscent of feudal lords and monarchs. Rather than enhancing freedom and democracy, these neoliberal experiments have proven to undermine both: they have been accompanied by "the most brutal forms of coercion" and have inflicted misery "on the collective body politic as well as on countless individual bodies" (ibid., 18). Whether we end up with hybrid economies or Abba Lerner's "controlled economy," the point is to care for people and their lives and not about the wealth of few multinationals. For Lerner, the issue, economically speaking, is to find an alternative to *laissez-faire* economics that differs from "collectivism" and that promotes "emancipation" (1947, 1). The three primary "tasks" of a controlled economy would be first, to fully utilize all natural and human resources (make sure anyone who wants to work can find employment); second, "abolish all dire poverty" and "diminish the tremendous inequality of income and wealth"; and third, "put an end to monopoly throughout the economy and the accompanying exploitation and economic waste" (ibid., 3). Controlling the economy, for Lerner, is the means by which the welfare of the general population can be enhanced, and in eschewing both pure capitalism and collectivism, he admits that "it is likely to earn the enmity of the devotees of both dogmas," yet it would become a "rationally organized democratic society" (ibid., 4). Lerner makes sure to explain in his treatise that the ultimate test for the success of any proposal like his own is the extent to which the general welfare is being improved, and not whether this or that segment of the economy is thriving at the expense of another (as Klein reports). One may call this a utilitarian moral theory, where the consequences are examined, rather than focusing on the moral means by which economic mechanisms are set up. For Lerner, what is important in justifying an economic model is not the quantitative tools that make it operate efficiently, but the qualitative assessment of what state of affairs it brings about.

In his approach, Lerner follows the welfare economists, such as Arthur Pigou, who among others insisted on shifting economic thinking from wealth (wealth creation and growth) to welfare (caring for the poor). In approaching the economy from this perspective, it's natural for Pigou to argue about minimum wages, for example, but not simply for its own sake or for its economic benefit, but in moral terms as well: "Economic welfare is best promoted by the establishment of national minimum, at such a level that the direct good resulting from the marginal pound transferred to the poor just balances the indirect evil brought about by the consequent reduction of the dividend" (1912, 395–396). Just as we noted above the Catholic Church's sense of communal welfare as community building and not charity, we can find this sentiment in welfare economics (ibid., 478). What distinguishes welfare economists is their insistence that financial inequalities are noxious in moral terms in addition to the financial harm of underconsumption. In Pigou's words: "The misery and squalor that surround us, the injurious luxury of some wealthy families, the terrible uncertainty overshadowing many families of the poor—these are evils too plain to be ignored. Whether the life of man ends with his physical death, or is destined to pass unscathed through that gateway, the good and the evil that he experiences here are real; and to promote the one and restrain the other is a compelling duty" (ibid., 488). For Pigou as well as others in this theoretical realm of welfare economics, just as it is for those who care about developmental economics, the moral dimension is not simply a by-product, but the main reason for studying economics and trying to use market tools to eliminate poverty. If poverty cannot be eliminated through market-capitalism we should find an alternative. Pigou quotes Comte to say that "it is for the heart to suggest our problems; it is for the intellect to solve them . . . The only position for which the intellect is primarily adapted is to be the servant of the social sympathies" (2013, 5). And these "social sympathies" harken back to Smith, as we saw above, but may have been forgotten by mainstream neoliberal economists. Pigou's policy recommendation is that the notion of transferring money from the "relatively rich" to the "relatively poor" should depend on whether this transfer (in the form of progressive taxation or direct government subsidies) adds to the "national dividend" or diminishes it (ibid., 705ff).

While Klein is outraged by the neoliberal infringement into the utopian zone of economic transformation, and while Pigou and Lerner offer modest reconceptualizations of the ways in which market-capitalism should be reformed, it's the utopian version offered by Jameson that still preoccupies us here. He is clear that he offers the third transitional option of utopian thinking, the dual-power model. For him, this third alternative is qualitatively better than the revolutionary and the reformist alternatives (as we saw in the previous chapter). The first is deficient because of its violent and destructive tendencies, and the second because of its negligent impact with incremental changes. In reintroducing the dual-power model, Jameson forces us to think creatively about what would make a difference right away in how we can move forward toward a communal ideal or a prosperity model. Perhaps what he offers is deficient as well, because he trusts the military apparatus too much or wishes to ignore some of its undemocratic practices, as we saw above. Just as the Catholic Church remains dogmatic and unwavering in claiming divine authority, so is the military the secular equivalent of this institutional organization. These are not community-based collectives that foster ongoing recalibration of ideas and practices from the bottom up. When welfare is offered to the poor a price is attached: adherence and compliance, obedience and silence. Whatever else they are, these models are undemocratic. Should they be? Some might argue that meritocracy should be at the heart of democracy, so that experts will guide the appeal to the collective will. Others may argue that the models we have enumerated have different intent at their core, whether salvation for the religious or national security for the military, and as such they cannot be useful inspirational tools for the prosperity model we have in mind. Before addressing them, we should attempt to distill the salient points of reference these institutions embody and free them from some of the frames in which they are lodged. Unlike Jameson's model, the current outline consciously cherry-picks whatever may be morally acceptable and worthy of emulation.

II: MANDATORY COMMUNITY SERVICE (SOCIAL CONTRACT)

As mentioned above, one of the most appealing features of the dual-power model for Jameson has been mandatory conscription. This single act can bring about the moment of classless society when every person, regardless of background, is part of and participates in military service. There is some appeal to classlessness as a unifying principle and practice on two levels: first, the temporary encounter of citizens with each other may enhance a sense of empathy; and second, national service may instill a communal sense of belonging. The drawback is also clear insofar as this isn't a voluntary but coerced service. What attitude will participants have if they feel they are forced to contribute to the well-being of others? Will it have the same uplifting spirit envisioned by Jameson's utopia, or instead breed resentment? Is the specter of warfare the only means by which, as the Greeks and Spartans have done before, to unite a people? It's one thing to say that only those who have trained for war are worthy of public office, as some Greeks have maintained, and quite another to say that everyone must train for war. Preparation for warfare is dangerous because it presupposes that warfare is inevitable and that one ought to be ready for it. And since the training for warfare is predicated on disciplinary behavior—following orders and being mentally ready to kill other people who are labeled enemies—this may undermine critical engagement among the population. There are better ways of socializing people into groups and into serving the greater good. If military service were to be replaced by paid civil service, say of one year sometime in one's life before the age of twenty, then we may rightfully expect a civic-minded populace to embrace it. We may also expect that fond youthful memories of communal life will transform one's outlook about individual struggle and ambition. Otherwise, we may suggest that a one-year civil service will be accomplished by the time someone is forty, so perhaps a certain skill set can be more fruitfully shared with the community. The insistence that this service be completed earlier rather than later hinges on the belief that this year will be formative for participants, that they will carry with them a sense of belonging to their community, that they will learn to interact with strangers empathetically, seeing how solidarity is practiced rather than studied in classrooms.

While Jameson's proposal is more concerned with how to get closer to the Marxian utopia, in this book the concern is to reconceptualize the notion of the social contract. For Socrates, this meant abiding by the laws of the State as long as you enjoy its protection. Your rights are contingent on your duties, so that without the latter being executed the former have no meaning. Responsible citizens are those who fulfill their duties first and only then can claim their rights. This isn't a chronological issue of doing one before the other, but more of a logical priority, first give up something in order to be entitled to something in return. In this sense, veterans should have the right to demand healthcare after their tour of military service; and other citizens can ask for roads to be paved after they paid their taxes. This is also the way in which Rousseau envisioned individuals giving up some freedoms to have them reinstated by the State, now with the full force of legitimate legal and enforcement systems. Despite the debates over the "general will" and its potential to be too authoritative and ad hoc, the point Rousseau was after was more about having some communal sense that transcended the amalgamation of individual wills, something that elevates—in the Hegelian sense of *aufhebung*—the communal spirit of civil society that remains the foundation of the more legalistic and regulated State apparatus. If the State is governed by democratic principles, there should be a level of compromise and consensus about what is best for the community. Perhaps what is at stake is the starting point for any cooperation, the kind we have noted in the kibbutz and communes, and the one that may be relevant for reinforcing a sense of camaraderie among complete strangers. Perhaps what is at stake as well is a shift from the exuberance of the Enlightenment figures who were still fighting the ghosts and in some cases the reality of slavery and indentured-like exploitation common in feudal societies. If we consider these two issues together, it would make sense to remind ourselves of the concerns with human nature already discussed in part I. Are we by nature selfish, self-centered, absolute egoists with malicious intent when encountering others? Taking for granted our (socially) given and (politically) legitimate freedoms, is it not more reasonable to assume, even if only provisionally, that we are cooperative by nature, that evolution has favored us as a species more because of our propensity to collaborate than because our brains became large enough to devise more sophisticated ways of hurting others to survive? Admittedly, we can learn much from ants and bees, as Wilson (2012) is fond of reminding us, emulating these species's behavior.

The spectrum of answers to these questions begins on the one extreme with the likes of Robert Axelrod, who argues that we are indeed selfish egoists by nature, but that we have learned to cooperate to improve our lot. Using elaborate and repeated computerized Prisoner's Dilemma games, he has concluded that "results from the tournaments demonstrate that under suitable conditions, cooperation can indeed emerge in a world of egoists without central authority" (2006, 20). He refers here to extended tournaments where the PD games are played repeatedly with numerous players who eventually recognize and appreciate the advantages of cooperation for optimal personal purposes. But just because the cooperators improve their individual positions does not mean that society as a whole has been well served by this cooperation. As Axelrod admits, "Getting out of Prisoner's Dilemma is one of the primary functions of government: to make sure that when individuals do not have private incentive to cooperate [as the game makes abundantly clear], they will be required to do the socially useful thing anyway" (ibid., 133). In other words, what is required is to avoid a general exploitation of PDs, and that is the role of government regulations. Admittedly, it's beneficial for participants to collaborate not because of any altruistic motive but because doing so will minimize their penalties. But if government agencies modify the payoffs from the game and promote cooperation by teaching "people to care about each other," it is possible to change young people's preferences toward the "welfare of others" (ibid., 134–135). Instead of limiting the potential for future cooperation, Axelrod is optimistic enough to suggest that despite humanity remaining egotistic at heart, if two prerequisites are met—reciprocity and the shadow of the future—then it would be possible to affect socialization in large groups of people (ibid., 173–174). But will education be enough? Even if reciprocity is enjoined, aren't there alternative strategies that take advantage of others' cooperation without reciprocity, what we recognize as taking advantage of others? Even if we prove to everyone that reciprocity is in their best interest, will individuals be able to think about the "shadow of the future" rather than their immediate gratification? As long as Axelrod maintains a certain egoist view of human nature, even his best educational efforts may fall short.

On the other extreme of this spectrum of answers to the questions about cooperation we find Matthew Lieberman, who argues that "we are wired to be social" (2013, ix). Looking at the evolutionary evidence, Lieberman reports that "while we tend to think it is our capacity for abstract reasoning that is responsible for *Homo sapiens'* dominating the planet, there is increasing evidence that our dominance as a species may be attributable to our ability to think socially" (ibid., 7). For him, humans' social adaptation is more crucial than any other feature about our species, and the three features of our human nature that contribute to this is our "connection," "mindreading," and "harmonizing" (ibid., 11–12). While the connection with others in our species lays the groundwork for socializing, and while mindreading is an innate trait that allows us to figure out what others are thinking, harmonizing refers to "the neural adaptations that allow group beliefs and values to influence our own" (ibid.). Dismissing the "axiom of self-interest" (ibid., 83ff), Lieberman continues to show with measurements of brainwaves activity that "*our brains are built to practice thinking about the social world and our place in it*" (ibid., 22, italics in the original). What is most upsetting about holding onto the "axiom of self-interest" is that it has become a "self-fulfilling prophecy," engendering a "self-reinforcing [cycle], becoming more and more engrained over time" (ibid., 96–97). There is a way out of this vicious cycle, a way to undermine the self-fulfilling prophecy of self-interest that we reinforce when we celebrate the success of the few at the expense of the many. We can intervene, both pedagogically and personally, and remind everyone who will listen that we are indeed wired to be social and that empathy isn't an esoteric idea associated with spiritual thinking (as we saw above with the Dalai Lama) but an intrinsic human quality we all share. Lieberman mentions David Rock, who has developed specific strategies for businesses to incorporate into their "work environment that enhances employee engagement and productivity" (ibid., 259). The application to the business community reveals that the binary of competition and cooperation is a false one. If we appeal to what humans already know deep down about their social environments, then the economy must be part of these environments and not outside of them. These overlapping social environments include one's family and friends, neighbors and acquaintances, coworkers and colleagues, perhaps even market and political spheres. Seeing the world from this perspective requires education as well, but unlike the education suggested by Axelrod to sway people to become cooperative, Lieberman's education is an appeal to who we already are, to our deep natural tendencies, behaviors we innately know and have experienced. The unconditional love of a mother or father for their child is not the exception to the rule (of human interaction) but symptomatic of human relations.

Somewhere in between human selfishness and cooperation there is another view expounded by Martin Nowak. He admits that "humans are selfish apes," but he insists that "competition does not tell the whole story of biology. Something profound is missing" (2011 xv). As far as he is concerned, despite the "dark" side of evolution that promotes competitive survival, there is a "bright" side that is seldom talked about: "The range and extent to which we work together make us supreme cooperators, the greatest in the known universe" (2011, xvi). For him, this is not simply a by-product of our interaction with other people, but more specifically that "would-be competitors decide to aid each other instead" (ibid.). This "bright side of biology" involves our intentional choices, numerous and repeatable decisions we have made historically, because "cooperation—not competition—underpins innovation" (ibid., xix). As far as Nowak is concerned, the key to creativity and the building blocks of any complex construction are always a cooperative effort that yields results much more fulfilling and progressive than if we relied on either individual ingenuity or the competitive drive. Instead of developing this third view of cooperation in spiritual terminology, Nowak's choice is to insert it as a third principle of evolutionary progress, one that complements (genetic) mutation and (environment-fitting) selection (ibid., xx). Even if historically we survived because of mutation and selection, we have come of age now where cooperation is essential for global survival. Nowak's approach combines Axelrod's surveys of PD tournaments and Lieberman's empirical reports, adding more of a biological than a cognitive dimension. The five mechanisms that Nowak emphasizes are applicable both to biology and sociology, and they include repetition, reputation, spatial selection, multilevel selection, and kin selection. "Using these five mechanisms of cooperation, natural selection has ensured that we are able to get more from social living than from the pursuit of solitary, selfish life" (ibid., 272). And though competition and cooperation seem to be at odds with each other, for Nowak the reverse is the case: "The essentially competitive drive of evolution can, in many circumstances, give rise to cooperation" (ibid.). The proof for this counterintuitive conclusion is that we can observe "love, friendship, jealousy, and team spirit . . . across all human societies" (ibid.). Being "hopeful, generous, and forgiving," or what may be considered incorporating "charitable attributes," is the basis for "the winning strategies of direct and indirect reciprocity" (ibid.). One hopes that these strategies are not limited to kinship relations of those within fairly homogenous communities but can extend to all diverse societies, small and large.

If we are willing to change our vocabulary and expand it to include cooperative strategies as endemic to human nature, perhaps our concern with social contract theories and models will change as well. The starting point will be how we work together, how we see others as part of our community, and as such see ourselves always already members of a community. If cooperation is front and center, then competition can be a supplemental strategy useful occasionally but not always. Likewise, when we help others it's not because we are charitable in religious terms, but because this is who we are, people who are innately compassionate (as Rousseau speculated and as Nowak and Lieberman prove empirically), and therefore instinctively driven to be of service to others. Once we realize that social Darwinism—the theory that justifies personal success at the expense of others as an extension of evolutionary natural selection as the survival of the fittest—is indeed a post hoc rationalization of greed, we can set it aside. Instead, we can promote the idea that we have been cooperative all along, that our success depends on others, and that cooperation and teamwork yield better results than debilitating competition. Can you imagine what social contract theory will look like with this in mind? The political philosophers we encountered in part I had to justify why we should enter a social contract; by now we can appreciate that some inclination of a social contract was always already there, perhaps not fully articulated as a "contract" but as well-established social relations we enjoyed. To think otherwise is both a biological and intellectual folly we should refrain from perpetuating. So, recommending civil service to everyone shouldn't be a novelty but a sensible expression of our inner inclinations. What policy to adopt can be disputed—age, length, kind of service, tax credit or payment for such service—but the very idea can be reasonably accepted. To be sure, if this language of cooperation takes hold, the resistance to the "mandatory" aspect of "communal service" may dissipate as well, since the binary of coercion and voluntarism will disappear in this case.

III: POWER RELATIONS

The more we think about *practopia* (practical utopia) and about community service, the more we should acknowledge that power relations must be addressed as well. Before we examine specific principles that should hold, the framework of political economy must be reexamined. What we have already alluded to in the previous two parts is that the realities and power of neoliberal market-capitalism have overtaken some of the most cherished ideals of democracy, from influencing who should be nominated by the major parties to the funding of campaigns, from the drafting of legislation by lobbyists to the promotion of a Gig Economy that deprives workers of any benefits. So, the reasonable starting point here must be one that puts political and social ideals before economic ones, that insists on the moral dimension of any policy recommendation and the ways in which it is eventually implemented, and that recognizes the economy as a means and not an end in itself. When political leaders, such as presidents Clinton and Bush, promoted private ownership of homes, they used the markets to bring this about: bank deregulation and access to mortgages. And when the financial industry ran amok with this idea and created a bubble, it was up to these leaders, by then presidents Bush and Obama, to curtail the markets and remind the public what idea they originally had in mind. This would have meant, policywise, that the government intervention they designed (Troubled Asset Relief Program of close to $1 trillion) should have been directed to the homeowners themselves and not to the private financial institutions that inflated debt ratings and exacerbated the eventual bursting of the bubble. They should have taken control of the markets not in the form of direct subsidies to the institutions that were responsible for what happened but given direct financial assistance to late-mortgage payers or those defaulting on their debts. If this sounds naïve, simply compare the relative success of "cash for clunkers" (about $3 billion) in stimulating the car industry through grants to owners of old, fuel-inefficient, and polluting cars and trucks with that of the mortgage assistance. Though we can debate on the success or failure of such programs, inspired by Keynesian thinking and not by neoliberal ideology, what matters here is the moral approach that should have been paramount: the political sphere should be responsible to harness, curtail, and regulate unbridled market exuberance and protect consumers.

Once the political dimension of political economy is not merely an adjective but an overriding category, and once the economy remains subservient to and dependent on moral and democratic forces to direct it, we are bound to have a more controlled economy, in Pigou's and Lerner's sense, instead of a reviled planned economy of the Soviet or Chinese variants. Democratic supervision can be enhanced with rigorous use of the Internet—letting the public vote with a click of the finger on policy recommendations—and market decisions can benefit from feedback information loops that are broadly shared and expertly examined. If we discard outdated binaries, such as unregulated markets and central planning, we can find alternatives that could improve our economic welfare. We can adopt from the political sphere three doctrines—rotation or term limits, checks and balances, and consensus—and apply them to markets. To be sure, benevolent dictatorships are more expedient and efficient in completing economic goals than democracy. If we skip the Cultural Revolution in China with its devastating results—starvation, human rights violations, and unjustified killings of millions—and move to the twenty-first century, we can see how State capitalism under the Communist Party's regime introduced public transportation (speed rails not seen in the United States yet) and reduced pollution (through solar energy) in a manner impossible in some Western democracies. But the price might be too high: surveillance and infringement on personal freedoms and rights. To be clear, maintaining the inefficiencies and at times awful results of democracy (racist and sexist elected leaders) remains our best political options outside of some utopian anarchy.

When we consider *leadership rotation* or what amounts to *term limits*, we safeguard against the concentration of political power in the hands of few incumbents who eventually care more about their own reelection than about what ails their constituents. The reelection success of the US House of Representatives from 1964 to 2016 exceeds in each election cycle 80 percent; in the US Senate, during the same period, only six out of twenty-seven cycles have seen rates below 80 percent. What does this tell us about the longevity of political leaders? How much experience must our political leaders have when career professionals run most government agencies? The dominance of incumbency is indisputable in many democracies, even though the ideal of the farmer-legislator of the American founding fathers could not foresee professional politicians. If all political leadership is continuously rotated, just as is done in egalitarian communes and kibbutzim or even in the military where there is a mandatory retirement age of sixty-two, political leadership will be about service and not about power. Only fifteen of the fifty states have enacted term limits. But if our concern is less with political expertise and more with the diffusion of political power, we should encourage service and rotation as a sensible policy. More in line with the general principle of community service, political positions would be then viewed not as positions of power, but as temporary sites where competent and charismatic leaders share their experiences and insights. The hallmark of democracy is the peaceful transfer of power, so that even when candidates win office who are objectionable, their opposition can be confident that they can lose their positions with the next election. Likewise, if leaders abuse their positions of power, they can be replaced without the violence of a revolution. The principle of rotation in politics will have a direct impact on the economy, because the lobbying appeal of corporate giants (to further exclusively their own interests) will diminish; if you add to this a rotation of economic leaders as well, it's the policies that would be under scrutiny and not those who are in power to manipulate them. By focusing more on policies and procedures rather than on the individuals who execute them, we might avoid the kind of power grab or obfuscation that takes place even when rotation and term limits are enforced; if we add to this the explicit notion of public service, we might make it less appealing to those hungry for power for its own sake or for personal enrichment.

The second principle worth mentioning in this context of a *practopia* is *checks and balances*, whether along the American constitutional model or other parliamentary systems. What is relevant here for critics of neoliberal market-capitalism is that in markets three powers (business, labor, and government) should keep each other in check. When multinationals exploit their power, government regulations can stop them; when business interests squeeze their laborers, organized labor can push back with government support; and when the labor market loses its luster, it needs government and business support to revitalize and retool it. The point of checks and balances is to curtail abuses and keep the parties in check, and to balance the power among participants. Introducing this principle in the political arena, as some democracies and republics have done, should inform economic models and their institutions. Economic leaders should be kept in check, not by their enabling boards but by employees and customers alike. And unlike the acrimonious relationship between business and labor in the United States, there are other models (Germany) where labor leaders are voting members of corporate boards. Under these conditions, we can bring about a sea of change where a more cooperative mindset informs the behavior of all the three market powers. When any party to a decision, an environmental agency or labor group, has a *de facto* veto power, a greater urgency to collaborate will be inevitable. Why would anyone propose a new idea or policy without first consulting with all the affected parties, the stakeholders? Would it not be more reasonable in a democracy with equally powerful constituencies and local councils to ask first? Feedback loops have been found more effective in enacting healthcare policies (Hall 2016) and energy-saving schemes (Rynn 2010). Any national organization that has economic impact, from utility companies (privately or publicly owned) to retailers (from Walmart to Amazon), would benefit immeasurably from listening to all the stakeholders. Even the most libertarian or anarchist customer is comforted by knowing that some agency along the long chain of supply has guaranteed the safety of products. This state of affairs is not the result of market self-policing but instead the active vigilance of customers and their representatives.

The third principle that relates to political power relations is *consensus* as practiced by Native Americans. The *Merriam-Webster Dictionary* defines the term as first, "general agreement: unanimity," second, "the judgment arrived at by most concerned," and third, "group solidarity in sentiment and belief." Leaving aside the high bar of unanimity—the consent by everyone— which itself is only one of the three options offered above, the sense of agreement or solidarity is more relevant in our context of the political eco- nomic spheres. If we find some level of agreement in the political sphere, it's reasonable to expect that some agreement (by most if not all) can be reached about economic policies. Native Americans, as we saw above, had to take their time and deliberate over their choices; they had to convince the mem- bers of the community that declaring war or moving to a new location was a good idea. The time it takes may seem too long or even wasteful; but what is forgotten is that the long process of listening and sharing concerns reinforces the sense of community. This sentiment is lost when legislation is passed with the thinnest of margins that imposes something on the rest of society without fully vetting the potential intended and unintended consequences. When we think ahead under "the shadow of the future" we may tamper our emotions. Some commentators have lamented the state of the political order in the United States in the past few years because of its legislative gridlock. But isn't the gridlock a true representation of an ideological rift in the cul- ture? As such, it's a symptom and not a cause, a consequence we must accept because no majority was clear until the latest election cycle when the Repub- lican Party gained control of all the branches of government. Mill's warning about the "tyranny of the majority" (1956, 7) is alive and well in the American republic where a president can be elected with a minority (of the popular vote, though majority of the Electoral College) that represents only 18 percent of the general population and 26 percent of those eligible to vote (McMaken 2016). The point of reaching consensus, both in the political and economic spheres, is that we would become more engaged as stakeholders who are responsible for decisions even when they backfire. The US political establishment made a mistake in invading Iraq, as journalists, economists, and even politicians now admit (not to mention the more compliant military leaders). But because of the post-9/11 frenzy of fear and revenge, the public was overwhelmingly supportive, allowing the Patriot Act to strip a basic "checks and balances" process where the executive must convince the judici- ary that surveillance of citizens is necessary. The point is not that consensus as such will always be informed or warranted, but that because a choice was made by consensus we should accept our own folly and not blame, for example, the Bush administration alone. Economic decisions need not be made by consensus, but when they are made by insulated executives they are likely to fail. Examples abound of ill-conceived ideas that fell flat or quickly disappeared from the market.

With the principles of rotation, checks and balances, and consensus build- ing, markets will no longer be politically protected from exogenous costs, as is the case of fossil-fuel corporate giants that enjoy federal subsidies while polluting the environment; instead, they will be responsive to the changing political agenda of a less entrenched group of political servants whose main concern is the welfare of the community. We can then more reasonably expect natural resources to be allocated with an eye on the long term, have their use contextualized among competing alternatives, and eventually come up with national policies that account for all the variables related to energy resources (such as military expenditures, environmental costs, and the health of the population). This approach neither reverts to the communist model of central planning—one agency knows it all—nor advocates ignoring financial matters. But when various constituencies are debating if to pursue the Keystone Pipeline (from Canada to the southern US coast), we cannot simply relapse into the old-fashioned binary of job creation and environmental hazards. The complexity of arguments and choices must be considered and a consensus should emerge even if it takes years and decades. As Native Americans understood already centuries ago, our decisions must be informed by past generations and be mindful of generations to come. Thinking only about our immediate situation is dangerous even in crisis situations; long-term solutions should be ready to implement way before such crises erupt. Slow deliberations are worthwhile, as the executives of Samsung would agree after one of their latest smartphones exploded when its battery heated up. Lengthening the time between developing and introducing a new technology may be beneficial for all concerned. And having public controls over private enterprises isn't a bad idea as some neoliberals claim. We should remember in this context how dependent—without acknowledgment—most corporate innovation is on the US government largesse. As already noted above, Mazzucato offers an amazingly informative record of how entrepreneurial the State has been in offering long-term investments in new technoscientific infrastructures, like the Internet and GPS, that eventually have been exploited by corporations. Most entertaining is her documentation of Apple's reliance on government patents for its so-called creative success (2014, chapter 5). To relegate politics to the realm of legislative and regulatory protection of the public from the potential abuses of corporations overlooks the essential role government agencies continue to play in our economic welfare. The market can easily be reorganized under principles different from the neoliberal ones for continued prosperity.

It is worth emphasizing this last point because the conflation or separation between the political and economic spheres may seem both arbitrary and impractical, especially if we pursue our *practopia*. If the State is indeed entrepreneurial and can manage and support innovation in its various agencies, then why not expand its reach even further? Though GPS was intended for military use at first, it wouldn't be far-fetched to think of its commercial applications; and once those potential applications were made clear, shouldn't other (private) entities offer this application free of charge? The public already paid for the research and development through taxes, so why must it pay a second time to telecommunication companies? Thinking about cooperation between public and private entities, perhaps a more reasonable cost allocation may ensue. This is not the place to articulate specific policies, but instead to promote a new framework of talking about innovation and creativity, how decisions ought to be made, and long-term communal benefits. The standard neoliberal argument about the necessity of intellectual property rights falls apart (as we saw above); likewise, the standard neoliberal distaste for the Commons is unwarranted (as corporations are beneficiaries more than their consumers). If we begin with the cooperative nature of humanity, the agreeable majority will overshadow minimal transgressions of some members. And this majority, we can reasonably expect, will be large and strong enough to affect political and economic policies alike.

IV: GOVERNMENTAL SOCIAL PROGRAMS

Having described the allure of utopian thinking, the need for rethinking the frames of reference we have historically assumed, we should also ask about the role of government. After the devastation of the two world wars in the twentieth century, many political philosophers and novelists thought it necessary to argue for governments that would protect citizens rather than descend into autocratic dictatorships in the name of utopian thinking (communist, fascist, and in all cases nationalist). Observing the similarly devastating consequence of neoliberal power grabs around the globe, always in the name of freedom and prosperity, we are now poised to figure out what countervailing power can regulate multinational corporate giants not to demolish public institutions and decimate the environment. What Bernard Russell was for the post–World War II era in *Authority and the Individual* (1949), Robert Reich is for the post–Great Recession era in *Saving Capitalism* (2015). To signal his good intentions, Reich adds in the subtitle, "For the Many, Not the Few." Like Russell before him, he takes for granted that government agencies are essential for the workings of any State, and that without them market dominance of the "few" will not be kept in check. The "solution" to the ongoing political discontent and the rise in income and wealth inequality (that leads to political disenfranchisement) is "an activist government that raises taxes on the wealthy, invests the proceeds in excellent schools and other means people need to get ahead, and redistributes to the needy" (2015, xiii). As we saw above, the overlapping of the economic and political domains as political economy is defined by Reich as "the study of how a society's laws and political institutions relate to a set of moral ideals, of which fair distribution of income and wealth was a central topic" (ibid., xvi). In this line of argument, he continues the work of welfare economists, from Pigou and Polanyi to Amartya Sen (1987), to reassess the functioning of markets in broader terms than financial growth. They share a conviction that markets need rules and that these rules are not simply legal instruments to protect market autonomy; they express the importance of human reciprocity and solidarity. This may be a tall order for a government, but as Russell astutely explained, economic security that accounts for human tendencies to compete and cooperate should be balanced and managed through rules and regulations, through public education and the preservation of national identities (or global identities if nationalism is a harbinger of potential nasty extremism).

Prescient in his concern with modern power relations, Reich explains his own approach by quoting Edward Ryan (as we already noted before): "Which shall rule—wealth or man; which shall lead—money or intellect; who shall fill public stations—educated and patriotic free men, or the feudal serfs of corporate capital?" (ibid., 45) As we are learning from the American presidential election cycle of 2016, these questions sound even more alarming, and a populist billionaire in charge of the largest political economy on earth outlined the answers to them. In his own exhortations, Reich echoes Stiglitz's critique of current capitalist practices (cited above). They both argue about the "vicious cycle" that characterizes the American political economy: "Economic dominance feeds political power, and political power further enlarges economic dominance" (ibid., 82–83; 157). This means that wealthy individuals fund and control political candidates and institutions that are supposed to regulate them, and through their lobbyists they in fact write the laws that Congress passes (London 2016). What Reich recommends is replacing the vicious cycle with a "virtuous cycle," one "in which widely shared prosperity generates more inclusive political institutions, which in turn organize the market in ways that further broaden the gains from growth and expand opportunity" (ibid., 84). In this he is no different from Stiglitz, who also talks about sharing the prosperity of market-capitalism. Though noble in their intent, they follow a long line of reformers who still want to "save capitalism" rather than abolish it; they want to find what Galbraith dubbed a "countervailing power" to reign in corporate excesses and guarantee that market participants have a fair share at its prosperity (ibid., 171ff). The issue, then, is not what size the government should be—and therefore what amount of taxes should be collected annually—but instead who the government is for, and what are its specific roles. As Reich argues, "The pertinent issue is not how much is to be taxed away from the wealthy and redistributed to those who are not; it is how to design the rules of the market so that the economy generates what most people would consider a fair distribution on its own, without necessitating large redistributions after the fact" (ibid., 219). Just like Stiglitz, Reich has faith in the rules of the game determining the results of the game; they believe in fairness as a principle by which all players abide, and with this faith they put their trust in market-capitalism. But is their trust warranted? Can the majority pressure the government to establish fair rules and enforce them? Or, as we have seen lately, will the people put their trust in the wealthy to set rules according to which they, too, can become wealthy? Are we not enamored by the lifestyle of the "rich and famous" and want to live vicariously through the pulp media's exposure of them? The idea that markets can be tamed and that by simply changing some rules or enforcing others more vigorously fairness can be guaranteed sounds naïve at this stage of market-capitalism.

The role of government is not limited to the perspective of neoliberal ideology. Not all social issues can be solved through markets, and not all policy choices should be made in financial terms. As much as the likes of Stiglitz and Reich—self-styled left-leaning critics—may seem to abhor market abuses, they refuse to abandon markets. As national security and protection of the elderly are sacrosanct with our self-image of a democratic State, we pull our resources, regardless of market efficiencies, to spend annually more than any other country on our defense forces; likewise, we have not abolished the mainstay programs of the New Deal, from Social Security and Medicare, to unemployment insurance and mandatory education for children. Whether this commitment finds its way to the rhetoric of politicians is less important than the admission that we are indeed fulfilling the principles imagined in Marx's *Communist Manifesto* (1848), especially the ten-point plan for communist policies (end of part II). The issue here is less the adherence to capitalist or Marxist principles and more the ways in which we think about our community and the responsibilities we have to all its members. Government agencies, as Rousseau already suggested, are nothing but representatives of our "general will," so we should look at them as fulfilling what we value as a community. Will the "saving" of market-capitalism bring about greater prosperity than market-socialism? This very question already commits us to reformulating market mechanisms instead of imagining different modes of human interactions. It would be more reasonable at this stage to abandon any commitment to either capitalism or socialism and adopt a post-modern posture of both/and, where we can transform both political economic models and bring about a novel formulation that draws from them without being beholden to their ideologies. Most of us would give up some freedoms for social enrichment, as is evident in social media platforms where individuals willingly share their private data to be "connected" to others. We do the same when we grant government institutions the right to surveil citizen's behavior so as to detect threats to our collective security. In the Digital Age, the balance between security and privacy is clearly leaning toward security; in the Age of Distraction, the balance between information and entertainment is clearly leaning toward entertainment; and in the Age of Complacency, the balance between the individual and the community is leaning toward the authority of community representatives, from teachers and police officers to politicians and experts.

Given the pervasive American distrust of government agencies because we have historically villainized the government as the "other" (in the Hegelian sense of the power relations between the Master and the Slave), we must find a reasonable starting point for our conversation about public policy. We should ask, would you let people die in the streets because they lack health coverage? We should likewise ask, would you agree that some people deserve more support than others regardless of their talents and potential contributions? Would you prefer to protect yourself rather than have a community-funded, dedicated, and professional security force? And with questions like these we can make explicit what we agree or disagree with; we can highlight where the community finds itself. Though criticized for being too liberal and beholden to market-capitalism, it seems that John Rawls (1971) had such concerns in mind when developing his notion of the "veil of ignorance," a means by which to demand our reflection on designing a State where our choices would be neutralized from biases because we wouldn't know how they would affect us personally. Kantian in tenor, the idea was to ensure "justice as fairness" in a system where neither justice nor fairness were framing the debates. Should we be each other's "keepers," show brotherly and sisterly love for our fellow community members? Have we lost Rousseau's sense of pity and compassion, Smith's sense of sympathy and empathy, and our own sense of humanity? The reason the Catholic Church was mentioned earlier was not for the sake of religious providence and the necessary adherence to its doctrine, but to remind us of our humanity and, as Native Americans have taught us as well, our intimate dependence on the environment of which we should be custodians and not rulers. The various roles we must ascribe to government agencies should be understood in this spirit. Our interdependence is not a result of educational training but a precondition for our species's survival. When we cooperate and share, we can thrive; when we compete ruthlessly with each other, we shall all perish.

The Preamble to the US Constitution states: "We the People of the United States, in Order to form a more perfect Union, establish Justice, insure domestic Tranquility, provide for the common defence, promote the general Welfare, and secure the Blessings of Liberty to ourselves and our Posterity, do ordain and establish this Constitution for the United States of America." This sanctified document has been argued about since its inception and was compromised to be ratified (Dahl 2002). The Preamble remains instructive, regardless of its origins among wealthy slave owners; their actions did not conform to their words, but as internal strife and conflict eventually brought to bear, we may have come closer to these ideals some two centuries later. Some critics would claim that this is not the case, that racism and sexism abound, and that these statements about our self-identification are hollow at best, and worse, a smokescreen behind which to hide our actions. If these promises inform our political economy, we can at least agree to be committed to "a more perfect Union." This goal could be contrasted with what is becoming evident in the EU where different countries, like our original colonies, feel less united and more divided. Similarly, the advocacy for justice, tranquility, and defense are mentioned alongside the need to "promote the general Welfare" and not personal riches. What would "general Welfare" mean today if not universal healthcare and minimum living wages? Would that not also mean Social Security and Medicare for the elderly as national obligations to maintain their collective "welfare"? Though we have come to think of the mandate to "secure the Blessings of Liberty to ourselves and our Posterity" at the expense of equality, all the other parts of the Preamble seem not to set liberty and equality at odds with each other. The use of terms, such as *We the people, common, general,* and *ourselves* in addition to the insistence on a more *perfect Union* clearly indicates the concern of a unified community. These terms complement the infamous statement of the Declaration of Independence: "We hold these truths to be self-evident, that all men are created equal, that they are endowed by their Creator with certain unalienable Rights, that among these are Life, Liberty, and the pursuit of Happiness." So, equality and liberty are considered parts of the same basic spectrum of moral principles on which the political economy should be established. Just as we have claimed that in order to understand Smith's *Wealth of Nations* we have to know his *Theory of Moral Sentiments*, so we have to assume that the *Declaration*'s insistence on equality was part of the *constitutional* sense of liberty, that the one was recognized as part of the other. With this, the roles of the government should not stray from promoting and protecting these ideals. The issue at hand is about the responsibility of the government to maintain not only the checks and balances among its three branches but also between the individual and the State.

More recently, behavioral economists have contributed to the discussion of the specific roles government should play in "nudging" young children to eat more healthy foods, encouraging adults to exercise regularly, and monitoring more closely the elderly to prevent disastrous outcomes. Understood as "libertarian paternalism," perhaps an oxymoron, they attempt to answer the question: How can one be left to choose freely and still have the paternal concern of a government? Richard Thaler and Cass Sunstein have made the case that "if incentives and nudges replace requirements and bans, government will be smaller and more modest" (2008, 14). Instead of limiting themselves to regulatory oversight and financial incentives—incentivizing one kind of behavior (e.g., personal deductions for mortgages and children) and discouraging another with heavy taxes (cigarettes and alcohol)—government agencies have enlarged their toolboxes to include pollution auctions and school cafeteria menu design. There are two points to appreciate in this "new

path": first, that every personal choice, however seemingly private and benign or within one's "rights," has a simultaneous social cost, one borne by
the community. You may choose to smoke and thereby contract cancer, you
may be willing to shorten your life span and suffer from debilitating lung
cancer, but in fact your choices are also inflicting certain pains on others,
from secondhand smoke to additional costs for insurance companies and
hospitals. Your costs are spread to others, and as we all subsidize your
personal choices, we are penalized unfairly without consultation or consent;
second, with this perspective, the discussion about the size of the government
is transformed into a smarter and more effective government. Perhaps a
smarter government might also be smaller, but being smaller does not guarantee being smarter.

Already in Kenneth Arrow's *Social Choice and Individual Values* (1963)
and Amartya Sen's *On Ethics and Economics* (1987), there has been a reasonable expectation that human behavior is ultimately a social matter that we
should all be concerned with because of its consequences. The ancient
Greeks acknowledged this fact just as classical economists have; and when
they examined the conditions under which self-sufficiency would obtain,
they admitted that one's virtues need to be socially contextualized. Government agencies that ignore social costs or treat them as exogenous costs (using
neoliberal terminology that justifies excluding environmental costs from economic models), do so not only at their own peril but at the expense of future
generations. Without becoming paternalistic, government representatives
have fiduciary duty to warn us of catastrophes, as the National Oceanic and
Atmospheric Administration is charged to do, to defend us from enemies,
both domestic and foreign, as the Department of Defense is supposed to do,
but also support our flourishing. This means anything from healthcare and
education to interstellar exploration and public entertainment. It's true that
some of these responsibilities have been undertaken by private enterprises,
but they, too, have been under the regulatory control (subsidies and censorship) of government agencies. Private enterprises have benefitted from the
protective net of public systems, from transportation and communication to
cyberspace and the tax code. To think that market initiatives require no
public support is a folly even neoliberals cannot claim. Instead, they just
want deregulation in the areas from which they may benefit most. While
enjoying the deregulation of the banking industry, they nevertheless accepted
government bailout; while they decry government corruption and bloat, they
reward themselves handsomely through government contracts even when
profits are elusive.

A short list of government responsibilities can be drawn from our experience in the more developed democracies around the world. Among the candidates to make it to the list—where government agencies must take the lead—
will remain public health (in the form of universal health), national security

(in the form of mandatory civil service), education (under special conditions that assist the least privileged and with benefits shared by a national Commons), finance (central bank that has the right to print money and set interest rates), infrastructure (across all regions with different priorities), transportation (highly subsidized public venues), law enforcement (with restrictive use of violence), environment (from parks to pollution controls), and food security (from production and distribution to consumption warranties). This would still leave various sectors of the economy where government agencies will be more regulatory and protective than interventionist, from manufacturing and agriculture to entertainment and exploration. Governments have the legal right to use violence in the name of the sovereign, understood as the people. But we should be critical about how far we want government agencies to curtail individual choices and to what ends they can use the threat of violence to accomplish social and even moral goals. Let's hope that Machiavelli is wrong in claiming that the price of political stability and social harmony is better accomplished by fear than love; and let's promote our innate social and cooperative tendencies (as discussed above).

V: GROWTH AND SUSTAINABILITY

Though we have critically discussed growth in part I, we should heed Pierre Proudhon's comment that "social truth cannot be found either in utopia or in routine: that political economy is not the science of society, but contains, in itself, the materials of that science, in the same way that chaos before the creation contained the elements of the universe. The fact is that, to arrive at a definite organization, which appears to be the destiny of the race on this planet, there is nothing left but to make a general equation of our contradictions" (1927, 580). As this book examines political economy and its moral features and human elements, and as we are bound to remain within a range of seemingly contradictory expectations, we need to outline these expectations. To begin with, Proudhon is correct that just as "chaos before the creation contained the elements of the universe," so the elements we enumerated in parts I and II are the basis for our concluding chapters of this book. But instead of merely reshuffling variables, we should try to find new vocabularies or at least juxtapose some concepts on established ones, and question the rhetorical and psychological damage that has been done in their name. This is especially true in the case of economic growth.

Growth has been understood in linear terms as a projectile whose trajectory toward progress and prosperity is unimpeded. But instead of thinking about it in the technoscientific terminology of being the economic engine that moves us ahead, and instead of pressing our politicians and corporate leaders to expand markets at all costs (to the environment), perhaps we ought to ask if such growth, as Marx beseeched us, would improve the potential of human emancipation (Therborn 2008, 124–25). Unless there is something positive that affects workers, why worry about growth altogether? Piketty illustrates that an average 2 percent growth has been with us for centuries, and looking far enough into the past, population and economic growth have been anemic at best, with some short periods (more recently) of bursts (2013). When contemporary debates over projected growth are presented in the media, it seems that unless it's in the 5 to 10 percent annual rate an economy is in trouble. We hear about the catastrophic slowdown in the Chinese economy, being only 6.9 percent in 2015, the "slowest in 25 years" (Magnier 2016), as if this is cause for alarm. The Chinese economy, unlike the US or EU economies, began so far behind that double-digit growth was expected; developing economies in general have greater rates of growth because of the introduction of new technologies. Should we be obsessively concerned over growth rates? What if we substituted growth with viability and sustainability? If the concern is with the effectiveness of providing for human comfort, wouldn't the psychological pressure to infinitely grow subside? Growth then becomes a by-product and not a goal.

There are those, like Tim Jackson, who distinguish between the needed growth of developing nations and the environmental requirements that should guide developed ones. According to him, at stake is the irreversible environmental damage we are causing the planet without any payoff in terms of increased satisfaction or happiness. If the planet's resources are indeed "finite," then we should strive for "prosperity without growth" (2010). Since the imaginative horizon is future generations, it stands to reason that we curtail our consumption, and protect and regenerate natural resources. It may be more reasonable to suggest that we should displace the arguments on behalf of growth with those of sustainability than simply argue that ongoing growth is unsustainable. This would mean that the infatuation with growth as the panacea with which to cure all human afflictions or the only way to fund public policies is unwarranted, even dangerous. Both Federal Reserve chiefs, Alan Greenspan after the Great Recession and Janet Yellen in more recent years, have admitted that their economic model—the dominant model of macroeconomics—is flawed. In a hearing before a House of Representatives committee, its Chair, Henry Waxman (D, CA) asked: "You had the authority to prevent irresponsible lending practices that led to the subprime mortgage crisis. You were advised to do so by many others. Do you feel that your ideology pushed you to make decisions that you wish you had not made?" And the most Greenspan (by then retired from the post) would admit is, "Yes, I've found a flaw. I don't know how significant or permanent it is. But I've been very distressed by that fact" (Andrews 2008). As the most powerful financial regulator in the world, all we could hear from Greenspan is that he "found a flaw." The promise of lower taxes that would trickle down the economy and deliver an economic boost was a sham, and the most we can learn is that perhaps there is a "flaw"; the flaw in the logic of the model is that growth is always available, that when it takes place there are no costs associated with it, and that in its name prosperity can be shared by a larger number of people. Less dogmatic but still intellectually handcuffed to this flawed model is the current chief, Yellen, who said at the Federal Reserve in Boston that "the events of the past few years have revealed limits in economists' understanding of the economy and suggest several important questions I hope the profession will try to answer" (Applebaum 2016). More circumspect, but still beholden to the limitations of economics, Yellen is still committed to adjusting interest rates to maintain growth.

Perhaps it's time to simply use a different vocabulary, one that looks fifty or one hundred years into the future of a nation rather than to what will or will not happen within the next quarter. It was Keynes who dismissed such long-term thinking because he quipped that in the long run we are all dead; but does this sentiment warrant condemning our unborn descendants as well? When we focus on the viability and stability of our economy, when we replace one technology slowly and methodically with another, we are not committing ourselves to being slow but to being responsible. In doing so, we provide optimal conditions for survival and potential success. This is true within the family structure, commercial enterprises in the economy, or democratic institutions that protect us. We admire community pillars whose longevity means loyalty, care, and pride; we deride those fly-by-night enterprises whose sole mission is to make a quick buck and disappear from one community into another (where they can exploit local hospitality and their own anonymity). Sustainability isn't the slogan of environmentalists alone, but the watchword that should guide political economists because it provides a level of psychological (if not material) comfort; it's where we can enjoy ourselves and the company of others; it's where we find a supportive environment for our ambitions and good luck. In short, to be able to sustain yourself is a feat worthy of much admiration, illustrating one's virtues. The ancient Greeks patiently extolled the virtuous life without dismissing the idea of the community. Their thinking about friendship follows a path less concerned with the increase of material comforts but with virtuous interactions with others. The socialist utopian Proudhon, though speaking more specifically about how to transform the banking industry, was right when saying, "The mutualist association is like nature, which is wealthy, beautiful and luxuriant, because she draws her wealth and her beauty from the creative force that is within her; in a word, because she produces everything from nothing. Nature in producing does not profit thereby" (1927, 88).

We should be taking Proudhon's view of nature with a grain of salt, as "Nature" contains not only the great attributes listed above but is also "ruthless" and "cruel" (in human terms, of course) insofar as it brings about its own "balance" or "equilibrium" on its own terms. This means, at times, that certain species disappear and others flourish, that preserving every element of its ongoing evolution is more of a human ideal than a natural one. Yet this great faith in natural phenomena and the lessons humans ought to learn from them can enlighten. Is there a way to produce and be creative, to innovate and prosper, without chasing growth and profits? Is there a way to harness, with great digital platforms, the best of humanity and share it generously without expecting profits from such gifts? In other words, can we sustain a stream of creative output without the "destruction" that supposedly accompanies them (as Schumpeter suggested)? Or, when we allow for some decay in a segment of the economy (because of redundancy or technological replacement), can we accommodate those who might be suffering from this decay (in the form of retraining, retooling, or simply retiring)?

VI: ON HUMAN LABOR AND THE COMMONS

We have seen in earlier parts how classical and contemporary thinkers have explained the intimate connection of the value of products and services to labor, and how this connection is related to individual freedom and property rights. This line of argument makes sense against the backdrop of slavery, either the outright ownership of humans or the indirect control of serfs by feudal lords; shouldn't it be revised to accommodate recent developments? Slavery as we have known it has been abolished, and indentured servitude is likewise illegal (even when practiced in some segments of the economy). A new vocabulary, therefore, is needed to rethink market relations and human interactions. It's true that most wage earners feel as if their lives are similar to those of indentured servants of yesteryear, and in many cases—the fast food industry comes to mind—they are indeed treated as such. Recent debates over the minimum wage and what qualifies as a "living wage" have made it into referenda across the United States, from cities to states, to increase the hourly payment to $15. The annual salary from this potential raise would be $31,200, hardly enough, after taxes, to qualify as a "living wage," especially in communities where the cost of living is high. This debate, however laudable as a first step toward improving the lives of hard-working individuals, is reformist at best and distracting at worst. What we should think about is the whole economy and the range of income disparities that are observed in all sectors. Regardless of the arguments in favor of income inequalities, and in order to reign in the excesses of the very rich, perhaps we should agree on a range of salaries that are morally defensible. What if we agreed that everyone in the country should never earn less than $50,000 and no more than $500,000 annually? The salary of the president of the United States is, after all, $400,000, and this position is admittedly the most powerful in the free world. Why should anyone earn more than that? Likewise, a guaranteed annual salary of $50,000 would allow people to follow their callings rather than submit to work conditions and careers they dislike. If about 70 percent of employees "hate" their jobs (Castillo 2015), shouldn't we be alarmed and try to change the whole matrix of jobs, careers, and work?

If we think of our work as a vocation or even a calling in the theological sense, we might avoid the kind of personal dissatisfaction and the toll it takes on our lives. If we distinguish between work and leisure and if we work to live rather than live to work, our whole outlook and morale suffer (Livingston 2016). Perhaps from the luxury of my own position as a university-tenured full professor I can imagine a world different from the one to which most people are regularly subjected. Professors, ideally, love what they do, from teaching and research to serving their own institutions and the community; and when they are asked to do more—give a public lecture in their area of expertise, participate in a forum on public policy, or serve as reviewers—they believe this is an extension of their vocation, something they are already engaged in and therefore do not expect extra compensation. Perhaps only some professions, such as mine (ideally and not under the neoliberal conditions of slave labor of part-time instructors who are exploited), can exemplify the notion that our lives can be fulfilling and community oriented. There are conditions, such as steady and well-paying-enough jobs, under which humans thrive and can devote their energies to what they love to do. Can this be expanded to public employees who love to take care of forests and parks? Can we think of engineers who are delighted to design a new bridge or rocket? These examples may sound too privileged to be scalable to the entire economy. Can we find those among us who will enjoy cleaning streets and grocery stores? Can we find enough people to take care of basic tasks and commit to lifelong menial labor? Perhaps here the answer is that as the Digital Age advances, robots will do more manual-labor jobs. This is already true in assembly lines and toll booths where robots and sensors are dominant and where Artificial Intelligence is being developed. So, what would people do?

Under ideal conditions, and indeed this last part is about a *practopia* that serves our moral and political principles, the issue will not be how to reach full employment, how to "create new jobs"; instead, we should be concerned with how those people who want to work can find fulfilling jobs, and how to work as little as possible in order to earn as little as $50,000 or as much as $500,000 annually. Our concern with optimal employment will be related to education and training, to lifelong learning and changing careers and vocations. What we wanted to do in our youth may not be what we want to do as we grow old. If minimal income is guaranteed, we can ask ourselves how we can help others and improve the state of the union. What if you could do anything you want and still get paid to do so? What if you could accomplish your weekly or monthly tasks, as contract software engineers do, in relatively short order and then have plenty of time to think, enjoy the outdoors, or just invent something playful? As we saw earlier, the Sharing Economy when coupled with the Gig Economy has some features that come close to this imagined economic reality. When possession isn't the ultimate measure of one's contentment and when private property is not perceived as a goal but a burden, we can transform it into the Caring Economy where sharing is a form of gifting and where altruism is common. Right now, only the rich can afford this luxury, perhaps some professionals; why not turn this into the norm rather than the exception? What if this became the duty of political leaders to organize? Science fiction authors have been the vanguard of utopian visions that explore the conditions under which abundance is the platform for social choices and where Marx's imaginative society is in fact fleshed out in detail. Whether they do so under the rubric of "work/play" as a category (Le Guin 1974, 92, 269) or by expecting some level of cultural awareness, what they point to is a different language with which to approach human labor, one that presupposes safety nets and flourishing rather that setting them as goals.

Money and markets may have a place in the current proposal, but they will be means rather than ends; they will help grease the wheels of commerce and human interactions as convenient tools and not as repositories of power and wealth. Since wealth will be unnecessary for accomplishing personal goals, and since no great wealth would ever be in the hands of the few (given rigorous and enforceable progressive tax policies), annual income would suffice for all needs and some wants. Doctors and nurses will want to treat patients rather than view their dedicated calling in monetary terms; bankers will become civil servants (all banks will be formally nationalized, as in fact they are already informally protected, insured, and bailed out by central banks) who care to safeguard sufficient liquidity in the market and that exchanges can be completed. To be sure, wealth will be progressively taxed to secure disincentives to accumulation, more aggressively than the flat global tax proposed by Piketty (2014). Instead of market-capitalism there will be a partial market-socialism where the community owns natural resources and where other crucial segments of the market, like finance and banking, are run by professionals who are public servants. The idea that government regulation impedes progress is false, as its main role is to protect people with policies reached by democratic processes. Likewise, the idea that public institutions are inherently inefficient is a myth perpetuated by neoliberal think tanks that advocate risk taking by the public (in the form of infrastructure and research and development programs) and profit taking by private corporations. This language and its conceptual framing must change. This change, to be sure, is not because a new ideology is proposed in its stead, but because the empirical evidence supports such change of mind. Just imagine what it would be like to live in a community where everyone is respected, everyone contributes to the well-being of the community, and everyone is supported by everyone else. This, as we saw above, is what soldiers feel like when they are in the military. Expertise will be needed, and compensation will not be monetary but one of extra responsibility and leadership. In positions of power (merit based and temporary), extra work and additional responsibility will be expected from those volunteering for them. Power relations will be governed by good practices—transparency and accountability— and their imperfections can be corrected. Leadership positions will be in the hands of those who reluctantly volunteer to fill them temporarily rather than those vying for them for personal gains.

The revival of the Commons in its new digital guises would enhance a sense of shared responsibility by the community. Educational institutions will accommodate new ways of thinking about one's worth, contribution, and personal well-being different from the grades they hand out or the money their graduates expect to earn. This isn't as difficult as it sounds, as one can observe around the globe numerous instances where communal living and working is a response to how life can be arranged differently. No one will be forced into this communal-like living, nor will anyone be indoctrinated. Try to have a discussion with young people about the possibilities that might obtain with a different framing of our collective potential, and you'll be surprised. My university students were eager to think of alternatives different from those available in the neoliberal toolbox; they have never been exposed to what can be the case, only to what is currently the case. And with current disregard to "facts" as bothersome inconveniences, neoliberal interpretation of economic conditions is fraught with misinformation about the evils of government practices and the ingenuity and innocence of private enterprises. This cycle of miscommunication must be broken and reframed, but, unfortunately, not necessarily under the "democratic" practices of the Internet. The Internet alone, just as markets alone, cannot bring about an Age of Integrity and good will; some basic rules of conduct are required, some level of objective critical examination, and a thorough protection of the public from powerful predators. Those in power are the political and economic elites that influence each other and that benefit from each other's support. As we said earlier, as long as the economy is at the service of democracy and as long as politicians follow the moral principles that undergird democracy we have some hope for optimism.

VII: CRITIQUES, REJOINDERS, AND DISCLAIMERS

In a recent piece in the neoliberal media outlet *The Wall Street Journal*, the state of the EU was critically examined in comparison and in relation to the

election of Donald Trump to the American presidency. The fascinating conclusion was that the populist movements around the world are responding
more to complaints about justice and not about economics. Arguments about
the expediency of globalization are set in moral terms, where questions of
government bailouts and unfair immigration policies overshadow the potential prosperity of free trade (Stephens 2016). The liberal cause, if one can
generalize without losing all intellectual respect, must be explained in moral
terms, not economic ones. People care about their pocketbooks, we were
always told, but this does not mean that they don't care about morality. The
rhetoric of populist right-wing extremists like Trump is based on complaints
and misgivings, on how individuals and groups have been hurt and treated
unfairly. This kind of rhetoric when accompanied by a few concrete examples of reasonable grievances are politically powerful. Instead of dismissing
them, we should listen to them and veer the conversation in the direction of
moral principles, the ones worthy of fighting for. This level of discourse was
attempted in this book, where basic assumptions and frames of references
were critically examined. If we all agree, liberals and conservatives, that the
neoliberal system of the last few decades doesn't work, what are the alternatives? What solutions do we propose? In this last chapter, several ideas and
policies were proposed, from mandatory national service to the ownership of
the Commons by the people, all the way to minimal and maximal annual
wages, endorsing universal healthcare and educational guarantees. These are
not radical proposals, perhaps not radical enough. But they should bring
about a radical transformation of the mindset with which we encounter each
other as community members and not as isolated nomads in space. We are
social human beings, and our species has thrived because of cooperation and
the ways we have incorporated new technologies. There is room for improvement, and greater leadership should be coming forth to instill and reward
social values. One doubts the rhetoric of some neoliberals that believe in
unfettered markets and the complete autonomy of individuals; what world do
they live in? How would they excel without the rule of law? Will they live
off the grid and cease all communication with others? The ideal of enjoying
the fruits and rights of the community without having to pay any price is
untenable and parasitic; it bespeaks of the worst in us. On the other hand,
thinking about our advantages and rights in terms of the fulfillment of our
obligations sounds much more reasonable, even practically necessary.

One way of reconceptualizing *the quest for prosperity*, as the title of this
book suggests, is by answering guiding questions that could transform our
understanding of "prosperity." Perhaps informed by the spiritual dimension
of humanity, perhaps influenced by the potential of human life, these questions might be useful to keep in mind. These questions can be answered even
when one remains agnostic about human nature and the human condition:

1. Do I have respect for myself? If yes, why?
2. Do I have respect for other members of society? And when I don't, on what ground is my judgment based?
3. How can I make sure that in this brief time on earth I can make a contribution beyond my own needs and wants?
4. Can I begin all interaction with other people by assuming that they mean well even when they fail?
5. How can I best share my ideas and concerns with others?
6. In which forum do I wish to participate? What best practices can guide this forum?
7. How can I minimize my carbon footprint while still enjoy what my community has to offer?
8. Who do I feel accountable to in my studies and in my work?
9. What is my calling or vocation? Am I pursuing it with all my heart?
10. Am I fulfilling my duties and obligations while enjoying my privileges and rights?
11. Do I keep my integrity, honesty, and goodwill in the forefront of my deliberation about my work, my relations, and my environment?

This is not an exhaustive list of questions. These are the kind of questions that follow Socrates' expectation that we should live an "examined life," critically evaluating what we are about to say or do. Some may argue that this luxury of critical contemplation is reserved for the few, not the many, because the many are frantically attempting to make a living, scrape by and survive under economic conditions that are daunting. But if we change these conditions—coupling abundance with technoscientific efficiency and guaranteeing living wages to all—then we are likely to have a few minutes here and there to reflect, to stop and think, to put a mirror to ourselves before we act.

Conceptually and methodologically what is recommended here and what should be made more explicit is the postmodern approach to solving practical problems. This approach insists on a plurality of options and models and on the ceaseless process of adjustment and reconfiguration. More specifically, this approach expects to account for whatever useful data and methods are available along the spectrum of ideas and frames of reference, one that transcends the binary of capitalism and communism or that sets in opposition the ownership of natural resources and the means of production in private or public hands. If conditions are favorable to carve out segments of the economy where private ownership is more efficient, so be it; if there are other segments where it's crucial to maintain public control of public lands, then any private intrusion in the form of leases can be monitored, regulated, and if needed, stopped. Barriers to private ownership should guarantee a fair and transparent process, the consequences of which enrich the community beyond what it could do on its own. Privatization should be argued for and proven on its resulting merits instead of presupposing that an ideological framework alone suffices as an argument (as neoliberals are fond of doing). This is not to say that ideology should not be discussed at all, but when we discuss its moral foundation and the merits of its proposals we should account for all the relevant variables (social and environmental costs and benefits) as opposed to ignoring them. The current approach to economic intervention that promotes public risks and costs and private profits and benefits has not served us well; it has been detrimental and in some cases, like the last financial crisis, disastrous.

Perhaps the way to bring this chapter to a close is to remind the reader that whatever is proposed here is provisional, based on reasonable arguments and empirical evidence of the past century. As we live through another Gilded Age where income and wealth inequalities have skewed the ideals of capitalism, we must take stock and critically engage economic proposals. Whether we come from the so-called left or right, we should keep in mind the moral commitments we have already endorsed two hundred years ago: freedom, equality, fraternity, solidarity, the perfectibility of humanity, and the democratic improvement of the human condition. These principles are philosophical and therefore incorporate political, social, and economic ones as well, and their entanglement may prove difficult to separate. Perhaps they should not be separated at all. These principles must be contextualized in terms of the others. Therefore, any ideological claim for unfettered liberty is nonsensical, and any claim for absolute equality is likewise misleading if guarantees for diversity are ignored. Since the individual never stands alone but is always already a community member, this membership should be understood and taught, explained and practiced. Great leaders have recognized their indebtedness to their teams and supporters. Similarly, scholars and critics recognize their contributions in terms of the work of others, and thereby remain humble participants in a long conversation that started before they were born.

Epilogue

The end of this book may be less satisfactory to those who want definitive answers, the kind offered so passionately by dogmatists, orthodox thinkers, and petrified ideologues on the political spectrum. But it will remind us of human kindness and the collaborative efforts we have made in the past to survive as a species and as a community. Crowd-funding is just one of many examples of how the digital revolution brought with it virtual connections, altruism, and goodwill. Since the context for this book has been the devastating effects of the Great Recession, infusing the conversation with existentialist morality is to be expected; it's a reasonable prerequisite to ward off claims for the "natural course" of the economy or for lack of human agency. How, then, should we rethink human interactions in the *digital age*? Here are some final suggestions.

First, the quest for prosperity should apply to everyone, and it shouldn't be exclusively analyzed in monetary terms, as we saw in the last chapter, where the contours of a model were delineated. My critical examination has been historically informed, philosophically inspired, and focused on political economy; it also resists the temptation to limit critical assessment to the linguistic, rhetorical, and visual tropes and memes that define our view of the economy and what ideological worldview we internalize. This approach is concerned with the material conditions of humanity as *Marx* already exposed them; it also recognizes the *Popperian* insistence that there is a reality out there with which we interact and that defines our responses. As we look at future interactions within and outside markets, the *postmodern* trepidation with any totalizing perceptions as well as with strictly binary views of our situation remains intact. Approaching the spectrum of options available to us is more informative than having to choose between only two options.

There has been little intellectual agreement among the three strands identified above—Marxist, Popperian, and postmodern. The guardians of these philosophical approaches have routinely criticized each other, discarded and dismissed anything outside their domains. In the name of reason, they behaved unreasonably; in the name of freedom, they confined their supporters to their own viewpoints. My own approach is more collaborative: any element that can be useful should be used, and any insight should be shared as widely as possible. This means that the Marxist critique of idealism is worthy of maintaining, that the dialectical method reminds us of the thesis and antithesis as we work toward a synthesis, and that the material conditions even of our cultural and virtual consumption are paramount in deliberations about potential transformations. The Marxist fight for the emancipation of the working class should not be erased because the Soviets or the Chinese erected a State apparatus that is personally oppressive and collectively totalitarian, or because class identity has turned out to be elusive and fluid.

As for the Popperian contribution, conjectures and refutations, falsification, and the refusal to expect *Truth* even in scientific matters is enlightening and liberating. Similarly, the insistence on incremental changes of social piecemeal engineering is crucial when the lives of so many are at stake and when revolutionary fervor may bring about uncontrollable violence. The notion of the logic of the situation can similarly help us in contextualizing more rigorously what sometimes appears as a broad generalization about economic circumstances. In short, it is not the case (as neoliberals and communists are fond of claiming) that one size fits all in Critical Rationalism.

And finally, postmodern critics who wanted to overcome the modernist strictures of Marx and Popper promote a pluralistic worldview where the old and the new, the familiar and the foreign, can comingle into a tapestry of options for any situation. Contextualization is a starting point coupled with the putative credibility of other opinions. Specific policy proposals should remain tentative and provisional. This is because any ideology that in the name of consistency becomes fanatic is of no use here, as circumstances are fast moving. Ideological convictions, such as freedom and equality, human dignity and communal cooperation, are useful starting points but not closing statements in deliberations about policy recommendations. It's lamentable that for some the very notion of an ongoing debate over the morality of policies seems frivolous. We must somehow convince them that civic engagement is a moral duty and not the luxury of academics, especially in an age where "tweets" represent more than just venting.

What Marxism, Popperianism, and postmodernism share is their critical concerns, their insistence on the fallibility of human inquiry, and on the need to acknowledge the (material and cultural) contexts within which models and theories come into existence. Following their common heritage, we might be able to avoid the strictures of their orthodox adherents, the guardians of their eternal flames. Perhaps we can cajole their disciples to let down the draw-bridge and allow the richness of their texts to be used more freely and without preconditions. It is an outright folly to believe that any one thinker, however great, could have anticipated the historical contingencies with which we operate in the present day. And as influential as these three schools of thought have been over the decades, they, too, have seen internal fractures and the fragmentation of their own theories; they have seen how novel ideas come forth as critiques or reconstructions. In short, they can appreciate an ongoing dialectical process of thinking.

Second, the present study suggests that the ongoing displacement we are experiencing in the *age of robotics* is about labor, scarcity, and our social contract with the State and therefore should be understood in terms of *power relations*. Behind every proposal or debate over the loss of jobs lurks a set of relations that will empower some and disempower others, that will liberate or enrich some while exploiting or discarding others (Livingston 2016). On some level, every critical analysis must account for the increase or decrease in the power of people to respond to their predicament. The consequences of robots replacing labor in certain sectors of the economy may not result in reverting back to some historical feudal epoch but may question the need for labor altogether. If certain tasks make some people "superfluous" rather than an exploited reserve army of the unemployed, then other human relations will be affected as well (Kolbert 2016). Endemic poverty and lack of educa-tion contribute to the imbalance between nation-states in regard to their workforce and the employment aspirations of young people.

This new reality raises the question: What should we do with all the unskilled or underskilled or differently skilled people for whom no work is to be found? Should we create work when none is needed? Or, should we give up on full employment as an outdated bourgeois (and Protestant) value and let people receive guaranteed monthly wages? Will this send us down a moral rabbit hole where mindless consumption reigns supreme? And who are the "we" who determine the answers to these questions? We could push this thought experiment a bit further and envision a day when resource allocation and manufacturing will be fully controlled by artificial intelligence cyborgs, and because of their lack of human fallibilities their conduct will be "per-fect." Would this, then, alleviate our concerns about human greed and immo-rality? Would such conditions establish the *ideal village*—now scalable globally—envisioned by Smith? The immense feedback-looped artificial in-telligence would guarantee efficiency without exploitation, and surpluses would pay for exogenous costs and be redistributed to pay for guaranteed wages. Has morality been extricated (by design) from the cyborgs that con-trol, run, and support markets? If so, human traits, such as curiosity and empathy, sociality and cooperation, will have to be enhanced to deal with nonmarket human interactions.

Third, thinking of exchange relations or what some have called the *Relational Economy* (Bathelt and Glücker 2011), we should not follow Dale Carnegie's (1936) best-selling manual that became a standard for salesmanship; instead, we should be concerned with moral relations and obligations we feel toward each other as members of the same species and as members of the same local community. Rather than concern ourselves with prosperity in terms of sales and profits (in the American model), we should focus on the criteria by which we condone or condemn our exchanges (no longer measuring financial success but moral fortitude). This outlook traverses the theoretical and practical terrain with a philosophical conceit that gaps can be bridged and that with a plurality of options an optimal one can be identified. Is this too much to ask for in the *age of distraction* when our information bandwidth is rapidly expanding? Is this too much to expect in our *digital* and *virtual* world? Is the promise of increased equality under these terms outdated, itself a distraction (from the realignment of new power relations)?

The inextricable features of the political and economic spheres as they work their way through our social and cultural spheres must always be related back to morality. Divorcing morality from political economy may suffer the sad result of leaving it up to (powerless) professional ethicists to philosophize about such matters in the sterility of academic institutions, and leaving (powerful) participants in market exchanges to completely ignore moral issues. Such a situation is dangerous. As educators and responsible citizens, we must accompany personal choices as well as public policies with an explicit assessment about their morality. Practically, we may find ourselves paying the price of inefficiency for the sake of protecting human or tribal rights and traditions (diverting an oil pipeline from Canada to the southern shores of the United States to respect Native American's sacred lands). The issue here is not just showing respect for native traditions, but a reasonable recognition of our role as custodians of the planet (regardless of who reminds us of this moral principle).

Similarly, we may find ourselves collecting more data than we thought was necessary, taking longer to examine these data, and then making a choice with the widest possible moral consensus: Is it fair to everyone? Are the benefits equitably shared? Can we defend this policy with respect to future generations? In subsuming expediency under the democratic principles of inclusion and participation, we may encourage the public to be more engaged in the affairs of the State. Moreover, as we move toward consensus we will be aware of the compromises we may have to make, the kind that are the cornerstone of any democratic governance that guards against the concentration of power in the hands of the few.

Fourth, the neoliberal pretense that money alone reflects public opinion and that people vote with their wallets misses the point of public engagement and empowerment. Likewise, neoliberal and communist reductionism subverts the notion of prosperity and presents it as if the overall economic benefits of a community are equally shared by its members. The moral price market neoliberalism and state communism exact from us is too high. Just think of the example of lead poisoning in the water system of Flint, Michigan, and you get the picture: in the name of cost-cutting (tax revenue has been minimized in the state), an emergency manager decided to switch the water source to one that was cheaper but hazardous. Cost cutting and efficiency are one thing; endangering the lives of residents is another. Was the danger unknown? Were its effects unforeseeable? Or was it simply a less affluent and predominantly black community whose political power was already diminished and therefore could be ignored?

Economic variables remain central in any critical discussion of *practopia*, but their privileged position should be restricted to the starting points for a democratic dialogue and not the final arbiters of what direction should be pursued. The residents of Flint, in the example above, should have been consulted from the start about changes in water sourcing. If there are sufficient data to give pause, if there is resistance from a community that knows the history of the rivers nearby (because they have fished there for decades), then the fateful decision should have been stalled. The consequences, as this outrageous case illustrates, are too much for any community to bear.

Fifth, perhaps we should worry less about labels and names, such as the Sharing Economy, Peer-to-Peer Economy, Crowd-Based Economy, Collaborative Economy, Gig Economy, Relational Economy, or Platform-Driven Economy, and worry more about what moral practices they embody. This reminds me of my colleague, Glenn Morris, who came to give a talk about Native Americans decades ago. I asked him how he should be introduced (being at the height of political correctness): Native American, Indigenous People, American Indians, or First People? Oh, he responded, don't you worry about it, I will introduce myself. With this quip, he licensed himself to start the lecture by telling the class that he was asked by me how to introduce him, and that he, too, was pondering this same question not long before. So, he continued, I asked my elders this question at the last sweat lodge meeting we had up north. And after three days of prayers and conversations, the eldest of them finally answered me: I don't care what they call us as long as they stop stealing our land! I tell this story every semester in my first day of class, reminding my students that how they address me is less important than how they treat or respect me.

The same goes for the infatuation with the Sharing Economy. If the only way "sharing" comes about is when you pay for it, then it might be technically sharing, but it's a far cry from sharing as a gift relationship, expecting nothing in return except some goodwill and fine memories. Similarly, the technoscientific emergence of platforms on which remote exchanges can be managed and rerouted (from virtual shopping malls to online legal services) doesn't change the fact that someone somewhere has control over these platforms and is charging a fee. Even if our services are "on demand" and therefore look like a musician's "gig," this alone isn't a sufficient condition to think that one isn't exploited or that market-like behavior has changed. Perhaps all that has changed is a mode of extracting more efficiently out of someone's expertise or presence (babysitting, housesitting, or tending to one's pets or farm animals) rather than radically changing the terms of the game. When we claim that a new mode of economic exchange is a "game-changer," we anticipate that a whole set of underlying conditions change as well, that maybe we are looking at each other as ends and not as means, as moral beings who deserve empathy and not charity. Let me be clear: if charity is genuinely given and received, it is indeed a blessing; but when it is a cover-up operation that overlooks or sugarcoats basic inequities in human relations and the institutions that preserve them, then it's a farce; it's a morally scandalous cover-up operation that hides predatory practices and institutionalized theft. Once we shed the essentialist claim about the inevitability of competition, we can more sensibly encourage cooperation among people, locally and virtually, because this is who we are as people and this is how we'd like to interact with each other.

Sixth, while it is correctly believed that some changes require a revolutionary or a "start-from-scratch" approach to wipe out detrimental habits and entrenched policies of social institutions, the inevitable price of violence and the consolidation of power should dissuade us from this approach. Would it not be more reasonable to have an *intellectual revolution* or a *radical change of heart* that could accomplish the same goal? Logically, we have four options: revolutionary thought and action, incremental thought and action, revolutionary thought and incremental action, or incremental thought and revolutionary action (the least likely combination). My own preference is revolutionary thought and incremental implementation. For this process to succeed, we should provisionally trust State institutions that can hold their ground and provide services under moral principles regardless of changes in leadership. Courts of law should remain powerful institutions that offer checks on the powers of new administrations, as is routinely the case with the US Supreme Court. As populist movements overtake party politics, the courts will be tested as the guardians of reason and the rule of law. Putting our faith in such institutions may seem unjustified, but the alternatives are even less promising (believing the benevolence of revolutionary leaders or the power of the people themselves to dictate the terms of their social contract). Admittedly, judges can be bribed and other officials may have ongoing conflicts of interest when fulfilling their duties, but journalistic institutions that are independent and offer public service (rather than profits alone) can expose such abuses.

Seventh, the present contribution is meant as a footnote (admittedly a long one) to what has already been written about the philosophical assumptions that frame political economy theories, trying to bring together strands that have stood apart in our great libraries. But if I had to commit to a way of thinking about political economy, I would find myself on the moral spectrum leaning toward the deontological end. The deontological approach (associated with Kant) claims that a principled procedure should be followed (without knowing its effects), while the consequentialist concedes to potentially immoral means to accomplish a moral result (the ends justify the means). What if the desired "end" is never accomplished? What if the promise for communal prosperity remains an unachievable ideal in the name of which we justify the accumulation of wealth in the hands of the very few? What if the promises of indefinite growth never materialize? A principled commitment to equality, for example, prior to the implementation of any policy, has a better chance of success (measured in moral terms) than if one always remains waiting in vain for the eventual "trickle down" of prosperity.

Leaning toward the Kantian extreme does not invalidate completely the consequentialist quest for justice; there are times and places where a principled choice is unclear and when human suffering outweighs the benefits that the few enjoy domestically (since we measure GDP averages, Gordon 2016, chapter 1) or internationally (when imperialistic propensities are still evident). In the case of the Great Recession, the deregulation of the banking industry (in the name of freedom) and the promotion of home ownership (in the name of responsibility as embodied in private property ownership) were State licenses for private investment banks to underwrite one of the worst financial debacles in years. The consequences are apparent as millions lost their homes (and jobs and marriages) and as private investment banks have been fined billions of dollars in the aftermath (for deliberately misleading clients, fraudulently reselling mortgages that were worthless, and inventing financial instruments whose sole purpose was to hide valueless mortgages from investors, homebuyers, and legislators). About four million homes were foreclosed on and about two and one half million businesses were bankrupted; depending on how one counts, about $260 billion in fines were paid in the past few years by banks and other financial institutions. And in case anyone has forgotten, the neoliberal (entrepreneurial) risks undertaken by private corporations were paid for by the tax-paying public (the bailout). Any clever economic argument that justifies this calamity must be drowned out by a simple (deontological) moral claim that corporate greed never justifies human suffering: one's gain should never be at the expense of someone else's pain.

Eighth, my proposals may seem not sufficiently radical or the outline of a model for political economy (and indirectly of all human relations) may seem not specific enough, so a postmodern note might be useful. When we speak of *postcapitalism* or of *postsecularism* we concede two intellectual moves at once: binaries are starting points that cannot be ignored even when we try to overcome them *and* despite their difference they remain bound with each other and lift our conversation to a new level of discursive insights. Different modes of thinking remain intertwined, inform each other, and maintain a dialectical conversation whose history they share. Some residues of market-capitalism will be evident in the Sharing or Caring Economy, even in my preferred *practopia*. This may be because of convenience or habit, because of certain efficiencies that are worthwhile to retain, or simply because people need multiple methods of evaluating their accomplishments. Just because we keep money and churches around does not mean that either money or churches control every facet of our lives. As was proposed in the last chapter, if everyone's annual compensation is within a reasonable range and everyone's accumulation of wealth is limited, then money will not have the same symbolic hold it has today. If we focus on human vulnerabilities and the ways in which we can have compassion and empathy toward others, we are bound to transcend unfettered neoliberal capitalism, the kind that leaves the human face behind a veil of rational choice and autonomy; the kind that classifies all human interactions in uniform, universal, and absolute monetary terms; or perniciously, the kind that measures human well-being in average per capita GDP terms. When we look around, we must admit that "there are fundamental moral issues at stake" (Stiglitz 2016, 324).

Ninth, the postmodern posture advocated here is also informed by the work of French *existentialists* of the post–world wars years. Having experienced the war years as refugees, resistance fighters, or witnesses, they dealt with moral questions on a personal level: How should I behave? What will posterity say about my stance to actively or passively resist the occupation and fascism? One of the concepts that permeated their discussion of personal culpability was *dirty hands* (later to be reintroduced in the ethics literature as the "trolley dilemma"), a way of thinking about the potential compromises when making moral choices (Bakewell 2016). They accepted the fact that there were no easy choices or clear-cut paths they could follow, that they had to choose under unbearable conditions the best they could, admitting that their moral calculus might be challenged in retrospect. Perhaps in the twenty-first century the moral calculus is made in financial terms rather than under military occupation terms (though still true in war-ravaged Syria, for example); perhaps it's easier to think of the suffering of those whose homes have been foreclosed than about atomic bomb victims. But as was noted above, isn't a thoroughly moral deliberation upfront preferable to a post hoc rationalization? Given our logical acuity, we can justify almost anything while "calculating" moral equivalences. If we think exclusively in *market* terms, are we willing to revert to the machination of slave holders in the Americas who somehow justified the buying and selling of human beings? Are we still beholden to a State apparatus that has denied basic human rights to one segment of the population?

A reminder of slave markets is not a thought experiment, but a reality whose socioeconomic and legal effects are still felt around us (when white police officers shoot unarmed black youths, when black citizens are disproportionately represented in the prison population, and when poverty itself is criminalized). Similarly, our founding fathers' hypocrisy (when it came to equality and freedom) should not be swept under a constitutional rug. Only under the moral weight of philosophical debates can we hope to appeal to a prosperity for which we must keep fighting as an ongoing revolutionary act. What is this revolutionary thought? It should begin with Rousseau-like compassion and Smith-like empathy, the emotions that bring about cultural expressions of unconditional love, a life of tranquility and health, a life not defined and limited by the acquisition of wealth. Perhaps in the *age of distraction* we have lost our way and have marginalized the issues that should concern us most. Perhaps we are duped into Zen-like postures (think of the prominence of yoga) so as to forget the *age of anxiety* that lurks around us and literally drives us crazy (think of the prominence of Valium, Librium, and Xanax as pharmaceutical coping mechanisms).

Finally, as the title of this book promised to speak of the "quest for prosperity" and as the major historical presuppositions we have examined have shown, we should conclude with two further points. The first is about wealth itself. Aristotle worried that wealth would produce the character of "a prosperous fool," because "wealthy men are insolent and arrogant; their possession of wealth affects their understanding." And he continued to explain that when "wealth becomes a sort of standard of value for everything else," and as this outlook colors their thinking, people start to believe that "there is nothing they cannot buy" (*Rhetoric*, Book II, chapter 16). There should not be a market for values we can buy and sell as there should not be a slave market. Whenever prosperity is equated with wealth and wealth becomes a means by which we cast moral principles aside, we are in trouble. Our understanding should not be affected by wealth, as Aristotle noted, but by the plight of those among us who suffer and whose voices are not heard in a democracy run by lobbyists. Our *collective wealth* should be used to forge a future where we improve the human condition and set in place a *social contract* based on *solidarity and empathy*. The neoliberal refrain about charity and philanthropy of the wealthy whose generosity we should admire misses the point that we would not need charity at all if everyone has enough, if the natural and human-made resources we collectively own are fairly shared to begin with. If we wish to be wise rather than fools, let us rethink the quest for prosperity in moral terms.

The second point relates to the neoliberal refrain that with hard work and some education anyone can succeed. This refrain, unfortunately, is made in bad faith. Education and hard work are both *necessary* ingredients in one's sense of nourishment and flourishing—that is, psychosocial prosperity. Only with a commitment to collaboration and cooperation and a transformation of notions of scarcity to those of abundance may the *sufficient* conditions for personal and communal prosperity be sensibly fulfilled. Let us aspire to be wise and virtuous rather than prosperous fools.

Bibliography

Abdelal, Rawi, and Adam Segal. 2007. "Has Globalization Reached Its Peak?" *Foreign Affairs*, January/February 2007: 1–7. Available at: http://www.wright.edu/~tdung/Globalization_peaked_ForeignAffairs.pdf. Accessed September 24, 2016.

Ahmed, Nafeez. 2014. "Inclusive Capitalism Initiative Is Trojan Horse to Quell Coming Global Revolt." *The Guardian*, May 28, 2014. Available at: https://www.theguardian.com/environment/earth-insight/2014/may/28/inclusive-capitalism-trojan-horse-global-revolt-henry-jackson-society-pr-growth. Accessed September 17, 2016.

Akerlof, George A. and Robert J. Shiller. 2015. *Phishing for Phools: The Economics of Manipulation and Deception*. Princeton and Oxford: Princeton University Press.

Althusser, Louis. 2014. "On Ideology" and "Ideology and Ideological State Apparatuses." In *On the Reproduction of Capitalism: Ideology and Ideological State Apparatus*. Translated by G. M. Goshgarian. London and New York: Verso.

Anderson, Richard G., and Charles S. Gascon. 2007. "The Perils of Globalization: Offshoring and Economic Insecurity of the American Worker." *Federal Reserve Bank of St. Louis*, Working Paper 2007-004A.

Anderson, Terry L. 1997. "Property Rights Among Native Americans." *Foundation for Economic Education*. Available at: https://fee.org/articles/property-rights-among-native-americans/. Accessed June 26, 2016.

Andrews, Edmund L. 2008. "Greenspan Concedes Error on Regulation." *The New York Times*, October 23, 2008. Available at: http://www.nytimes.com/2008/10/24/business/economy/24panel.html?_. Accessed October 15, 2016.

Ante, Spencer. 2008. *Creative Capital: Georges Doriot and the Birth of Venture Capital*. Boston: Harvard Business Press.

Applebaum, Binyamin. 2015. "Perils of Globalization When Factories Close and Towns Struggle." *The New York Times*, May 17, 2015. Available at: http://www.nytimes.com/2015/05/18/business/a-decade-later-loss-of-maytag-factory-still-resonates.html?_r=0. Accessed September 21, 2016.

———. 2016. "Why Isn't the Fed Raising Rates? It's Complicated, Chief Says." *The New York Times*, October 14, 2016. Available at: http://www.nytimes.com/2016/10/15/business/economy/federal-reserve-janet-yellen.html?. Accessed October 15, 2016.

Ariely, Dan. 2008. *Predictably Irrational: The Hidden Forces That Shape our Decisions*. New York: HarperCollins.

Aristotle. 1958/1946. *The Politics*. Translated by Ernest Barker. London, Oxford, and New York: Oxford University Press.

Armeni, Damon T. 2013. "Moral Principles for Taking a Volunteer Force to War." *Armed Forces Journal*, December 19, 2013. Available at: http://armedforcesjournal.com/moral-principles-taking-a-volunteer-force-to-war/. Accessed October 29, 2016.

Arnuk, Sal, and Joseph Saluzzi. 2012. *Broken Markets: How High Frequency Trading and Predatory Practices on Wall Street Are Destroying Investor Confidence and Your Portfolio.* New Jersey: FT Press.

Aronowitz, Stanley. 2014. *The Death and Life of American Labor.* London and New York: Verso.

————. and William DiFazio. 2010. *The Jobless Future* [1994]. Minneapolis and London: University of Minnesota Press.

————. and Fredric Jameson. 2014. "An American Utopia: Fredric Jameson in Conversation with Stanley Aronowitz." *YouTube*, March 20, 2014. Available at: https://www.youtube.com/watch?v=MNVKoX40ZAo. Accessed October 29, 2016.

Arrow, Kenneth J. 1963. *Social Choice and Individual Values* [1951]. New Haven and London: Yale University Press.

Association of Research Libraries. 2016. "Copyright Timeline: A History of Copyright in the United States." Available at: http://www.arl.org/focus-areas/copyright-ip/2486-copyright-timeline -.WOaWURLyujg. Accessed September 26, 2016.

Axelrod, Robert. 2006. *The Evolution of Cooperation* [1984]. New York: Basic Books.

Ayres, Clarence E. 1973. *Science: The False Messiah* [1927]. Clifton: Augustus M. Kelley, Publishers.

————. 1978. *The Theory of Economic Progress: A Study of the Fundamentals of Economic Development and Cultural Change* [1944]. Kalamazoo, MI: New Issues Press, Western Michigan University.

Bair, Jennifer. 2011. "Constructing Scarcity, Creating Value." In *The Cultural Wealth of Nations*, edited by Nina Bendelj and Frederick Wherry. Stanford, CA: Stanford University Press.

Bakewell, Sarah. 2016. *At the Existentialist Café: Freedom, Being, and Apricot Cocktails.* New York: Other Press.

Baptist, Edward E. 2014. *The Half Has Never Been Told: Slavery and the Making of American Capitalism.* New York: Basic Books.

Baran, Paul A., and Paul M. Sweezy. 1966. *Monopoly Capital: An Essay on the American Economic and Social Order.* New York and London: Modern Reader Paperbacks.

Barker, Ernest (Editor). 1960. *Social Contract: Essays by Locke, Hume, and Rousseau* [1947]. London, Oxford, and New York: Oxford University Press.

Bathelt, Harald, and Johannes Glücker. 2011. *The Relational Economy: Geographies of Knowing and Learning.* Oxford: Oxford University Press.

Batson, Daniel. 2015. "The Egoism-Altruism Debate: A Psychological Perspective." In *Caring Economics: Conversations on Altruism and Compassion, Between Scientists, Economists, and the Dalai Lama*, edited by Tania Singer and Ricard Matthieu. New York: Picador.

Baudrillard, Jean. 1998. *The Consumer Society: Myths and Structures* [1970]. London: Sage Publications.

Bender, Frederic L. 2003. *The Culture of Extinction: Toward a Philosophy of Deep Ecology.* New York: Humanity Books.

Benkler, Yochai. 2006. *The Wealth of Networks: How Social Production Transforms Markets and Freedom.* New Haven and London: Yale University Press.

Bergeron, Suzanne. 2001. "Political Economy Discourses of Globalization and Feminist Politics." *Signs* 26, no. 4, Globalization and Gender: 983–1006.

Berman, Elizabeth Popp. 2014. "Not Just Neoliberalism: Economization in US Science and Technology Policy." *Science, Technology, & Human Values* 39, no. 3: 397–431.

Bernanke, Ben S. 2015. *The Courage to Act: A Memoir of a Crisis and Its Aftermath.* New York: W. W. Norton & Company.

Berry, David M. 2008. *Copy, Rip, Burn: The Politics of Copyleft and Open Source.* London: Pluto Press.

Bettelheim, Bruno. 1969. *The Children of the Dream: Communal Child-Rearing and American Education.* London: The Macmillan Company.

Botwinick, Aryeh. 1981. "Politics in a World of Scarcity: Theories of Justice and Political Obligation." *Journal of Social Philosophy* 12: 7–15.

Braverman, Harry. 1974. *Labor and Monopoly Capital: The Degradation of Work in the Twentieth Century*. New York and London: Monthly Review Press.

Brown, Wendy. 2015. *Undoing the Demos: Neoliberalism's Stealth Revolution*. New York: Zone Books.

Buchanan, Allen. 1985. *Ethics, Efficiency, and the Market*. Totowa, NJ: Rowman & Littlefield.

Budd, Edward C. (Editor). 1967. *Inequality and Poverty*. New York: W. W. Norton & Company, Inc.

Bussell, Ari. 2009. "Mandatory Military Service Works in Israel." *NewsBlaze*, November 26, 2009. Available at: http://newsblaze.com/world/israel/mandatory-military-service-works-in-israel_11173/. Accessed October 30, 2016.

Butler, Judith. 2015. *Notes Toward a Performative Theory of Assembly*. Cambridge and London: Harvard University Press.

Byanyima, Winnie. 2015. "Richest 1% Will Own More Than All the Rest by 2016." *Oxfam International*. Available at: https://www.oxfam.org/en/pressroom/pressreleases/2015-01-19/richest-1-will-own-more-all-rest-2016. Accessed June 17, 2016.

Caring Economics. 2016. Available at: http://www.caring-economics.org/. Accessed March 20, 2017.

Carnegie, Dale. 1936. *How to Win Friends and Influence People*. New York: Simon and Schuster.

Cassidy, John. 2010. *How Markets Fail: The Logic of Economic Calamities* [2009]. New York: Farrar, Straus and Giroux.

Castillo, Stephanie. 2015. "'I Hate My Job,' Say 70% of US Employees: How to Be Happy at Work." *Medical Daily*, January 29, 2015. Available at: http://www.medicaldaily.com/i-hate-my-job-say-70-us-employees-how-be-happy-work-319928. Accessed December 13, 2016.

Chambers, Samuel A. 2014. *Bearing Society in Mind: Theories and Politics of the Social Formation*. London and New York: Rowman & Littlefield International.

Champeau, Serge, Carlos Closa, Daniel Innerarity, and Miguel Poaires Maduro(Editors). 2015. *The Future of Europe: Democracy, Legitimacy and Justice after the Euro Crisis*. London and New York: Rowman & Littlefield International.

Clark, John Maurice. 1936. *Preface to Social Economics: Essays on Economic Theory and Social Problems*. New York: Farrar & Rinehart, Incorporated Publishers.

Closa, Carlos. 2015. "The Transformation of Macroeconomic and Fiscal Governance in the EU." In *The Future of Europe: Democracy, Legitimacy and Justice After the Euro Crisis*, edited by Serge Champeau et al. London and New York: Rowman & Littlefield International, 37–56.

Coid, Jeremy, Min Yang, Simone Ullrich, Amanda Roberts, and Robert D. Hare. 2009. "Prevalence and Correlates of Psychopathic Traits in the Household Population of Great Britain." *International Journal of Law and Psychiatry* 32, no. 2 (2009): 65–73.

Coleman, Charly. 2014. *The Virtues of Abandon: An Anti-Individualist History of the French Enlightenment*. Stanford: Stanford University Press.

Commons, John R. 1990. *Institutional Economics: Its Place in Political Economy* [1934]. New Brunswick and London: Transaction Publishers.

Conscious Capitalism, Inc. 2016. Available at: https://www.consciouscapitalism.org/about. Accessed September 18, 2016.

Cowspiracy. 2016. Available at: http://www.cowspiracy.com/facts. Accessed January 10, 2017.

Cox, Jeff. 2015. "Misbehaving Banks Have Now Paid $204B in Fines." CNBC, October 30, 2015. Available at: http://www.cnbc.com/2015/10/30/misbehaving-banks-have-now-paid-204b-in-fines.html. Accessed October 8, 2016.

Creative Commons. 2016. Available at: https://creativecommons.org/about/mission-and-vision/. Accessed September 27, 2016.

Cunliffe, Barry. 1988. *Greeks, Romans and Barbarians: Spheres of Interaction*. New York: Methuen.

Dahl, Robert. 2002. *How Democratic Is the Constitution?* New Haven and London: Yale University Press.

Das, Satyajit. 2016. *The Age of Stagnation: Why Perpetual Growth Is Unattainable and the Global Economy Is in Peril.* Amherst, NY: Prometheus.

Davidow, William H. 2011. *Overconnected: The Promise and Threat of the Internet.* Harrison, New York, and Encino, CA: Delphinium Books.

DePaulo, Bella. 2015. How We Live Now: Redefining Home and Family in the 21st Century. New York: Atria Books.

Desilver, Drew. 2016. "In the U.S. and Abroad, More Young Adults Are Living with Their Parents." *Fact Tank,* May 24, 2016. Available at: http://www.pewresearch.org/fact-tank/2016/05/24/in-the-u-s-and-abroad-more-young-adults-are-living-with-their-parents/. Accessed September 30, 2016.

Diamandis, Peter, and Steven Kotler. 2012. *Abundance: The Future Is Better Than You Think.* New York: Free Press.

Dolan, Maura. 2012. "Christian Louboutin Holds on to His Red Soles." *Los Angeles Times,* September 5, 2012. Available at: http://articles.latimes.com/2012/sep/05/news/la-ar-christian-louboutin-red-soles-20120905. Accessed September 30, 2016.

Donnan, Shawn. 2016. "Inequality Declines after Global Financial Crisis." *Financial Times,* October 2, 2016. Available at: https://www.ft.com/content/5aae6948-88a2-11e6-8cb7-e7ada1d123b1. Accessed October 4, 2016.

Drucker, Peter F. 1993. *Post-Capitalist Society.* New York: Harper Business.

Earl, Peter E. (Editor). 1988. *Psychological Economics: Development, Tensions, Prospects.* Boston, Dordrecht, Lancaster: Kluwer Academic Publishers.

Eaves, Elisabeth. 2008. "Who Gives The Most?" *Forbes,* December 26, 2008. Available at: http://www.forbes.com/2008/12/24/america-philanthropy-income-oped-cx_ee_1226eaves.html. Accessed October 28, 2016.

Edsall, Thomas B. 2015. "Can Capitalists Save Capitalism?" *The New York Times,* January 20, 2015. Available at: http://www.nytimes.com/2015/01/21/opinion/can-capitalists-save-capitalism.html Accessed January 21, 2015.

Ehrenreich, John. 2016. *Third Wave Capitalism: How Money, Power, and the Pursuit of Self-Interest Have Imperiled the American Dream.* Ithaca and London: Cornell University Press.

Eichner, Alfred S. (Editor). 1978. *A Guide to Post-Keynesian Economics.* New York: M. E. Sharpe, Inc.

Epictetus. 2004. *The Art of Living: The Classical Manual on Virtue, Happiness and Effectiveness* [125]. Edited by Sharon Lebell. New York: HarperOne

Eriksen, Erik O. 2015. "The Eurozone Crisis in Light of the EU's Normativity." In *The Future of Europe: Democracy, Legitimacy and Justice After the Euro Crisis,* edited by Serge Champeau et al. London and New York: Rowman & Littlefield International, 248–262.

Fawcett, Henry. 1871. *Pauperism: Its Causes and Remedies.* London and New York: Macmillan and Co.

Fellowship for Intentional Community. 2016. Available at: http://www.ic.org/the-fellowship-for-intentional-community/. Accessed October 29, 2016.

Ferguson, A. T. (Editor). 1976. *Revolution or Reform? A Confrontation* [1972]. Chicago: New University Press.

Ferguson, Niall. 2008. *The Ascent of Money: A Financial History of the World.* London: Penguin Books.

Fink, Richard H. 1982. *Supply-Side Economics: A Critical Appraisal.* Frederick, MD: University Publications of America, Inc.

First. 2016. The International Award for Responsible Capitalism. Available at: http://www.firstmagazine.com/Awards/Default.aspx. Accessed September 17, 2016.

Francis, Pope. 2013. "*Evangelii Gaudium* (The Joy of the Gospel): Apostolic Exhortation on the Proclamation of the Gospel in Today's World." November 24, 2013. Available at: http://www.papalencyclicals.net/Franc/index.htm. Accessed October 22, 2016.

Fraser, Steve. 2015. *The Age of Acquiescence: The Life and Death of American Resistance to Organized Wealth and Power.* New York, Boston, and London: Little, Brown and Company.

Friedman, Benjamin M. 2005. *The Moral Consequences of Economic Growth.* New York: Vintage Books.

Friedman, Milton, and Rose Friedman. 1979. *Free to Choose: A Personal Statement.* New York and London: Harcourt Brace Jovanovich.

Fuller, Steve, and Veronika Lipinska. 2015. "Towards a Proactionary Welfare State." In *The Future of Social Epistemology: A Collective Vision*, edited by James H. Collier. Lanham: Rowman & Littlefield, chapter 22.

Galbraith, John Kenneth. 1962. *Economic Development in Perspective.* Cambridge, MA: Harvard University Press.

Genetics Home Reference. 2017. "Can Genes Be Patented?" U.S. National Library of Medicine. Available at: https://ghr.nlm.nih.gov/primer/testing/genepatents. Accessed February 23, 2017.

Gigerenzer, Gerd. 2002. *Calculated Risks: How to Know When Numbers Deceive You.* New York: Simon & Schuster.

Giroux, Henry A. 2004. *The Terror of Neoliberalism: Authoritarianism and the Eclipse of Democracy.* Boulder: Paradigm Publishers.

Goffman, Erving. 1974. *Frame Analysis: An Essay on the Organization of Experience.* Boston: Northeastern University Press.

Gongloff, Mark. 2014. "45 Million Americans Still Stuck Below Poverty Line: Census." *The Huffington Post.* September 16, 2014. Available at: http://www.huffingtonpost.com/2014/09/16/poverty-household-income_n_5828974.html. Accessed October 22, 2016.

Gordon, Robert J. 2016. *The Rise and Fall of American Growth: The U.S. Standard of Living since the Civil War.* Princeton and Oxford: Princeton University Press.

Graeber, David. 2014. *Debt: The First 5,000 Years* [2011]. Brooklyn and London: Melville House.

———. 2015. *The Utopia of Rules: On Technology, Stupidity, and the Secret Joys of Bureaucracy.* Brooklyn and London: Melville House.

Grenoble, Ryan. 2016. "Elizabeth Warren Takes on Uber, Lyft and the 'Gig Economy.'" *The Huffington Post*, May 19, 2016. Available at: http://www.huffingtonpost.com/entry/elizabeth-warren-gig-economy-uber-lyft_us_573e06dfe4b0aee7b8e9589c. Accessed October 10, 2016.

Griffiths, Simon. 2014. *Engaging Enemies: Hayek and the Left.* London and New York: Rowman & Littlefield International.

Gross, Michael, and Mary Beth Averill. 1983. "Evolution and Patriarchal Myths of Scarcity and Competition." In *Discovering Reality*, edited by Sandra Harding and M. D. Hintikka. Dordrecht, Holland: D. Reidel.

Habermas, Jürgen. 2009. *Europe: The Faltering Project* [2008]. Translated by Ciaran Cronin. Cambridge: Polity Press.

———. 2015. *The Lure of Technocracy* [2013]. Translated by Ciaran Cronin. Cambridge: Polity Press.

Hall, Susan D. (2016). "Feedback Loops on Patient Health Data Key to Engagement." *Fierce Healthcare*, March 8, 2016. Available at: http://www.fiercehealthcare.com/it/feedback-loops-patient-health-data-key-to-engagement. Accessed November 13, 2016.

Hammond, Allen L. 2001. "Digitally Empowered Development." *Foreign Affairs* 80, no. 2: 96.

———. and C. K. Prahalad. 2004. "Selling to the Poor." *Foreign Policy* 142: 30–37.

Harari, Yuval Noah. 2015. *Sapiens: A Brief History of Humankind.* New York: HarperCollins Publishers.

Hart, H. L. A. 1963. *Law, Liberty, and Morality.* Stanford, CA: Stanford University Press.

Harvey, David. 2014. *Seventeen Contradictions and the End of Capitalism.* Oxford and New York: Oxford University Press.

Hill, Michael. 2012. *Cannibal Capitalism: How Big Business and the Feds Are Ruining America.* Hoboken, NJ: John Wiley & Sons, Inc.

Hill, Richard. 1992. "Continuity of Haudenosaunee Government." In *Indian Roots of American Democracy*, edited by Jose Barreiro. Ithaca, NY: AKWE:KON Press, Cornell University.

Hobbes, Thomas. 1968. *Leviathan* [1651]. Edited by C. B. Macpherson. New York: Penguin Books.

Hobson, Sophie. 2015. "Apple's Record Value Is Bigger Than All But 19 countries' GDP." *LondonlovesBusiness*, February 11, 2015. Available at: http://www.londonlovesbusiness. com/business-news/tech/apples-record-value-is-bigger-than-all-but-19-countries-gdp/9751. article. Accessed September 24, 2016.

Hollis, Martin, and Edward Nell. 1975. *Rational Economic Man: A Philosophical Critique of Neo-Classical Economics*. Cambridge: Cambridge University Press.

Holyoake, George Jacob. 2012. *The Co-Operative Movement To-Day* [1903]. Reprinted by Forgotten Books.

Huddleston, Tom, Jr. 2015. "5 Times Pope Francis Talked about Money." *Fortune*, September 14, 2015. Available at: http://fortune.com/2015/09/14/pope-francis-capitalism-inequality/. Accessed October 23, 2016.

Hume, David. 1970. *Writings on Economics* [1752–1758]. Edited by Eugene Rotwein. Madison: The University of Wisconsin Press.

———. 1978. *A Treatise of Human Nature* [1738–1740]. Editor L. A. Selby-Bigge. Oxford: Oxford University Press.

Hymer, Stephen. 1978. "The Multinational Corporate Capitalist Economy." In *The Capitalist System*, edited by Richard Edwards, Michael Reich, and Thomas Weisskopf. Englewood Cliffs, NJ: Prentice-Hall, Inc., 481–92.

Investopedia. 2016. "Development Economics." Available at: http://www.investopedia.com/ terms/d/development-economics.asp?ad=dirN&qo=investopediaSiteSearch&qsrc=0&o= 40186. Accessed April 12, 2017.

Jackson, John H. 2000. "The Perils of Globalization and the World Trading System." *Fordham International Law Journal* 24: 371-82.

Jackson, Tim. 2010. *Prosperity without Growth: Economics for a Finite Planet*. London: Routledge.

Jameson, Fredric. 2016. *An American Utopia: Dual Power and the Universal Army*, edited by Slavoj Žižek. London and New York: Verso.

Jennings, Christopher. 2016. *Paradise Now: The Story of American Utopianism*. New York: Random House.

Josephy Jr., Alvin M. 1968. *The Indian Heritage of America*. New York: Bantam Books.

Kahneman, Daniel. 2011. *Thinking, Fast and Slow*. New York: Farrar, Straus and Giroux.

Kant, Immanuel. 1970. *Kant's Political Writings*. Edited by Hans Reiss. Translated by H. B. Nisbet. Cambridge and London: Cambridge University Press.

Keitheley, Paul. 2015. "Popular Capitalism: Economic Reality of Wishful Thinking?" *Politics & Policy*. Available at: http://politicsandpolicy.org/article/popular-capitalism-economic-reality-or-wishful-thinking. Accessed September 16, 2016.

Keynes, John Maynard. 1963. "Economic Possibilities for Our Grandchildren" [1930]. In *Essays in Persuasion*. New York: Norton.

———. 1964. *The General Theory of Employment, Interest, and Money* [1936]. New York and London: Harcourt Brace Jovanovich.

Klein, Naomi. 2007. *The Shock Doctrine: The Rise of Disaster Capitalism*. New York: Metropolitan Books.

Kolbert, Elizabeth. 2016. "Our Automated Future." *The New Yorker*, December 19 and 26, 2016, 114–18.

Kolhaktar, Sheelah. 2016. "The Anti-Uber: An Upstart Tries Out a Bold Strategy in the Ride Wars." *The New Yorker*, October 10, 2016, 40–46.

Kornai, Janos. 1980. *Economics of Shortage*, 2 vols. Amsterdam: North-Holland Publishing Company.

Krugman, Paul. 1993. "The Fall and Rise of Development Economics." Available at: http:// www.wws.princeton.edu/pkrugman/dishpan.html. Accessed September 22, 2016.

Kuhner, Timothy K. 2014. *Capitalism v. Democracy: Money in Politics and the Free Market Constitution*. Stanford: Stanford University Press.

LaMagna, Dal. 2016. "Responsible Capitalism: Corporate Social Responsibility." Available at: http://www.dallamagna.com/responsible-capitalism. Accessed September 17, 2016.

Lanier, Jaron. 2010. *You Are Not a Gadget: A Manifesto*. New York: Vintage Books.

Lazzarato, Maurizio. 2015. *Governing by Debt* [2013]. Translated by Joshua David Jordan. South Pasadena, CA: Semiotext(e) Intervention Series, 17.

Le Guin, Ursula K. 1974. *The Dispossessed.* New York: Harper Voyager.

Lekachman, Robert. 1959. *A History of Economic Ideas.* New York: McGraw-Hill Book Company.

Lerner, Abba P. 1947. *The Economics of Control: Principles of Welfare Economics.* New York: The Macmillan Company.

Lessig, Lawrence. 2008. *Remix: Making Art and Commerce Thrive in the Hybrid Economy.* New York: The Penguin Press.

———. 2011. *Republic, Lost: How Money Corrupts Congress—and a Plan to Stop It.* New York and Boston: Twelve.

Levine, David. 1988. *Needs, Rights, and the Market.* Boulder, CO: Lynne Rienner Publishers.

Levitt, Steven D., and Stephen J. Dubner. 2005. *Freakonomics: A Rogue Economist Explores the Hidden Side of Everything.* New York: William Morrow.

LexisNexis PCLaw. 2016. "Rehabilitation—What Is Rehabilitation." Available at: http://law. jrank.org/pages/1933/Rehabilitation-What-rehabilitation.html. Accessed: June 21, 2016.

Lieberman, Matthew D. 2013. *Social: Why Our Brains Are Wired to Connect.* New York: Broadway Books.

Livingston, James. 2016. *No More Work: Why Full Employment Is a Bad Idea.* Chapel Hill, NC: The University of North Carolina Press.

Locke, John. 1947. *Two Treatises of Government* [1690]. Edited by Thomas I. Cook. New York and London: Collier Macmillan Publishers.

London, Nell. 2016. "It's Common for Lobbyists to Write Bills for Congress. Here's Why." *Colorado Public Radio,* May 10, 2016. Available at: http://www.cpr.org/news/story/its-common-lobbyists-write-bills-congress-heres-why. Accessed November 28, 2016.

Lyotard, Jean-Francois. 1984. *The Postmodern Condition: A Report on Knowledge* [1979]. Translated by Geoff Bennington and Brian Massumi. Minneapolis: University of Minnesota Press.

MacEwan, Arthur. 1978. "Capitalist Expansion and the Sources of Imperialism." In *The Capitalist System,* edited by Richard C. Edwards, Michael Reich, and Thomas Weisskopf. Englewood Cliffs, NJ: Prentice-Hall, Inc., 492–99.

Mackey, John, and Raj Sisodia. 2014. "'Conscious Capitalism' Is Not an Oxymoron." *Harvard Business Review,* August 22, 2014.

Macpherson, C. B. 1962. *The Political Theory of Possessive Individualism: Hobbes to Locke.* London: Oxford University Press.

Machiavelli, Niccolo. 1977. *The Prince* [1513]. Translated and edited by Robert M. Adams. New York and London: W. W. Norton & Company.

Madrick, Jeff. 2014. *Seven Bad Ideas: How Mainstream Economists Have Damaged America and the World.* New York: Alfred A. Knopf.

Magnier, Mark. 2016. "China's Economic Growth in 2015 Is Slowest in 25 Years." *The Wall Street Journal,* January 19, 2016. Available at: http://www.wsj.com/articles/china-economic-growth-slows-to-6-9-on-year-in-2015-1453169398. Accessed December 3, 2016.

Malenbaum, Wilfred. 1975. "Scarcity: Prerequisite to Abundance." *Annals of the American Academy of Political and Social Science* 420: 72.85.

Malthus, Thomas Robert. 1970. *An Essay on the Principle of Population* [1798]. Edited by Anthony Flew. New York: Penguin Books.

Markovic, Mihailo. 1974. *From Affluence to Praxis: Philosophy and Social Criticism.* Ann Arbor, MI: University of Michigan Press.

Marx, Karl. 1972. "The German Ideology" [1845–1846]. In *The Marx-Engels Reader.* Edited by Robert C. Tucker. New York: W. W. Norton & Company, Inc.

———. 1975. "Economic and Philosophical Manuscripts" [1844]. In *Karl Marx: Early Writings.* Translated by Rodney Livingstone and Gregor Benton. New York: Vintage Books.

———. 1976. *Capital* [1867]. Volume I. Translated by Ben Fowkes. New York: Vintage Books.

———. 1988. *The Communist Manifesto* [1848]. Edited by Frederic L. Bender. New York and London: W. W. Norton & Company.

Maslow, Abraham H. 1943. "A Theory of Human Motivation." *Psychological Review* 50: 370–96.

Mason, Paul. 2015. *Postcapitalism: A Guide to Our Future.* New York: Farrar, Straus and Giroux.

Matthews, Eric. 2015. "Young People Can Afford Homes, They Just Don't Want to Be Homeowners." *Fortune*, August 18, 2015. Available at: http://fortune.com/2015/08/18/young-people-can-afford-homes-they-just-dont-want-to-be-homeowners/. Accessed October 8, 2016.

Maurice, Charles, and Charles W. Smithson. 1984. *The Doomsday Myth: 10,000 Years of Economic Crises.* Stanford, CA: Hoover Institute Press.

Mazzucato, Mariana. 2014. *The Entrepreneurial State: Debunking Public vs. Private Sector Myths.* London and New York: Anthem Press.

McAdams, David. 2014. *Game-Changer: Game Theory and the Art of Transforming Strategic Situations.* New York and London: W. W. Norton & Company.

McCloskey, Dierdre N. 1998. *The Rhetoric of Economics.* Second Edition. Madison: University of Wisconsin Press.

McMaken, Ryan. 2016. "26 Percent of Eligible Voters Voted for Trump." *Mises Institute*, November 9, 2016. Available at: https://mises.org/blog/26-percent-eligible-voters-voted-trump. Accessed November 13, 2016.

Mill, John Stuart. 1956. *On Liberty* [1859]. Edited by Currin V. Shields. Indianapolis and New York: The Bobbs-Merrill Company, Inc.

———. 1965. *Principles of Political Economy* [1848]. Edited by J. R. Robson. Toronto, Canada: University of Toronto Press, Toronto.

Miller, Timothy. 1998. *The Quest for Utopia in Twentieth-Century America.* Syracuse: Syracuse University Press.

———. 1999. *The 60s Communes: Hippies and Beyond.* Syracuse: Syracuse University Press.

Mirowski, Philip. 2011. *Science-Mart: Privatizing American Science.* Cambridge and London: Harvard University Press.

Mullainathan, Sendhil, and Eldar Shafir. 2013. *Scarcity: Why Having Too Little Means So Much.* New York: Henry Holt and Company.

Myrdal, Gunnar. 1970. *The Challenge of World Poverty: A World Anti-Poverty Program in Outline.* New York: Random House.

Nelson, Richard R., and Sidney G. Winter. 1982. *An Evolutionary Theory of Economic Change.* Cambridge and London: Harvard University Press.

North, Douglass C. 1990. *Institutions, Institutional Change and Economic Performance.* Cambridge and New York: Cambridge University Press.

Nowak, Martin A. 2011. *SuperCooperators: Altruism, Evolution, and Why We Need Each Other to Succeed.* New York: Free Press.

Nozick, Robert. 1974. *Anarchy, State, and Utopia.* New York: Basic Books, Inc., Publishers.

Paine, Thomas. 1797. "Agrarian Justice." Available at: http://xroads.virginia.edu/~hyper/Paine/agrarian.html. Accessed June 27, 2016.

Panitch, Leo. 2014. "'Responsible Capitalism Is Nonsense—the Left Must Offer a Real Alternative." *The Guardian*, August 4, 2014. Available at: https://www.theguardian.com/commentisfree/2014/aug/04/responsible-capitalism-left-alternative-ed-miliband. Accessed September 17, 2016.

Perelman, Michael. 1987. *Marx's Crises Theory: Scarcity, Labor, and Finance.* New York: Praeger Publishers.

Pew Research Center. 2013. "The Global Catholic Population." Available at: http://www.pewforum.org/2013/02/13/the-global-catholic-population/. Accessed October 22, 2016.

Phelps, Edmund. 2013. *Mass Flourishing: How Grassroots Innovation Created Jobs, Challenge, and Change.* Princeton and Oxford: Princeton University Press.

———. 2015. "What Is Wrong with the West's Economies?" *The New York Review of Books* LXII, no. 13 (August 13): 54–56.

Pigou, Arthur C. 1912. *Wealth and Welfare.* London: Macmillan and Company, Ltd.

———. 2013. *Economics of Welfare* [1920]. Hampshire: Palgrave Macmillan.

Piketty, Thomas. 2014. *Capital in the Twenty-First Century* [2013]. Translated by Arthur Goldhammer. Cambridge and London: Harvard University Press.

Pinker, Steven. 2002. *The Blank Slate: The Modern Denial of Human Nature.* New York: Penguin.

Polanyi, Karl. 1957. *The Great Transformation: The Political and Economic Origins of Our Time* [1944]. Boston: Beacon Press.

Polderman, Tinca J. C., Beben Benyamin, Christiaan A. De Leeuw, Patrick F. Sullivan, Arjen Van Bochoven, Peter M. Visscher, and Danielle Posthuma. 2015. "Meta-Analysis of the Heritability of Human Traits Based on Fifty Years of Twin Studies." *Nature Genetics* 47, no. 7 (2015): 702–9.

Popper, Karl. R. 1957. *The Poverty of Historicism.* New York: Harper & Row, Publishers.

Prahalad, C. K. 2005. *The Fortune at the Bottom of the Pyramid.* Upper Saddle River, NJ: Pearson Education, Inc.

Proudhon, Pierre Joseph. 1927. *The Solution of the Social Problem* [c1851]. Edited by Henry Cohen. New York: Vanguard Press.

Ramdas, Kavita, Matthew Bishop, and Michael Green. 2011. "Point-Counterpoint: Philanthro-capitalism." *Stanford Social Innovation Review*, December 15, 2011. Available at: http://ssir.org/point_counterpoint/philanthrocapitalism. Accessed September 18, 2016.

Rattner, Steven. 2016. "What's Our Duty to the People Globalization Leaves Behind?" *The New York Times*, January 26, 2016. Available at: http://www.nytimes.com/2016/01/26/opinion/whats-our-duty-to-the-people-globalization-leaves-behind.html. Accessed September 21, 2016.

Raustiala, Kal, and Christopher Sprigman. 2012. *The Knockoff Economy: How Imitation Sparks Innovation.* Oxford and New York: Oxford University Press.

Rawls, John. 1971. *Theory of Justice.* Cambridge, MA: Harvard University Press.

Reich, Robert B. 2015. *Saving Capitalism: For the Many, Not the Few.* New York: Alfred A. Knopf.

Rifkin, Jeremy. 2014. *The Zero Marginal Cost Society: The Internet of Things, the Collaborative Commons, and the Eclipse of Capitalism.* Hampshire, UK: Palgrave Macmillan.

Robbins, Lionel. 1935. *An Essay on the Nature of Significance of Economic Science* [1932], Second edition. London: Macmillan.

Rodrick, Dani. 2011. *The Globalization Paradox: Democracy and the Future of the World Economy.* New York and London: W. W. Norton & Company.

————2016. "Put Globalization to Work for Democracies." *The New York Times*, September 17, 2016. Available at: http://www.nytimes.com/2016/09/18/opinion/sunday/put-globalization-to-work-for-democracies.html. Accessed September 21, 2016.

Rorty, Richard. 1989. *Contingency, Irony, and Solidarity.* Cambridge: Cambridge University Press.

Rosenstein-Rodan, Paul N. 1943. "Problems of Industrialization of Eastern and South-Eastern Europe." *Economic Journal* 53 (June–September 1943): 202–211.

————. and Dragoslav Avramovic. 1984. "Natura Facit Saltum: Analysis of the Disequilibrium Growth Process." In *Pioneers in Development.* New York: Oxford University Press, 205–21.

Roseveare, Henry. 1969. *The Treasury: The Evolution of a British Institution.* New York: Columbia University Press.

Rothbard, Murray N. 2009. "Aristotle on Private Property and Money." *Mises Institute*, December 7, 2009. Available at: https://mises.org/library/aristotle-private-property-and-money-0. Accessed June 27, 2016.

Rousseau, Jean-Jacques. 1964. *The First and Second Discourses.* Editor Roger D. Masters. Translated by Judith R. Masters. New York: St. Martin's Press.

————. 1978. *On the Social Contract* [1762]. Editor Roger D. Masters. Translated by Judith R. Masters. New York: St. Martin's Press.

Russell, Bernard. 1949. *Authority and the Individual.* London: Routledge.

Rynn, Jon. 2010. "Renewable Energy: The Power of Positive Feedback Loops." *Grist*, August 18, 2010. Available at: http://grist.org/article/2010-08-17-renewable-energy-the-power-of-positive-feedback-loops/. Accessed November 13, 2016.

Sachs, Jeffrey D. 2008. *Common Wealth: Economics for a Crowded Planet*. New York: The Penguin Press.

Sahlins, Marshall. 1971. *Stone Age Economics*. Chicago: Aldine Atherton Inc.

Said, Edward. 1978. *Orientalism*. New York: Pantheon Books.

Samuelson, Paul A., and William Nordhaus. 1973. *Economics*, ninth edition. New York: McGraw-Hill.

Sariel, Aviram, Daniel Mishori, and Joseph Agassi. 2015. "The Re-Inventor's Dilemma: A Tragedy of the Public Domain." *Journal of Intellectual Property Law & Practice* 10, no. 10: 759–766.

Sassower, Raphael. 1988. "Ideology Masked as Science: Shielding Economics from Criticisms." *Journal of Economic Issues* XXII: 167–79.

———. 1990. "Scarcity and Setting the Boundaries of Political Economy." *Social Epistemology* 4, no. 1: 75–91.

———. 2009. *Postcapitalism: Moving Beyond Ideology in America's Economic Crises*. Boulder and London: Paradigm Press.

———. 2013. *Digital Exposure: Postmodern Postcapitalism*. Hampshire, UK: Palgrave Macmillan.

Schawbel, Dan. 2013. "John Mackey: Why Companies Should Embrace Conscious Capitalism." *Forbes*, January 15, 2013. Available at:http://www.forbes.com/sites/danschawbel/2013/01/15/john-mackey-why-companies-should-embrace-conscious-capitalism/#64498356a3f4. Accessed September 16, 2016.

Schumacher, E. F. 1973. *Small Is Beautiful: Economics as If People Matter*. New York: Harper & Row.

Schumpeter, Joseph A. 1954. *History of Economic Analysis*. New York: Oxford University Press.

———. 1975. *Capitalism, Socialism and Democracy* [1942]. New York: Harper & Row, Publishers.

Sen, Amartya. 1987. *On Ethics and Economics*. Oxford: Basil Blackwell Ltd.

Sen, Sudhir. 1974. *A Richer Harvest: New Horizons for Developing Countries*. New York: Orbis Books.

Sennett, Richard. 2006. *The Culture of the New Capitalism*. New Haven: Yale University Press.

Shirky, Clay. 2010. *Cognitive Surplus: Creativity and Generosity in a Connected Age*. New York: Penguin Press.

Singer, Tania, and Ricard Matthieu, eds. 2015. *Caring Economics: Conversations on Altruism and Compassion, Between Scientists, Economists, and the Dalai Lama*. New York: Picador.

Slade, Maxwell (Editor). 2016. "Copyright." *Legal Information Institute*. Cornell University Law School. Available at: https://www.law.cornell.edu/wex/copyright. Accessed September 26, 2016.

Smith, Adam. 1937. *An Inquiry into the Nature and Causes of the Wealth of Nations* [1776]. New York: Random House, Inc.

———. 1976. *The Theory of Moral Sentiments* [1759]. London: Penguin.

———. 1978. *Lectures on Jurisprudence* [1762–1766]. Edited by R. L. Meek, D. D. Raphael, and P. G. Stein. Indianapolis, IN: Liberty Classics.

Spiro, Melford E. 1970. *Kibbutz: Venture in Utopia* [1956]. New York: Schocken Books.

Sraffa, Piero. 1960. *Production of Commodities by Means of Commodities: Prelude to a Critique of Economic Theory*. Cambridge: Cambridge University Press.

Stehr, Nico. 2008. *Moral Markets: How Knowledge and Affluence Change Consumers and Products*. Boulder and London: Paradigm Publishers.

Stephens, Bret. 2016. "The System Didn't Work." *The Wall Street Journal*, December 6, 2016, A15.

Stevenson, Leslie. 1974. *Seven Theories of Human Nature*. New York and Oxford: Oxford University Press.

Stigler, George J. 1982. *The Economist as Preacher and Other Essays*. Chicago: University of Chicago Press.

Stiglitz, Joseph E. 2002. *Globalization and Its Discontents.* New York and London: W. W. Norton.

———. 2013. *The Price of Inequality* [2012]. New York and London: W. W. Norton & Company.

———. 2016. *The Euro: How a Common Currency Threatens the Future of Europe.* New York and London: W. W. Norton & Company.

Strauss, Ilana E. 2016. "The Hot New Millennial Housing Trend Is a Repeat of the Middle Ages: Communal Living Is Hardly a Departure from Tradition—It's a Return to How Humans Have Been Making Their Homes for Thousands of Years." *The Atlantic*, September 26, 2016. Available at: http://www.theatlantic.com/business/archive/2016/09/millennial-housing-communal-living-middle-ages/501467/. Accessed October 25, 2016.

Sundararajan, Arun. 2016. *The Sharing Economy: The End of Employment and the Rise of Crowd-Based Capitalism.* Cambridge and London: The MIT Press.

Surowiecki, James. 2004. *The Wisdom of Crowds.* New York: Anchor Books.

———. 2015. "In Defense of Philanthrocapitalism." *The New Yorker*, December 13, 2015. Available at: http://www.newyorker.com/magazine/2015/12/21/in-defense-of-philanthrocapitalism. Accessed September 18, 2016.

Suzor, Nicolas. 2013. "What Motivates Free Software Developers to Choose between Copyleft and Permissive Licenses?" Opensource.com, August 8, 2013. Available at: https://opensource.com/. Accessed September 27, 2016.

Svetlova, Margarita, Sara R. Nichols, and Celia A. Brownell. 2010. "Toddlers' Prosocial Behavior: From Instrumental to Empathic to Altruistic Helping." *Child Development* 81, no. 6 (2010): 1814–1827.

Tawney, R. H. 1948. *The Acquisitive Society* [1920]. New York and London: Harcourt Brace Jovanovich.

Thaler, Richard H. 1992. *The Winner's Curse: Paradoxes and Anomalies of Economic Life.* Princeton, NJ: Princeton University Press.

———. and Cass R. Sunstein. 2008. *Nudge: Improving Decisions About Health, Wealth, and Happiness.* New Haven, CT: Yale University Press.

The Economist . 2016. "The Birth of Philanthrocapitalism." February 23, 2006. Available at: http://www.economist.com/node/5517656. Accessed September 18, 2016.

Therborn, Goran. 2008. *From Marxism to Post-Marxism.* London and New York: Verso.

Titmuss, Richard M. 1970. *The Gift Relationship: From Human Blood to Social Policy.* New York: The New Press.

Trivett, Vincent. 2011. "25 US Mega Corporations: Where They Rank If They Were Countries." *Business Insider*, June 27, 2011. Available at: http://www.businessinsider.com/25-corporations-bigger-tan-countries-2011-6. Accessed September 24, 2016.

Tusi, Nasir ad-Din. 1964. *The Nasirean Ethics* [1235]. Translated by G. M. Wickens. London: George Allen & Unwin Ltd.

Tverberg, Gail. 2016. "Twelve Reasons Why Globalization Is a Huge Problem." *Our Finite World*, July 11, 2015. Available at: https://ourfiniteworld.com/2013/02/22/twelve-reasons-why-globalization-is-a-huge-problem/. Accessed September 24, 2016.

US National Conference of Catholic Bishops. 1986. "Economic Justice for All: Pastoral Letter on Catholic Social Teaching and the U.S. Economy." Washington, DC: United States Conference of Catholic Bishops Inc.

———. 1996. "A Decade After 'Economic Justice for All': Continuing Principles, Changing Context, New Challenge." November 1995. Washington, DC: United States Conference of Catholic Bishops Inc.

Veblen, Thorstein. 1953. *The Theory of the Leisure Class: An Economic Study of Institutions* [1899]. New York and Toronto: The New American Library.

Venables, Robert W. 1992. "The Founding Fathers: Choosing to Be Romans." In *Indian Roots of American Democracy*, edited by Jose Barreiro. Ithaca, NY: AKWE:KON Press, Cornell University.

Ward, Adrian F. 2012. "Scientists Probe Human Nature—and Discover We Are Good, After All." *Scientific American*, November 20, 2012. Available at: http://www.scientificamerican.

com/article/scientists-probe-human-nature-and-discover-we-are-good-after-all/.   Accessed: June 21, 2016.

Weeks, Kathi. 2016. "Utopian Therapy: Work, Nonwork, and the Political Imagination." In Frederic Jameson, *An American Utopia: Dual Power and the Universal Army*, chapter 9, 243–265.

Weisskopf, Walter A. 1971. *Alienation and Economics*. New York: E. P. Dutton & Co.

———. 1978a. "Imperialism and the Economic Development of the Third World." In *The Capitalist System*, edited by Richard C. Edwards, Michael Reich, and Thomas Weisskopf. Englewood Cliffs, NJ: Prentice-Hall, Inc., 492–499.

———. 1978b. "The Irrationality of Capitalist Economic Growth." In *The Capitalist System*, edited by Richard C. Edwards, Michael Reich, and Thomas Weisskopf. Englewood Cliffs, NJ: Prentice-Hall, Inc., 395–409.

Williams, Raymond. 1961. *The Long Revolution*. London: Chatto & Windus.

Wilson, Edward O. 1975. *Sociobiology: The New Synthesis*. Cambridge: Harvard University Press.

———. 2012. *The Social Conquest of Earth*. New York and London: W. W. Norton & Company.

Wolff, Richard D. 2012. *Democracy at Work: A Cure for Capitalism*. Chicago: Haymarket Books.

Worstall, Tim. 2015. "The True US Poverty Rate Is 4.5%, Not 14.5%." *Forbes*. March 15, 2015. Available at: http://www.forbes.com/sites/timworstall/2015/03/15/the-true-us-poverty-rate-is-4-5-not-14-5/#69d3876d5562. Accessed October 22, 2016.

Yunus, Muhammad. 2007. *Creating a World without Poverty: Social Business and the Future of Capitalism*. New York: Public Affairs.

Zaretsky, Eli. 2012. *Why America Needs a Left: A Historical Argument*. Cambridge, UK: Polity Press.

Zoref, Lior. 2012. "Of Oxes and the Wisdom of Crowds." *TED Talk*. Available at: http://blog.ted.com/of-oxes-and-the-wisdom-of-crowds-lior-zoref-at-ted2012/. Accessed October 8, 2016.

Index